Instruments of Desire

Instruments of Desire

The Electric Guitar and the Shaping of Musical Experience

Steve Waksman

Harvard University Press
Cambridge, Massachusetts
London, England   1999

Copyright © 1999 by the President and Fellows of Harvard College
All rights reserved
Printed in the United States of America

Library of Congress Cataloging-in-Publication Data

Waksman, Steve.
    Instruments of desire : the electric guitar and the shaping of
musical experience / Steve Waksman.
        p.   cm.
    Includes bibliographical references, discography, and index.
    Contents: Playing with sound : Charlie Christian, the electric guitar, and the Swing
Era—Pure tones and solid bodies : Les Paul's new sound—Mister Guitar : Chet
Atkins and the Nashville sound—Racial distortions : Muddy Waters, Chuck Berry,
and the electric guitar in Black popular music—Black sound, black body : Jimi
Hendrix, the electric guitar, and the meanings of blackness—Kick out the jams : the
MC5 and the politics of noise—Heavy music : cock rock, colonialism, and Led
Zeppelin.
    ISBN 0-674-00065-X (cl. : alk. paper)
    1. Electric guitar—History.   2. Popular music—Social aspects.   3. Gender identity
in music.   4. Sex in music.   5. Music and race.   6. Guitarists.   I. Title
ML1015.G9W24   1999
787.87'19—dc21   99-39764

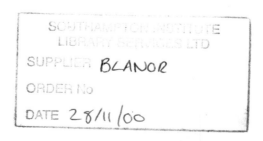

Acknowledgments

Chapter 6, "Kick Out the Jams!: The MC5 and the Politics of Noise," was previously published in slightly altered form in *Mapping the Beat: Popular Music and Contemporary Theory,* edited by Thomas Swiss, John Sloop, and Andrew Herman (Malden, Mass.: Blackwell Press, 1998), pp. 47–75.

Portions of chapter 7, "Heavy Music: Cock Rock, Colonialism, and the Music of Led Zeppelin," have been published in the *Journal of Popular Music Studies,* vol. 8 (1996), pp. 5–25.

Thanks to my graduate committee: Richard Leppert, Maria Damon, David Roediger, John Wright, and Paula Rabinowitz. Special thanks to Richard, as excellent an adviser as one could hope to have, and to Maria, for cool times and good talks in Cambridge.

Big thank you to Betty Agee at the Program in American Studies, University of Minnesota, for all of her help in facilitating the completion of a long-distance doctorate after my move from Minneapolis.

Special shout out to my good friend Carol Mason, for moral support, intellectual encouragement, and many a fine drinking session.

Hats off to the boys of 22 Warner St., Somerville, for providing a place to party while this project was coming to a close.

Completion of this project was made much easier by the Norman Johnston DeWitt fellowship at the University of Minnesota, and by a travel grant from the Program in American Studies, University of Minnesota.

Many thanks to the staffs at the Country Music Hall of Fame Archive in Nashville, Tennessee, the Blues Archive at the University of Mississippi in Oxford, Mississippi (especially Edward Komara), and the Minneapolis Public Library.

Extensions of gratitude to Jonathan at the Michael Ochs Archive in Venice, California, Jim Fricke at the Experience Music Project in Seattle, Washington, Pete Strayer at Gibson Musical Instruments, and to Frank Driggs, Jon Sievert, Leni Sinclair, and Valerie Wilmer for help in assembling the photographs contained herein. Special thanks to Jim Fricke, for his strong support and dogged effort.

Multitude of thanks to Lindsay Waters for his faith in this project, to Kim Steere for her administrative help in putting this book together, and to Kate Brick for her sharp editorial eye.

Finally, thanks to Mom and Dad, for their patience and untiring support in all manner of ways.

Contents

Illustrations

Introduction

Going Electric

Within the mythology that often stands in for the history of rock 'n' roll, one of the key turning points is Bob Dylan's performance at the 1965 Newport Folk Festival, the performance during which the singer went electric. There is a lack of agreement as to the uniformity of the outrage that Dylan's use of electric instruments generated, but his performance had at the least a divisive effect upon the attending crowd and upon the subsequent history of the folk movement. Indeed, Robert Cantwell began his recent study of the folk revival by referring to Dylan as a figure who "personally terminated the popular folksong revival, some thought, by picking up an electric guitar and sending his message around the world with it."[1] Brandishing an electric guitar, Dylan assaulted the ideal of an authentic musical community held by the most devoted folk enthusiasts, within which acoustic instruments were valued for the intimacy they promoted as people gathered around to hear the musician. An acoustic guitar was just loud enough to make music, but not so loud as to drown out the voice of the singer, or of any in the audience who wanted to sing along. An electric guitar, by contrast, made too much noise, and in so doing converted an audience comprised of individuals into a mass whose attention was overwhelmed by the sound of it all.

Cantwell is only the most recent in a long line of music critics and historians who have pointed out that the ideal of the people and of people's music held by folk music enthusiasts was an ideal rooted in social privilege and in the belief that they existed above the mass of listeners who were drawn to musical forms like rock 'n' roll.[2] However, I am less interested in what Dylan's performance at Newport suggests about the folk music constituency, or about Dylan himself, than I am in what it suggests about the position of the electric guitar in the popular music of the 1960s. If Dylan, by incorporating the electric guitar, gestured toward a new hybrid of folk and rock sensibilities, the controversy stirred by his use of the instrument also indicated the extent to which the electric guitar by 1965 had become an object invested with deep significance among certain segments of the pop music audience.

That year was a turning point in the history of the electric guitar, but not only or even primarily because of Dylan's new musical direction. Before Dylan's turn to electricity, before even the Beatles' ascent to pop music megastardom, the sales figures for guitars, and for electric guitars in particular, began to skyrocket in the United States. For the Gibson company, one of the leading names in guitar manufacturing, electric guitars had come to dominate sales figures by the mid-1950s, when the first stirrings of rock 'n' roll were met with a surge in electric guitar manufacturing.[3] The upstart Fender company first issued its innovative Stratocaster in 1954, which has since become one of the most enduring icons of late twentieth-century popular culture. The real peak of activity, though, began around 1963, when total sales figures for all guitars almost doubled from the previous year, from just over 300,000 to over 600,000.[4] By 1965, total guitar sales had jumped to 1.5 million; the Fender company alone was producing 1,500 guitars a week, most of them electric models.[5] Complementing and in some ways motivating this wave of production was the heightened popularity of guitar-based music, not only the oft-noted folk revival and British invasion but the earlier and less recognized trend of electric guitar–driven instrumentals by the likes of Duane Eddy, Dick Dale, Link Wray, and the Ventures (and in England, the Shadows).

By the middle of the 1960s, then, as rock 'n' roll historian Philip Ennis noted, "the boy with his guitar became a national phenomenon."[6] The situation was notable enough for *Life* magazine to feature a full-color two-page spread on the rising popularity of electric guitars in 1966, with an array of guitars laid out dramatically across the pages and grouped according to price. This was no consumer's guide, but an attempt to reduce a wide-ranging cultural phenomenon to the bottom line. "It's Money Music," ran the headline, and the accompanying text told a tale of the electric guitar's new ubiquity that stressed the instrument's role as a commodity.

With an electric guitar today, a teen-ager can make not only a big noise but he can also make money. Starting out with one of the modest instruments . . . to amuse himself, he soon finds that people—even friends—will pay to hear him play in a combo at their parties. So he moves up until he owns an electronic marvel costing hundreds of dollars . . . Teen combos are fast becoming the country's most popular form of musical entertainment, and sales of electric guitars—along with the nation's decibel level—have nearly doubled each year for the past three.[7]

Despite its condescending cheekiness, *Life*'s brief account does highlight some unique features of the electric guitar's economic value. A commodity in its own right, the electric guitar also played an increasingly prominent role in the creation of a second product, pop music itself; and the music, in turn, served as the best vehicle for promoting the instrument. The *Life* account, however, misrepresents the motivation of the young guitarists who were bent on buying more and better gear. The amount of money to be made by the average "boy with his guitar" was rather dismal—certainly not enough to explain the intense growth in sales. There was something more to this phenomenon, something that was not strictly economic but that had to do with a different kind of investment in the electric guitar.

That "something more" is what this book is about—those qualities of the electric guitar that made it an outrageous presence at Newport, and that have made the electric guitarist into something of a culture hero among a significant segment of the audience for popular music. Attempting to explain this latter phenomenon, journalist and B. B. King biographer Charles Sawyer sought to capture the essence of the electric guitar's appeal to young white audiences of the 1960s. According to Sawyer, the public fascination with figures such as Michael Bloomfield, lead guitarist for the Butterfield Blues Band, had as much to do with the instrument as with the personality. The electric guitar was "ideal for representing the culture that embraced it," proclaimed Sawyer, who continued:

It is primitive in the extreme: six strings stretched on a board, hand picked and hand fretted; no moving parts; more rudimentary than a harpsichord; an ancient instrument. But, the instrument is also high technology: electromagnetic signals, generated by tiny magnets beneath the strings, amplified by electronics and fed to a bank of speaker cones. The sound it makes is full of urban clash and clang and has more percussion in it than the piano and vibraphone combined. It requires extreme dexterity and precision to play well. The electric guitar is the mediation between the two poles: the primitive hand-held harp and the highly technological synthesizer.[8]

The terms of Sawyer's description—extreme primitivism on the one hand, high technology on the other—play upon a set of cultural oppositions similar to those at work in the uproar over Dylan's performance at Newport.[9] If folk music enthusiasts perceived the electric guitar to be a technological intrusion into their idealized, untouched community, adherents of the electric guitar saw the instrument as a means of reconciling these elements, of blending "primitive" simplicity with "technological" complexity.

There is also a racial subtext here within which the primitive stands for the African-American influence upon electric guitar performance, whereas the technological stands for white contributions. For it was during this period that the electric guitar came to embody a certain set of countercultural desires that hinged upon the transference of racial and sexual identity between African-American and white men. African-American bluesmen became the ideal type of electric guitarist after whom legions of young white musicians (like Michael Bloomfield) sought to pattern themselves; and the resulting "rebellion" reproduced patterns of racism and sexism even as it aimed to produce an effective model of resistance rooted in musical practice. The dynamic involved is similar to that described by Eric Lott in his study of blackface minstrelsy, *Love and Theft,* in which white efforts to mimic or appropriate elements of African-American musical traditions speak of a "profound white investment in black culture" born from the internalization of the color line among white performers and spectators.[10] The putting on of blackness, or of elements of black style, is from this perspective an attempt to compensate for a perceived lack in the composition of whiteness; and this lack is, according to Lott, most often experienced in terms of gender and sexuality. Thus electric guitar performance in the 1960s, like blackface minstrelsy in the 1840s, followed a "gendered logic of exchange" within which white males sought to compensate for their supposed deficiency by drawing upon the sexual excess that African-American men were thought to embody.[11]

How did the electric guitar come to figure so prominently within this dynamic of racial and sexual desire? The often-noted male bias of the instrument cannot be fully grasped without examining how the varieties of masculinity that have taken shape around the electric guitar have resulted from such a convergence of race, gender, and sexuality. The music of hard rock and heavy metal forebears such as the MC5 and Led Zeppelin provides perhaps the most explicit enactment of the racialized nature of rock's favored mode of phallocentric display, with the electric guitar as a privileged signifier of white male power and potency. Yet at issue is not a one-way line of transmission from black to white performers, but a system of racial, sexual, and musical meanings that have influenced both black and white musicians. Paul Gilroy thus noted the intermingling of sexuality and authenticity in the career of Jimi Hendrix, whose apparent adoption of the sexual codes inherited from minstrelsy dramatized the "antagonism between different local definitions of what blackness entailed" among the diverse audiences of 1960s popular music.[12]

For Hendrix, the electric guitar was crucial to the creation of a demonstrative sexual persona. Like the white guitarists who were his peers, he manipulated his instrument onstage to accentuate his physical presence. Unlike them, however, he was not seen to be aspiring toward some ideal of authentic musical performance rooted in race and sexuality, but was believed to personify that ideal by many of the whites in his audience. Among black onlookers he was more often criticized for his willingness to play to white expectations of how a black man should act. This division of judgment was not drawn so neatly along racial lines as I have made it sound. However, the discursive confusion over Hendrix's ultimate meaning as a black performer lays bare the extent to which he crossed easy lines of racial categorization through his distinctive style of electric guitar performance.

Viewed in this way, the electric guitar joins the history of the body as it has been formulated by Michel Foucault and Judith Butler, among others: the instrument is used to invest the body of the performer with meaning, to confer upon it a unique identity whose authentic, natural appearance works to conceal its reliance upon artifice and technology.[13] Just how deep-rooted the assumption of the electric guitar as a male instrument can be, for instance, is revealed by Jennifer Batten, a guitarist who spent several years touring with Michael Jackson as his lead guitarist. Recounting her experiences on tour, Batten noted that "it's a shock for some people to see a woman playing the guitar. All over the world, on the Michael Jackson tour, people would ask me whether I was a man or a woman. Just because I played guitar, they assumed I was a guy." Her interviewer, Joe Gore, responded astutely, "You mean it was easier for them to believe that the guitar player was a man who *looked* like a woman than that she was actually female?" "Yeah. It was a drag," stated Batten, "I'd stand there with my blonde hair, red lipstick, and caked-on stage makeup, thinking, 'Thank you, Poison! Thank you, Cinderella! You've confused the children of the world.'"[14] Batten refers to the prevalence of a sort of gender ambiguity among male hard rock bands in the 1980s that was designed not to call masculinity into question so much as add an air of excitement to the proceedings, playing upon the sexually charged question of "is he or isn't he." Her observations are more valuable, though, for exposing the way the electric guitar is habitually read in the context of rock performance and the processes through which the instrument carries certain associations that are inscribed onto the body of the performer.

These points of intersection between the electric guitar and the history of the body are only part of the instrument's significance. To return again to Dylan's performance at Newport, amid the range of associations that contributed to the controversy, what stands out is that the electric guitar was offensive because of its *sound*. A similar incident at Newport just three years later demonstrates this matter. The incident is narrated by Ellen Willis, who sets the scene by noting the relative informality of it all. It was a Saturday afternoon in the summer of 1968, and the festival's attendees were circulating among a number of folk music workshops designed to promote a more intimate brand of contact between performers and audiences than was available at the larger concert held during the evening. But, in Willis's account, "into this pastoral carnival crashed the sound of—electric blues."[15] Willis goes on to explain that "the workshops were not supposed to use amplification, but for obvious reasons this rule could not apply to City Blues, so a minimum of sound equipment had been set up on the amphitheater stage" to be used by the featured performers, black Chicago blues performers Junior Wells and Buddy Guy.[16] Even by the amplified standards of Chicago blues, Wells and Guy were loud performers; at Newport, they were so loud as to interfere with the other workshops, prompting the festival's director to request that they turn it down—a proposition that both the performers and the assembled crowd soundly rejected. And so the music continued, with guitarist Guy announcing to the audience, "This is my first year at Newport, and now you people have to come to Chicago. We play *loud!* I'd like this mike even louder."[17]

In this instance, the source of conflict was the "great divide" between acoustic and electric sound. Amplification represented a louder, more demonstrative style of musical performance that put the performer at the center of attention. For performers like Guy and Wells, the use of electric instruments was part of a musical strategy that stemmed from ghetto clubs in Chicago, where the attention of the audience could not be taken for granted but had to be won. A flamboyant performer, Guy, like Jimi Hendrix, used volume, feedback and other effects made possible by amplification to enhance his showmanship and draw attention to his mastery of his chosen instrument. Far from mere grandstanding, however, his use of such effects was the result of an aesthetic preference for sounds that cut against the grain of a smooth musical surface. At Newport, Guy's presence assumed the status of noise, of an approach to sound that could not be readily assimilated into the presiding social and aesthetic assumptions of the festival. In the broader world of American and British popular music during the 1960s, though, it was precisely this noise that guitarists used to forge new affective alliances between audiences and performers.

The line between acoustic and electric sound stands as a fundamental boundary in the recent history of popular music. Yet the electric guitar has a much broader importance with regard to sound than the electric/acoustic divide would suggest. Considered over the course of its history since its invention around 1930, the electric guitar is notable less for its connection to any one sound than for the general mutability of its sound. The distortion and excessive volume favored by musicians like Guy was but one possible set of sounds, and moreover one that gained currency only gradually over the course of the 1950s and 1960s, during which time it moved from African-American blues clubs to the broader national and international scene of popular music production. More influential during the early years of the instrument's career was the pure tone crafted by figures like Les Paul and Chet Atkins, guitarists who combined their interest in the electric guitar with new recording techniques, and who sought to eliminate the unwanted resonances and excessive noise of improperly amplified guitars as a means of increasing overall sonic clarity. In contrast to the sonoric excesses that were favored in later years, the sound cultivated by Paul and Atkins was calculated not to disturb the existing conventions of pop, but to assimilate the electric guitar into those conventions. As such, their actions laid the groundwork for the subsequent mass acceptance of the instrument.

Electric guitarists have been notable for the attention they have devoted to the quality and the character of the sounds they produce, and for their creative use of electric technologies in the making of popular music. As a history of the electric guitar, then, this book is also a history of certain modes of musical practice and of the engagement of musicians with particular ways of shaping sound. Similarly, in his history of digital instruments, Paul Théberge situates digital sound technologies within the broader history of musical reproduction in the twentieth century, noting that such instruments are an outgrowth of the tendency to treat musical sound as an increasingly autonomous and manipulable element.[18] This tendency resulted in large part from the advent and refinement of sound recording, which demonstrated that sound could be shaped in ways that were not systematically bound to the original act of musical performance. According to Théberge, digital instruments have blurred the line between recording and performance, between musical production and reproduction, by making available to musicians an array of sounds "already there," prerecorded sounds that can be tapped as the source for a new musical performance.[19] He goes on to observe that "musicians today . . . often speak of having a unique and personal 'sound' in the same manner in which another generation of musicians might have spoken of having developed a particular 'style.'" For Théberge, this concept of a "sound" is irremediably tied to the development of recording technologies, which have conferred upon sound a new materiality.[20] The electric guitar stands as a product of an earlier era. Although Théberge recognizes the instrument's flexibility in terms of sound, he also asserts that it cannot be considered a fully "electronic" musical device. The electric guitar retains too many of the features of traditional musical instruments, including a sound mechanism that relies on "a more-or-less direct relationship between player, technique, and instrument." By contrast, digital synthesizers, samplers, and drum machines "rely less on acoustics than on electronics and digital logic, and their sound-producing hardware is completely independent of the user 'interface'—the device that allows them to be played."[21] This shift in the basis of sound production is for Théberge what makes digital instruments "hybrid" objects that blend elements of musical production and reproduction.

Théberge's distinction between the basic step of electrifying sound and the later move toward an electronic approach to music is useful, particularly in light of the way that the electric guitar has often been cast as the guarantor of musical authenticity in opposition to the self-conscious fabrication promoted by synthesizers since the 1970s. In making this distinction, however, Théberge overlooks the ways in which the electric guitar set the stage for the hybrid objects and processes that are his main subject. If the electric guitar did not in itself contain the possibility for blending sound production and reproduction, the number of electric guitarists who have concentrated on both sides of this musical equation certainly furthered the tendency toward technological fusion and hybridization. Les Paul's simultaneous efforts to develop the solid-body electric guitar and techniques of multiple track recording are only the most explicit example of how guitarists have viewed the electric guitar not simply as a way of making music, but as a means of shaping sound. Playing with sound preoccupied all of the musicians I discuss, and their different approaches bring to light the role of the electric guitar in the history of twentieth century sounds as well as the role of sound in the cultural politics of twentieth century popular music.

French musicologist Jacques Attali provides another theoretical approach to sound and the significance of musical instruments that complements Théberge's work, but is broader in its implications. Attali's work has recently begun to garner considerable attention,[22] but few have noted the crucial role played by musical instruments in his theoretical framework. The omission is easily explainable, since the musicologists and cultural studies scholars who have found Attali's insights most useful have themselves paid scant attention to the role of instruments in the making of music. While nonacademic literature on the history of the electric guitar, for example, has grown exponentially over the past several years, due largely to the increasing value of the instrument as a "collector's item,"[23] one can count the number of significant academic discussions of the electric guitar on one hand. Robert Walser's analysis of the guitar-based virtuosity that reigns in heavy metal music is notable, and I build on Walser's many suggestive observations regarding the electric guitar in hard rock and heavy metal.[24] Other recent studies of popular music and aesthetics dwell upon the electric guitar in more than passing detail, but have tended to overgeneralize about its importance rather than examine it in different contexts to explore the range of meanings surrounding the instrument.[25] It is with the range of the guitar's meanings and uses that I am most concerned, by which I mean two things: the ways in which the electric guitar has been integrated into a diverse set of existing musical contexts, and the ways in which the electric guitar has reshaped those contexts, and has created new fields of knowledge within the history of popular music.

Attali is most relevant to the latter of these issues. Instruments play a key part in his larger effort to theorize the role of music as a prophetic social force, one that contains within it the principles of cultural, economic, and political power. In the first chapter of his book, *Noise,* Attali outlines his inquiry in terms that make manifest his overarching belief in the capacity of music to embody and, indeed, herald the social order:

> Fetishized as a commodity, music is illustrative of the evolution of our entire society: deritualize a social form, repress an activity of the body, specialize its practice, sell it as a spectacle, generalize its consumption, then see to it that it is stockpiled until it loses its meaning. Today music heralds—regardless of what the property mode of capital will be—the establishment of a society of repetition in which nothing will happen anymore. But at the same time, it heralds the emergence of a formidable subversion, one leading to a radically new organization never yet theorized, of which self-management is but a distant echo.[26]

The historical trajectory of Attali's argument is at once critical and utopian: in the past and present of musical organization he perceives both the seeds of political disaster—a new totalitarianism based on an economy of repetitive desire—and the possibility of a transformation that would restore music to the hands of its makers.

Underlying each of these potentialities is the fundamental quality of music as a means of structuring difference, a quality within which the main source of conflict and opposition is between musical "order" and "noise." His book traces

> the political economy of music as a succession of *orders* (in other words, differences) done violence by *noises* (in other words, the calling into question of differences) that are *prophetic* because they create new orders, unstable and changing. The simultaneity of multiple codes, the variable overlappings between periods, styles, and forms, prohibits any attempt at a genealogy of music, a hierarchical archeology, or a precise ideological pinpointing of particular musicians. But it is possible to discern who among them are innovators and heralds of worlds in the making.[27]

Attali here formulates a dialectic of musical development predicated not simply upon the changing structure of music as such, but upon the changing modes of social organization that music represents. "Noise" is that mode of sound that interrupts the existing codes according to which music is understood, and in so doing proposes a new way of musical understanding that could also lead to new ways of structuring power and difference. Noise, then, is not a strictly musical category, not to be equated with dissonance; rather, it refers as much to ways of making music, or of experiencing music, as to the music itself.

This grounding of "noise" in musical practice is most clear in the theoretical priority assigned by Attali to "the instrument" as a device that might lead the way toward new modes of musical perception and understanding. As he writes in the last chapter of *Noise,* "Music should be a reminder to others that if *Incontri* was not written for a symphony orchestra, or the *Lamentations* for electric guitar, it is because each instrument, each tool, theoretical or concrete, implies a sound field, a field of knowledge, an imaginable and explorable universe."[28] In such passages, it becomes clear that Attali's goal is not to theorize *about* music but *through* it, to use music as a "tool of understanding" that can open a "sound form of knowledge."[29] Instruments are crucial to this search for knowledge through sound because they are the nexus at which the abstract codes of music-making meet the material acts through which music is produced.[30] They are the points at which new theories of music-making first begin to take shape:

> In music, the instrument often predates the expression it authorizes, which explains why a new invention has the nature of noise; a "realized theory"

(Lyotard), it contributes, through the possibilities it offers, to the birth of a new music, a renewed syntax. It makes possible a new system of combination, creating an open field for a whole new exploration of the possible expressions of musical usage. Thus Beethoven's Sonata no. 106, the first piece written for the piano, would have been unthinkable on any other instrument. Likewise, the work of Jimi Hendrix is meaningless without the electric guitar, the use of which he perfected.[31]

For Attali, instruments contain the possibility of reorganizing musical practice. Indeed, he describes his ideal model of musical freedom, "Composition," as a process of taking "pleasure in the instruments, the tools of communication."[32] In Composition, the musical worker uses his instrument to create his own musical code in which noise no longer signifies an unwanted dissonance but rather demarcates the autonomy of desire. Yet Attali adds a qualification here: "inducing people to compose using predefined instruments cannot lead to a mode of production different from that authorized by those instruments. That is the trap."[33] The instrument must, in a sense, be reinvented lest it merely reproduce the existing terms of domination through the regulation of noise.

With Attali's framework in mind, the ability of the electric guitar to generate noise assumes a new significance. The issue is not whether the instrument created volume, distortion, and other sonic effects, but whether the creation of these effects, the noise of the electric guitar, marked a reorganization of musical practice or a reconceptualization of social and political differences through music. My answer is a qualified "yes," with a qualification similar to Attali's that such a reorganization does not always move in a progressive or liberatory direction. The innovations of Les Paul are one example of a genuine rethinking of the process of making music that left existing relations of power and difference intact, particularly with regard to gender. Moreover, the achievement of new effects always contains within it the potential of becoming normalized. Like the instruments that produce it, noise itself has to be continually reinvented if it is to avoid becoming the basis for a new, restrictive musical order. One might well claim that this is the legacy of the 1960s, when the noise of the electric guitar, which seemed to hold so much promise as a means of establishing new sorts of musical relationships between audience and performer, instead solidified the influence of capital upon musical production.

This book therefore does not present a progressive narrative of musical and political achievement with regard to the electric guitar. Especially when one considers the electric guitar's impact upon the race and gender dynamics of popular music, any notion of radical or even steady progress fades quickly from view. The instrument has, if anything, strengthened the male bias of public musical performance during the twentieth century. Its impact upon race has been less clear, but when one examines the fact that, despite the overwhelming influence of African-American musical practices, the electric guitar is today cast as an overwhelmingly white instrument, it is hard to escape the conclusion that the instrument has participated in a significant act of racial expropriation. If the electric guitar has not entirely restructured the musical performance of difference, it has been an agent of change, shaping the mode of musical production and the experience of difference in and through popular music. Furthermore, I hope I encourage readers to think about *why* the most far-reaching possibilities opened by the electric guitar have not come to pass, and to think about alternative strategies for using music, and musical instruments, as tools of social and cultural (as well as aesthetic) transformation.

Chapter 1

Playing with Sound

Charlie Christian, the Electric Guitar, and the Swing Era

Soundings

One night in Bismarck, North Dakota, in 1938, a young guitarist named Mary Osborne went to hear Charlie Christian play at a local jazz club. Christian was a rising musician in the jazz world, whose notoriety came not only from his talent but from his use of a fairly new invention, the electric guitar. Inside the club, Osborne heard a sound "much like a tenor saxophone strangely distorted by an amplification system." When she saw Charlie, she realized that she was listening to an electric guitar "playing single line solos, and voiced like a horn in an ensemble with the tenor sax and trumpet." She continued, "I remember some of the figures Charlie played in his solos. They were exactly the same things that Benny [Good-man] recorded later as *Flying Home, Gone with 'What' Wind, Seven Come Eleven* (sic) and all the others."[1] Osborne was impressed by Christian's virtuosity as a jazz soloist, but was most fascinated by the unfamiliar sounds emanating from Christian's guitar.

Today the electric guitar does not sound so foreign. We take its extreme volume or its ability to cut through a full band almost as a matter of course. Since at least the 1960s, the electric guitar has been the principal solo instrument of popular music, and electric guitarists have become cult heroes around whom many fans perceive the music to revolve. Such was not the case in the 1930s. During the 1930s and early 1940s, the electric guitar was transformed into a solo instrument by musicians like Charlie Christian. Though not the first to play the electric guitar, Christian used the new sounds made available by the instrument to forge a unique single note style that broke jazz guitar out of its confinement in the rhythm section. With Christian the electric guitar became a major instrumental voice, on a level with the horns that dominated the swing jazz style of the time.

Christian's innovative use of the electric guitar drew heavily upon the musical traditions of the Southwest, where he grew up. Born in Texas and raised in Oklahoma City, Christian came of age in an area where black and white folk styles mixed, and where music was a pervasive element of social interaction.[2] By the late 1920s, Oklahoma City was second only to Kansas City as the leading jazz center of the southwestern United States; musicians traveled back and forth between the two cities, participating in a circuit of musical exchange that centered around jam sessions and public competitions between the hottest big bands.[3] Christian's own musical style was shaped by the blues-based swing that dominated the southwestern jazz scene, and he transplanted this style to the East when he joined Goodman's band in 1939. Christian's history is therefore part of the story of how regional musical styles were incorporated into a broader system of commercial and musical exchange, a process that was largely mediated by the recording industry.

This process of transmission was central to what jazz historians have labeled the swing era, the period when jazz became fully integrated into the commercial mainstream of American culture.[4] The music of the swing era was dominated by the big bands (generally featuring ten to fifteen instruments). While often heavily arranged, the best big band music created a sense of spontaneity and rhythmic immediacy that made it the most popular dance music of the Depression. As such, swing music was an important avenue of advancement for musicians. Those who sat in the orchestras of Benny Goodman or Count Basie had made it to the top of their profession.

By 1940, however, this degree of fame and financial success was not enough for a number of young musicians who were dissatisfied with the stylistic stagnation of swing. Charlie Christian was one of a small number of young black musicians who participated in the formation of bebop, a musical style that featured small groups improvising over complex chord changes. Bebop was oriented toward allowing more room for individual creative expression, while at the same time shaping a music of such rhythmic and harmonic complexity that only musicians initiated in the new style could participate. For black musicians, such efforts were in part a frustrated response to the situation in swing whereby the bulk of the profit went to white musicians and bandleaders.[5] Perhaps more important, bebop represented a self-conscious attempt by black musicians to modernize their music, and to create new forms of expression that confronted the dominant culture.[6] The new music therefore emerged as a resistant practice, designed so as not to be easily borrowed or easily appreciated.

Charlie Christian played a central role in this modernization of the black jazz voice until his death in 1942 at the age of twenty-five, participating in Harlem jam sessions with future innovators like Thelonius Monk and Dizzy Gillespie. His role within the formative stages of bebop was made distinctive by the degree of success that he had already attained as a featured performer with Benny Goodman's Sextet. As the most successful of the young bebop experimenters, Christian, perhaps more than any other musician, straddled the increasingly separate realms of swing and bebop. Moreover, Christian's participation in the search for a new jazz vocabulary paralleled his attempt to create a new voice for the guitar. The electric guitar followed him in his move from local jazz hero to swing virtuoso to proto-bebop innovator. Through these transitions and transformations, the guitar was itself transformed both as musical instrument and as commercial object.

Charlie Christian's Guitar

Ralph Ellison, in his book, *Shadow and Act,* remembered his days as an aspiring young trumpet player in Oklahoma City: "Sometimes, inspired by the even then considerable virtuosity of the late Charlie Christian (who during our school days played marvelous riffs on a cigar box banjo), I'd give whole summer afternoons and the evening hours . . . to practicing hard-driving blues."[7] Having grown up in a family of musicians, Christian cultivated his talent at an early age. He mastered blues technique on a makeshift instrument, a cigar box banjo that was undoubtedly homemade. One can imagine the sounds that such an instrument would emit: thin, tightly drawn, and most likely not well-tempered.

Stringed instruments such as the banjo and the guitar have been prominent in American music for over two centuries. A prototype for the banjo was brought by African slaves, and was picked up by white minstrel performers as early as the 1830s.[8] The guitar similarly entered the American continent through the slave trade. Both instruments were central in the creation of African-American musical forms; Robert Palmer has described how the guitar's "flexibility in terms of tuning made it the ideal instrumental vehicle for the non-tempered, microtonal melodic language of the blues."[9] Early "race record" blues releases by performers such as Blind Lemon Jefferson and Charley Patton often featured only guitar backing behind the vocals, while solo or duet guitar instrumentals were not uncommon.[10] The acoustic guitar thus became an essential component of the rural bluesman, one of the central images of the early recording industry.

Growing up as a musician in the black neighborhoods of Oklahoma City, Christian absorbed the influences of acoustic blues through his everyday encounters as well as through records and radio. Blues were by no means the only influence available to the young Christian. Ellison vividly describes the musical culture of the city, where "a number of the local musicians were conservatory-trained," and "harmony was taught from the ninth through the twelfth grades" in the high school he and Christian attended.[11] Moreover, Christian, his father, and his brothers regularly strolled through white neighborhoods playing "light classics as well as the blues"; his brother Edward later led his own jazz band and played with members of the famed Blue Devils Orchestra.[12] Christian therefore had a direct connection to the city's jazz scene in his own family, and more generally had access to a broad range of musical styles during his youth that were not strictly limited to local forms of folk expression.

The dance band styles popularized during this period reflected contemporary processes of musical cross-fertilization. In southwestern swing, musicians applied the loose melodic structure and rhythmic variations of the blues to standard jazz instruments like the saxophone and trumpet. Black jazz bands also drew heavily upon a repertory of vaudeville songs that were decidedly not of African-American origin. Just as much a product of musical hybridization was western swing, a big band style that combined rural white fiddle music with many of the same principles that drove the black jazz bands, including an emphasis on improvisation and a driving dance-oriented rhythm section.[13] White and black musicians rarely played together, at least publicly, but each group was listening to the other. Music, then, transgressed the racial boundaries that shaped social interaction.

Early uses of the electric guitar further reflected the interracial dynamics of the southwestern music scene. By the middle of the 1930s, musicians in both western swing bands and swing jazz bands were using the electric guitar, influencing each other over the radio and through recordings. White guitarists such as Leon McCauliffe and Bob Dunn, and black guitarists such as Eddie Durham and Christian were all simultaneously experimenting with amplification, seeking to transform the guitar from a rhythm instrument into a medium for single-note improvisation.

At the time, the guitar was a fairly recent addition to the emergent jazz band style. In the earliest years of jazz, the guitar lacked the sheer volume necessary to work effectively in combination with the much louder horn instruments that dominated the music. Banjos rather than guitars were the mainstays of jazz rhythm sections throughout much of the 1920s, because the banjo generated considerably more sound than its six-stringed counterpart. Yet the banjo's sharp, penetrating tone began to clash with the smoother rhythmic flow that dance bands were seeking. By the end of the decade, an increasing number of bands began substituting guitar for banjo in their rhythm sections, since the guitar's tone blended better with the changing jazz band sound.[14] The problem still remained, however, of how to ensure the guitar's audibility within the larger band context.

In response to this matter, a small number of artisans, inventors, and entrepreneurs began experimenting with ways to amplify the guitar. By 1930, the Dobro company had produced what was probably the first commercially manufactured electric guitar. Only a year later Rickenbacker came out with its "frying pan" model.[15] The frying pan's odd shape, which looked more like a banjo with an elongated neck than a standard guitar, was fairly typical of the permutations that characterized the earliest electric guitars. Yet the most notable characteristic of the electric guitar was the inclusion of an electromagnetic device called a pickup, which transmitted the vibrations of the strings so that the guitar's sound could be amplified. It was with the incorporation of the pickup onto the body of the guitar that the electric guitar as such was "born," for

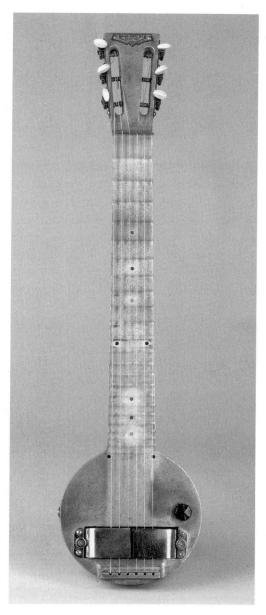

1.1. The Rickenbacker "Frying Pan," the earliest commercially manufactured electric guitar, first issued to the market in 1932. Courtesy of the Experience Music Project.

this innovation in design marked the first real acknowledgment of the integral role of electricity to the instrument's changing function.

In 1936, Rickenbacker's company catalog portrayed the electric guitar as a "miracle" of sound that tapped into an elemental or even divine source of electric energy.[16] Meanwhile, guitar companies began to standardize the shape of the new invention. A year earlier, the Rickenbacker had introduced its first Spanish-body electric models, which integrated electric sound technology with a more conventional shape and design not far removed from the acoustic guitar. That same year, the Gibson company produced its first electric guitar, a finely crafted Spanish-body instrument called the ES-150. As a "long-established leader" in instrument manufacturing, Gibson gave the electric guitar legitimacy while also improving both the aesthetic and the technical qualities of the instrument.[17] The ES-150 was the foremost expression of the guitar as a commercial object during the 1930s, combining the modernism of the new sound technology with a neoclassical design that signified craftsmanship and respectability.

Electric guitars did not circulate only through commercial channels, however. Many musicians engaged in their own attempts to amplify the guitar. Eddie Durham, a musician and arranger with several successful bands of the period, experimented with ways to increase the volume of his guitar, independently creating his own resonating devices until he bought a National resonating guitar in 1933.[18] By 1938, Durham was recording solos on electric guitar with the Kansas City Six, a small-group offshoot of Count Basie's band. A year earlier, he met twenty-year-old Charlie Christian in an Oklahoma City pool hall, where Christian asked the older musician how he got his unique sound. Durham recalled the encounter in an interview in 1979:

> He asked me to give him some pointers, like what to do if you want to play the instrument with class and go through life with the instrument. He wanted to know technical things, like how to use a pick a certain way . . . I said, "Don't ever use an up-stroke, which makes a tag-a-tag-a-tag sound; use a down-stroke." It takes an awful fast wrist to play a down-stroke—it gives a staccato to sound, with no legato, and you sound like a horn.[19]

By his own account, Durham was already aware that the electric guitar might open new musical avenues, and he passed this on to Christian.

1.2. The Gibson ES-150 electric guitar, first produced in 1936. Charlie Christian used an ES-150 for much of his early career, and the bar pickup included on these guitars has since become known as the "Charlie Christian" pickup. Courtesy of the Experience Music Project.

Channels of exchange and communication among musicians were at least as important as commercial channels in the success of the electric guitar.

Exchanges among musicians were by no means free of commercial influence, though. Shortly after his encounter with Durham, Christian bought his first Gibson electric guitar, probably an ES-150, and also probably the same model played by Durham.[20] Similarly, Mary Osborne, after seeing Christian play, "scouted the local music stores until she found a Gibson like his—bar pickup and all," while another local store displayed the latest electric guitar "as featured by Charlie Christian."[21] Instruments gained an aura of prestige through their association with established musicians, an aura that was perhaps further enhanced by the company logo that appeared on the headstock of every Gibson guitar.

Whatever status the electric guitar may have conferred upon a musician was significantly heightened when Christian joined the Goodman band in 1939. An article written by Christian for *Down Beat* magazine in December of that year reveals how the electrification of the guitar enhanced his career. Entitled "Guitarmen, Wake Up and Pluck! Wire for Sound; Let 'Em Hear You Play," the article reads as a veritable manifesto for the electric guitar. Christian asserts that most bandleaders see guitarists only as robots "plunking on a gadget to keep the rhythm going." After several paragraphs that more or less reiterate this point, he goes on to declare that "the dawn of a new era is at hand for all those fine guitarists who had become resigned to playing to feed their souls but not necessarily their stomachs. Electrical amplification has given guitarists a new lease on life."[22] The connection between the electric guitar and newfound prosperity dominates the rest of the piece. Christian recounts how amplifying the guitar led to his big break playing with Benny Goodman, before concluding with a plea for "all you starving guitarists" to "take heart."

> I know, and so does the rest of our small circles, that you play damned fine music, but now you've got a chance to bring the fact to the attention of not only short-sighted leaders but to the attention of the world. And I don't think it'll be long before you're feeding your stomach as well as your heart. Practice solo stuff, single string and otherwise, and save up a few dimes to amplify your instrument.
>
> You continue to play the guitar the way it should be played, and you'll make the rest of the world like it.[23]

For Christian, playing guitar "the way it should be played" meant using the instrument as a means of personal artistic expression. Music was sustenance for the soul; yet talent and creativity did not put food on the table. According to Christian's rhetoric, economic concerns were inseparable from artistic ones. The electric guitar represented the "dawn of a new era" not because it would enhance guitarists' creativity (which according to the article was already impressive) but because it would allow them to be heard, and to capitalize upon their talent. Christian therefore constructs an image of the electric guitar as an instrument of opportunity, a representation that had special resonance after years of economic depression. Meanwhile, Christian could use his successful image to promote guitarists and the electric guitar as integral to jazz performance, and thus to fully participate in the commercial benefits of the swing era.

Movement

In August 1939, Charlie Christian stands in front of a train that will take him to Los Angeles, where he will audition for Benny Goodman. Smiling broadly, dressed casually, with hat in hand, Christian shakes hands with trumpeter James Simpson, while Eddie Christian smiles and watches at his brother's side.[24] Read literally, the image captures a significant point in Christian's career, the point at which he moved from local jazz hero to commercial jazz star. Read symbolically, the photograph illustrates one of the central motifs in the history and mythology of jazz: that of movement, in its many manifestations, whether it be the relocation of a musician to capitalize on commercial opportunities, the transmission of styles across geographical areas, or the moment at which stylistic experiments engender a new jazz vocabulary.

Charlie Christian moved into the jazz mainstream by virtue of his talent and his creative use of the electric guitar. Yet he was also part of the broader integration of southwestern swing into the increasingly nationalized jazz economy. The Southwest was a hub of jazz activity during the Depression, particularly in Kansas City, where political corruption created an economic shield that permitted the development and sustenance of a flourishing night life.[25] Musician John Tumino described the unique situation in Kansas City: "Well, hell, everybody, the rest of the country,

1.3.   Charlie Christian getting ready to board the train to Los Angeles, where he will audition with Benny Goodman, in the summer of 1939. Courtesy of Frank Driggs.

was in the Depression . . . Now I'm talking about deep depression. They couldn't afford three dollars a night for a musician. But in Kansas City, every damn little joint had musicians. They came from Oklahoma and New Orleans and Omaha and . . . the whole Midwest. They all came to Kansas City because every joint had a place for 'em."[26] Kansas City stood at the center of a jazz network that ran through the Southwest. Musicians traveled from all over and moved about regularly, exchanging ideas while they competed with each other for recognition from both the public and their peers.

Competition was a central feature of the Southwest's musical culture. Advertisements for shows regularly announced the staging of "battles" between the bands on the showbill. "Astounding music! Phenomenal music! Continuous dancing to the exhilarating tunes of 8 great bands," proclaimed one poster from the early 1930s, which went on to emphasize the presentation of "A Battle of Music!" between the bands of Thamon Hayes and Bennie Moten: "HAYES' BAND AND MOTEN'S VICTOR RE- CORDERS—two crack orchestras—will work off a sportsmanlike grudge when they finish up with a battle royal to decide which of them is the better band. Don't miss this!"[27] More than a simple advertising strategy, battles between bands shaped the relationship between band and audience, giving the audience a major participatory role in the performance. A band judged how well it was playing by the response of the crowd, by the energy of the dancing that accompanied each number, and the enthusiasm of the appreciation that followed the songs.[28] Within such an environment, a successful band might extend a single composition for an hour or even longer, as the musicians' improvisatory flights derived sustenance from spirited audience reaction and interaction.

Relationships among musicians were also marked by this sense of competitiveness, particularly in the jam sessions that were so much a part of the region's jazz scene. Musicians would stay up all night and into the early morning participating in "cutting sessions," where they would take turns improvising over familiar compositions, often trying to upstage one another through the exhibition of creativity and virtuosity.[29] The session was more than a forum for musical showboating, however. Jo Jones, long-time drummer for Count Basie's band, emphasized that the sessions were held "for the joy of playing."

> Now those were pretty tough times and yet the guys did take the time to study, and when they had found something new they would bring it up to the session and they would pass it around to the other musicians, no matter what instrument they played. So they would try that particular riff or that particular conception at a session and perfect it. The idea of the jam session then wasn't who could play better than somebody else—it was a matter of contributing something and of experimentation.[30]

Experimentation often worked in conjunction with the spirit of competition. Musicians looked for new ideas or techniques to cut their challengers, and to mark themselves as deserving respect for having something unique to play. Yet experimentation was also a crucial part of the musical exchange that occurred in the sessions, as musicians shared new ideas with one another, and worked out their ideas collectively. Jam sessions therefore fostered a sense of social camaraderie within competitive circumstances.

The southwestern swing style combined the tendency toward experimentation and personal expression so prominent in the jam sessions with

1.4. Charlie Christian jamming with saxophonists Sam Hughes *(left, with horn lowered)* and Dick Wilson *(right, blowing hard)* at Ruby's Grill in Oklahoma City, where the guitarist played a regular gig with pianist Leslie Sheffield before moving to join the Goodman band. Photo by Buddy Andersen, courtesy of Frank Driggs.

a smooth rhythmic drive that made the music extremely popular for dancing. Compositions were centered around riffs, short melodic statements that were repeated in unison, often with variation, throughout a given piece. These riffs gave structure and unity to a composition through repetition, and also served as a basis for the improvisations of individual soloists. Like the dance-ready 4/4 rhythm that drove the music, the solo lines of the best southwestern musicians flowed with an air of relaxation, with notes often landing on either side of the beat, and resting in between points of harmonic progression.[31] Such was the style of Lester Young, who played tenor saxophone with the Basie band and had a strong influence upon the young Charlie Christian. Young eschewed sheer technical display for expressiveness, and relied upon musical understatement to turn his solos into condensed narratives of musical and emotional experience.[32] His solos are filled with pauses and long notes that leave the listener uncertain of where the line may go next, though providing a sense of resolution in the end. Through Young's influence, Christian learned to play "like a horn" and to seek ways of extending the language of jazz.

Count Basie, Lester Young, and Charlie Christian were all "discovered" in the mid- to late 1930s by John Hammond, a record producer and talent scout for Columbia Records. Hammond brought to his relentless search for unrecorded talent a concern for maintaining the integrity of the music he recorded, especially when that music was performed by black musicians. He had an uncommon attraction to African-American music and, despite his association with Benny Goodman, seemed to believe that blacks were more natural, authentically talented musicians than were whites. In the program notes to the "From Spirituals to Swing" concert that Hammond produced in 1938, he and James Dugan asserted that the "best hot musicians are men of profound feeling, even if this feeling is inarticulate," before announcing that they wanted to show the audience some "real" jazz by "presenting some of its best Negro practitioners."[33] Despite the condescension of such statements, Hammond, a committed jazz fan as well as a producer, treated black musicians with respect and, as the manager of Benny Goodman, was one of the key figures in breaking down the racial segregation of the swing bands. In 1936, Goodman, strongly supported by Hammond, hired pianist Teddy Wilson as part of his trio, thus becoming the first white bandleader to hire a black musician.[34] Less than four years later, Hammond traveled to Oklahoma City to hear Charlie Christian, and was so impressed he almost immediately brought him to Los Angeles to audition for Goodman.

The story of Christian's audition with Goodman has become legendary within the history of jazz. By Hammond's account, Goodman initially had been dismissive of Christian, and expressed little interest in the idea of incorporating an electric guitar into his band. During an intermission at one of Goodman's shows, Hammond and bassist Artie Bernstein sneaked Christian's equipment onto the stage. Upon returning, the perturbed Goodman called for the band to play the tune "Rose Room." Hammond continues the story:

I am reasonably certain Christian had never heard "Rose Room" before, because it was a West Coast song not in the repertoire of most black bands. No matter. Charlie had ears like an antennae. All he had to do was hear the melody and chord structure once and he was ready to play twenty-five choruses, each more inventive than the last . . . Before long the crowd was screaming with amazement. "Rose Room" continued for more than three quarters of an hour and Goodman received an ovation unlike any even he had before.[35]

Only twenty-two years old at the time, Christian joined Goodman's Sextet with a burst of creativity, overturning any doubts Goodman might have had about featuring the electric guitar as a solo instrument. The young guitarist was now employed by one of the most popular bandleaders in the country: he had "made it."

Yet the question remains of what this success meant to Christian, and more specifically, what did it mean for Christian, as a black musician, to join the band of a white bandleader? Such a move was undoubtedly an advancement in economic terms. John Hammond declared that Christian's salary went from $7.50 per week to $150 per week upon joining Goodman's band.[36] Christian could also reach a much broader audience than before and could attain new heights (for him) of public recognition, as shown by his repeated victories in *Down Beat* readers' polls from 1939 to 1941.[37] However, being so much in the spotlight also meant being much more visible to whites, who composed the majority of the jazz audience during the swing era.[38] Joining Goodman's band therefore also meant assuming a certain image for Christian, a look of respectability that justified his new status.

A publicity photo from Christian's first year with the band offers some insight into his position relative to the Goodman organization. The picture features Goodman at center, flanked by Christian and guitarist Arnold Covey, who tended to hold down the rhythm in the Goodman big band. Christian wears the formal costume of the professional jazz musician, participating in a masquerade of respectability that was part of the ritual of being a professional. For Christian, this was probably both a self-representation and a representation imposed upon him by Goodman, one which distinguished his playing from forms of distinctly African-American performance like the blues. Moreover, the centrality of the leader within the frame leaves no doubt as to the controlling presence.

1.5.   Charlie Christian flanking bandleader Benny Goodman's left side, holding his Gibson ES-150 guitar. On the right is guitarist Arnold Covey, who regularly performed with the Goodman big band. Photo by Charles Nadell, courtesy of Frank Driggs.

The guitarists seem almost peripheral, and Christian's guitar here is literally placed before him, figured as a further badge of his new status, and held out with a prideful stance.

The sound of Christian's guitar was central to the music of Goodman's Sextet during his brief two-year career with the band. James Lincoln Collier, a jazz historian, has discussed the way in which the Sextet played with sound, using the contrasting timbres of the various solo instruments to add variation to the fairly simple riff-based song structure.[39] This use of sound reached its fruition by late 1940, when the group featured three horn soloists—Goodman on clarinet, Georgie Auld on tenor saxophone, and Cootie Williams on trumpet—with markedly different sounds alongside Christian's hornlike guitar playing. Meanwhile, Christian's solos with the group extended the blues-based vocabulary of southwestern swing into new terrain, both musically and socially. Ralph Ellison described the meaning of musical style for black musicians during the 1930s:

> [T]here is a conflict between what the Negro American musician feels in the community around him and the given (or classical) techniques of his instrument. He feels a tension between his desire to master the classical style of playing and his compulsion to express those sounds which form a musical definition of Negro American experience . . . Among the younger musicians of the thirties, especially those who contributed to the growth of bop, this desire to master the classical technique was linked with the struggle for recognition in the larger society, and with a desire to throw off those non-musical features which came into jazz from the minstrel tradition.[40]

The basic tension described by Ellison is fundamental to understanding Christian's career with Goodman. Christian's move to join Goodman's band was itself an expression of his desire for "recognition in the larger [read: white] society." Yet Christian himself was never fully integrated into the band. While he had a prominent role in the Sextet, he rarely performed with the more popular large orchestra, a situation he shared with the other black musicians hired by Goodman during the 1930s, like pianist Teddy Wilson and vibraphonist Lionel Hampton. Nascent attempts at integration thus coexisted with continued segregation during the swing era. The parity that Charlie Christian's guitar gained with respect to other solo instruments was not equaled by his own parity with respect to white musicians.

A pair of front-page articles from the October 15, 1939 issue of *Down Beat* further illustrates this point. Written in response to Goodman's decision to bring Christian into his band, the articles articulated the ambivalence of the jazz community toward the matter of integration. Answering the question, "Should Negro Musicians Play in White Bands?" a host of musicians responded in the negative, with one anonymous source highlighting potential danger of black male musicians making sexual overtures to white female patrons as the principal reason for opposition.[41] Even some of those who supported Goodman's move did so in divided terms. Bandleader Woody Herman, for instance, declared his band's admiration for black musicians and their devotion to musical styles of African-American derivation such as the blues. However, Herman went on to state that despite their sentiments regarding African-American music and musicians, he and his bandmates would not consider the addition of a black member: "We have too much respect for the vitality and imagination of Negro musicians to ask any one of them to sacrifice his integrity."[42] Such tacit support for continued segregation was set alongside more unflinching praise for Goodman's choice from both white and black musicians, including Goodman and Christian's bandmate, Teddy Wilson. Amid all these voices, what perhaps is heard most clearly is a description of the move toward integration as a unilateral decision: it is Goodman who is to be commended or criticized, not Christian, whose agency is effectively effaced along with his voice, notably absent from the list of those questioned.

That black musicians were not empowered to define the terms of their recognition during the swing era comes as no surprise. Jazz historians, and the few cultural historians who write about jazz, have continually defined the rise of bebop as the moment when black musicians began to define for themselves the terms of musical performance and creativity, in direct confrontation with the hierarchies that existed within the swing orchestras. Yet the opposition between swing and bebop should not be drawn so starkly.[43] During the swing era, black musicians like Charlie Christian sought to combine creativity with commercial success. More important, Christian's image as a member of Goodman's band was one that mediated between the minstrel tradition of black performance and more modern, self-reflective forms of presentation. The mask of respectability that Christian assumed perhaps was projected to appease white expectations, but was also a mark of self-assurance that expressed his willingness to mix up sounds and play the changes in front of any audience, black or white. Similarly, Christian's use of the electric guitar reflected his desire to be heard at the same time as it expressed a demand to be heard differently. He would articulate this demand more clearly in the jam sessions held at Minton's nightclub in Harlem.

Changes

The language of African-American modernism is an insider's language projected outside, an attempt to bring the secrets that have been contained behind the minstrel mask to the direct attention of white listeners while still keeping those listeners in the dark as to what is being said.

Houston Baker describes the modernist strategy as one in which the black performer exhibits at once a mastery of the "skills and knowledge of a 'master culture'" and a firm understanding of vernacular "modes of existence."[44] Baker's framework is very close to that articulated above by Ellison, in which black performers adopted "correct" styles of performance in their quest for recognition. However, for Baker the process involved is more explicitly one of appropriation and reconfiguration, in which style, whether it be musical or literary, is used to challenge white cultural dominance.

Bebop was not an essentially black musical language. Like southwestern swing, it was a fusion of African-American and Euro-American influences, a mixing of rhythmic variation, melodic improvisation, and complex harmonic structures. During the years (1940–1942) that Charlie Christian was jamming in Harlem with Thelonius Monk, Kenny Clarke, Dizzy Gillespie, and other young jazz players, the music was only starting to sound new, to assume a sound that would later be identified as modern. Nonetheless, even during these early years, the music played by (mostly) black musicians in the Harlem jam sessions assumed the status of an insider's language, removed from the jazz mainstream, in which the conventions of jazz performance were extended and, ultimately, transformed.

Minton's Playhouse was mostly where the new music was played, a place of mythological importance within the history of jazz. Countless creation myths concerning the formation of bebop have been written with Minton's as the Eden where jazz was reborn into modernism. Yet the descriptions provided by musicians are more modest than those put forth by critics and historians. Mary Lou Williams and Carmen McCrae, for instance, remembered Minton's in the following terms:

> Minton's Playhouse was not a large place, but it was nice and intimate. The bar was at the front, and the cabaret was in the back. The bandstand was situated at the rear of the back room, where the wall was covered with strange paintings depicting weird characters sitting on a brass bed, or jamming, or talking to chicks.[45]

> Minton's was just a place for cats to jam. People didn't pay too much attention to what was going on, I mean those people there that weren't musicians. So when you went in you'd see cats half-stewed who weren't paying much mind to what was happening on stage. But the musicians were.[46]

Minton's gave musicians a place to congregate and to play away from the formality of their regular engagements. The jam sessions at Minton's were occasions for social and musical exchange like those held in Kansas City. Yet the context had changed. Many of the musicians playing at Minton's had made the same move as Charlie Christian, a move to integrate their careers into the commercial mainstream of the swing era. The jam sessions at Minton's, unlike those in Kansas City, were more clearly an alternative social and creative space to the dance halls and the large bands that dominated jazz performance at the time.

At Minton's, and in bebop more generally, performers organized themselves into small groups that aimed to increase the space for individual solos and improvisation. Gone were the large, heavily arranged orchestrations of the big bands, but also gone were the tight, ordered unison lines that constituted the central structural element of Goodman's Sextet. The new music was more sparse, dominated by single-note improvisations over unconventional harmonic structures. "Playing the changes" was the central musical attribute of early bop, the musical element at which Charlie Christian most excelled. Musician James Moody recalled that when the band at Minton's used to play "Stompin' at the Savoy," a jazz standard, "Charlie Christian would be playing on it, and he'd start playing, and on the outside of it he would just be going along slowly, and as soon as he came to the difficult part, the bridge, he would tear it up, he would dive in. Now I know that was intentional, it was beautiful."[47] "Playing the changes" meant digging into the chord structures underlying a composition to find notes that weren't explicitly stated by the harmonic logic of the piece. Such a style of improvisation increased the freedom of melodic development, which was no longer tied to a composed theme. Moreover, standard tunes were regularly defamiliarized and recomposed by imposing a new set of chord changes upon the melody. Harmonic improvisation was thus the critical point of experimentation in the Minton's jam sessions, through which soloists were liberated to play at the limits of established jazz methods.

Charlie Christian regularly attended these Harlem sessions to the point where he left an amplifier permanently on the Minton's bandstand. In his playing at the club, Christian moved the electric guitar even further in the direction of single-note improvisation than he already had in his performances with Goodman. The few recordings made during the sessions show Christian soloing for minutes upon end, while the tone of his guitar sounds sharper than it had with the Sextet, possessing a trebly edge that cuts through the sparse accompaniment. Moreover, as Gunther Schuller describes in his book, *The Swing Era,* Christian's melodic lines were "almost completely linear" in his playing at Minton's, at times threatening to elude the underlying harmonic structure.[48] Schuller goes on to suggest that Christian was the most advanced of all the young experimenters, expressing hints of a new jazz vocabulary that was only beginning to assume clarity and focus.[49]

Unfortunately, Christian died before bebop had stylistically matured. While his innovations gave impetus to the music's development, he became frail and weak from tuberculosis, exhausting himself through his participation in the all-night jams. At the time of Christian's death in 1942, bebop remained, as Ellison described it, "a texture of fragments, repetitive, nervous, not fully formed," a music still in the process of becoming.[50] Similarly, the racial consciousness that would later become an explicit element of the music was not so strongly articulated amid these early experiments. Only after 1945 would bebop become a fully "anti-assimilationist sound" that conveyed in musical terms the separateness of African-American experience.[51] During the years of Christian's participation, bebop's separateness was more musical than racial, a collective search for intensely personal forms of expression. At Minton's, improvisation and innovation were the combined means by which young black musicians like Christian demonstrated their newfound creative freedom among themselves. They created a unique musical language, an inside phenomenon that only later emerged as a public expression of a new racial sensibility.

Playback

In his book, *The Art and Times of the Guitar,* Frederic Grunfeld states the significance of Charlie Christian in no uncertain terms: "There is the guitar before Christian and the guitar after Christian, and they sound virtually like two different instruments."[52] The electric guitar *was* a different instrument, offering sonic possibilities that allowed the guitar to break away from its standard role in the jazz rhythm section. However, the uses to which the new invention would be put were far from inevitable. Christian's achievement lay in tapping into the electric guitar's potential, not simply to make his playing more audible, but to expand the instrument's vocabulary. Largely through his innovations, the electric guitar was integrated into American popular music, and gained a new aura of prestige and legitimacy both as a musical instrument and a commercial object.

This theme of integration, both racial and musical, runs through Christian's career, emerging again in his move to join the Benny Goodman band. Yet the young musician was compelled to keep moving, to look for alternative outlets where he could extend and transform existing musical conventions. In this context, the electric guitar was a crucial part of Christian's search for a more personal form of musical expression. He used the sounds offered by the instrument to forge an innovative musical style, participating in a collective move toward experimentation among young black musicians that marked at once an affirmation of individual creativity and a search for new forms of racial expression. As such Christian laid the groundwork for one of the principal dynamics in the history of the electric guitar: the use of the instrument by African-American musicians to stake out a middle ground between widespread popular acceptance and local, more racially exclusive networks of musical and cultural exchange.

Chapter 2

Pure Tones and Solid Bodies

Les Paul's New Sound

The New Sound

The year was 1946, and Les Paul had a problem. Two problems, really, but both centered around the difficulty he was having in achieving the right sound. First of all, he had become frustrated with the poor quality of the recordings he made in commercial studios: "I walked out of a contract and I decided that I was never gonna record in a studio again . . . because I never could hear myself; that's how bad the recording techniques were."[1] As a long-time electronics enthusiast with a penchant for taking apart his various devices (guitars, radios, phonographs) and building them up anew, Paul figured he could achieve a clearer sound on his own, and in fact had already begun work toward that end with experiments in sound recording and electric guitar design. Adding to his determination was his second problem, one more personal in nature:

> My mother came backstage and she told me that she had heard me on the radio. "Lester," she said, "you were fine." Only I knew it wasn't me; I hadn't been on the radio. Then I found out that it had been George Barnes [a noted Chicago jazz guitarist]. No reflection on George, of course, but I figured that my own mother had a right to know when her son was playing. So I walked out of the theater, just like I did out of the recording contract, and I decided that I wasn't gonna record or go on the radio or anything until I could work out something so much me, that my mother would know that that was her Lester playing.[2]

Thus, by Paul's account, he went on to form his "new sound," a sound that would lead him and his wife, Mary Ford, to become among the most successful U.S. recording artists in the years immediately preceding the rise of rock 'n' roll. Paul's new sound hinged upon two distinct but related technological innovations that he had a significant hand in developing: multiple-track recording and the solid-body electric guitar.

For Les Paul, the search for a readily identifiable sound, a unique musical identity, went hand in hand with technological experimentation. As Chet Flippo observed in 1975 in *Rolling Stone*, Paul regarded every guitar he owned as "an imperfect object to be rebuilt," a quality that led Flippo to further comment, "That's why Les Paul may well be the most important figure in popular music in the last two-and-a-half decades. He is not interested in music per se; he is an electronics technician and inventor (self-taught) whose mania is music *delivery systems*."[3] Large as Paul's influence looms over the general history of popular music, it is even larger within the history of the electric guitar; he is one of a select few individuals who are regularly cited as key architects of electric guitar design by historians of the instrument, and his namesake Gibson Les Paul guitar is one of the two or three most popular models of the last forty-five years. Yet what I find most fascinating about Paul is not merely his dedication to technical innovation, but his application of these innovations to music. Despite Flippo's claim that Paul was not interested in music per se, he has enjoyed a long career as a performer, and his inventions were clearly an outgrowth of his performing career. In his efforts to master both the technical elements of guitar playing and the technological trappings of his instrument, Paul stands at the intersection of technology and musical practice, his career a shining example of Michael Chanan's dictum: "The changes that have revolutionized musical perception and practice over the past hundred years are part of a protracted dialogue between music and science, technology and the sonic imagination . . . The imagination of the inventor discovers in the aesthetic domain of music a space for the free play of technical ideas."[4] To this interplay between musical and technological ideas I would add a further element, economics, which for Paul translated into the desire to succeed in a capitalist-driven economy of musical production, a key motive behind his search for a sound that he could call his own.

Les Paul—guitarist, inventor, entrepreneur—is the subject of this chapter, and if such a rich combination of activities did not provide enough matter for discussion, I will add a further dimension of his career, one hinted at in his narrative of the origins of his "new sound." Paul's wry comments about his mother's misidentification uncover a private, familial motivation behind the innovations that brought him mass acceptance. In a similar vein, the music Paul made with his wife Mary Ford was continually framed by their domestic partnership; the theme of Les Paul and Mary Ford "at home" ran through popular representations of the duo, including their own radio and television shows. At the center of this combined domestic/professional union was Les's continually expanding home recording studio, the product of his endeavors to gain control over his recorded sound. Les and Mary's recording studio and Paul's other favorite device, the electric guitar, became part of the more general incorporation of technology into American middle-class homes in the years following World War II. Lynn Spigel and Keir Keightley have shown how television and hi-fidelity stereo were part of a re-visioning of domestic space during the 1950s. Modern technical conveniences introduced into the home both new possibilities for marital or family togetherness and new arenas for potential conflict.[5] These works provide a critical starting point for understanding how Les Paul and Mary Ford contributed to the gendering and, indeed, to the domestication of technologies like the electric guitar, and conversely how technology mediated Les and Mary's own relationship, as manifested in the music they made and in the private life they led so publicly.

What ultimately connected Les Paul's endeavors as an inventor with his music and his performing career was an overriding preoccupation with sound, and specifically with the sound of the electric guitar. Whereas Charlie Christian was lauded for playing guitar "like a horn," it was largely through the efforts of Les Paul that the electric guitar assumed a distinct sound in its own right. The sound that Paul sought to achieve through his work in developing the solid-body electric guitar was characterized by its lack of distortion or any extraneous noise. This quest for tonal or sonoric purity complemented Paul's musical taste for unfettered melody, free of the dissonances and off-beat changes that dominated much of the jazz of the period (which was, of course, an extension of the proto-bebop experiments in which Charlie Christian had participated in the last years of his life). Though he had spent many years playing jazz, the music that Paul recorded with Mary Ford was pop music, designed to have the broadest possible appeal, and also designed to be generally devoid of obvious ethnic or racial markers. The style of pop purveyed by Paul and Ford and the ideal of tonal purity that Paul pursued had significant implications for the construction of pop music during the early 1950s and the ability of such music to absorb the influence of other musics (whether African-American, Latin, or varieties of gypsy music, in the case of Paul and Ford). Although pop music absorbed these influences, it did so silently, without directly acknowledging the ethnicity of either performers or audience.

Inventing the Solid-body Guitar

It is difficult for people today to realize what music was like before amplification. Acoustic music by its very nature was intimate, designed for a smallish audience . . . For music to be widely disseminated it had to be notated and played over and over again, or be picked up through the oral tradition, endlessly altered and finally lost in its original form.

Even when microphones and loudspeakers entered the scene, music couldn't get too loud. Feedback was the bane of the industry. A mishandled amplified acoustic guitar could suddenly start howling like a supercharged coyote.

. . . The solid-body electric guitar solved all that; henceforth feedback was either an avoidable error or a deliberate aesthetic device. Suddenly, after 1948, an instrument was available that was inexpensive . . . easily transportable, simple to play . . . and capable of megasymphonic amounts of noise.[6]

John Rockwell's brief history of amplification, taken from a 1976 article on another noted guitar manufacturer and inventor, Leo Fender, posits the solid-body electric guitar as the culmination of an evolutionary process from localized acoustic performance to a brand of music making that could easily fill a room (or a stadium). Rockwell's perspective is informed by the hindsight of one who had lived through the rise of the electric guitar in the 1960s, when the instrument's potential for producing feedback, distortion, and other sonic effects was put to creative use by a generation of young musicians. Although the solid-body electric guitar marked a departure from earlier ways in which the electric guitar had been approached, the new modes of noise made possible by the solid-body were, if not a wholly unintended consequence, certainly a secondary consideration. For Les Paul, at least, the purpose of the solid-body electric was not to facilitate the production of noise, but to eliminate noise altogether; moreover, he hoped his innovations would increase rather than diminish the intimacy that his music conveyed.

Before proceeding with an investigation of Paul's role in developing the solid-body electric guitar, some general observations are in order. The invention of the electric guitar in the years around 1930 occurred simultaneously in several locations, through the work of several individuals and groups of individuals. So it was with the solid-body electric. Les Paul is one of at least three who are alternately credited with building the first solid-body—Leo Fender and Paul Bigsby (working from suggestions by country guitarist Merle Travis) are the other two. Beyond the matter of assigning credit lies the more complex issue of determining when a new invention can be said to exist; in the case of the solid-body electric, do the early prototypes developed by Les Paul and Paul Bigsby take precedence over the mass production efforts of Leo Fender?

Thomas Hughes has addressed some of these issues in his monumental study of American technology, *American Genesis.* Therein, Hughes makes a useful distinction between invention and innovation, the latter being the process of bringing the former into use. Invention necessarily precedes innovation, according to Hughes, but both are crucial when assessing the cultural impact of a particular technological artifact. Hughes goes on to challenge the idealization of invention as a heroic activity resulting from qualities of individual genius and spontaneous creativity, declaring instead that "invention is rarely if ever an act, but usually a process involving the conceptualization, probably visualization, of various means to an end of solutions to a problem; the embodiment of these in models; and subsequent experimentation with the models to discover how well the means fulfill the end in mind."[7] Les Paul's experience in constructing a solid-body electric guitar would certainly bear out such a pragmatic understanding of the inventive process. As Paul himself admitted, there were no major "eureka moments"; rather, the instrument emerged through a long process of trial and error. "It was all accidental," he demurred in a 1985 interview. "You never can tell when [a new invention] will happen . . . It's odd, but you can think of something and actually build it or patent it and then find out that it's already been sitting out there somewhere."[8] Not one to shy away from assuming credit for his achievements, Paul nonetheless refuses to romanticize his technological endeavors. His design for a solid-body electric guitar, like his techniques for multiple-track recording, arose not from a flash of inspiration but from the imperatives of his professional career and his more general enthusiasm for tinkering with electronic devices.

As legend would have it, Les Paul built his first electric guitar when he was a teenager performing in the parking lot of Beekman's barbecue stand in his hometown of Waukesha, Wisconsin. Mary Shaughnessy opens her biography of Paul with the story of his first electric instrument. Performing as a one-man band, equipped with guitar, harmonica, and washtub drum, the young musician would play through a carbon microphone attached to his mother's radio speaker—barely audible to most in the parking lot. Determined that his act reach his captive audience, young Lester appropriated the speaker from his father's Kolster radio-phono set and put it to creative use.

> That night he taped the arm of the Kolster phono set to the top of his guitar, stuck the needle into the wood, and fed the sound through the phono input. Then he cranked the volume up as high as it would go. The speaker occasionally squealed with feedback, but the peculiar new sound attracted even more curious onlookers. They drifted over from the produce stand and gas station across the road, and Lester's tips tripled. Then and there he knew "the electric guitar spelled money."[9]

The "peculiar new sound" produced in its nascent form by Paul in his parking lot performances would, in modified form, become one of the most profitable commodities in the history of popular music. Also important is the technological resourcefulness exhibited in the above narrative. At the age of fourteen, Paul already had considerable facility with fairly new household objects like radio and the phonograph, enough so that he could disassemble them and use them toward ends of his own making.

Exceptional though Paul's activities might seem, they were but one manifestation of a much broader phenomenon, the growth of technological enthusiasm and electric tinkering among white middle-class boys and young men in the early decades of the twentieth century.[10] The center of activity for such tinkerers was the crystal radio set, which assumed the aura of a "new frontier" in the years before commercial broadcasting dominated the airwaves. Amateur radio operators measured success by their ability to tune into distant stations; they were continually adjusting the controls of their instruments to achieve better reception and improve the quality of sound coming through their headsets. According to Susan Douglas, this subculture of amateur radio operators represented a unique sort of pop culture audience, one that sought active control over the technological means of distribution and that resisted efforts by corporate interests and the military to exert control over their activities.[11]

It is no simple coincidence, then, that both Les Paul and his primary counterpart in the development of the solid-body electric, Leo Fender, were wholehearted radio enthusiasts before they designed guitars, and that both men worked primarily as independent inventors who believed they could improve upon the instruments built by established guitar manufacturers. Fender's guitar factory in Fullerton, California grew out of a radio repair shop he ran in the 1930s. Forrest White, longtime Fender plant manager, recounted that "by the time Leo graduated from high school in 1928, he was already hooked on electronics. He had an amateur 'ham' radio station with the call letters W-6-DOE," and was building amplifiers and PA systems that were rented by local musicians.[12] Paul, for his part, built his first crystal radio set around 1927, only a couple of years before his electric guitar. His interest in radio fueled a more general interest in electronics.[13] Soon thereafter he too transmitted his own broadcasts from the basement of his mother's house. During the next decade, when he was a professional musician in New York, he and his bandmate Jim Atkins (brother of Chet Atkins) would broadcast jam sessions from their apartment building under the name "Booger Brothers Broadcasting Company," attracting musicians from all over the city until they were stopped when their signal interfered with the air traffic flying overhead.[14]

Sometime between these two phases of Paul's life, his idea for a solid-body electric guitar began to crystallize. During the early 1930s, when he was leading a dual life as a jazz and hillbilly musician (under the pseudonym Rhubarb Red) over the Chicago radio airwaves, Paul began to recognize that "when you've got the top [of the guitar] vibrating and a string vibrating, you've got a conflict. One of them has got to stop, and it can't be the string, because that's making the sound."[15] This conflict, a result of the resonant body of the hollow electric instruments that were the order of the day, led Paul to search for a guitar with a more stable surface: "So in 1934 I asked the Larson Brothers—the instrument makers in Chicago—to build me a guitar with a ½″ maple top and no f-holes. They thought I was crazy. They told me it wouldn't vibrate. I told them I didn't *want* it to vibrate, because I was going to put two pickups on it."[16] The two-pickup design was as odd as the solid-body concept by the conventions of the day, and both give evidence of the extent to which Paul was thinking of the electric guitar in very different terms from most instrument makers of the period. Electric guitars were still a fairly new invention, and were still generally conceived as acoustic guitars equipped with the resources to allow for amplification. Even when Charlie Christian burst onto the national music scene five years later, his main guitar, the Gibson ES-150, followed this basic design, though the guitar it was developed from, the L-5, was one of the choicest acoustic jazz instruments then available. But Les Paul was not satisfied with such an instrument; as an electronics enthusiast who had spent years trying to improve the sound of his radio, he foresaw the possibility of an instrument in which the tone generated by the electric signal could be more effectively isolated from the acoustic properties of the guitar.

One result of Paul's quest for "pure string vibration" was a cumbersome but tonally rich solid-body prototype he built in 1941 and dubbed "the Log." The Log has become one of the most fabled instruments in the history of the electric guitar, as much for its oddity as for its sound. To build it, Paul procured use of the Epiphone guitar company's factory, which he visited every Sunday for weeks until the instrument was finished. The end product was essentially a 4″ × 4″ strip of wood with an Epiphone neck and pickups designed by Paul, but the instrument was so unsightly that he added "wings" cut from the sides of a standard acoustic jazz guitar in order to normalize its appearance.[17] Like the Rickenbacker "frying pan" and other early electric guitar models, the Log was an instrument "in the making."

Strange though its appearance may have been, the Log was a perfectly functional instrument with a rich tone and greater sustain than other available guitars of the period. Paul used it to record a number of songs. Recognizing its design as something of a breakthrough in terms of sound, he tried at one point to sell the concept behind it to the Gibson company, but was flatly refused by M. H. Berlin, head of Gibson's parent corporation, Chicago Musical Instruments. At the time there was no perceived

2.1. Les Paul, photographed in 1977, showing off his "Log" guitar, first built in 1941. The Log's unusual design is seen to good effect here, with Paul holding one of the instrument's wings apart from the solid central plank that formed the core of the instrument. Photo © Jon Sievert.

market for a solid-body guitar, especially not one that looked like a broomstick with a pickup.[18] Undaunted by rejection, Paul continued with his experiments, constructing a series of modified Epiphone and Gibson guitars with pickups of his own making and blocks of wood or metal inserted into the body to reduce vibrations. Jim Atkins offered an evocative description of one of Paul's more curious efforts from the late 1940s, one that involved a piece of railroad steel.

> He went down to the railroad yards and found a rail that was jutting out over another bunch of rails. He suspended, with a piece of piano wire, a ninety-pound piece of steel rail. Then he put an electronic pickup next to the string in about the proper position a guitar pickup would be on a regular guitar. When he came back to New York in 1948 he told me, "J., that's the most beautiful sound you ever heard. There is absolutely no vibration interfering from any direction, and you get nothing but pure tone." He said, "When we can build an electric guitar that'll do that, we'll have it made."[19]

This search for a pure tone would eventually lead to Paul's namesake Gibson solid-body electric guitar, First, though, he would have to convince the management at Gibson that it was an idea worth considering.

Paul's growing success as a recording artist certainly helped in this matter. In 1945, the year before his Log was rejected by Gibson, Paul's guitar playing and innovative recording techniques were featured prominently on a hit single by Bing Crosby, "It's Been a Long, Long Time." With Crosby's encouragement, Paul began to focus more attention upon his recording endeavors, building a small studio in the garage of his Hollywood home. Over the next three years he would perfect the sound-on-sound recording practices that he used so prominently in his career with Mary Ford, producing a number of songs featuring his guitar playing in intricate multi-track arrangements, and in the process landing a deal with Capitol Records. By 1948, after two decades as a professional musician, Les Paul was surging toward celebrity, and his increased notoriety gave his idea for a solid-body guitar new credibility, for his association with the instrument would now be a key promotional device.

A more pressing consideration for Gibson, though, was the success of the Fender Telecaster guitar, the first solid-body instrument to be produced for widespread consumption. Originally released onto the market in 1950 as the Broadcaster (it was quickly renamed at the request of the Gretsch company, which had a drum set of the same name), the redubbed Telecaster met with quick acceptance among musicians even as it was ridiculed by other guitar manufacturers. Like Les Paul's Log, the Telecaster broke the rules of guitar design; it was distinctly plain in appearance, with no sumptuous curves or eye-catching finishes. Yet this lack of ornamentation also meant the guitar was easy to reproduce, and thus ready for distribution on a scale unheard of for guitars of comparable quality. Moreover, while the Telecaster paralleled Paul's Log in its lack of conformity to standards of guitar design, it represented a more pragmatic blend of innovation with the demands of the performing musician. Its compact design was built for easy use onstage as well as in the studio, whereas the Log was really only useful as a recording instrument.

Discussing the concept behind the Telecaster, Leo Fender stressed two factors. He readily acknowledged that appearance was a secondary consideration. His main concern was with the utility of the instrument, a preoccupation that he attributed to his long experience working with radio and electronics.[20] Fender also emphasized the importance of the sound of the electric steel guitar, which had featured in the Western variants of country music that flourished near his guitar shop in California. Unlike standard electric guitars of the time, which were fashioned after their acoustic counterparts, the electric steel guitar is played in a "table top" manner, with the instrument resting on its back rather than being held sideways. Electric steels presented a solid, flat surface to the musician with considerably less body mass than standard electric guitars. Consequently, steel guitars also emitted a different sound, one that Fender worked to emulate in his solid-body designs: "On an acoustic electric guitar you have a string fastened to a diaphragm top, and that top does not have one specific frequency. If you play a note, the top will respond to it and also to a lot of adjoining notes. A solid guitar body doesn't have that, and so you're dealing with just a single note at a time."[21] Fender thus articulated the same basic idea as Les Paul: the desire to capture "pure string vibration" and thus to create a "clean" sound "that had sustain and a lack of feedback."[22] Although Paul insists that Fender was aware of his experiments, Fender has disclaimed prior knowledge of existing solid-body electrics in building his instruments. Without being able to state authoritatively which version of the story is correct,[23] it seems clear that by the mid- to late 1940s the solid-body electric guitar was gaining a certain cultural momentum, that it was no longer an isolated concept but an invention so widely recognized that it stimulated experimentation on a number of different fronts.

Thus Gibson began to warm up to the idea of incorporating a solid-

2.2.   The Fender Telecaster guitar, first released in 1950 as the "Broadcaster."
Criticized for its plain appearance, the commercial success of the Telecaster set
the stage for the broader commercialization of the solid-body electric guitar.
Courtesy of the Experience Music Project.

body guitar into its line of electric instruments. According to Ted McCarty, who became president of the Gibson company in 1950, Fender's success was viewed with interest and no small amount of caution by rival guitar manufacturers. McCarty believed that the solid-body guitar, as built by Fender, required considerably less craftsmanship than the hollow-body instruments that were the mainstay of Gibson's electric line; he feared that moving too quickly in marketing a solid-body guitar would risk the company's reputation as a maker of fine instruments.[24] Yet the unabated popularity of the Fender model forced Gibson's hand, and an internal research team began work on solid-body designs. "We had a lot to learn about the solidbody guitar," recalls McCarty, "It's different to the acoustic. Built differently, sounds different, responds differently."[25] The decision was made to enlist the assistance of Les Paul, though accounts vary as to how large a role Paul played in the design of the Gibson solid-body. McCarty insists that a core of Gibson employees, including himself, completed their solid-body prototype before approaching Paul. When the guitarist was presented with the instrument, he reportedly turned to partner Mary Ford and said, "I think we'd better join them, they're getting too close to me!"[26] However, Paul insists with equal vigor that he was brought into the project before the guitar was completed, and had a much larger impact on the final design.[27] Investigating these competing claims, A. R. Duchossoir, a Gibson historian, concludes that "Les primarily set the standards of performance for the new instrument. In other words, he gave CMI/Gibson a detailed brief as to what he wanted, particularly sound-wise, but strictly speaking he did not take a part in the engineering of the guitar."[28]

Whatever Paul's role in developing the instrument may have been, the Gibson solid-body that hit the market in 1952 bore his name, and represented an effort to blend the innovations made by Paul, Fender, and others with some of the aesthetic flourishes that characterized Gibson instruments. Notable in this regard was the arched top, produced with carving equipment that the smaller Fender company neither had nor could readily afford.[29] Another key distinguishing feature was the finish, which was available in a choice of either black or gold. Les Paul explained the significance of the colors: "I had two models in mind right from the very beginning, [what came to be known as] the standard gold-top, and the black Custom . . . I picked gold because no one else had one, and because it's always associated with quality, richness. And I picked black because it's classy, like a tuxedo, and also because a player's hands—if the guy were white—would show up onstage against the black finish."[30] To counter the plain Telecaster design, then, the Les Paul was cast as a high-class instrument, one that signified upward mobility and professionalism (a guitar to be worn like a tuxedo), and this set of associations also bore upon the assumed racial identity of the imagined consumer. Just how crucial this visual conception of the guitar was to Gibson's overall idea of the instrument can be gathered from the company's original advertisement for the Les Paul. Set against a hazy, almost surreal backdrop, Les Paul stands to the left side; dressed in a sharp suit (not a tuxedo), he is shown with his hands poised in playing position on a guitar, his gaze cast down at the instrument. Yet the guitar he holds is only an outline; the Les Paul in all its detail is projected ahead of him in the picture, its curved, luminescent body and long neck cutting a swath through the center of the ad, indeed cutting Paul off at the legs to give him the appearance of floating on air, or rather floating on the sensational qualities of his namesake instrument.

Of course, visual appeal was only a part of the Les Paul design. Equally important to the marketing of the guitar, and arguably more important for the musicians who would purchase the instrument, was its sound. The text of the above advertisement advised its audience that "you have to see and hear it to appreciate the wonderful features and unusual tone of this newest Gibson guitar."[31] Meanwhile, a brief article on the Les Paul from the 1952 NAMM (National Association of Music Merchants) convention emphasized that "those who played it . . . said that all traces of feed-back and overtone have been eliminated in the Les Paul model Gibson. Those hearing it agreed that it produced a wealth of contrasting tonal effects, from brilliant treble to full, deep bass, with a good solid in-between voice for rhythm."[32] Through such statements, the ideal of tonal purity that Paul had pursued for over a decade entered mass circulation as a desirable commodity, complementing the "classy" exterior of the Les Paul guitar with an electric sound that was stripped of excess and balanced in all its dimensions. Moreover, marketing and commercial success worked to legitimize what had once seemed an unruly invention among guitar makers.

The advent of the solid-body guitar was only one product of the quest

2.3. "It's a Sensation!" The first advertisement for the Gibson Les Paul guitar, from a 1952 catalogue. Courtesy of Gibson Musical Instruments.

for pure tone. Another key development was the humbucker pickup, the result of yet another set of experiments conducted by Gibson's staff. As explained in the previous chapter, the pickup is what electrifies the electric guitar, converting the vibrations from the guitar's strings into an electronic signal through an electromagnetic charge. Les Paul had long recognized the centrality of pickup design to the overall sound of the guitar. His solid-body innovations were continually accompanied by reconstructed pickups, and he even observed at one point that where the electric guitar is concerned, "nothing can be right if the pickup isn't right."[33] However, it was left to Gibson employee Seth Lover to produce a pickup that further diminished the amount of extraneous noise generated by the electric signal. The specific target of Lover's attention was the electronic hum that was generated by the intersecting fields of the pickup and the guitar amplifier. Lover explained,

> I thought at the time, if we're going to have a new pickup, we should have something that does away with this curse of the hum that we were always running into. The guitar player, he would have to stand and turn around to find a place to minimize the hum. That wasn't too bad when there was only one amplifier but, when there were two or three, what was right through one amplifier was wrong for the others! . . . So, I decided that we ought to make a pickup that would do away with that noise.[34]

Lover's solution to the problem of hum was to double the number of coils in the existing pickup design. Standard pickups of the time consisted of a single coil of copper wire wound around six small magnets, one for each string; by adding a second coil and a second set of magnets, Lover found that magnetic hum could be reduced or eliminated, for the humming signal produced by one of the coils would be canceled by the signal of the other.[35] Completed in 1955, the humbucker was slowly incorporated onto Gibson instruments due to delays in securing a patent for the design. By 1957, it was available on a number of Gibson models, including a revamped Les Paul Custom model that featured three humbucker pickups running through the center of the guitar's body.[36] Over time, humbucking pickups would become one of the distinguishing features of Gibson electric guitars, and would be identified as a primary source of the Les Paul guitar's unique tone.

Nothing essential happens in the absence of noise.

—*Jacques Attali (1985), p. 3.*

In 1971, a reader of *Guitar Player* magazine submitted a set of questions to Les Paul about his role in the development of the electric guitar. Asked about the solid-body concept, Paul reasserted the importance of achieving "a great sustaining tone" and eliminating "the resonant peaks that would make one note louder than another." In hindsight, the main principle behind the solid-body was the creation of an instrument marked by uniformity of response "so that the notes would sustain evenly on each fret all the way up and down the fingerboard." The reader also asked Paul about humbucking pickups. "The reason for the humbucking coil was to eliminate the hum," Paul plainly stated, and went on to discuss the great improvements in pickup design that had occurred in the preceding two decades. "The most noise that we are getting out of them now . . . is the thermal noise of the resistance of the wire . . . The greatest advantage of the humbucking coil," he concluded, "is to get rid of unwanted noise."[37]

Les Paul's career as inventor has been oriented toward giving musicians greater control over the boundary between desirable and undesirable noise, a boundary that has been continually renegotiated throughout the recent history of popular music. Indeed, the electric guitar has been central to this process of negotiation since its invention (and reinvention). Guitar historians have tended to characterize the solid-body electric and accompanying innovations like the humbucker pickup as devices that increased the electric guitar's capacity for the production of noise. The passage by John Rockwell that opened this section is indicative of this line of interpretation: the solid-body electric made possible the experimentation with electronic sound that occurred among blues musicians in the 1950s and, especially, among rock guitarists of the 1960s. Tom Wheeler has seconded such an impression of the solid-body electric, declaring with regard to the Les Paul that "most guitars are designed to fit a style of music; it is no exaggeration to say that rock & roll guitar styles were shaped in part by the Les Paul."[38] Speaking more generally of the electric guitar's role in 1950s popular culture, Wheeler claimed that the instrument "best symbolized the blend of faith in all things American, the excitement of technological horizons, and the kinetic energy of consumer society's sudden superstar, the teenager."[39] Associating the electric guitar with the rise of rock 'n' roll plays into the mythos of the instrument as a beacon of energy and a device that facilitated the loosening of social constraints, a perpetually appealing idea that has no small degree of historical basis. However, I want to draw attention as well to the ways in which the solid-body electric, as conceived by Les Paul, was intended primarily as a means of regulating the musical production of noise, and ensuring that melodic or tonal purity would not be overtaken by perceived sonic disorder. Through Paul's efforts and influence the electric guitar achieved new levels of standardization and uniformity of performance, and the clean, sustaining tone produced by his innovations would become a key component of the "new sound" he created with his wife and performing partner, singer Mary Ford.

The House that Les and Mary Built

Portrait of two lovers with guitar: a publicity photo from 1952 presents Les Paul and his wife, Mary Ford, sitting atop a Gibson Les Paul, thus giving new meaning to the concept of the solid-body guitar, an instrument apparently strong enough to support the weight of two bodies. Straddling his namesake guitar, Paul sits upon the most solid part of the instrument. His position beneath Ford plays into the notion that his presence is the weightier of the two, while Ford's place atop the slender neck of the guitar lends her an aura of lightness. Their relative positions also cast Mary as the primary object of the viewer's gaze; poised on something of a pedestal, she occupies the visual center of the image, a place reinforced by Les's direct, adoring gaze. Mary looks only obliquely at Les, averting her eyes from the camera. Other contrasts between the two figures emphasize the differences between Les and Mary. Paul's black suit, pictured against the bright background of the guitar, is countered by Ford's light-colored outfit, offering a complementary connotation of lightness to the one noted earlier, both of which bear upon her supposed purity as a white woman. This suggestion of whiteness can also be read into the different poses that Les and Mary assume. While Paul straddles the guitar with his legs spread, only one leg visible to the camera, Ford sits sidesaddle on the neck of the guitar, her legs held together in a gesture that partially undermines the sexual connotations of the instrument as it protrudes upward from Paul's crotch. Ford is open to the gaze of both Paul and the viewer,

2.4.   A Capitol Records publicity shot of Les Paul and Mary Ford perched atop a giant Les Paul guitar. Courtesy of the Michael Ochs Archives, Venice, California.

but as a romantic rather than a strictly sexual object. Her body is to be idealized rather than overtly eroticized, and the electric guitar reinforces this image of her.

Above all, what this picture suggests is the extent to which the electric guitar, and by extension Paul's involvement with technology, mediated their public relationship. When the couple reached the number one position on the national record charts with their version of "How High the Moon" in 1951, all attention was focused on the technical accomplishments of Paul's recording methods, on the "sound" he created through his inventiveness. Yet that sound depended upon Ford's voice as much as it did upon Paul's ingenuity as guitarist and recording technician; her multi-tracked vocals complemented his overdubbed guitar lines to produce the "new sound" that became their trademark. Moreover, that "new sound" was created not in the commercial recording studios of the day but in the different houses that Les and Mary shared during the course of their performing career. Paul's home studio originated out of his frustration with the quality of commercial recordings and his desire to have full control over the production of his music. Recording at home, he could supervise all the technical details of the process and also work on songs whenever he chose rather than be tied to an external schedule. Yet the development of a home studio also meant collapsing the strict boundaries between public and private life in a manner at once unique and in keeping with some of the patterns of 1950s domesticity. As Les and Mary's home became centered around the technologies used to produce their music, so their home life became a central element in their public persona, providing a model of domestic space reinvented by technology.

> It is possible that the existence of something mass and public makes possible something that is at the same time intimate and private.
> —*Warren Susman (1987), p. 50.*

Les Paul began experimenting with multiple recording techniques in the 1930s, long before he met Mary Ford. His recording techniques first emerged out of a desire to play with accompaniment at times when other musicians were not around.[40] Paul played along with the sound of his own guitar in private for almost a decade before applying some of the techniques he'd developed to the aforementioned Bing Crosby song, "It's Been a Long, Long Time," which became a number one single in 1945. It was at this time that Paul first met Colleen Summers, a young country singer on the southern California scene whom he auditioned to appear on his radio show. Paul's marriage was failing, and smitten by Summers, he began an affair that would develop into a personal and professional partnership of close to two decades.

It was Paul who decided upon Summers's name change, first to Mary Lou and then to Mary Ford, so that in performing with him she would appear as a different personality from the country singer who was already well known in the Western region. After an initial set of performances for Paul's show, they did not perform together publicly until 1949. In the interim, Paul further refined his recording methods, applying them to the production of music made for commercial use.

Paul's efforts in this direction took shape during a period of extreme unrest within the music industry, when the growing prioritization of recordings generated considerable conflict between musicians and record manufacturers. James Kraft has documented this aspect of popular music history in his recent book, *Stage to Studio*. As Kraft recounts, the first quarter of the twentieth century was something of a heyday for American musicians; musicians found opportunities for work not only in nightclubs but also in the proliferating movie theaters, vaudeville, and other commercial establishments. Because of the growing popularity of recordings during the late 1920s and into the 1930s, however, thousands of jobs were lost by musicians in an industry that defended itself by proclaiming the value of technological progress. The new role of technology within the production of popular music also meant a loss of control among musicians over the process of making music, a condition that for Kraft was most clearly represented in the refashioned broadcast and recording studios that became the standard location of commercial musical production. Such studios were organized around control booths, which in turn included as their most prominent feature the mixing board, a device that regulated the input and output levels of the various microphones. The mixing board was run by a sound engineer trained in the technical aspects of sound reproduction rather than by a band leader trained in musical performance.[41] Musicians were thus largely divested of control over their labor as the new studios demanded a sort of specialized knowledge that had less to do with musical practice as such than with regulating the results of performance and shaping them into musical objects suitable for transmission and commodification.

This reorganization of musical work offers a crucial bit of context for understanding Les Paul's drive to gain control over the means of musical reproduction. Yet it has to be noted that Paul's response to the situation was far from typical. During the first years of the 1940s, the common strategy of musicians, embodied in the policy of their union, the American Federation of Musicians, was simply to resist the incursion of new technologies. James Petrillo, who became head of the AFM in 1940, proclaimed as early as 1928 that "the living musician . . . must be consulted and his services utilized" in the deployment of technology "or else the machine will be silent."[42] Willingness to silence the machine eventually led to the infamous AFM recording ban of 1942–1944, during which time union members refused to perform on any commercial recordings, a move that won significant concessions from the major record companies but ultimately left the trend toward centralization of the music industry intact.

After the War, the AFM continued to pressure record companies to give musicians a greater say in the uses of technology, but to little avail; the postwar consumer boom combined with growing anti-union sentiment to consolidate corporate power within the music industry, and the AFM was placed in a defensive position. Meanwhile, Les Paul pursued a dream made possible by his distinctive acquisition of both musical and technical knowledge and motivated by his single-minded drive for personal success. Withdrawing into the garage of his Hollywood home, he converted the space into an overcrowded control room, with just enough space for "a disk-recording lathe, mixing console, turntable, and monitor," along with the various tools Paul would use to continue his experiments in guitar design.[43] It was here that Paul devised the techniques that would become known as his "new sound," continually testing different styles of microphone placement, altering the tape speed of his recording equipment to achieve unique sonic effects by thoroughly electronic means, and most significant, "producing overdubbed recordings that were relatively free of surface noise and distortion," which he managed to achieve "by squeezing the recording frequency down and painstakingly filtering out unwanted sound."[44] Tracks were recorded onto shellac disks (this was in the days before tape was a readily available medium), and each new track was overlaid onto the previous ones in a fashion so that no single track was retrievable once recorded. A mistake meant starting over from scratch; as Paul put it, "You can never go back—you can only keep going on. So you just don't make a mistake."[45] This almost excruciating degree of technical precision and Paul's already-noted pursuit of pure sound in his recording techniques both contributed to his singular goal—the minimization of unwanted noise.

After roughly two years of intensive experimentation, much of which he accomplished in isolation and relative secrecy, the guitarist came up with a recording that showcased his sonic inventiveness in an accessible, melodic context. "Lover," a Rodgers and Hart composition first featured in the 1932 film *Love Me Tonight,* became in Paul's hands a multi-tracked orchestra of eight guitars with skeletal rhythmic accompaniment on drums (all parts performed by Paul). The song opens with a moderately paced statement of the melody, during which Paul's method of layering tracks of guitars is fully in evidence. In the background is a single bass track providing harmonic counterpoint, played on the lower strings of the guitar; the midrange is covered by a set of tracks that outlines the melody through a lilting chord progression with a single-note turnaround; and the foreground of the piece is occupied by a chorus of upper-register, picked, mostly arpeggiated lines that elaborate on the melody. Halfway through, the song pauses, only to speed up the tempo considerably. The high-pitched parts create a swirl of sound that dances around the main melody with a rapidity that is partly due to Paul's sure technique as a guitarist, and partly due to his manipulation of the speed of his recording equipment.

As a solo performance, "Lover" presented a new conception of the recording artist, moving away from the notion that the recorded object need bear any one-to-one relationship to the act of musical performance.[46] Describing the piece, Paul explained, "until 'Lover,' I'd never been able to combine all my inventions and recording techniques into one bag of tricks—to use the delay, echo, reverb, phasing, flanging, sped-up sounds, muted picking and everything else on a multiple recording."[47] This range of effects was an outgrowth of Paul's insistent belief in the mutability of sound, and his interest in technology was the outlet. Just as significant as the technical achievements of "Lover," though, was the essential musical conservatism of the song. Paul's style of foregrounding the melody indicated his impulse to avoid the complex harmonic directions that jazz music had recently begun to follow.[48] Even the quick-fire embellishments in the tune's second half remained thoroughly consonant with the main line of melodic development, however much they might have impressed the listener. Indeed, it was this blend of sonic inventiveness with melodic conservatism that set the stage for Paul's subsequent success as a recording musician. On the strength of "Lover," he secured a contract with Capitol records, whose A&R head Jim Conkling expressed amazement at Paul's skills as a recording engineer: "He was feeding in the bass end and top end of the scale all at the same time, which was a feat I never understood."[49] Capitol's recording engineers were similarly puzzled, and Paul's technological expertise became valuable to the company.

In fact, it was Capitol's publicity department that first came up with the phrase "new sound" to stir interest in Paul's recordings. The strategy proved successful: "Lover" went as high as number twenty-one on the national sales charts in February 1948, while its companion piece, "Brazil," went to number twenty-two—impressive showings for a pair of instrumental tracks. Yet, as luck would have it, Paul's first success as a recording artist would coincide with an auto accident that left him in the hospital for months and almost led to the amputation of his right arm. During this interruption, Capitol continued to release songs that Paul had recorded during his initial wave of multi-track activity, but these met with less enthusiasm than "Lover," and there was a sense among the company's management that Paul's "new sound" would need to be renewed in order to find further success.

At this juncture Paul decided to incorporate Mary Ford into his act full-time, in the hope that adding vocals to his instrumental mix would increase the commercial appeal of his music. Ford was not featured strictly as a vocalist, however. Also a guitarist, she played along with Les as part of his trio, touring the country with a show that split the difference between Paul's former allegiance to jazz and his new affinity for smooth vocal pop. Early reviews of the trio in concert emphasized the ease with which they performed and Les's penchant for punctuating his music with chatter and gags to amuse the audience.[50] Over the years, the routines developed between Les and Mary would become key to their popularity, and would also reveal some of the not-so-subtle interpersonal dynamics that characterized their public relationship. One of the more illuminating examples of their onstage interaction comes from Mary Shaughnessy's biography of Paul. Shaughnessy describes a bit in which Les and Mary "traded increasingly complicated guitar solos," which came as something of a surprise to the majority of fans who viewed Mary solely as a singer. "Les would feign bewilderment when Mary echoed his first few licks with ease. Then he'd pick out a run at breakneck speed, grinning and winking at the crowd to signal his confidence that she would fall on her face. When it became apparent that she was going to replicate his fancy finger work, though, he'd take a swipe at her strumming hand or rip the plug out of her electric guitar."[51] Through such measures, Paul worked to ensure that instrumental virtuosity remained his domain even as he showcased Ford's own musical skills, and managed to do so with levity. The power imbalance characteristic of Paul's maneuvers pervaded the couple's careers, and effectively reinforced their image as a couple who observed the boundaries of gender propriety during a period when those boundaries were being defended with renewed force.

Lucy O'Brien has written of the major role postwar pop music played in reasserting the value of domesticated femininity through the figure of the female singer.[52] Citing Doris Day and Peggy Lee as the new breed of white, strikingly blond woman vocalists, O'Brien highlights the extent to which such singers were valued as much for their glamorous image as for their vocal abilities. They served as icons of conspicuous consumption at a moment when the economy demanded consumer activity to effect the transition from wartime production. Just as important, they presented a version of womanhood that was designed to be visually or even sexually appealing without appearing unduly aggressive or independent, playing within the confines of their assigned positions rather than seeking to upset the norms that governed the music industry.[53] Central to those norms was the assumption that female performers were best suited to be vocalists, not only because as vocalists they were placed at the visual center of the musical group, but because in singing women could present the illusion that their musicality was inseparable from their physicality, that it was the result not of instrumental mastery but of a more "natural" expression of self.

Despite her instrumental skills, Mary Ford was cast into this role when she joined Les Paul's act. Yet to suggest that Ford helped to naturalize Paul's overwhelmingly technological sound is to simplify her place within their music. To begin with, Ford's vocals were overdubbed as much as Paul's guitar. Eight tracks of singing vied for space with an equivalent number of tracks for guitar in the typical recordings of the duo. Moreover, Ford's vocal style tended toward the crooning of male performers like Perry Como, a manner of singing that relied on the microphone for its effectiveness. Crooning used the microphone to make audible soft tones, and therefore created a sense of intimacy, a set of private musings overheard. When Les Paul discussed his approach to recording, he regularly stressed this sort of intimacy as one of his goals. In a 1954 article for *Down Beat* magazine, for instance, Paul commented upon the need to exercise restraint in applying technical effects like echo, which "can destroy intimate sound, and intimate sound is, to say the least, very hard to capture."[54] Some years later, he articulated the same desire in somewhat different terms, declaring, "All I really want to do is to reproduce sound as it really is, and with depth perception so you can *see* the performer."[55] Both of these statements reflect Paul's tendency to conceptualize sound in spatial terms, and in so doing to imagine technology as a means of bringing recorded sounds closer to the listener. Paul thus developed techniques of "close miking," placing the microphones as close as possible to the sources of sound; and Ford's style of singing similarly played into the ideal of intimate sound.

The spatial dimensions of Paul's sonic ideal assume a more specific character when considered alongside the domesticated image that Les and Mary worked to convey. As early as 1949, when their professional relationship first began to cohere, the couple presented themselves in radio broadcasts as Les Paul and Mary Ford "at home," a motif that would frame their public image throughout the 1950s. A 1957 ad for Gibson guitars shows Les and Mary at home with their matching Les Paul guitars, offering a suggestive representation of the electric guitar as a domestic object rather than the more common perception of the instrument as a device of youthful rebellion. For Les Paul and Mary Ford, the electric guitar and their electronic recording and broadcasting equipment *were* a key part of their domestic ideal. Home represented both intimacy and productivity, as reflected in the ad copy for Gibson guitars: Les and Mary were at their best "selling music . . . selling their sponsor's products . . . selling records—and *Selling Gibsons.*" Performing over radio and television, or having their records played over hi-fidelity systems designed to reproduce the attention to sonic detail that Les purveyed, Les and Mary would play from one home to another, publicly transmitting a version of domestic life predicated upon the incorporation of electric technologies into the comfortable privacy of middle-class homes.

At the core of this domestication of technology was a fundamental paradox: the technologies perceived to reinforce the comfort of the home also worked to connect the private to the public sphere. Whereas Les Paul's innovations produced a more private, intimate sound, new electric technologies like television and radio gave private space a new public dimension. To some extent this was effected by converting the home into a site for modes of leisure and amusement that had previously been tied to going out. Yet as Lynn Spigel observes in *Make Room for TV,* radio and television also enabled the suburban household to selectively maintain its

2.5.   Les Paul and Mary Ford "At Home" in a 1957 advertisement for the Gibson Les Paul. Courtesy of Gibson Musical Instruments.

connection to the outside world, filtering out undesirable sounds and images.[56] Les Paul's desire to employ electricity to purify the sound of the electric guitar here finds a parallel; and given the priority assigned to domesticity in the public image put forth by Paul and Mary Ford, one can infer that Paul was working to achieve a similar kind of "antiseptic electrical space" in his innovations.

Household electrical objects like television, radio, and the more elaborate audio systems that became common during the 1950s were also sources of conflict and negotiation between men and women in the home. Radio, for example, became the basis for a masculinized cult of technological enthusiasm during the 1920s among young men like Les Paul, who would convert the basement or the garage into veritable electronic laboratories. Television was more problematic, placed squarely at the center of what Lynn Spigel calls the "family circle." While radio served as a means for men to assert their territorial rights within the domestic sphere, television was often depicted in popular representations as having a pacifying, or feminizing, influence upon the men who watched it, and further contained male pleasure by placing it under the surveillance of women.[57] Women who watched TV, by contrast, were portrayed as watching while working, incorporating the TV not only into their leisure time but into their domestic work. The cultural logic of television therefore entailed something of an inversion of standard patterns of active male and passive female approaches to technology, although this dynamic ultimately reinforced the notion that the home was a woman's sphere.

High fidelity stereo units, by contrast, assumed a role in the 1950s similar to that of radio in the 1920s, offering a new outlet for men to tinker with technology within the home. In an analysis of gender and high fidelity, Keir Keightley notes that hi-fi enthusiasts set themselves apart from the more general "feminizing" and homogenizing impulses of television and mass culture.[58] According to Keightley, the hi-fi unit was believed to assert the individuality of its owner, with separate components matched according to personal taste. The integrated console phonographs that bore a close resemblance to television consoles "were seen by marketers and hi-fi fans alike as feminine equipment, as opposed to the *separate* individual components of a masculine rig."[59] Perhaps most significant, though, was the value placed by hi-fi enthusiasts upon the "faithful reproduction of aural phenomena," a phrase that echoes Les Paul's desire to "reproduce sound as it really is."[60] In both instances, sonic authenticity becomes a means of establishing a sort of male territorial dominion in the home, apart from domesticating influences.

As close collaborators, Les Paul and Mary Ford did not inhabit strictly separate spheres of technology, but their relationship nevertheless reinforced many traditional gender boundaries regarding technology in the home. Public attention turned with new interest to Les and Mary's home in 1953, after the couple had completed construction of a house in Mahwah, New Jersey that was, according to Mary Shaughnessy, "a monument to the 'New Sound.'"[61] Paul's home studio concept was here taken to a new extreme, as the entire house was centered around the creation of Les and Mary's music, along with Paul's continual modification of his various electric guitars. A 1957 *Metronome* article offered a telling description of the new residence: "A Sound Studio with the very latest electronic equipment, around which a beautiful home has been built."[62] Paul had achieved a reorganization of domestic space of which other men might only dream. His new home featured a main studio that included a one-of-a-kind eight-track tape recorder that he had developed with the assistance of the Ampex company. The eight-track gave him greater control over the separate channels of sound that went into the recordings he created with Ford. Paul's home was "one of the most complete audio control centers" imaginable, and it allowed him more flexibility in his approach to recording than any other working musician of the time.[63]

The effect of Les and Mary's new home on the pair became clear in a pair of articles from 1953. Writing for the *Saturday Evening Post,* Amy Porter emphasized how the residence was set up to allow its inhabitants to record whenever inspiration might hit them. "Because Les may want to get something down on tape at any time," said Porter, "he also has a recorder and a sound mixer in the living room and connecting mikes scattered around the house." Porter continues, "A much-used mike is the one that hangs above Mary's kitchen sink. If she is busy washing dishes when Les yells to her to please sing something, she can oblige and still keep on with her household chores. She puts on earphones to hear Les's guitar accompaniment from wherever she happens to be."[64] While their New Jersey home presented new possibilities for musical production and reproduction, then, it also was a space within which the gendered division of labor remained more or less intact. The new technologies that made

Paul's work as recording engineer less difficult also compounded the difficulty of Ford's household duties.

A *Newsweek* article from the same year discussed Les and Mary's home in a photo essay depicting a day with the couple. Of the five photos included, only two show Les and Mary in the same room. One of these is in the studio, "making records" (with bass player Wally Kamin in the background, who was married to Mary's sister, Carol), and the other is of the couple relaxing after a day's work in their "vista-windowed living room." Another picture shows Les and Wally in the "workshop," laboring over an electric guitar in a state of disrepair, while Wally appears alone in one photo, working as a secretary in the home office from which business was conducted. Perhaps the most telling image, though, is that of "Mary and Carol in the kitchen." Carol is doing the dishes while Mary leans against the opposite counter, singing, with sheet music in hand; far in the background but positioned at the center of the photo is Les, shown through several doorways in a room far removed, with guitar in hand.[65]

These images reveal the ambivalence underlying the ostensible domestic harmony of Les and Mary's career, an ambivalence shaped by the couple's use of technology. Within the house that Les and Mary built, technology simultaneously brought the couple together and kept them at a distance from one another, a pattern also evident in the earlier photograph of the two perched on a guitar. Though connected by Les's adoring gaze, in this photo they appear on different planes, the space between them taken up by one of Paul's technological endeavors. The ability of electricity to conquer space assumes a curious, even ominous tone, and the ideal of intimate sound espoused by Paul is revealed to be no more than an auditory illusion.

An episode of Les and Mary's radio show from early in their partnership offers a final bit of insight. Titled "The Case of the Missing Les Paulverizer," the episode revolves around Paul's inability to locate the gadget that allowed him to create his multi-track recordings. (The "Les Paulverizer" was the fictitious code Paul used for his overdubbing techniques.)[66] As the show starts, Paul complains to the audience: "Now if someone hadn't stole my electric Les Paulverizer I'd be sittin' here strummin' this one guitar and it'd sound like six." Also missing is Mary Ford, who would otherwise be adding vocals to the show; so Les launches into a brief performance of the pop standard "Avalon" that manages to employ several tracks of his guitar playing despite the absence of his Paulverizer (Paul made no claims to being a good scriptwriter). Completing the song, he continues to ponder his situation until struck by a flash of insight; recalling that Mary had recently been asking a lot of questions about his invention, he calls into their basement after her and is met by a chorus of "Mary"s in response. Paul chastises Mary for stealing his Paulverizer and cautions her about touching its dials, but to no avail, and the two engage in a silly exchange that features their voices twisted and turned in all manner of sonic permutations, often in imitation of other noted radio personalities like Jack Benny and Amos 'n' Andy. More banter leads into another song, the "Hawaiian War Chant," which Mary introduces with the proclamation, "Now with my Mary Forderizer I throw this switch

> and now I'm three
> and now I'm three
> and now I'm three."

Mary's claim upon technology remains short lived, however. Upon finishing the piece Mary cries for Les's help—the machine has begun to smoke from misuse, and Paul has to rescue her from the imaginary contraption. "Didn't I tell you something would happen," he counsels, soliciting a plaintive apology from Ford. "And you promise never again to fool with my inventions . . . and will you remember that it's the Les Paulverizer and not the Mary Forderizer," to all of which Ford readily consents. After another piece featuring Les's guitar(s), he asks Mary whether she is at all tired of "playing second fiddle to the guitar" in their marriage. In response, she expresses frustration not with his interest in guitars but with the way their life is centered around "these crazy electrical gadgets." Paul decides on the spot that he is "through with electronics" (a promise he will keep until the next episode of the show). First, however, he wants to know one last thing from Mary: why did she take his Les Paulverizer in the first place? "Well, I thought if the thing could make one guitar sound like six," replies Mary, "I could plug in my new Hoover vacuum cleaner and clean the house six times as fast."

The interaction between Paul and Ford in this show sets up Paul as the virtuoso, the master of music and technology whose authority is challenged, if ineffectually, by his wife. That electric technology could have reinforced such a conservative pattern of gender relations comes as a surprise only if one is convinced by the narrative of technological and cultural progress that tends to be projected onto such devices. To argue that the electric guitar was exclusively a conservative influence within 1950s popular culture, or even within the more narrow confines of Les Paul and Mary Ford's career, would be to overlook the range of new possibilities produced by the instrument. Nonetheless, the combination of technological innovation with social and musical conservatism found in Les Paul's achievements seems to bear out Simon Frith's contention that "What is most startling about the history of twentieth-century sounds is not how much recording technology has changed music, but how little it has."[67] One might add that even the most progressive technological achievements do not necessarily entail significant shifts in social relations. By containing his mastery of sound technologies within the framework of domesticity, Paul persuaded consumers that his music was genuinely innovative, but would not upset the conventional order of household relations, a crucial point to put forth in a cultural economy where the home was the main site of musical consumption. He also convinced the public that his innovations would not disturb the normal listening pleasures associated with popular music: as the "pure" sounds he produced would ideally reinforce domestic harmony, so too would they leave intact the standard melodies of pop.

Pure Pop

Asked in 1983 how he would categorize himself musically, Les Paul recounted the string of stylistic shifts that characterized his long musical career.

> I started out as a hillbilly; I loved bluegrass. I started out playing bluegrass, country and writing country songs, but as time went on I gave up the country scene altogether, and changed my name from Rhubarb Red to Les Paul. As Les Paul I wanted to be a jazz artist. Every night I'd be up in Harlem, with Art Tatum and Lester Young, playing with them. I nearly lived there . . . and I learned from all the black players, my friends up in Harlem.[68]

Fascinated as he was by the sounds coming from Harlem in the late 1930s, though, Paul would not adhere to a path of playing straight jazz, nor would he classify himself as a jazz musician. Moving through the different stages of his career, the term he settled on most comfortably to describe his stylistic preference was "commercial music," which for him meant developing a style "which changes to what the public wants." Having a distinctive way of playing was certainly important—recall the story of how Paul came upon his "new sound"—but his key was to maintain a personal style without having to educate the public into appreciating the music he had to offer.[69] Paul's philosophy of commercial music was a peculiar variant of populism that assumed that people only authentically desire what they already know they want, and which viewed the function of the performing musician as providing them with just that. The guitarist explained this perspective more fully in an interview conducted some thirty-two years earlier with *Down Beat*.

> Okay, so you make great sounds. The people you're playing for, they work all day, they don't go to music schools and study harmony. They pay their dough, they come in, they listen.
>
> If they don't understand what you're doing, they walk out. What are you supposed to do, tie 'em with a rope while you explain you're playing great music?[70]

In his drive for accessibility, Paul was only one of a number of white musicians whose inclusion in the mainstream of American popular music placed him outside the boundaries of identifiable categories like jazz, blues, and country music. Kay Kyser, a white bandleader who enjoyed considerable success in the late 1930s and early 1940s, played a style of music that was heavily influenced by jazz, but softened at the edges so as to appeal to that segment of the pop audience who preferred sweet melodies over blues-based riffing. According to Krin Gabbard in *Jammin' at the Margins,* Kyser has been written out of jazz histories because of the persona he adopted. Where white bandleaders like Benny Goodman approached jazz with a degree of seriousness that bespoke their desire for respectability and their respect for the music, Kyser, as a bandleader, was more of a clown who often danced and made faces while his musicians took off on their solos (practices reminiscent of Les Paul's own taste for continually joking with the audience, framing his music with banter and choreographed comic routines). Kyser was a figure who, in Gabbard's analysis, "was reassuringly free of any trace of Otherness"; even as his band swung with conviction, Kyser's antics and his lack of identifiable ethnic markers worked to discourage "those aspects of swing era performance that hinted at darkness."[71] For Gabbard, the salient point is that Kyser represents an era when jazz was defined very differently, and the historical gap between these notions of jazz has led to the exclusion of performers like Kyser from contemporary accounts of the music's history. Les Paul, on the other hand, shows how mainstream musicians might deliberately avoid the jazz label at a time when jazz was increasingly defined as high art rather than popular music and was increasingly linked to the improvisatory excursions of bebop, a mode of jazz performance designed to deliberately exclude those not accustomed to its rhythmic and harmonic conventions.

Paul expressed his ambivalence toward bebop in a 1952 *Down Beat* article, in which he admitted he did not always "get the message" of the music, but did find it to be of value. "I think it's great because it's going to be a stepping-stone to the future," he said in response to a Miles Davis horn solo, "but I don't think I could listen to five hours of that record. I'm afraid I would become very nervous. It's nervous music."[72] What in particular about bebop made Paul feel nervous was unclear—whether it was the distinctive approach to rhythm, the tendency to turn standard chord changes inside out, or the fact that the music represented the effort of African-American musicians to assert themselves as artists with new authority. What is clear is that Paul hoped his music would have quite a different effect upon his audience. He therefore rehearsed several different versions of a song in front of the crowds that came to see him perform before settling upon a version to record, so that he could gauge audience responses and ensure that he would release music that would satisfy established tastes.

The idea of listening to a record for five hours might seem daunting to even the most devoted listener, but Paul here touches upon one of the key qualities of popular music in its mass-produced form, its ability to stand up to repetition without provoking undue nervousness. Considering the history of music in the context of the industrialization and mechanization of sound, Jacques Attali suggests that repetition is not merely a quality of music, or a way in which music is consumed, but a distinct mode of production that places music in the service of technology rather than the other way around.[73] Attali further observes that these methods of processing music work to stifle possible means of articulating difference. Under repetitive conditions music continually reproduces what is most readily assimilable, manufacturing a plentiful homogeneity that effectively silences divergent trends. Musical forms like bebop that produce uncomfortable degrees of noise for the average listener are pushed to the margins, while the mainstream is occupied by performers like Paul, who cultivate familiarity even as they are championed for their innovation.

Les Paul's approach to sound, as much as the specific content of his music, defined him as a commercial or pop performer. Indeed, listening to the body of work he produced with Mary Ford, it is hard not to be struck by the diversity of influences that appear: not only jazz and hillbilly, but also blues, Russian folk music, Spanish and Latin American melodies, music of the Hawaiian islands, and varieties of what might be called gypsy music (courtesy of Django Reinhardt, the French gypsy jazz guitarist who was Paul's primary musical influence). The results of Les and Mary's efforts in this direction were often little more than ethnic kitsch. "Hawaiian War Chant," a song featured in the episode of the couple's radio show, was a particularly silly example of ethnic influence, with Mary's lyrics evoking Hawaiian language through a melody of nonsense syllables while Les multi-tracked a sprightly rhythm that has only the barest resemblance to any identifiably Hawaiian sounds. In other instances, though, they drew upon foreign or ethnic styles to expand their melodic palette, or alternately to convey a sense of pathos.

The former strategy can be heard in Paul's many instrumentals. It was in his instrumental recordings that Paul generally took the most stylistic chances, and allowed himself to move the farthest afield. Spanish-derived melodies in particular assumed a pronounced role in the crafting of Paul's multi-tracked instrumentals, and three such songs recorded by the guitarist reached the top twenty of the national sales charts between 1952 and 1954: "Carioca," "Lady of Spain," and "Mandolino." None of the songs was indigenous to Spain or Latin America. "Carioca" and "Lady of Spain" were written by white American songwriters who were seeking to capture something of the Latin mystique, while "Mandolino" was Paul's own composition. Yet the line of influence is clear enough, however mediated, within the song titles and within the content of the songs themselves. There is no straining for authenticity, but rather a more basic desire to achieve certain musical effects through the combination of a vaguely exotic melody with Paul's characteristically strict adherence to melodic regularity.

"Carioca," from 1952, exemplifies Paul's musical approach on these songs. Opening with a dark modal passage enlivened by the spiraling lines of Paul's guitar, the song then bursts into its principal melody, which Paul supplements with layers of background guitar that are alternately strummed, sped up through tape effects, and picked rapidly to approximate the sound of Spanish guitars. This pattern repeats once more, and then the modal passage returns a third time as a means of concluding the song. Paul's method is much the same as it was in "Lover," with a multitude of guitars put in the service of a melody stripped to its most basic elements. In this context, the emulation of Spanish sounds took shape as another of the tricks that Paul sought to work on the ears of his listeners through his mastery of sonic technologies.

A south-of-the-border aura[74] also pervaded many of Les and Mary's ballad recordings, which highlighted the second of their aesthetic objectives, conveying a sense of pathos. Ballads were a central element of the couple's repertoire, and were the principal medium for Paul to showcase his techniques for close-miking Ford's voice, producing those qualities of intimate sound upon which he laid such stress. Paul's guitar consequently played a background role on vocal ballads; it was Ford's voice that was foregrounded, with its hushed, languorous tone. The sources of Les and Mary's ballads were varied, but their most successful such recording was in their "south-of-the-border" mode. "Vaya con Dios" was released in June of 1953. By the end of the month it had moved to the number one position on the national sales charts.[75] A hymn to a departed lover, "Vaya con Dios" supplemented its Spanish-language vocal hook with a smattering of further Spanish guitar effects by Paul, including a brief solo section in which the guitarist simulates the sound of a mandolin. Yet the Spanish or Latin American influence is present principally in the atmosphere of the song. Fleeting references to the "hacienda" and the "village" ground the song in a sense of place that is at once specific and ambiguous, and provide the perfect setting for Mary's plaintive vocal inflections.

Rather than drawing any kind of simple opposition between the natural sources of authentic music and the technologically shaped sounds of commercial pop, or condemning Paul and Ford for their appropriative tendencies, I am asking how Paul and Ford could draw upon such a range of sources while still presenting a distinct performing identity that remained thoroughly ensconced within the conventions of mainstream pop. The best explanation of this curious dynamic can be located in Les Paul's sound, and more specifically in the ability of his pure, electronically produced tones to contain the intimations of otherness that his eclecticism might otherwise suggest. Paul's attempt to remove extraneous noise from his music and from the sounds produced by his electric guitar merged in these instances with the symbolic erasure of unruly ethnic or racial signifiers. His version of pop resided within the mainstream not because of the absence of foreign elements, but because of its power to purify those elements while incorporating them into its substance.

Paul's aesthetic strategies paralleled those of another musical style that enjoyed considerable success during the 1950s, mood music. In his study of the varieties of easy listening that have arisen during the past several decades, Joseph Lanza draws a connection between mood music and Muzak, both of which seek to organize the emotional response of the listener through the technological means of ordering sound. While Muzak was single-mindedly oriented toward cultivating sounds that soothed rather than frayed the nerves (a suggestive parallel to Paul's comments regarding the undesirable "nervousness" of bebop), mood music "functioned as Muzak's id," according to Lanza, engaging in "volatile mood swings" that transported the listener through a range of emotional states via the medium of high fidelity.[76] This emotional tourism was often accompanied by a fascination with exotica that strongly echoed the content of Paul's music. Describing the music of Les Baxter, Martin Denny, and others, Lanza refers to "an enchanting, teeming, intoxicating, and festering easy-listening sub-genre that vexed many an unsuspecting ear with the dark forces of 'foreignness' while staying within the bounds of propriety."[77] Such music regularly exhibited the mutability of electronic sounds as enthusiastically as did that of Les Paul and Mary Ford. If the evocation of exotica was one means of holding the listener's interest, so too was the foregrounding of electronic effects like those pioneered by Paul, all geared toward the production of a form of electronic music that was "not the weird machine-made sounds usually associated with the term, but music based on popular melodies, and played on conventional instruments that have been ingeniously electrified."[78]

The ingenious use of electricity was at the core of Les Paul's career as musician and inventor. Largely through his efforts, the electric guitar became just that, an instrument capable of producing an electronic tone relatively independent of its acoustic properties. Similarly, the process of sound recording assumed striking new forms of flexibility through Paul's experiments in layering tracks and manipulating sound through electronic means. Paul's significance was divided in its effects: though regularly championed as an innovator of significant proportions (more than one commentator has labeled him the Edison of the electric guitar), he is also notable for applying new technologies in a manner that displayed their accessibility as well as their novelty. The range of new sounds he produced was continually framed by familiar melodies and by the comfortable personas he and Mary Ford crafted, which avoided unsettling any musical or social boundaries. At the same time, Paul's career with Ford was indicative of the ambivalence that surrounded electric technologies as they were incorporated into white middle-class homes during the 1950s. For the couple, the electric guitar and the recording studio paralleled more common items like the television and the high-fidelity stereo, objects that brought about a reorganization of domestic space and affected gender and power relations in the home.

Visiting Les Paul's house in 1983, two decades after his marriage with Mary Ford had dissolved (and also years after her death in 1977), Peter Mengaziol commented with amazement on the state of the residence. For Mengaziol the home presented a sort of "living archive," each room containing past and present experiments that bespoke of Paul's many achievements and also of his tireless energy. "The house is in controlled disarray," he noted, observing equipment in various states of disrepair. "It's a tinkerer's paradise but a suburban housewife's nightmare."[79] Without a "woman's touch" to organize the surroundings, Paul had completely colonized the domestic space that he and Mary Ford had once shared with his technological endeavors.

Thoroughgoing as Paul's interest in technology remained, he expressed a special affection for the guitar among the various devices that occupied his space and attention over the years.

> You take all your gadgets, all you want, and play around with them, but finally you go back to the guitar. And that's *it,* just to play that guitar . . . Anyone who's a guitar player well knows that they don't need all those gadgets, all they want it [sic] just plain six strings on that guitar and they can have a field day. It's the greatest psychiatrist, the greatest housewife, the greatest doctor, the greatest thing a person can have in their hands, just those six strings on a box . . . An organ or synthesizer is a passive mechanical device; a guitar *talks.*[80]

Paul's remarks reflect a common tendency among musicians to humanize their instruments, and to view the guitar as a companion of the highest order, a result of the expressive qualities the guitar is considered to possess and the amount of time that guitarists spend alone with their instruments. Paul also refers to the special role that the electric guitar occupies within the history of technology as it bears upon musical production. Despite the hours of research and experimentation he had put into modifying electric guitar design, for Paul the instrument could not be reduced to its technical details. Insofar as Les Paul can be said to have had a romance with technology, it is in his more specific romance with the electric guitar, a romance that continues for him and scores of other musicians who prize the instrument's ability to "talk," to offer the advantages of technology while still bending to the needs and desires of the musician.

Chapter 3

Mister Guitar

Chet Atkins and the Nashville Sound

Uptown

Sometime between the late 1950s and the late 1960s, country music was said to have relocated, to have moved uptown. The phrase "gone uptown" stood for a perceived shift in country music, a softening of the edges that made it easier listening for segments of the pop music audience who had historically shunned country. Having gone uptown, it was feared that country music would leave its traditional core of fans—its rural southern base—behind. Major record labels like RCA and Decca sought to expand the audience for country music by removing the coarse melodies of the fiddle and the high-pitched, plaintive whining of the steel guitar, putting in their place smooth vocal choruses, lush string sections and the "round warm tones" of hollow-body electric guitars.[1]

By the 1960s this merger of country songs with pop sounds had been popularized in the national media as the Nashville Sound. At the center of much of the attention was a guitarist of formidable talent who, since 1957, had served as A&R (artists and repertoire) man for the Nashville division of RCA records and had produced many of the albums recorded under the label's heading. Chet Atkins was, by all accounts, the primary architect of the Nashville Sound, the man who had taken country music uptown through his combination of musical knowledge, skill with electronics, and flair for selecting good songs and good singers. A professional musician since the 1940s, Atkins spent years of struggling before earning a reputation for being one of the finest guitarists in all of popular music; by the early 1950s he carried the title "Mr. Guitar," worked regularly as a session guitarist for scores of singers, and was releasing album upon al-

bum of guitar-based instrumentals under his own name. Well before the
Nashville Sound had become anything like an identifiable commodity,
Chet Atkins was in a sense laying the groundwork for the later, more
widespread fusion of country and pop elements on his own albums, demonstrating for the listening public that "a pop song could sound country
when fingerpicked à la Atkins."[2] Moreover, the versatility of Atkins's
finger-picking guitar style was not limited to pop or country; classical
music became another key element of his repertoire, a means of presenting an image that spanned the musical and cultural spectrum from low to
high and that asserted the guitarist's respectability in the face of hillbilly
stereotypes.

Country guitar historian Rich Kienzle notes that Chet Atkins's virtuoso
playing made the guitar accessible to a wider audience of music enthusiasts and country music fans.[3] Important as Atkins's accomplishments with
the guitar have been, though, his virtuosic status is best considered not in
isolation but in conjunction with his role as an architect of the Nashville
Sound. Specifically, what Atkins brought to his dual roles as producer and
musician, besides the already-noted willingness to cross stylistic boundaries, was a concern with crafting sound by electronic means. Like Les
Paul, Chet Atkins combined intense devotion to the guitar with an interest in electronics. Atkins not only helped to solidify the position of the
electric guitar in country music, he also applied many of the recording
techniques pioneered by Paul in his production efforts. In so doing, he
worked to move country music away from the naturalistic aesthetic that
had so long dominated the genre. Electronic technology smoothed the
edges of the music and made it accessible to a broader range of listeners
than the music had previously attracted. Meanwhile, the guitar, and the
electric guitar in particular, served as the anchor of Atkins's performing
identity through his stylistic permutations; whether playing an old Tennessee fiddle tune or a Bach minuet, his role as "Mister Guitar" worked to
hold things together.

"Mister Guitar" was not such a clearly integrated figure, however. As
Atkins sought to test the boundaries of country music through the creative application of electric sound technologies in combination with his
own wide-ranging musical eclecticism, so was he perceived by many to
exemplify a crisis of definition within country music. Many fans and
critics of the genre had little desire to be taken uptown. They preferred

country music precisely because of its resistance to such impulses, and viewed Atkins as the figure who was leading country music down the wrong path. Taking such a perspective into account, I want to present a portrait of Atkins not as someone who led country music in a "progressive," pop-oriented direction, but as a figure whose career contained many of the contradictions that resided within country music during a crucial era in the music's history. During the two decades following World War II, country music expanded its audience significantly, and the base of country music production became increasingly centralized within the burgeoning Nashville studio system. These changes in turn generated a paradoxical set of pressures within the genre: on the one hand, there was a desire to respond to swelling commercial demand by accommodating the music to the broader tastes of the pop market; on the other hand, there was a desire to maintain, or even reassert, a sense of rootedness and tradition in the face of outside influences and interests. Atkins's career was largely shaped by these competing pressures, which serve as something of a thematic linchpin in the pages that follow.

The Nashville Sound

Describing the rise of Nashville's Music Row in his autobiography, *Country Gentleman,* Chet Atkins makes a telling comparison between the seat of Nashville recording and Tin Pan Alley. "Tin Pan Alley got its name because of the tinny sounds of the dozens of pianos in the demonstration rooms of music publishing houses. Music Row began to get the same sound; however, the dominant instrument was the guitar and not the piano."[4] The change of instrumentation was tied in Atkins's mind to a way of making music that he found characteristic of Nashville's developing music industry. Where the piano signified a more formal approach to composition and musicianship, one premised on the ability to read and write music, the guitar-based songs put together on Music Row were mostly self-taught and in a traditional style, presumably in keeping with the oral modes of transmission that had driven rural southern music. However, Atkins continues, these traditional practices eventually blended "with improvisation and the styles of other musicians," giving the music produced in Nashville "a different, modern style."

The mix of qualities evoked here by Atkins can be taken as a working definition of the Nashville Sound: frenetic musical activity signified by the cacophony of multiple guitars, motivated by the hope of getting a song purchased by an established publisher, and having it sung by an established performer. It was an informal approach to playing music set within a highly structured musical economy—elements of "traditional" music were fused with jazz and contemporary pop. What the Nashville Sound represented, then, was not so much a sound as a process of syncretization and centralization. A generation of white southern musicians who had been raised with one ear to local musical traditions and the other to the increasingly expansive musical world of radio came together in Nashville during the 1950s to redefine country music.

Or at least so one version of the story goes. Another version is that the Nashville Sound was a defensive maneuver put into practice by Atkins and his mentor at RCA records, Steve Sholes, among others, to maintain the commercial viability of country music in the face of rock 'n' roll. "The commercial threat was rockabilly," wrote John Morthland in the *Journal of Country Music,* "which split the heretofore-unified country audience into young and old. Given the defection of youth, the decision was to try broadening the market of older people, including those who had moved from the country into the suburbs."[5] The music that resulted was notable for a new emphasis on vocals over hot instrumental picking and a soft, loose beat that contrasted markedly with the sounds being created by the hillbilly cats recording at Sun studios just a couple hundred miles west. "If rockabilly was to take over as rural dance music, country would become primarily listening music, even *easy* listening music, radio music."[6] This conception of the Nashville Sound as a transformation of country music into easy listening music was also put forth by Bill Malone in his book, *Country Music U.S.A.* Noting that the Nashville Sound has also been called the "Chet Atkins compromise," Malone goes on to assert that "Chet Atkins deliberately tried to create a middle-of-the road sound (his 'compromise') which would preserve the feel and ambience of 'country' music while also being commercially appealing to a broader audience which had no experience with rural life and no liking for the harder sounds."[7] According to Malone, insofar as this compromise won a new audience for country music it was an audience of older pop fans whose taste for easy-listening pop had been unsettled by the musical shifts of the 1950s.[8] In making such a compromising gesture country music risked losing much of what made it distinctive. From this perspective, the dominant impulse of the Nashville Sound was not modernization but homogenization, and country music aligned itself with a set of musical and commercial values that were decidedly unchallenging to the many listeners.

The contrasts and tensions embedded in these different accounts of the rise of the Nashville Sound cut to the heart of the ways in which genre categories shape the production of popular music.[9] Within the histories of country music, the Nashville Sound might be classified as a transgressive moment, when proponents of the genre were forced to reexamine their understanding of the music's significance.[10] Before the Nashville Sound, country and pop coexisted uneasily. While there were periodic points of crossover, the most definitive country music performers remained rooted in a set of performance traditions that predated commercial recordings. It is thus no accident that country music histories seem almost obligated to start at the beginning, to tell the whole story of the music's development from a set of local and regional folk practices to a commercially distributed form, and to posit the supposed conflict between local folkways and commercially driven impulses toward homogenization as an ongoing theme in the music's history, if not the overarching driving force.

In his book, *Bluegrass Breakdown,* Robert Cantwell rejects the folk art versus commercial art dichotomy that has woven its way through so much of the writing on country music. Cantwell plainly asserts that hillbilly music is "entrepreneurial and commercial, prospering in the one commodity which in America is ever in short supply—the past."[11] The point, then, is not to mourn the loss of tradition in the face of commerce but to examine how commercial forms work to construct an imagined past, or the illusion of the past in a present-day performance. The process of recording was crucial to this illusion. Discussing the earliest hillbilly recordings made in the 1920s,[12] Cantwell notes: "It isn't simply that the recordings of 'old-time' music have become old . . . The hillbilly recordings . . . were *already old-fashioned* when they were recorded."[13] Recording became the medium by which a particular idea of the southern rural past was not so much preserved as created through the manipulation of sound; and this was the process that, according to Cantwell, shaped much of what we now recognize as country music.

What Chet Atkins transgressed or compromised in his function as a primary architect of the Nashville Sound was something more specific than the ostensible boundary between country music and the pop mainstream, a boundary predicated in large part upon the desire to maintain country music as an essentially folk way of making music. The key innovation of the Nashville Sound from a recording standpoint was an approach to sound that sought to conceal rather than foreground the old-fashioned sound of the music being recorded. Until the 1950s, country music had more or less adhered to a method of recording similar to that described by Folkways founder Moses Asch: "I always believed in the 'one mike' theory—I hate the stereo recordings, and mixing can never give you the accurate sense of the original sound."[14] Contrast this with Atkins's description of recording the first major hit he produced, Don Gibson's "Oh Lonesome Me":

> The record was different because we miked the bass drum, and I don't think that had ever been done before; I never had heard it, if it had. Back in those days, everybody'd just gang around the mike. You know, we had an engineer, Jeff Miller, who would just put one of those old condenser mikes in the middle of the floor and put the bass, drums, rhythm guitar, and everything on it . . . I remember it was impossible to get an intimate sound because he wouldn't let any singer get up too close to the mike . . . But as I said, we put a mike on the bass drum, and E-Q'd it . . . It was a new sound, so fresh and different for the time.
>
> When we miked, we had piano, bass, drums, and rhythm guitar—that was four. And one mike for the group, and one for the singer, so probably six.[15]

Atkins, like Les Paul, sought an intimate sound in his recordings, a sense of private communication through a public medium. The "one mike" theory espoused by Asch, on the other hand, was a way of representing sound that conjured a sense of origins. The sound of the performance was presented not merely "as it is" but "as it *was*," and was designed to conjure a sense of the time and place when the sounds heard were first developed. Chet Atkins, meanwhile, saw the separation and equalization of sound as a means of creating something new, a sound that asserted its discontinuity with the past as it had been constructed within country music. "I'm a country boy myself and I've played the Opry," said Atkins in a 1971 interview, "but this music has to continue to urbanize and keep up with the times . . . I don't reminisce about the old days. I'm in the business of selling records."[16] Advances in recording technology assisted

Atkins in his efforts to create a product imprinted with presence that, eschewing the idealization of old methods and old sounds, assimilated a wider range of listeners.

At the center of the debate concerning the historical significance of the Nashville Sound, and indeed at the center of the Nashville Sound itself as it took shape during the 1950s and 1960s, is a multi-tiered system of meanings and points of conflict. Most prominent is a concern with the role of the past in the production of country music: To what extent should country music carry a sense of its own past into present day performances, and to what extent can that past be said to precede, temporally and ideologically, the moment of recording? This latter question brings us to another component of the debate over the effects of the Nashville Sound: What role should technology play in the production of country music? Should the emphasis be on the transparent use of technology for the purposes of reproducing the effect of an old southern sound, or should it rather be upon the standardization of a country music sound in keeping with the broader conventions of mainstream pop? Finally, both of these sets of issues lead to the matter of commerce: Should country music strive to appeal to the broadest possible audience, or should it reserve its appeal for those committed to the music not only by taste but by background and experience?

In his approach to recording, Chet Atkins sought to negotiate among these various possibilities, and the methods he helped to establish have brought him both acclaim and castigation. By the mid-1970s, Atkins himself came to express a certain ambivalence about the role he had played in fostering the Nashville Sound. He explained his reservations most fully in a 1976 interview in *Rolling Stone,* responding to the question, "Haven't you since apologized for the Nashville Sound?"

> I've said that I hope country music doesn't completely lose its identity—and I apologized for anything I did in taking it too far uptown, which I did because we were trying to sell records. To sell records you gotta surprise the public, give them something different all the time . . . The point I was making was that if it was *my* fault that country music had moved farther uptown, well, I was sorry. But I want to sell records, too.[17]

Atkins here lends his support to an economic interpretation; the Nashville Sound was created to make money, and whatever other consequences that followed were unintentional. However, economic motives cannot be abstracted from the broader range of issues that came together in the production of the Nashville Sound. Moreover, for all the economic impetus, and for all the attention given to the agency of Atkins the producer in the crafting of country music's sound, the creation of the Nashville Sound was primarily led by musicians. Or more precisely, the Nashville Sound was created by a group of musicians whose convergence in Nashville was a key part of that city's emergence as the commercial and cultural center of country music.

*   *   *

When Chet Atkins came to Nashville in 1946, the key attraction of the city for aspiring musicians was the Grand Ole Opry. Nashville had yet to develop any significant base for recording activity, but the Opry had become perhaps the key country music institution, a broadly heard showcase where established stars held sway and up-and-comers struggled for a place in the spotlight. The Opry was also something of a bearer of country music tradition, an image that the show's founding announcer, George Hay, had long worked to promote. Despite the air of conservatism around the Opry, though, there were significant changes in the air. One of the show's biggest stars and staunchest traditionalists, Roy Acuff, had left over a contract dispute. His replacement was to be Red Foley, a southern-born singer who had spent the past several years of his career performing on Chicago's National Barn Dance. Though a talented and popular singer in his own right, Foley was viewed with suspicion by many Opry loyalists who perceived him as an outsider with a singing style that was overly smooth and modern.[18] Yet the deal had been made, and in April 1946 Foley would take the stage of the Opry for the first time with a band that included a young Chet Atkins on lead guitar.

In his book, *Kentucky Country,* Charles Wolfe described the Opry debut of Red Foley and Chet Atkins as "one of those curious watersheds" in the history of country music, when both the sound and image of the music were poised to undergo significant revision.[19] Though most of the attention that night was focused upon Foley (who was received enthusiastically by the Opry audience), Atkins was given his moment in the spotlight, playing a song called "Maggie" unaccompanied on acoustic guitar just before the show's commercial break.[20] According to Atkins, that moment represented the fulfillment of a long-held wish to be featured on the

Opry, a show he had listened to since childhood. Yet the time of fulfill-ment was to be short-lived. By his own description, his style was too "quiet" for the Opry audience: "I was playing acoustic guitar and the Opry House is absolutely the worst place, I guess, to work. The audience is very noisy."[21] Electric guitars were still something of an anomaly at the Opry; despite their use by one of the show's biggest attractions, Ernest Tubb, the instruments were perceived to clash with the show's traditional image. Reconciled to playing acoustic guitar, Atkins could not effectively project himself to the Opry crowd, and his solo spot was cut within six months of joining the show by mandate of the network officials in New York. His bandleader, Red Foley, tried to encourage him to stay on, but Atkins was not happy being limited to the role of sideman, so he quit.

Atkins would not come to Nashville again for another four years. Dur-ing the interim, he was fired from two more radio jobs, but also managed to attract the attention of Steve Sholes, an executive at RCA records in New York. Boosted by Sholes's support, Atkins began recording with RCA under his own name as well as playing with other singers on the label. At the same time, he settled into a position with one of his former employers, WNOX in Knoxville, where he formed a loose association with the guitar and mandolin duo Homer and Jethro and hooked up with the act that would lead him back onto the Opry stage, the Carter Sisters and Mother Maybelle.

Upon his second move to Nashville, Atkins found only a few changes from his first time through, but they were significant. For one, Steve Sholes had begun doing much of his recording of country performers in Nashville rather than transporting them up north to Chicago or New York, hence Nashville started to become a center of recording as well as performing activity. Having gained Sholes's trust and admiration during his brief association with RCA, Atkins became Sholes's main musical contact in Nashville, often helping to organize recording sessions; his work in this capacity laid the groundwork for his later efforts as a pro-ducer and A&R man. Meanwhile, at the Opry the main change Atkins noted was the addition of electronic instruments. "In the beginning they didn't have *any*," he wrote in his autobiography, "but little by little the electronic age crept in. By the time I returned to Nashville this second time, there were lots of them."[22] In particular, there was a new group of guitarists at the Opry by 1950 who shared Atkins's taste for pushing at the boundaries of country music, and who had taken up the electric guitar as part of a strategy of creating a new solo role for the guitar that was closer in some ways to jazz than to traditional country.

Over the next few years, Atkins, Hank Garland, Billy Byrd, and Grady Martin would enliven the backstage area of the Opry with impromptu jam sessions in which they would trade solo parts over chord changes that stretched the usual three-chord, major key structure of country music. These same guitarists, along with another, Harold Bradley, would also become key session musicians as more and more performers began to record in Nashville. By the end of the 1960s, each had been featured on literally hundreds of recordings. As such they helped to lay the groundwork for the intensely centralized studio system that arose in Nashville during the 1950s and came to fruition in the 1960s, a system based upon the musicians' familiarity with each others' style, allowing arrangements to be created on the spot in the studio. This process was noted for its casualness, but also facilitated maximum productivity and standardization of musical product as different singers recorded with the same core of musicians. And because of the preponderance of guitarists involved in the process, guitars came to dominate the sound of country music, especially on the records produced by Chet Atkins.

Among these guitarists, Billy Byrd was something of an elder statesman as well as a figure of some prestige due to his role as lead guitarist for Opry icon Ernest Tubb. Though his parts for Tubb tended toward melodic simplicity, Byrd's primary musical affection was for jazz, and his main musical influence was Charlie Christian. Drawn to Christian's ability to "take a guitar and phrase it like a horn," Byrd was described by Owen Bradley, a producer, as one of the first Nashville guitarists to play the electric guitar, and in a style that was more pop than country.[23] According to Byrd, he turned to country music primarily out of economic necessity. He continued playing pop and jazz in his club performances throughout the 1940s, and "jazzed up the country as much as I could" when appearing on the Opry.[24]

When younger guitarists Hank Garland and Harold Bradley came to town, Byrd offered professional guidance and also tutored them in the ways of jazz guitar. Garland became an especially proficient pupil who went on to record *Jazz Winds from a New Direction* with a jazz quartet featuring vibraphonist Gary Burton in 1960. By the mid-1950s these guitarists, along with a coterie of other musicians like bassist Bob Moore, saxophonist Boots Randolph, and pianist Floyd Cramer, were holding regular jam sessions at the Carousel Club, located just blocks from the Ryman Auditorium, home of the Opry. Although on the Opry stage they still had to follow country conventions fairly closely, the Carousel was a place for stretching out, where the collective taste for jazz improvisation held sway. David Halberstam, writing in the Nashville *Tennessean* newspaper, reported on the affinity for jazz among the city's hillbilly musicians in a 1959 article, noting the existence of a new breed of musician, the "jazz-billy," within Nashville's musical landscape and highlighting guitarists Garland and Chet Atkins as particularly notable examples of musical versatility.[25]

To observe that jazz served as a musical crossroads where country music changed into a modern, sophisticated form accessible to a broad audience is only to scratch the surface of the phenomenon through which jazz entered the vocabulary of so-called "country" musicians. Jazz was itself a highly unstable musical category in the years following 1940. The growth of bebop and the reclamation of jazz by African-American musicians like Charlie Christian, Charlie Parker, and Dizzy Gillespie had created a situation in which jazz was perceived to be increasingly distant from popular music. By the 1950s jazz was widely understood to be an avant-garde form, detached from the tastes of the average listener; thus did Les Paul deride the music for its "nervousness" and its inaccessibility to listeners with no musical training. Chet Atkins expressed similar reservations about jazz at several points in his career. In *Country Gentleman,* for instance, he writes of the apparent "militancy" of jazz musicians who show no regard for the melody of a tune, suggesting that it seems "as though the musicians are putting on the public."[26] Meanwhile, Atkins described himself in a 1967 biography as "strictly a melody man," and went on to explain that "one reason jazz has never been a great success is because it is improvisation, and the public loses the melody . . . Music should have a melodic line somewhere that is appealing and I try to keep this in mind in all my recordings."[27] This popular taste for melody led to a preference for a style of improvisation that owed more to swing styles of the 1930s than to the harmonically complex and even dissonant forms of jazz that had taken shape since the 1940s. The Charlie Christian that was admired by guitarists like Billy Byrd was the Christian of the Benny

Goodman Sextet, not the more adventurous figure who took the stage night after night at Minton's in Harlem;[28] and Atkins's primary jazz influence, Django Reinhardt, was also a musician whose approach was rooted in the melodic improvisations of the swing era.

By the same token, the uses to which the electric guitar was put by these musicians was calculated to blend with the melody of a tune. As session musicians, the guitarists associated with the Nashville Sound were noted for their ability to blend into any musical framework without calling undue attention to themselves, a philosophy clearly articulated in a Monument records publicity release for Grady Martin. "Fuzztone, gut-string fills, straight neck dobro, Echoplex, and double neck guitar are but a few of the terms that would come up in a technical article on Grady Martin's relationship to the guitar," reads the brief biography, which goes on to note Martin's "knack for playing precisely what each song needed rather than his own personal style."[29] Expanding the range of possible tones was in this instance part of the process of tailoring a song; though the guitar played a prominent role, its function was primarily complementary. Yet this attention to sound was also a key element of the guitarist's craft as it was understood in Nashville, whether one was playing a session for another artist or recording a solo instrumental. Writing about Hank Garland, James Sallis noted that "Hank was a tinkerer, an experimenter, always trying different guitars, new ways of stringing or tuning them—anything to get a sound he wanted."[30] Out of such efforts, Garland came to co-design with Billy Byrd the Gibson Byrdland guitar, a successful model released in 1955 that sought to effect a compromise between the two principal guitar designs on the market at the time, large-bodied hollow guitars and smaller but heavier solid-body instruments.[31] This guitar bore the mark of the heavy attraction to jazz that the two players shared, and the compromise design showed a preference for smooth electric tones not unlike those preferred by Les Paul, tones that were easy on the ears and paved the way for the incorporation of pop music conventions into country music.

The Byrdland was but one of many examples of country guitarists' influence upon the shape and sound of the electric guitar during the 1950s. On the West Coast, Leo Fender routinely appealed to country guitarists to try his new designs and offer suggestions for improvement. One of these musicians, Bill Carson, has been credited with contributing

3.1.   Advertisement for the Gibson Byrdland guitar, designed with the input of Nashville studio guitarists Billy Byrd and Hank Garland. Courtesy of Gibson Musical Instruments.

to the design of Fender's most successful guitar, the Stratocaster.[32] By the mid-1950s, Chet Atkins too would have an electric guitar on the market that bore his name and followed many of his own design concepts. The line of guitars produced by the upstart Gretsch company under Atkins's sponsorship would enjoy considerable success and remain in production until the 1980s, when Atkins severed his relationship with the company. Atkins's role as a guitar sponsor was an outgrowth of his intense engagement with the guitar as a musical instrument and a technological device. Indeed, of the Nashville guitarists he was the figure most noted for tinkering with electronics and playing with sound. Moreover, Atkins was set apart from his Nashville peers by his distinctive finger-style approach to the guitar, an approach that established him as one of the most regarded solo guitarists of his time. His style of playing, in turn, made unusual demands on his development as a guitarist—demands that fueled his interest in the sonoric qualities of the electric guitar.

Finger Style

The most basic definition of finger-style guitar is a mode of guitar playing in which the musician picks at the strings using his fingers rather than a flatpick. However, the term "finger style" as it is generally used tends to have a more specific connotation.[33] Rich Kienzle offered a concise statement on the nature of finger-style guitar in a 1984 article for *Guitar Player* magazine. "The basic fingerpicking style . . . consists of the right-hand index finger picking out the melody while the thumb, usually equipped with a pick, plucks out a constant alternating bass accompaniment. The net result is a self-contained, rich, varied sound that gives the illusion of a lead and rhythm guitar being played simultaneously."[34] This last suggestion, that finger-style guitar creates the sense of more than one guitar being played at a given time, is crucial to the mystique surrounding the style, especially as it applies to Chet Atkins, who modified the basic finger-style method to employ not just the index finger and thumb but the middle and ring fingers as well to produce a wider array of melodic and harmonic combinations. When asked to explain the origins of his style for a publicity piece written shortly before his return to Nashville in 1950, Atkins replied, "There was nobody to play duets or trios with, the six years I was in Georgia, so what would you do? I tried making my playing sound like two guitars, and after awhile . . . it worked!"[35] In truth, though, the development of Atkins's style was not so self-contained; rather, Atkins's acquisition of finger-style technique demonstrates the complex lines of musical transmission at work in the rural South during the early decades of the twentieth century.

Historians and folklorists have located the roots of finger-style playing in the area around Muhlenberg County in western Kentucky. The style was most likely of African-American derivation, a product of the influential but largely ignored black string band traditions that flourished in parts of the South during the late nineteenth and early twentieth centuries, to be largely displaced by the popularization of blues.[36] Arnold Shultz, a near-mythic figure in the history of old-time music whose influence was felt by scores of performers in the western Kentucky area, was perhaps the most notable early guitar player using finger-style technique. Shultz played with several white string bands in the region. The locus for such interracial activity was the musicians' common occupation working the Kentucky coal mines.[37] During the course of the 1920s and into the 1930s, a small group of white guitarists adapted the style to an unusual blend of old-time and popular melodies. A player named Kennedy Jones was apparently the first white musician to directly apply methods learned from Shultz. Following him were two guitarists who worked for a while as a team, Mose Rager and Ike Everly; and it was they who influenced the man who first popularized the style to an audience outside of Kentucky, Merle Travis.

There is perhaps no better measure of Merle Travis's profound influence on the history of country guitar than the name now commonly used for finger-picking on the guitar, "Travis picking." Yet Travis has always been quick to assign credit to his guitar-playing forebears in Kentucky when discussing the development of his style. As he wrote in an unpublished autobiographical sketch, "When I was barely in my teens I discovered Mose Rager and Ike Everly. They played with a thumb pick on their thumb, playing an accompaniment with the thumb alone, while the forefinger picked a melody on the higher pitched strings." Drawn to their style, Travis made sure to attend the house parties and outdoor gigs that the two guitarists played, and after hearing them "did exactly what some young fellow will do tomorrow after hearing his favorite singer or musician. I went home and tried to play what they had played."[38] Through their influence, Travis formed a heavily syncopated style that relied on rapidly thumb-picked bass lines and high-register arpeggios that slid up and down the neck of the guitar with considerable facility. His best known solo guitar piece, "Cannon Ball Stomp" (alternately known as "Cannon Ball Rag"), shows the style to good effect, with Travis bringing the ragtime melody to a series of crescendos over the course of a minute and twenty seconds, the bass line at times threatening to overtake the song through sheer force of execution.[39]

Showing little desire to work in the local mines, Travis began hoboing across the upper South and lower Midwest around 1936, carrying little more than a guitar. By the end of the 1930s he had more or less resettled in Ohio, where he established a niche for himself as guitarist for WLW radio in Cincinnati. While in Cincinnati Travis would also record for an obscure independent label named King, which became one of the most significant and successful independent labels of the next several years, featuring a strong list of both country and rhythm and blues performers, the most famous of whom was James Brown. However, Travis's recording career for King was cut short when he was drafted into the military toward the end of World War II. Upon being discharged, he relocated to southern California, where he became a part of that region's growing country and western scene and formed an association with yet another newly formed record label, Capitol Records. There he acquired a reputation as a strong songwriter as well as a talented guitarist. One of his songs, "Sixteen Tons," would eventually become a number one hit in 1955 in a version by Tennessee Ernie Ford.[40] It was also after moving to California that Travis made his own contribution to the history of the electric guitar with a sketch he drew for his friend, guitar maker Paul Bigsby.

The Bigsby/Travis solid-body electric guitar, built in 1948, arose out of Travis's desire for a guitar with greater sustain. Like Leo Fender, his idea for a solid-body guitar arose out of listening to the sound achieved by the electric steel guitars that were featured in the western swing ensembles that ruled the southern California bandstands. As Travis recalled in 1979, "I kept wondering why steel guitars would sustain the sound so long, when a hollow-body electric guitar like mine would fade out real quick. I came to the conclusion it was all because the steel guitar was solid."[41] Broaching his idea to Bigsby, Travis, an amateur cartoonist, drew out a design on a piece of scratch paper and gave it to his friend; some weeks later, Bigsby had finished the guitar to Travis's specifications, including distinctive features like placing all six tuning pegs on one side of the headstock and inlaying mother-of-pearl fretboard markings shaped after the four suits in a deck of cards.

Guitar historians have debated at length over what significance to attribute to the Bigsby/Travis solid-body. The main point of controversy has to do with whether the guitar preceded Leo Fender's formulation of the solid-body concept, and whether the Bigsby/Travis design had any direct influence upon Fender's first successful solid-body model, the Esquire. Travis himself has claimed on many occasions that Fender borrowed the guitar and used it as the basis for his solid-body experiments; Fender, for his part, has consistently denied that such a thing ever happened. In *American Guitars,* Tom Wheeler concludes that Fender had in fact begun the process of developing a solid-body electric before Bigsby built his guitar for Travis. Wheeler goes on to draw a parallel between the Bigsby/Travis guitar and Les Paul's Log, suggesting that the two guitars were more notable for their connection with famous players and for their "exalted but commercially untenable status of being ahead of their time" than for the influence they had on subsequent guitar designs.[42] However, former Fender plant manager Forrest White more recently asserted that the Bigsby/Travis guitar did indeed influence Fender's designs, and his assertions are backed up by Richard Smith in his authoritative history of Fender guitars. According to Smith, there is clear evidence that Fender had seen the Travis/Bigsby guitar before completing his own solid-body model. Weighing the extent to which the differences of Fender's ultimate design outweighed the similarities (a considerable amount), Smith states that Fender by no means copied the Bigsby/Travis guitar, but did find it to reaffirm "the feasibility and obvious utility of a solidbody guitar."[43] Just as important, the Bigsby/Travis guitar stands as yet another example of the crystallization of the solid-body concept in the years following World War II, in this instance driven by the desires of a finger-picking country guitarist from Kentucky who had happened to migrate to an area where electric guitar design and performance were flourishing.

* * *

Throughout his career, Chet Atkins has routinely cited Merle Travis as the biggest single influence upon his guitar playing. Atkins's story of how he acquired finger-style technique differs markedly from that of Travis, though. While Travis learned the style through face-to-face encounters with other musicians, Atkins seems to have received little guidance from other players. Not that he was completely isolated from other musicians—his father was a music teacher, and his half-brother Jim was a guitarist and singer of considerable ability who left home while Atkins was still a boy to pursue a career in music. Atkins furthermore lived in the mountains of East Tennessee, where music was a part of the daily routine. Picking and singing sessions were a common recreation at the end of the workday, and community dances happened regularly on the weekends. Yet the musicians who exerted the greatest impact upon the formation of Atkins's style were not the ones with whom he came into direct contact, but the ones he heard through his favorite device (next to the guitar), the radio.

Like Les Paul, Chet Atkins was addicted to tinkering with technology, and radio was the primary focus of his early interest. "The Sears and Roebuck catalog and *Popular Mechanics* were the most important publications in the world," wrote Atkins of his youth. "I dreamed through the catalog and built things from the magazine. A two-tube radio was the most important dream."[44] This fascination with radio was fueled in part by the fact that his brother Jim could be heard week after week playing on the National Barn Dance under the pseudonym Tommy Tanner, alongside another pseudonymous guitarist, Rhubarb Red, otherwise known as Les Paul.[45] Yet Atkins also valued radio more generally for the access it provided to a world removed from his daily life, and to musicians performing in a range of styles, both familiar and unfamiliar.

As an aspiring guitarist, Atkins regarded the radio as his teacher. When barely past the age of ten, he began trying to copy the sounds he heard from professional musicians over the airwaves, a process that forced him to experiment with the guitar in a way that learning face-to-face did not. Robert Cantwell evocatively described the difference between these two modes of musical learning in *Bluegrass Breakdown*. "Traditional music in folk communities is . . . never as purely auditory as the message transmitted by radio or phonograph," states Cantwell, who describes the value attributed to direct contact with musicians of ability and experience in local musical traditions. "The most dedicated [students] . . . follow the revered musician to wherever he is to be found," as Merle Travis followed his models Mose Rager and Ike Everly; "five minutes under his tutelage will impart what hours of poring over his recordings will not—the *how,* as well as the *what* of his music."[46] By contrast, the radio or record "reflects only the audial facet of a many-faceted tradition; but in reflecting it," asserts Cantwell, "it frees it . . . And the music, freed from the sometimes dazzling processes of performance, presents itself to the ear *as* itself, an aural effect for which the musician, by a kind of musical detective work, must contrive a physical and mechanical cause, discovering techniques of his own as he goes."[47]

Such was the process by which Chet Atkins came upon his finger-style approach. In his autobiography he stresses the absence of any models for finger-style playing in his immediate environment. Rather, his style began to crystallize only after he moved to the relative isolation of northern Georgia to live with his father, a region where music was far less prevalent than in his birthplace near Luttrell, Tennessee. Forced to spend most of his guitar-playing hours by himself, Atkins "began to experiment picking the guitar with my fingers instead of using a hard pick. It felt natural, and since there was nobody around to teach me anything else I began, little by little, to develop a finger-pickin' style."[48] According to Atkins his movement in the direction of "finger-pickin'" had already started before he came upon the music of Merle Travis, but it was Travis who gave him a sense of what could be accomplished with the style, and the night he first found Travis playing guitar over the radio on station WLW occupies a pivotal place in Atkins's autobiography. About Travis, Atkins wrote,

> His guitar style was closer to that sound I had been searching for than anything I had ever heard. The clever way he played melody and rhythm at the same time knocked me over. I knew he was finger picking, but I didn't know how he was doing it. I would pick up WLW and Merle about once a month when conditions were right. When I couldn't pick him up on the radio, I would try to invent things that sounded like him. He was deeply influenced by traditional and folk music and his style was complex. If I'd heard him more often I would have wound up playing exactly like him.[49]

Atkins's comments here bear out Cantwell's discussion of the "detective work" involved in learning to play music from aural sources. The odd rhythm of this process—occasionally hearing Travis while regularly trying to copy his playing—allowed Atkins to avoid direct imitation, and to develop a style of finger-picking that, while derived from his model, took on unique qualities, like the use of three fingers on his right hand rather than relying on the thumb-and-index-finger approach typically used by Travis.[50]

Radio was also the means by which Atkins first became acquainted with the electric guitar. Even before he discovered the playing of Travis, he was attracted to the sound generated by guitarists like Les Paul and George Barnes, another genre-hopping Chicago musician who was using an amplified guitar as early as the 1930s. "When I first started playing seriously, electric guitar was just starting," remembered Atkins in 1976. "So it was a case of wanting to sound like somebody you heard on the radio, and the persons I heard of course were Les Paul and George Barnes. They played electric guitar and, you know, it was a bigger, nicer sound."[51] Like his taste for the playing of Merle Travis, then, Atkins's affinity for the electric guitar began as a purely aural phenomenon.

In this regard, Atkins's developing interest in the electric guitar can be taken to represent something of a transition in the history of the instrument, particularly where country music is concerned. The early use of the electric guitar in country music was largely shaped by the conditions of performance, and was tied to the rise of new commercial spaces where the music was presented. These dance halls, or honky-tonks, as they came to be called, proliferated throughout the Southwest during the 1930s and 1940s, and were noted as much for their role as social gathering spots as for their role as places to hear music. Musicians often had to use their resources to compete with the din of the dance-hall crowd, and the electric guitar became one means of ensuring that a guitarist could be heard. Over time, the sound produced by amplification became valuable in itself, and the dance halls became a key space for the transmission of the electric guitar on a local level, a place where performers who had not yet "plugged in" learned of amplification from musicians who had already acquired the new technology. Through this process, the electric guitar also began to be featured on more and more recordings, which were played in the dance halls via the newly developed medium of the jukebox.

Ronnie Pugh, biographer of Ernest Tubb, illustrates this course of development with an anecdote concerning the honky-tonk singer's decision to incorporate an electric guitar into his act. Tubb remembers a conversation with a jukebox operator in which the man told the singer that his records were played regularly during the afternoon hours, when things were quiet in the bars. "But as soon as the crowd gets in there and gets noisy, they start dancing, they can't hear your records, they start playing Bob Wills. They're not playing your records: you need to make them louder."[52] Lacking the funds to hire a larger band, Tubb's solution was to buy his guitarist a pickup and urge him to play electric guitar. Over the years the sound of electric lead guitar became a key element of Tubb's sound; and when he joined the Grand Ole Opry in 1943 he became the first performer on the show to regularly feature the instrument as a part of his act.

Although competitive conditions initially led performers in dance halls to seek out the electric guitar, soon it was recognized as a means of achieving new sounds, not simply audible volume.[53] For early proponents of amplification like steel guitarist Bob Dunn these two aims often coexisted,[54] but for guitarists coming of age a few years later, the electric guitar need not have borne any necessary relationship to the dance halls or to the imperatives of performing in front of a crowd. Radio and recordings removed the sound of the electric guitar from its immediate surroundings, and in the process distilled that sound into something desirable in itself for people listening at different times in different places.

Chet Atkins was one of the many guitarists whose first contact with the electric guitar came strictly via its sound. Having already developed some facility with electronics through his interest in radio, Atkins decided while a teenager to convert his acoustic instrument into an electric one. He went out and bought an amperite pickup and then ordered an amplifier through the mail. When his amplifier arrived with broken tubes, the young guitarist waited impatiently for replacements—"The guitar was all ready, with the pickup installed"—so that he could finally assemble the whole unit.[55] Atkins's moment of triumph was short-lived, however. Now that he had successfully assembled his electric guitar, he came face to face with another problem: his home, and the Georgia town where he lived, were not yet equipped with electricity. To power his new instrument, he would have to go to his schoolhouse, or travel twenty-five miles to the town of Columbus, where his father made regular trips to give music lessons and lead choir at a local church. He debuted his new instrument at school the next day—relieved to find that it actually worked—and thereafter made regular trips to Columbus with his father, about which he has said, "I would plug in and play and afterwards take it all back home again and wish for electricity."[56]

Atkins, then, began to use an electric guitar well before his debut at the Grand Ole Opry in 1946. As he moved into a career as a professional musician, he found his electric instrument to be less than satisfying in performing situations. The finger-style approach that he used made certain demands upon the sound of a guitar that his crudely amplified instrument could not meet. In a 1979 interview, Atkins described the problems he faced in properly amplifying his guitar:

> I used a DeArmond pickup, and the strings were not properly balanced. That pickup was the adjustable kind that you attach to the tailpiece, so it was kind of hard to balance each string so that they were all at the same volume. It was difficult to play fingerstyle on an electric guitar then because of the imbalance. Those pickups tended to work with the bass strings and the first string pretty well, but the wound third didn't pick up at all.[57]

Had Atkins employed a more standard single-string solo style like that used by Charlie Christian or Les Paul, in which individual notes were picked with emphasis and changes in register occurred less frequently, he would have experienced less trouble with early amplification techniques. But finger-style guitar entailed a quick alternation between the thumb-picked bass and the finger-picked treble and mid-range strings, and could only be effectively conveyed by a system of amplification that allowed for proper balance between the different registers of the guitar. Atkins therefore still relied on acoustic instruments during much of his early career, and began to feature the electric guitar more regularly only after 1947, when he could afford pickups that allowed him to adjust the volume of his guitar to fit his specifications.

Combined with Atkins's established interest in electronics, his finger-style method led him to continually search for ways of improving his sound over the next few years, when he began to find greater success as a performer and recording artist. His guitar sound changed dramatically in the singles he recorded from the late 1940s to the early 1950s. On his first successful single, the instrumental, "Galloping on the Guitar," from 1949, his sharp, trebly tone strikes a sort of middle ground between acoustic and electric, sounding very much like an acoustic guitar equipped with a pick-up. By the time of "Country Gentleman," recorded in 1953, the electric tone he achieves sounds smoother, more "pure" in the sense that Les Paul used the term, and Atkins's playing correspondingly flows through the piece with a greater sense of ease.[58] Accompanying this change in tone was a stylistic shift between the two pieces: the rapidly-paced, syncopated group interplay of "Galloping on the Guitar" gave way to a gradual, loping beat and an understated melody in "Country Gentleman," qualities that would become Atkins trademarks as he made a more concentrated move to fuse country and pop.

The stream of singles Atkins released between 1947 and 1954 helped to establish him as one of the most widely heard guitarists in the popular music of the period. Moreover, by the early 1950s he had caught on as a major Opry attraction, regularly playing as many as three solo spots every Saturday night for the show and broadcasting twice a day during the rest of the week for Nashville station WSM.[59] Thus was it no surprise that when the Gretsch guitar company went looking for "its own Les Paul," a well-known player whom they could use to generate new interest in their guitar line, they approached Atkins.[60] At the time Gretsch enjoyed only moderate success as a guitar manufacturer, and was more noted for the off-beat finishes of their guitars than for the quality of their instruments. In Atkins they found not only a valuable endorser, but a musician whose concern with sound and facility with electronics also made him an effective collaborator. Tom Wheeler described the multi-faceted appeal of Atkins to the Gretsch company in *American Guitars:*

> Among official recommendations the Atkins seal of approval was all any manufacturer could hope for in the mid 1950s. First, he was incandescent with talent. Second, he was an eminently trustworthy gentleman: if Chet says it's good, it's good. Next, he sold records by the truckload and appeared on TV, and to top it off he was a guitar designer associated with electronic experimentation . . . Chet Atkins was a perfect blend of folksy charm, electronic wizardry, and guitar genius, and as far as modern electric models are concerned, his say so put Gretsch on the map.[61]

Meanwhile Atkins, for his part, was excited by the possibility of having his name on a guitar, perceiving it as a legitimization of his status as a guitarist of high regard.[62] The association between Atkins and Gretsch was mutually beneficial, and helped to solidify the commercial process begun by the Gibson Les Paul whereby guitarist and guitar lent prestige to one another via the medium of the guitarist's name, a name that signified in turn a range of desirable qualities that the guitar would ideally confer upon potential consumers.

The first Gretsch Chet Atkins guitars were issued in 1955, after Atkins had met with company engineers to discuss the design. Two models were originally issued, a hollow-body and a solid-body that was really only semi-solid, composed of separate pieces of wood. This latter model was not to Atkins's liking, but the hollow-body that Gretsch designed would become his favorite guitar over the next several years of his career.[63] The Gretsch Chet Atkins hollow-body, model 6120, was a curious blend of Atkins's ideas with those of the Gretsch design team. To increase the sustain of the guitar and give it greater balance of tone, Atkins suggested using smaller f-holes than were customary on Gretsch models (later these "holes" would only be painted on); to facilitate the use of tremolo techniques that Atkins had developed over his years of playing, he recommended the inclusion of a tremolo arm and tailpiece designed by Paul Bigsby, the same guitar maker who had designed Merle Travis's solid-body prototype. Yet the look of the guitar was all of Gretsch's making, with a bright orange finish and assorted western features like a branded "G" on the upper right side of the body, an inlaid cattle head on the headstock, and that same cattle head alongside various imprinted cactus shapes on the fretboard, all designed to capitalize on an image of country music that had little bearing upon Atkins's own persona.

Atkins was none too pleased with the faux western trappings of his namesake guitar, and in subsequent years Gretsch phased out these elements of the guitar's appearance. Even less to his liking were the DeArmond pickups used by Gretsch, which lacked the proper balance he sought and also generated an annoying hum that was difficult to control in performing situations. To correct the situation he turned to an associate, Ray Butts, another electronics enthusiast whom Atkins had met shortly before forming his association with Gretsch. In 1954 Atkins had purchased from Butts a distinctive guitar amplifier equipped with an electronic echo unit, one of the many electronic effects he would feature on his recordings from that era. Now he asked for Butts's assistance in designing a new pickup that would cut down on extraneous noise and

3.2. The Gretsch Chet Atkins hollow-body guitar, first issued in 1955.
Note the branded "G" in the lower left corner. Courtesy of the Experience
Music Project.

provide a tone more suited to Atkins's style of playing. Within months, Butts independently designed a humbucking pickup very much like that produced by Seth Lover at Gibson, a double-coil pickup that reduced the unwanted hum while providing a thicker, less trebly tone than single-coil pickups.[64] The invention of the humbucking pickup paralleled that of the solid-body guitar, the result of the distinct efforts of two different electronic design specialists—an occurrence indicative of the growing value being place upon an aesthetic of tonal purity. At Atkins's urging, Gretsch soon added Butts's innovation to its line of Atkins-endorsed guitars, and the guitarist was better equipped to play electric finger-style guitar.

*   *   *

If Chet Atkins was never noted for his purism as a country musician, he expressed through much of his career a concern with purity of tone that echoed Les Paul, one of his principal influences. In part, this was due to the requirements of his chosen guitar technique; as Atkins stated in a 1969 interview, "If an amp is too loud, it bothers me . . . it makes it hairy to play if you're getting feedback when you've got your volume up too high and are playing finger style."[65] For Atkins, the effective use of finger-style methods entailed a high degree of sonic clarity so that the different ranges of the guitar could be heard. At the same time, however, this pursuit of a pure tone acquired a value of its own for the guitarist. Though he would feature a range of electronic, sound-altering effects on his many albums from the 1950s and 1960s, the dominant tone by far was a clean, smooth tone with a proper balance of bass and treble, a sound Atkins described on more than one occasion as "pretty."[66]

This self-conscious pursuit of a pretty, pure tone was a key aspect of Atkins's easy-listening strategy. Like his stated commitment to melody, Atkins's use of pretty guitar sounds was designed to cater to an audience that demanded comforting rather than enervating music. Moreover, the tone of Atkins's guitar worked to smooth the stylistic transitions from song to song on his albums. Insofar as his finger-style technique proved to be amazingly versatile, Atkins's pursuit of pure tone can be read as an effort to contain the most unsettling implications of that versatility. On *Finger-Style Guitar*, for instance, a 1957 release regarded by many as the quintessential Atkins album from the 1950s, the guitarist moves from the pop melodies of "In the Mood" and "Glow Worm" to classical pieces like

"Petite Waltz" and "Gavotte in D," with a Merle Travis tune thrown in for good measure. With such a diverse assortment of songs, Atkins achieves a striking degree of unity (some might call it homogeneity) throughout the album, an effect owed in no small degree to his use of electric guitar on each of the performances, classical as well as pop. Finger-style technique combines with purity of tone in this instance to forge a middle ground between elevated and popular musical forms where Atkins can assert his skill and make claims upon a sort of respectability rarely accorded to country musicians.

For Chet Atkins, the guitar was not only a means of making music, but a device that signified at once his connection to his rural upbringing and the distance he had imposed between himself and the circumstances of his childhood. "I remember malnutrition," asserted Atkins in 1976, "I remember being hungry. I said to myself when I was a kid, I'll never be that way again. I guess for me the guitar is the symbol of that."[67] Much as Atkins regarded the guitar as a symbol of his achievements in overcoming poverty, his success with the instrument also signified for him an effective counter to hillbilly stereotypes. In his autobiography, Atkins noted the shift from hillbilly to country during the early years of his musical development, a shift that signified at once the spread of the music's popularity outside of the South and the growing sense of dignity attached to the music.[68] The Nashville Sound was one result of this change; Atkins's distinctive brand of finger-style electric guitar was another. As his interest in classical music grew over the course of his career, Atkins would turn more and more to acoustic instruments. By the end of the 1960s he was playing nylon-string acoustic guitar almost as often as electric. One instrument he almost never featured in this later stage of his career, though, was the acoustic steel-string guitar, the sharp tone of which was one of the distinguishing features of traditional old-time music. Whether playing acoustic or electric, Atkins eschewed the "old southern sound" in favor of a tone more in keeping with the dignity and professionalism he sought to project.

One can see further traces of these currents running through Atkins's career in his various television and concert performances that have been preserved on video. A recent Shanachie Records video compilation, for instance, features performances by Atkins and honky-tonk singer Webb Pierce, culled from a series of mid-1950s television appearances on the

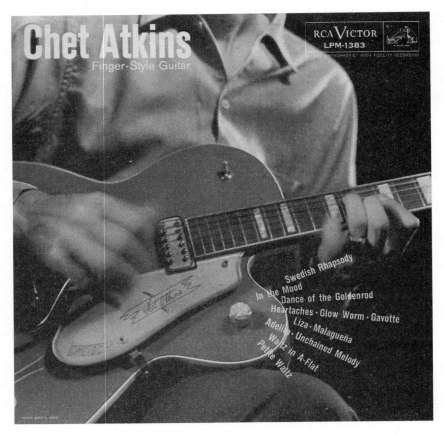

3.3. *Finger-Style Guitar.* The cover from Atkins's esteemed 1957 album shows the guitarist's fingers in a blur of motion.

Country Music Show in Nashville. The contrast between the two performers says much about the range of styles that occupied country music during the 1950s, and also sheds light upon Atkins's distinctive position in the genre. Pierce, one of the classic honky-tonk singers, comes out with a different suit for almost every song, and each outfit is a model of the verging-on-garish flair that many country musicians have used to mark out their distinctive look. Bright yellows and reds abound, with musical notes hovering abstractly on collars and sleeves, or record label imprints on each breast. Yet for all his visual flair, Pierce blends into the setting of the show. The many spectators and regular cast members who crowd the stage area are all done up in varieties of western apparel that differs from

Pierce only in the degree of spectacle. Thus does Atkins seem rather anomalous in his staid suit and tie, presenting a calm, almost too studied character amid the bouncing, enthusiastic crowd. Atkins's singularity is further marked by his guitars, alternately burnt orange or bright orange electric Gretsch models that provide further visual contrast with Pierce, who wields a full-bodied acoustic steel-string guitar through each of his performances. And then there is Atkins's music, with his rapidly finger-picked lines shaping melodies that shift from point to point across the fingerboard and yet retain their consistency, even as he ranges across material from the most traditional country ("Wildwood Flower") to the most standard pop ("Mr. Sandman").

Another video collection, featuring "rare" Atkins performances over the span of years from 1955–1975, presents a broader overview of the guitarist's career, and also finds him performing in a greater variety of settings. Opening with yet more of Atkins's 1950s television appearances, the tape goes on to show segments of two Atkins concerts in Norway, filmed a decade apart (1963 and 1973), as well as two further television appearances from the 1970s. Of the different segments, perhaps the most striking is the 1973 Norway performance, during which Atkins alternates between acoustic classical guitar and his trademark Gretsch electric, all the while supported by a full orchestra. Here Atkins's genre-hopping proclivities explicitly join his desire to craft an "elevated" form of musical expression. Yet the performance comes across as something less than a successful synthesis. Interestingly, Atkins eschews the more classical elements of his repertoire; there are no Bach minuets, but instead a sweep through some of his greatest hits. Meanwhile, the orchestra plays a principally additive role, with a few swells and flourishes here, a few rich harmonic textures there. But the orchestra fulfills an extra-musical function as well. Surrounding Atkins with the trappings of musical respectability, it also bequeaths to him the authority to lead the musical procession, allowing him to hover in that middle zone where elevated and popular tastes do not so much meet as uneasily coexist.[69]

Country Gentleman

1960 saw the release of *The Other Chet Atkins,* the first album on which Atkins played an acoustic guitar exclusively. The collection of songs was a rather standard assortment for the guitarist, with perhaps a bit more of a

Spanish emphasis. On the cover of the album, though, was a drawing of Atkins that indicated that this album marked a departure from Atkins's usual fare. The light-haired, blue-eyed guitarist was depicted here with dark features, dressed in the suit of a Spanish gentleman, standing in a courtyard with a piercing gaze and a nylon-string acoustic guitar poised beside him. This, we are led to believe, is the other Chet Atkins, a musician whose change of instrument engenders another sort of transformation. Demonstrating his skills with the acoustic guitar, Atkins displays his intimacy with the reputed birthplace of the guitar through an act of masquerade that literalizes his capacity to move in different musical realms.

This portrayal of Atkins as his own "other" might be seen to contain traces of minstrelsy, with the darkened features connoting not only the assumption of an alternative ethnicity but of an alternative masculinity; Atkins's pointed gaze and erect posture signify a more aggressive sort of masculinity than was usually associated with him.[70] Indeed, Atkins, like so many white southern performers born in the first decades of the twentieth century, performed in blackface as a boy in a local minstrel show, an episode he remembered fondly in his autobiography.[71] Yet the obvious differences from minstrelsy need also be noted: Atkins's mask is not African American but a version of darkness associated with the romance of southern Europe. Whereas an idealized conception of African-American masculinity provided white men of the 1950s and 1960s with the basis for a countercultural masculinity (albeit one that contained strong elements of racism and sexism), Chet Atkins strove for a different effect. The African-American influences upon his playing were progressively downplayed in favor of a sort of cosmopolitanism within which the connection to Europe figured strongly. By the ethnic conventions of the time, Atkins's darkness was still white enough, via its connection to Europe, so as not to unsettle the boundaries that were in place between respectable pop and music of clear African-American derivation.

Whatever machinations of identity formation and transformation are at work in this representation of Atkins, what I find most intriguing about the album's cover and the concept underlying it is that that the guitarist's otherness is so closely linked to his change of instrument. From this perspective, the image of Atkins put forth on *The Other Chet Atkins* is congruent with a more general tendency to depict him as a musician whose identity is closely tied to his choice of instrument. The title that Atkins has carried through much of his career, "Mr. Guitar," is perhaps the most obvious example of this aspect of Atkins's celebrity, indicating his connection with a set of values and meanings that circulate around the instrument.

Some clue as to the nature of those values and meanings can be gleaned from the story of Atkins's acquisition of his first guitar, a story that became an RCA publicity staple. Drawn to the guitar by his half-brother Jim, the young Atkins yearned for an instrument of his own. Following his parents' separation, his mother took up with a man who routinely brought a guitar with him when he visited the house. Willie Strevel would soon become Atkins's stepfather; and when he came home one day having traded an old Model T car for fifteen dollars and a Silvertone guitar, Atkins began trying to scheme a way of getting the instrument for himself. Using two guns left to him and his brother Lowell by his father, Atkins made a trade with his stepfather for that guitar.

> It was beat-up, but it was a milestone in my life. That guitar, and the others that followed it, would absorb almost every moment I could find for it for the rest of my life. I would lean on it for the love I never seemed to have enough of and depend on it for the friendships I didn't always find.
>
> I was so shy that most of the time people didn't even know I was around. So they ignored me. But now it didn't matter. I had what I had dreamed about as long as I could remember. And it would communicate for me . . .
>
> [T]he guitar was different [from Atkins's other childhood possessions]. It was not a toy. It was life itself to me. I dreamed of someday becoming a great star, though using it to make money never crossed my mind. I couldn't imagine getting paid for anything as wonderful as playing the guitar for people. I would have *paid* to play on radio—if I had had the money.[72]

From this single incident—the purchase of a guitar—Atkins leaps into a rush of associations that testifies to the overarching value of the instrument for him. The detail that would stand out, though, as the story was retold in RCA publicity releases and liner notes to Atkins's albums, was that he had traded two guns for a guitar, a gesture in keeping with Atkins's image as a gentle, civilized being devoted not to the wild pastimes associated with rural southern masculinity, but to the pursuit of musical excellence through his engagement with the guitar.[73]

Atkins's image as the "country gentleman" complemented his status as "Mr. Guitar." Together they worked to construct an image of the guitarist as a refined, sensitive, and creative musician who retained just enough of a connection to his rural southern background to ensure that he was still "country," however "pop" he might have sounded. Just how delicate of a balance this could be is evident in the liner notes to Atkins's 1959 album, *Mister Guitar,* written by Don Halberstam. Beginning with the suggestion that the album is something of a "homecoming" for Atkins, Halberstam presents some of the details of Atkins's background and his path to success, emphasizing the prominence of the guitar in the folk traditions of the East Tennessee mountains (without noting that Atkins's main influences came from outside the area) and the important role of music in the Atkins family. However much the guitar may have been rooted in the social and cultural setting of his youth, however, Halberstam notes that the guitar primarily figured for Atkins as a way of "getting out." As Atkins's style and repertoire broadened, so his reputation spread, and, as Halberstam notes, "there is now something of a controversy as to whether he is a country guitarist, pop guitarist, folk guitarist, or just an American guitarist. In fact, at present Atkins's records sell better at Nashville's two major record-and-book stores which cater to the local eggheads, than they do at the country-oriented Ernest Tubb record store."[74] "That," Halberstam concludes, "is why this record is something of a homecoming"—because Atkins had chosen to feature a few more country selections than on some of his previous releases, but also because someone at RCA decided it was time for Atkins to reassert his connection to the country audience at a time when his image was becoming so broad as to appear indistinct. Atkins's perceived refinement is clearly part of the problem; despite his best efforts at being a popular guitarist, the suggestion is that his appeal is primarily to a cultivated segment of the audience who has little investment in the maintenance of country traditions (a judgment that says as much about how the country audience was being constructed as it does about Atkins).

While the liner notes to *Mister Guitar* articulate some of the tensions between the country and noncountry aspects of Atkins's persona, the cover of the album offers an image worth pondering over in its own right. A rocking chair stands at the center of the picture, and sitting in the chair

3.4. "Mister Guitar." The cover to Atkins's 1959 album. Photo by Irv Bahrt.

is not Chet Atkins but his guitar (suitably, a Gretsch Chet Atkins hollow-body). Atop the "head" of the guitar rests a straw hat, while a red bow tie is secured around its neck. A pair of shoes is poised on the floor beneath the chair, assumedly where the guitar's feet would be if it had any feet. On the arm of the chair is a tall, cool drink, perhaps an icy lemonade, ready to offer refreshment to the leisurely instrument.

    This portrait of Atkins's guitar "sitting in" for the guitarist literalizes the dynamic whereby Atkins's identity is inextricably caught up with that of his instrument. Several other of Atkins's albums employ a similar motif, such as *Christmas with Chet Atkins,* on which Atkins's orange guitar is superimposed upon a snow-covered winter scene; and perhaps the strangest of all, *Caribbean Guitar,* on which the Gretsch, dressed with a grassy island hat, lies atop a picture of black fishermen working in their boats, the blue water sparkling about them. The mobility of Atkins's guitar in these images might be taken to indicate the guitarist's own mobility, with each album packaged to evoke a certain mood, place, or season. Yet I think this easy substitution of the guitar for the guitarist also points to some of the more curious and complicated elements underlying the title of "Mr. Guitar" that is so regularly attached to Atkins. Jerry Reed, another finger-style guitarist who was influenced by Atkins, said of his mentor, "If he weren't Chet Atkins, he'd have to be a guitar."[75] Reed meant to draw attention to Atkins's devotion to the guitar, his unflagging interest in the instrument and his determination to consistently seek to improve himself as a musician. The intimation of the virtual interchangeability of Atkins and his instrument, however, raises the question of just how literally we are to take the title "Mr. Guitar."

It is hard not to detect some strong points of ambivalence residing not so far beneath the surface of Atkins's appellation. In particular, Atkins as "Mr. Guitar" often comes across in RCA publicity as a lonesome character whose relationship with his instrument is one of virtual dependence. Writing the liner notes to Atkins's 1956 release, *Chet Atkins in Three Dimensions,* for instance, Noel Digby described the guitarist as a "custom-breaker" whose tendency to deviate from the norms of country music was part and parcel with his status as a "loner," as "one man playing one guitar."[76] Pursuing this notion a step further, David Halberstam writes in the notes to *Chet Atkins' Workshop* of the guitarist's home studio, a creation much like that used by Les Paul. Whereas Paul's home studio had been characterized as the perfect blend of commerce and domesticity by the popular press, Atkins's own studio is here represented as "the lonely man's room, and Atkins when he's working is a lonely man," proclaims Halberstam.[77] Atkins's wife and daughter are not mentioned, and the workshop is cast as a space where the lone musician can withdraw into the solitude he requires for effective recording.

Within this scenario of solitary creativity, the guitar itself readily assumed the status of a compulsory object, necessary not only to Atkins's musicianship but to his sense of being. On the back cover of the 1965 release, *My Favorite Guitars,* Atkins wrote: "I have guitars at home, guitars in my office and guitars when I travel. In this age, when everything is explained away in terms of neuroses, tensions and compulsions, I should probably be pegged in the 'compulsive guitar picker' category. Fact is, I feel quite incomplete if one isn't nearby."[78] Perhaps the strangest example in this vein comes from an anonymous article in *Billboard* magazine, included in a special supplement to the June 3, 1967 issue, which celebrated Atkins's tenth anniversary as an RCA executive and his twentieth anniversary as a recording artist with the company. Titled "The Guitar Is More Than a Facade," the article briefly detailed the experience of conversing with Atkins. "Talking to Chet Atkins is a distracting experience," the piece begins, for "he plays the guitar as he converses. While this may be unnerving at first, and brings about a feeling of inattention, one quickly realizes that every word is getting through. The guitar is more than a facade; it is a form of hearing aid."[79] The inversion at work here—that the guitar, typically an instrument that one either plays or listens to, helps Atkins to hear those around him—echoes the sense of incompleteness articulated by Atkins in his liner notes to *My Favorite Guitars*. According to such representations, Atkins is so absorbed in his instrument of choice that he could barely be said to exist apart from it. If we take this observation figuratively, then the logic of the "Mister Guitar" title becomes clear, and the photographic substitution of guitar for guitarist on the cover of the *Mister Guitar* album takes shape as a mere extension of this broader set of meanings at work in Atkins's career.

As to the reasons behind this series of representations, I believe there are three distinct impulses at work. First, the image of the lone musician involved in an intense communion with his instrument casts an aura of genius around Atkins, and places him within a romantic myth of individual creative force. Second, these images tap into another mythos, one more readily associated with country music: that of the frontier, and of the artist as a sort of lone frontiersman carving out a unique space through his wits and resourcefulness. This second concept sheds particularly strong light on the story of Atkins's acquisition of his first guitar, with the substitution of guitar for gun connoting a shift toward the cultivation of new, more civilized frontiers. Finally, Atkins's status as the lone, guitar-bearing figure placed him squarely on the margins of country music practice even as it acknowledged his talent and influence. In his guise as "Mr. Guitar," Atkins came forth as a musician whose principal adherence was not to any one genre of music, not even country music, but to an instrument that he used to cross styles and genres. Such were the themes and tensions that ran through Atkins's public persona, and that in many ways defined the contours of his career.

There is more to this story, however, for any attempt to explain the significance of Atkins's role as "Mr. Guitar" has to acknowledge that it was not just any guitar, but an electric guitar with which Atkins was so closely associated, at least during the first decades of his long career. By no means standard "country" instruments, despite Gretsch's best efforts to dress the guitar in country/western trappings, the electric guitars that bore Atkins's name were in many ways emblematic of his strange relationship to country music. With their state-of-the-art technology and their bright orange finish, the Gretsch Chet Atkins models (of which there were several over the years) departed from the naturalistic aesthetic that was so firmly engrained in country music's ethos and ideology, much as Atkins's recording techniques departed from the established conventions of sound production and reproduction.[80] During the 1950s and into the 1960s, when country music moved ever closer to the pop mainstream, the electric guitar was a key vehicle for the changes that the music was undergoing and a symbol of the willingness of musicians like Chet Atkins to broaden the music's range. If the results had the effect of establishing a new, even more constricting set of country music conventions, as some writers have suggested, they also played a part in establishing the music as a significant subset of the pop music industry with Nashville as its institutional base.

Chet Atkins was by no means solely responsible for these changes, but he has often been used to embody them, like his guitar was used to embody him on so many album covers. In a pivotal account of the Nashville music scene from 1970, Paul Hemphill used Atkins in just such a manner, declaring that "few people were more prepared to guide Nashville through its most trying period than Chet Atkins, who had the back-country roots of all the great country musicians but had gone a giant step further by developing interests in such diverse areas as poetry, classical music, philosophy and electronics."[81] A sort of country music renaissance man, Atkins managed to wield considerable influence upon the sound of country music and the structure of the country music industry through his combined activities as musician, producer, and executive. Furthermore, he exerted a parallel influence upon the electric guitar, codifying and extending innovations introduced by two of his principal influences, Les Paul and Merle Travis.

*　*　*

I think people appreciate purity. I think gadgets come and go but purity is what will be remembered . . . I think a guitar is meant to sound like a guitar and I can't understand why people try to make it sound like another instrument.

—*Chet Atkins, quoted in Flippo (1976), p. 35.*

Interviewed by Chet Flippo in 1976, Atkins expressed alongside his ambivalence about taking country music uptown a concern with the effects of technology upon music. Though he had worked to refine the sound of his own guitar playing and of the music he produced for others by electronic means, he still believed that a guitar should sound "like a guitar," that it should retain a certain purity. As I have argued in the last two chapters, the pursuit of sonic purity was one of the primary motives driving the use and development of the electric guitar during the years from roughly 1940 to 1960. More specifically, the pure electric tone associated with the solid-body guitar and humbucking pickups that were created during these years became a key element of music produced for the pop mainstream, music directed at the broadest possible audience but guided by the perceived values of a white middle-class listenership. Les Paul demonstrated the value that pure tones and uncomplicated melodies could have in the pop-music marketplace; Chet Atkins used the lesson of Paul's success in order to refashion country music. That two guitarists should have had such an impact upon the sound of American popular music should come as no surprise, for in its early years the electric guitar was part of a broader wave of technological enthusiasm that was largely focused upon ways of producing, reproducing, and transmitting sound. While Paul and Atkins were enacting their innovations, however, another group of guitarists was putting technology to uses not so readily assimilable to the average contemporary ear. In Memphis, in St. Louis, and especially in Chicago, African-American musicians were turning to the electric guitar to accommodate their music to the rhythms of postwar urban life. Electric blues, rhythm and blues, and rock 'n' roll all emerged out of this process, and the electric guitar would be used to produce an array of new sounds that unsettled the boundaries between acceptable and unacceptable noise in American popular music.

Chapter 4

Racial Distortions

Muddy Waters, Chuck Berry, and the Electric Guitar in Black Popular Music

Encounters

In the late summer of 1941, Muddy Waters was recorded for the first time by folk song collector Alan Lomax. As legend has it, Lomax was traveling through the South searching for fabled blues performer Robert Johnson (unaware that Johnson had died some years earlier of poisoning), and was more generally recording songs for inclusion in the Library of Congress. During his travels, he was advised by many of the locals in Coahoma County, Mississippi, to check out Waters (whose birth name was McKinley Morganfield), a young guitarist and singer well known in the area who had yet to do any recording.

Though Waters often performed with a string band in the area's joints and gatherings, these first recordings were of Waters solo, singing with acoustic slide guitar accompaniment. Using a portable recorder, with a microphone set up in the front room of Waters's Stovall Plantation residence, Lomax was immediately struck by the power of the pieces Waters played, particularly the song "Country Blues," a variation on a theme covered by both Johnson and Waters's most direct musical mentor, Son House.[1] Waters had been initially suspicious of the white man's motives, thinking at first that Lomax might have been "one of them smart police" investigating Waters's whiskey bootlegging activities.[2] Overcoming his reservations, Waters settled into the recording process rather easily, but was nonetheless taken aback by the sound of his own performance played back to him on Lomax's equipment: "That was the great thing of my life—never heard my voice on records, man, and to hear that, man, that was great, man . . . when I played a song and he played it back then I was *ready* to work. Never heard that voice before, you know, and I was *ready.*"³ Two years later, in 1943, he would make the move from Mississippi to Chicago, the established center of blues recording, to begin a career as a recording musician.

Just over a decade later, in 1955, a very different sort of African-American performer would find his way to Chicago. Chuck Berry came north not from Mississippi but from Saint Louis, Missouri; his music bore the influence of deep blues performers like Muddy Waters, but blues was only one element in the mix of black and white pop styles that came together in Berry's sound. Nevertheless, he made sure to catch Waters's act upon hitting Chicago, and it was Waters who directed Berry to the studio of Chess Records, by then among the most notable and profitable of the independent record companies that had sprung up to record blues and other black musical styles in the years following the Second World War.

Leonard Chess, who ran Chess Records with his brother Phil, was no folk song collector, but an entrepreneur who had carved out a significant niche in the blues market through his recording of Muddy Waters, Howlin' Wolf, and other black performers who used the electric guitar and other amplified instruments to modify their blues from its rural acoustic roots into a style ready for the boisterous clubs of the Chicago scene. Chuck Berry was no folk music performer either. Unlike Muddy Waters, he had adapted to the electric guitar well before he made his way to Chicago, and he approached Leonard Chess with the express purpose of recording his music for commercial distribution. Berry was also no newcomer to the recording process; though he had never before made commercial recordings, he had been experimenting at home with a microphone and tape recorder in anticipation of an opportunity.⁴ When Chess asked for a tape of his band, Berry promised him one, and returned home to rehearse a set of original compositions with his musical partners Johnnie Johnson and Ebby Hardy. The guitarist came back to Chicago with tape in hand, featuring four titles; the song that captured Leonard Chess's attention was "Ida May," a hillbilly-style number that Chess hardly believed "could be written and sung by a black guy."⁵ At the suggestion of Chess, "Ida May" was retitled "Maybellene," and the song began a rapid commercial rise that would change the fortunes of Chess Records as much as those of Chuck Berry.

Muddy Waters and Chuck Berry are rarely linked in scholarship on African-American music, or linked only in passing. Muddy Waters adhered to down-home, traditional blues despite his move to incorporate amplified instruments (unthinkable, according to scholarly conventions, that it would be because of such a move). Chuck Berry, prime rock 'n' roll innovator, used his electric guitar to jump start a brand of music-making designed to appeal to a younger audience than that of Waters, and a whiter audience as well (at least during the 1950s). Waters was dead set on demonstrating his manhood in the face of a history and a presence of violence against black men, whereas Berry tried his best to capture the rhythms of adolescence in a culture of consumption oriented toward the myth of abundance and the value of the new and the young. Despite the differences between these two musicians (differences that scholars have tended to leave implicit rather than treat explicitly), their careers intersected in Chicago, at Chess Records, where African-American musicians were putting amplification to a new set of uses that would considerably alter the soundscape of American popular music.

The stories of Berry's and Waters's first encounters with the recording process highlight a number of important shifts and transitions that marked the history of African-American popular music between the years 1941 and 1955: the changing concentration of blues performers in rural and urban areas, as well as between north and south; the displacement of field recording practices in favor of studio recording; the growing African-American acquaintance with technologies of sound production and reproduction like the tape recorder and the electric guitar; and the increased potential of African-American music, and of black performers, to "cross over" into success with white audiences. Thus can Waters and Berry be taken as examples, at once representative and exceptional, of the complex range of processes that shaped African-American popular music and were shaped by black performers in the years surrounding and following World War II.

More specifically, these were the years that saw the overlapping development of electric blues and rock and roll, two musical styles that were significantly affected by, and even derived from, changes in amplification and the role of the electric guitar. The ascent of the electric guitar to a position of relative supremacy in the instrumental hierarchy of popular music was in many ways led by blues performers; the figure of the wailing blues soloist issuing high-pitched, emotion-drenched guitar improvisations remains a powerful pop-cultural icon and one of the most common images of the electric guitarist at work. Yet the role played by the electric guitar in the growth of post-1945 blues styles was far more complex than such an image would suggest. Indeed, one might well argue that the most significant strain of Chicago blues, that promoted and performed by Muddy Waters, placed little emphasis on the guitar solo as it is understood today, instead exploiting the electric guitar and amplification more generally to create a total effect through the complementary elements of a tightly knit electric blues ensemble. Chuck Berry, by contrast, was a more familiar sort of guitar soloist by contemporary standards; his playing, as much as that of any one person, set the tone for much of what would follow in the next decade, when the electric guitarist became something of a culture hero. Drawing upon blues and jazz styles that were rooted more in the Southwest than Mississippi (Berry cites Charlie Christian, for instance, as one of his main influences), Berry turned the electric guitar into a spotlight instrument for the burgeoning style that became known as rock 'n' roll.

Amplifications

Much has been written of the "moldy fig" mentality[6] that has pervaded so much blues criticism, but no blues commentators have yet identified the converse of this phenomenon, the insistent celebration of black musicians as technological innovators and conspirators who drew upon their cultural resources to open new avenues of sonic experimentation via electronic means. Robert Palmer has been the most notable of these writers. In his essay, "The Church of the Sonic Guitar," Palmer all but disavows the significance of electric guitar innovations of the 1960s, declaring that "virtually every innovation associated with rock guitar playing in the 1960s can be traced back to black musicians of the middle and late 1950s."[7] This pronouncement works well as a corrective to the common tendency to hold up the 1960s as the most innovative of musical eras, a viewpoint that too often washes away the achievements of musicians in earlier decades, and that also too often casts African-American musicians in a supporting role. However, there is a deeper impulse driving Palmer's desire to cast black guitarists of the 1950s in a position of ultimate supremacy where sonic innovation is concerned. For Palmer, such musicians as Guitar Slim, Ike Turner, and Pat Hare played with a dangerous sort of creativity, stretching musical limits by twisting amplified sounds into all manner of permutations, following paths of musical excess that were paralleled by lifestyles that often bordered on or crossed the lines of criminality.[8]

That the electric guitar and amplification have become part of a powerful cultural fantasy surrounding the blues, a fantasy primarily held by white critics and musicians, is further evident in a comment by Ry Cooder, guitarist and *de facto* folklorist, concerning Robert Johnson. Considered by many to be the quintessential bluesman,[9] Johnson recorded with an acoustic guitar exclusively during his brief career (which ended with his murder in 1938), and was never known to have played or owned an electric instrument. Discussing Johnson's 1936 recording sessions, though, Cooder spins an elaborate interpretation of the guitarist's approach to sound that culminates in the hypothesis that Johnson would have turned his attention to the electric guitar had his life not ended when it did. About Johnson's preference for playing his guitar into the corner of a room during the sessions, Cooder claims that "he was sitting in the corner to achieve a certain sound that he liked," a sound shaped by the acoustic properties of the plaster wall, which worked to eliminate "most of the top end and most of the bottom end and [amplify] the middle, the same thing that a metal guitar or an electric guitar does."[10] Cooder goes on to suggest that Johnson "would have liked somebody to say, 'Robert, I'm going to boost the midrange' . . . I bet if you could have done that with equalizing and headphones in the modern era, he'd have been very glad. I'll bet you if you'd given him a Marshall amp to play through, he would have been *extremely* glad. But sitting in the corner, he could achieve something like that."[11] The flow of associations, from sitting in a corner to shaping a sound through electronic equalization to playing through a Marshall amplifier, says much about the ways in which technological developments have sought to fill in where the resourcefulness of the musician once had to suffice. More to the point, Cooder attributes a set of desires to Johnson with regard to technology and amplification that only make sense when one considers how charged with significance the turn to electricity has come to seem in the context of the blues. As the most ostensibly modern and innovative country bluesman, Robert Johnson would have to have considered amplification, for amplified blues pointed the way to the future, to the formation of a sound that would push popular music past its established limits and toward a new sort of musical energy.

A further piece of this fantasy comes from Michael Lydon, writing in a 1971 piece on Bo Diddley. For Lydon, as for Palmer, the locus of musical and cultural transformation was the 1950s. "In the early 1950s," observed Lydon, "music in America was in healthy shape"; there was a good dose of diverse activity, with solid contributions coming from performers in blues, country, and even modern classical music.[12] "Yet in one sense all was stagnant, for music had not yet boldly crossed its latest frontier: electricity, the only absolutely new addition to music-making for genera-tions." Lydon continued,

> Electricity was up for grabs, and the question (which I doubt anyone asked) was, who would get it? Who would find that music to make records music, not copies of it; to make radio a medium, not a transmitter? Who could make beautiful music on electrical instruments? There was quite a prize for the winner, for that musician who could put electricity in the service of his art might bring down walls higher than Jericho's.
>
> Who got it? The niggers, they got it.[13]

Where Palmer's theory of pop music history celebrates the accomplish-ments of the 1950s and discounts what came after, Lydon's theory works in the opposite direction, to devalue what came before. Asserting that it was the "niggers" who were the first to "get" electricity, Lydon effectively elides the efforts of Les Paul and others who had established a working aesthetic of electric sound production and reproduction centered around the value of tonal purity. Moreover, such an elision is necessary to Lydon's thesis, not only because he could not support his argument otherwise, but because to acknowledge the importance of other alternatives would be to undermine his understanding of electricity. For electricity is no mere tech-nological effect in Lydon's analysis; electricity gave black music its inten-sity and served as the generative impulse of rock 'n' roll, "that intensity that made non-believers call it noisy when played low, but made believers know it had to be played *loud*."[14] Others may have used electricity before, may even have taken it in new directions, but it was black musicians (or whites in love with black music, Lydon allows) who used it in the *right* way.

I cite these three instances of cultural fantasy surrounding the incorporation of amplification into black popular music to demonstrate just how intimately the blues has become caught up with electricity in the critical, if not the popular, imagination, and just how powerful that association has become. The African-American electric guitar–playing bluesman is a potent symbol, for reasons to which I will return. Furthermore, these interlocking views on blues and electricity serve to establish some of the terms of historical debate where the electric guitar is concerned (for history is always laden with images of cultural fantasy). Embedded in the series of reflections above is the belief that amplification marked, to a greater or lesser degree, a break with the past of African-American music and American popular music more generally; even for Cooder, the suggestion is implicit that Robert Johnson would have been happy with the prospect of amplification because he was already tuned into a forward-thinking approach to sound. Yet Cooder's hypothetical reflections in particular also suggest the turn toward amplification as a point of continuity with earlier musical practices, or with the practices of musicians in fields other than blues. His description of Johnson's desire for a particular sound, a sound that could be best achieved through electric means, echoes the desires of Les Paul and Chet Atkins; if Johnson had not begun to use amplification, other African-American musicians had as early as the mid-1930s, and many others would with an attention to sonic detail that paralleled the efforts of their white counterparts. How, then, did these parallel activities yield such different results?

To answer this question, we first need to acknowledge the distinct approach to sound in African and African-American musical traditions. Samuel Floyd, following the observations of Olly Wilson, has discussed the preference in African music for "timbres that contrast rather than blend," describing the resultant sound as a "heterogeneous fusion" of disparate sonoric elements.[15] According to Floyd, this "heterogeneous sound ideal" was retained by black slaves in the United States, and has continued to shape African-American music through the twentieth century. In blues this ideal has often been accomplished with the basic pairing of guitar and voice, both of which have been manipulated in accordance with principles of timbral distortion and flexibility. On guitar, the development of slide techniques allowed musicians to bend and manipulate notes in a manner well removed from the Euro-American preference for tempered notes and timbral clarity. Fretting the guitar with the dull edge of a knife or the broken end of a bottle allowed access to those notes between the frets of the instrument, and opened methods of "worrying" notes and even full chords by shaking the slide device on the strings, creating vibrato effects that gave each note a ring of indeterminacy.

Muddy Waters played guitar in just such a manner. It was this set of techniques, developed on acoustic guitar, that he transferred to electric after moving to Chicago. Not that Waters was alone in this transition; Chicago became perhaps the most important blues location of the postwar era not on the strength of a single performer, but on the widespread migration and proliferation of blues musicians throughout the city. Performers such as Buddy Guy, Louis Myers, Willie Dixon, Junior Wells, and Robert Lockwood, Jr. contributed significantly to the development of blues in Chicago, and of the electric blues style that became the city's trademark. As many have noted, though, it was Waters who in a sense presided over the scene, whose early recordings for Chess set the stage for the company's success with a style of blues that harked back to the South even as it made use of electric instruments. Moreover, it was Waters and his band who formed "the first important electric band, the first to use amplification to make their ensemble music rawer, more ferocious, more physical, instead of simply making it a little louder."[16] And so it is Waters who will stand at the center of this account of the place of the electric guitar and amplification in postwar Chicago blues.

*   *   *

When Muddy Waters moved to Chicago in 1943, the city was already a center of blues activity and home to a popular strain of urban blues. Bluebird Records, a subsidiary of RCA/Victor, was the primary studio associated with the emergent blues style of the period. Under the supervision of white record producer and executive Lester Melrose, musicians such as Big Bill Broonzy, Memphis Minnie, and Tampa Red came together at Bluebird to form what became known to many as the "Bluebird

Sound." The lone country blues guitarist was replaced by tightly knit and polished ensembles within which blues took on some of the polish of jazz and white pop styles. Just as significant as the musical changes involved in the "Bluebird Sound" was the change enacted by Melrose in the structure of recording. The group of musicians recording for Bluebird performed as accompanists on one another's records, forming what Mike Rowe has called "the greatest rationalization in blues recording" until that time.[17] For Rowe and many other historians, this period represents an unfortunate homogenization of the existing diversity of blues, from which the development of the harder-edged postwar styles marked a point of release and revitalization. Others judge the Bluebird era of Chicago blues recording as a more significant point of transition; Jas Obrecht, for instance, described in a piece on Bill Broonzy "the driving guitar/piano/string bass ensemble sound that sealed the evolution from '30s acoustic blues to postwar urban styles."[18] In effect, the sound associated with Bluebird records added a more regular, danceable beat that was driven by a guitar/piano/bass combination. The inclusion of the piano was a particularly notable innovation, marking a new degree of rootedness in blues styles (where the guitar had long been favored by migratory musicians) and an increased regularization of blues tonality. All but eliminated were the unpredictable rhythmic variations of acoustic country blues, as well as the harsh timbres favored by rural musicians, elements that would be reintroduced by the new wave of musical migrants that would hit the city in the decade surrounding World War II.

Another innovation linked to this period of blues activity was the use of the electric guitar, which began appearing on recordings by Broonzy and Memphis Minnie by the end of the 1930s and became even more common in the bars that doubled as performance spaces for Chicago musicians. Minnie's early use of amplification and prominent position within the city's blues scene is worth pausing over, for her presence at least partly destabilizes the narrative of masculine achievement that blues history so often becomes. In a study of Minnie's music and career, Paul and Beth Garon draw attention to the tendency among blues historians to describe an easy and clear transition from "classic blues," the blues style associated with female performers such as Bessie Smith and Ma Rainey that dominated the market in the early 1920s, to country blues, the style linked with figures like Robert Johnson which, by all accounts, laid the groundwork for the later florescence of electric Chicago blues.[19] According to the Garons, Minnie stands as evidence that female performers were not so thoroughly replaced, and further attests to the existence of a number of female performers who have remained hidden from history, who played in the country style and assumed the drifting, mobile lifestyle commonly associated with the itinerant bluesman. Minnie's early use of the electric guitar also proved to be a formative influence upon the sound of Chicago blues, and the Garons suggest that her local prestige played no small part in establishing the value of the instrument among the city's musicians.

Muddy Waters, for his part, testified to the presence of the electric guitar on the Chicago scene: "I started playing amplified guitar when I came to Chicago. Everybody else was playing them and I had to get something to go with that too."[20] The noisy conditions of the taverns dictated a turn to amplification, but as the electric guitar became more of a common presence, it acquired a quotient of desirability in its own right, if only as a means of remaining competitive in the local music marketplace. Yet Waters was also something of a relative latecomer to the electric guitar; others of his generation did not wait until they moved north to acquire the instrument. As early as 1939, Robert Lockwood, Jr. had gotten hold of one, and began to feature it in his broadcasts with Sonny Boy Williamson (Rice Miller) on the King Biscuit Show out of Helena, Arkansas, the most important blues radio show of its time. When Lockwood moved north, his replacement, Joe Willie Wilkins, continued to feature an amplified sound. It was Wilkins who introduced the electric guitar to Jimmy Rogers, a Chicago musician who became Muddy Waters's main collaborator from the mid-1940s to the mid-1950s. As Rogers remembered in a 1992 interview:

> The first electric guitar that I ever had in my hands was Joe Willie Wilkins's guitar . . . That was the prettiest sound I ever heard and that got me really interested in electrifying guitars. So, I finally did get a De Armond pickup. Muddy, when he came to Chicago, he bought him one . . . that's what the style was then. For electric you could take an acoustic and mount this pickup on it. It didn't have but one tone, loud or low; it was just turn it on, turn it up louder or cut it low.[21]

Rogers's comments indicate the difficulties faced by rural musicians in obtaining electric instruments. By 1940, electric guitars had been in production for a few years. Yet in the Delta region of Mississippi and Arkansas, and similar regions around the country, no music stores carried such items. So black rural musicians resorted to the same tactics as white rural musicians like Chet Atkins, acquiring the necessary parts and adding them to existing acoustic instruments. The resulting products were limited in the range of sounds they had to offer. But resourcefulness and experimentation led to greater control; Rogers, for instance, modified his tone by playing with his right (picking) hand at different positions along the strings, an approach that worked especially well in combination with another guitarist who would similarly alter his position to achieve contrasting but complementary tones.

Playing off of such contrasts was central to the collaboration between Rogers and Waters, for the two approached the guitar in markedly different ways. Where Waters's main influences were Delta slide players like Son House and Robert Johnson, Rogers was more drawn to the urbanized style that had already taken hold in Chicago. Playing together, they divided responsibilities equitably, according to their strengths, with Rogers holding down the rhythm on the bottom strings of the guitar and Waters giving shape to the melody through his distinctive slide work. It was the tension between urban and rural elements, and between the impulse to adapt to the demands of the Chicago bars and the desire to preserve the sounds of the Delta, that gave the pair's music much of its force. Waters described some of the nature of this tension:

> When I went into the clubs, the first thing I wanted was an amplifier . . . You get a more pure thing out of an acoustic, but you get more noise out of an amplifier . . .
>
> A lot of people here [in Chicago] didn't hear Son or Robert Johnson 'cause they didn't get a chance to. But all by itself that sound never would have made it in Chicago. I guess I'm just one of the first people who was thinking of that sound and kept it in my mind, learning on that sound, and when I got here I found peoples that could get close to that sound.[22]

Although Waters retained a strong preference for the acoustic slide sound of his mentors, a sound that had characterized his own music until 1944, he perceived the turn to amplification to be more than a simple necessity. Both he and Rogers heard in the electric guitar a sound that opened new possibilities, and entailed a reconsideration of the Delta blues style. As Rogers observed that "you could get sounds from the electric that you couldn't get from the acoustic," so Waters observed shortly before his death that the electric guitar offered "a very different sound, not just louder . . . That loud sound would tell everything you were doing. On acoustic you could mess up a lot of stuff and no one would know that you'd ever missed. So electric was really rough."[23]

Making new demands upon the guitarist, the electric guitar also formed the basis for a new sort of musical interplay. The dual-guitar format used by Waters and Rogers became a central component of the Chicago blues sound, with the interlocking electric guitar parts fusing melody and rhythm in ways that fully capitalized upon the qualities of amplified sound. Such a format was furthermore well-suited to the accompaniment of the harmonica, another instrument that was becoming more prominent in the blues of the period. The popularization of blues harmonica can be attributed to two individuals, both of whom went by the performing name of Sonny Boy Williamson. By general agreement, John Lee Williamson, a musician associated with the Bluebird sound, was the original "Sonny Boy." But it was the second Sonny Boy, Rice Miller, who arguably exerted the greater impact through his long-running radio show, the aforementioned King Biscuit Time. Featuring electric guitarists like Robert Lockwood and Joe Willie Wilkins as his accompanists, Miller worked to complement their sound by amplifying his harmonica with the help of a microphone. As Lockwood and Wilkins would help to convince their guitar-playing counterparts of the value of amplification, so Miller would similarly affect many of the harmonica players tuned in to his show.

Three Miller disciples would pass through Muddy Waters's band at different times during the 1940s and 1950s: Little Walter Jacobs, Junior Wells, and James Cotton. Of the three, Walter was the first and in the judgment of most blues critics the best. He was also the player who would go furthest in applying amplification to the harmonica. Walter first hooked up with Jimmy Rogers while the harmonica player was working on Maxwell Street, the commercial crossroads of Chicago's West Side, where musicians would regularly congregate and set up to play for passing change. As Rogers remembered, the "strange harp sound" coming from Walter's playing caught his ear. Soon the two began to work the clubs together, following a demanding routine outlined by Rogers: "We'd go from one club to the other, we were playin' for the kitty . . . We were out by 8:00 at night, and different taverns started around 9, so by the time the taverns closed at 2:00, we maybe done hit four or five, maybe six different taverns, and we had a pocket of money apiece, maybe 15, $20 apiece."[24] It was only after Walter cut out of town for a time that Rogers formed his association with Waters (and at first Rogers played harmonica to Waters's guitar). When Walter returned to the scene several months later, Rogers was quick to inform his partner about the young musicians' talent, and readily conceded his role as harmonica player to fill in as second guitar.

Thus was the first Muddy Waters band formed, with three musicians who had recently migrated to Chicago from points south, who had all spent time in the Delta region of Mississippi and Arkansas, and who had all adapted, in varying degrees, to musical styles and practices of the urban north. As the youngest of the three, Little Walter showed the strongest preference for contemporary black urban styles. His harmonica playing demonstrated a taste for the swing and jump blues sounds of Louis Jordan, and the recordings he made under his own name after 1952 would lean increasingly in the direction of rhythm and blues. At this early stage, though, Waters and Rogers worked to fit the young harmonica player into their own musical blend, concentrating particular attention upon his sense of rhythm, which showed the lack of discipline of a performer unaccustomed to having to fit his playing with that of other musicians.

As Neil Slaven pointed out in an overview of Little Walter's career, it was only some years later that Walter began to move his sound more in the direction for which he would earn his reputation, applying amplified effects to the sound of his harp in a concerted fashion.[25] Even at this early stage, though, the combination of Waters, Rogers, and Little Walter, joined by Elgin Evans on drums, proved a popular and formidable club attraction, gaining the title "The Headhunters" for their capacity to blow other bands off the stage, a practice rooted in the intensely competitive musical environment of Chicago where musicians were plentiful and club owners had their pick of who might rule the stage. Within such a context, amplification was how small groups like the Headhunters or the Four Aces, another guitar-and-harmonica ensemble featuring the brotherly duo of Louis and Dave Myers on guitars and Junior Wells on harp, could compete with the larger, horn-driven groups that stood at the other end of the city's black popular music spectrum.

During the early 1950s the Four Aces and the Headhunters were probably the leading Chicago bands of their type. Their connection was such that in 1952 the two groups traded harmonica players, with Little Walter moving to the Aces and Junior Wells moving to Waters's band, a shift generated largely by Walter's desire for greater independence than he was afforded by Waters. Like Muddy Waters's group, the Four Aces were a fully electric ensemble. Myers and his brother Dave paralleled Waters and Rogers in their division of responsibility and their skill as accompanists, and Wells approached the harmonica in a horn-like way very similar to Little Walter's style. About the style of guitar playing that marked the two ensembles, Junior Wells had some sharp observations in a 1994 interview. Wells remembered both pairs of guitarists fondly, and held them up as models for a brand of group-oriented playing that, in his experience, had become increasingly less common. On Waters and Rogers, Wells proclaimed that "these guys really knew how to back up a harmonica. Everybody doesn't know how to back up a harmonica. They think that when you take a straight pick and start playing real fast that you are backing up a harmonica player, but you're not."[26] About the Myers brothers, Wells offered similar praise, commenting that "they were two people that was made to play with a harmonica player . . . If you really want to get down, you get two guitar players and have one play the bass parts on a guitar and the other play lead on the guitar—then you gettin' down. Nobody did that better than Louis and Dave."[27] For Wells, the key to effective guitar accompaniment lay in downplaying the higher registers and concentrating on laying down the sorts of "funky" turnarounds that moved the beat forward. He further saw the two-guitar format to be more versatile and rhythmically complex than the guitar/electric bass combination that would become common in later years, retaining a fluidity that, to Wells, was lost amid the "boom, boom, boom" of the bass.[28]

While Wells sheds some light on the rhythmic value of the electric guitar in Chicago blues, his former bandmate, Louis Myers, provides perhaps the most vivid description of the effect that amplification had upon the context of live performance. Myers's discussion concerns the period after which Little Walter had moved to join the Four Aces, a time after Walter had begun to amplify his harp on a large scale.[29] Recounting the edge that amplification gave the Four Aces over bands that were less equipped with the technology to get their sound across, Myers also gives an evocative sense of how the band's sound was itself transformed (or at least of how the perception of that sound was transformed):

> Do you realize how strong an amplifier is just blowing an instrument out of it? Can you imagine an upright bass gonna sound as loud as an electric bass? . . . Now you imagine we gone all amplifiers and here's these cats still playing the old style, just sitting up there playing drive-along-jimmy no amplifiers . . .
>
> How could a small four piece group do any harm to a big band? All they had to do was look at what we had and look at what they didn't have. We had amplified music . . . we would chop them bands—Walter was playing like forty horns man. His amplifier would sound like that sometimes, put his echo on and God!! Music was hittin' the walls and bouncing back to us, bouncing all over the place and they'd say "Them cats sound like a giant band and there ain't but four of them."[30]

The joy that Myers took in the ability of his group to overpower other, larger bands on the same bill testifies to the degree to which competition was no mere defining economic condition of the Chicago club scene, but a value wrapped up with pride in one's musicianship. As such the Chicago scene paralleled the musical activity of Kansas City and other southwestern locations during the 1930s. Battles between bands, or among musicians, were a common feature of the Chicago clubs, and served as important ritual events whereby the existing hierarchy of the scene might be either upheld or challenged. Bands such as the Headhunters or the Four Aces were noted for their ability to outperform their competitors, and as Jimmy Rogers observed, the presence of these bands on a bill was more often than not welcomed by other performers, because they drew a good crowd and because other musicians "were tryin' to get into the beat that we had, see, and they would like to hear it."[31]

Similarly, staged battles among guitarists or harmonica players were regularly held, and were an important proving ground for young musicians on the scene. At such events, musicians sought to stretch the conventions of performance, adopting an increasingly flamboyant stage presence as the 1950s moved forward. Buddy Guy, who migrated to Chicago from Louisiana in 1957 and would eventually accompany Muddy Waters and many others, was among the first musicians in the city to regularly stand up while he performed. Inspired by the wild antics of the New

Orleans–based Guitar Slim, who used a guitar cord as long as 350 feet to allow himself freedom of movement all about the clubs in which he performed, occasionally even stepping outside while continuing to play, Guy used similar tactics to gain a competitive edge over the other guitarists on the scene.[32]

> When I came to Chicago, everybody was sitting down: Muddy, Junior, the Wolf, Walter, and all of them were in chairs playing this beautiful music that still is the best blues you ever heard of. And we used to have the Battle of the Guitars . . . So I said, "Oh, jeez, these guys is playing way more than I can play. I got to figure out something else to do to be a winner." The winner got a bottle of whiskey and at that time I didn't drink whiskey. I had a little friend who weighed about 300, and he said, "I'll make you win this whiskey, because I don't have a nickel." It was snowing, and he said, "You remember that thing you told me Guitar Slim used to do?" I had this 150-foot lead wire, and he said, "I'm going to take this wire outside, and you sit in the car. I'm going to plug it in while you're in the car. You come out of this car playing and sliding in the snow, and we got the whiskey" . . .
>
> And when they called me, I stepped out of the car. He opened the door and said, "You all want to see him, come out here." The place was packed, and I had the streets full. So when I walked in, there was Magic Sam and a few more guitar players . . . They had the bottle of whiskey, and it was empty. They told me, "You won it, but we done drinked it all!"[33]

Guy's story highlights the rough mix of competition and camaraderie that characterized the "guitar battles," with the winner's prize being subsumed by his friends and fellow guitarists. Yet underlying the story is the sense that the stakes involved were greater than the ostensible prize of the whiskey. For Guy, a relatively new presence on the scene, winning the battle was a means of gaining both the respect of his peers and the attention of possible future employers; it was largely on the strength of his performance at such events that he secured regular gigs in the Chicago clubs and became a favorite accompanist to many of the city's leading blues musicians.

Paul and Beth Garon derive a deeper, more symbolic meaning from the changing styles of performance that were overtaking the Chicago clubs, a meaning they link to the new uses to which amplification was being put: "Standing up was one of the more silent 'sounds of the city,' but its implication of assertion and resistance was another sign of the times."[34]

Dismissing the reductionist historical explanation of the rise of amplification that has so often been told, Garon and Garon perceive in the move to perform standing up and the move to play loud related gestures driven by an aesthetic and political recognition of the conditions of ghetto life, conditions in which the performers had to "put out" to be noticed. Their understanding of amplification and of the more assertive gestures associated with blues performance during the 1950s complements the narratives of Myers and Guy, adding a political and historical dimension often missing from the musicians' comments. At the same time, though, one senses that there is both more and less to the significance of amplification than what the Garons suggest. To return to Myers's discussion of the Four Aces, what stands out is the sheer physicality of the sound being produced: the strength of the sound and the music hitting the walls and bouncing around the room contrasted with the sight of the four musicians on stage. This audio-optical illusion is also crucial to Guy's story, for one might easily say that the key to his winning strategy was his ability to displace himself and his instrument from the site at which the sound of his guitar seemed to emanate, the stage where his amplifier was located. What Paul and Beth Garon term the sound of the city was also, then, a sound of surprise in which the relationship between the performing body (or bodies) and the sound being produced became increasingly unstable. Les Paul also disturbed the relationship between the performing body and recorded sound through multi-track recording, but Guy's alternative may have been more unsettling in live performance, where the integration of sound and sight tends (or tended) to be a fixed expectation.

If amplification had the effect of altering the relationship between sound and sight in musical performance, its more significant impact was on the sound itself. The use of musical effects like feedback and distortion would have to wait until the second half of the 1950s to gain any sort of currency among Chicago musicians. Even in the earlier phase of the city's blues scene, though, the phase during which the electric blues sound first crystallized in the bands of Muddy Waters and the Four Aces, musicians used amplification with considerable attention to the kinds of sounds being produced, striving to capitalize upon the novelty of electronic effects while maintaining some of the feel of older blues styles. Talking about his guitar style, Louis Myers stated that the primary focus was tone: "I'm playing tone and this is what makes the whole world go around in music."[35] Muddy Waters described his own music, and the blues in general, in strikingly similar terms: "When you play blues, you may play blues, but you ain't got no tone; but you see blues, it's tone—deep tone with a heavy beat."[36] For Waters it was tone and rhythm, more than melody or harmony, that drove his blues; he believed the primary innovation of his early band to have been "putting time to our lowdown Mississippi blues," placing a new emphasis upon rhythmic accents that was built upon interaction between the drums and the electric guitars.[37] Using the technology of amplification in such a manner reinforced black cultural priorities in ways that presaged the use of technology by rap musicians. Like contemporary black rap producers, Waters and his Chicago peers "worked in the red," manipulating sound by pushing technology beyond the limits for which it was designed in order to meet a distinct set of musical and cultural values.[38] The Chicago clubs were the spaces where this fusion of new and old sounds first came together, but it was in the recording studio that the sound was further developed and refined for wider transmission, particularly at the studio run by Leonard and Phil Chess, with whom Muddy Waters would spend the better part of his career recording.

Chess Games

Among the songs recorded by Alan Lomax during his 1941 encounter with Muddy Waters was "I Be's Troubled," a tune that set a driving acoustic rhythm against a mournful lyrical stance. Waters opened the piece with an instrumental passage that sets the tone and structure for the song: three sharp, high-pitched notes voiced with the help of a bottleneck slide, descending from D to B♭ to G (V-flat III-I),[39] punctuated by rhythmic accents struck on the middle and bass strings of the guitar. A repetition of the three-note melody leads to a third statement in which the three notes are extended to six, the tonic G being struck twice and then giving way to a B♭-G hammered and pulled off on the open G string at an octave below the original melody. The next few bars find Waters rounding out the song's progression with more emphasis on the bass and midrange of the instrument, though he continues to work creatively among the different registers of the guitar, building rhythmic tension by pausing on the middle G, working the note with his slide before shifting to the B♭-G transition on the lower strings, then moving back to the upper register for the final melodic movement. Waters inserts a quick shift to A, introducing a note of harmonic ambiguity, before settling back into the open G blues figure that guides the song. The progression has come full circle, only to be started anew as Waters begins his vocal:

> If I'm feelin' tomorrow
> Like I feel today
> I'm gonna pack my suitcase
> And make my getaway
> 'Cause I'm troubled
> I'm all worried in mind
> And I never been satisfied
> And I just can't keep from cryin'

With the lyrics in place, Waters's guitar and voice work with and around one another, the vocal melody following that of the guitar, but in the lower register characteristic of Waters's singing. As the lyric progresses, the rhythm turns around (the characteristic blues turnaround noted by Junior Wells). Where the first syllable is stressed during each of the first four lines, the accent shifts to the later part of the vocal phrase during the last four, with "troubled" carrying particular weight in combination with the stretched midrange G note that serves as a point of rhythmic and harmonic tension, and "never" carrying similar emphasis in line with Waters's modulation to A in the next to last line of the verse.

"I Be's Troubled" is marked by complex interplay at a number of levels: among rhythm, harmony, and melody; between voice and guitar; and among the different pitch registers available on the guitar, which Waters exploits to good effect through the use of his bottleneck slide. As such, the song is indicative of Waters's mastery of the country blues form, a manner of performance that stressed the resourcefulness of the lone bluesman who brought to the conventional song structure an approach to sound and rhythm that marked the performance as his own. Notably, "I Be's Troubled" would also be Waters's first successful recording under his own name, as well as the first significant hit for Aristocrat Records, the independent Chicago label that later changed its name to Chess. Rerecorded in 1948 under the title "I Can't Be Satisfied," the new studio-recorded version of the song retained the basic melody and structure of the earlier performance, as well as the lyrical refrain concerning Waters's troubled, worried mind. Waters made a number of lyrical modifications, and the clarity of the recording is considerably greater than that of the 1941 version. The new song included the playing of Ernest "Big" Crawford on string bass, and featured Waters on electric slide guitar.

Crawford's bass accompaniment was included at the suggestion of Leonard Chess. It filled in some of the space left in the mix by Waters's guitar, and supplied a consistent harmonic and rhythmic underpinning to the song, which added a note of urbanity to what was otherwise a rather straight country blues performance. Waters's electric guitar performance also infused urban style into a country form, although what stands out about "I Can't Be Satisfied" is how relatively little the electric guitar changed the sound of Waters's blues. Indeed, "I Can't Be Satisfied" found Waters playing to his strengths as a musician, deliberately moving away from the "modern" blues styles he had been encouraged to pursue during his first Chicago recording sessions. Waters explained in an interview with Jim and Amy O'Neal, "Ah, you don't know, when you wanted to record and want to make a record that was probably gonna sell, you don't know what you want to record—you record anything you say. But they threw the fat in the fire when they let me did the one by myself, bass, with just me and a bass, and that's what did it . . . When I came out and *different,* what the people *thirsted* for it."[40] Waters came out "different" by adhering to the style of blues he had learned and developed in Mississippi. While "I Can't Be Satisfied" was consistent with the Lomax-recorded "I Be's Troubled," it was unusual in the context of the Chicago blues market, which was dominated at the time by swing-influenced jump blues styles. The song found quick favor with the wave of new migrants who had joined Waters in moving to Chicago to take advantage of what they hoped were the greater opportunities of the North; "I Can't Be Satisfied" sold out its initial pressing in a matter of hours after the record had been distributed to local shops, taking both Muddy Waters and Leonard Chess by surprise.

If Waters determined the style and content of his first successful record for Aristocrat (and all accounts suggest that Chess recorded the song grudgingly), Leonard Chess would exert considerable influence over the subsequent direction of Waters's recording career and the sound of Waters's records. Though Waters's performing band with Rogers, Little Walter, and "Baby Face" Leroy Foster alternating on guitar and drums had already come together by 1948, Chess continued to record Waters in the stripped-down format that marked "I Can't Be Satisfied" for some time; occasionally Waters was accompanied by piano and bass, but he did not record for Chess with members of his own band until late in 1950. Yet Leonard Chess's influence upon Waters's recording career, and upon the more general output of Aristocrat and, later, Chess Records, was not so simply confining. Like Sam Phillips at Sun studios in Memphis (from whom Chess licensed many of its releases during the early 1950s), Leonard Chess and, to a lesser extent, his brother Phil, had their own ideas about how records should sound. Along with Willie Dixon, the songwriter and bassist who became an in-house producer and all-purpose company man at Chess during the 1950s, the Chess brothers worked with performers like Waters and Howlin' Wolf to shape the electrified sound of postwar Chicago blues. Moreover, the company drew in a wealth of new talent as their success grew over the course of the decade. With Chuck Berry and Bo Diddley, Chess played a crucial role in the promotion of rock 'n' roll that both complemented and, ultimately, undermined the company's success in blues recording.

*   *   *

Leonard and Phil Chess, Jewish immigrant brothers from Poland, began Aristocrat Records in 1947 as a means of capitalizing upon the popularity of some of the musicians who performed in bars and nightclubs that the two brothers owned. At the time of its formation, Aristocrat was a decidedly small-time operation, one of many such labels set up in Chicago and other urban centers of black musical activity in the years before and after World War II. This was a volatile period for popular music, during which the stronghold that major record labels had upon the popular market gave way for a time to a proliferation of smaller, more specialized interests. In Chicago, Bluebird Records, the RCA subsidiary that had dominated the city's blues recording during the 1930s and the early part of the 1940s, had stalled its activity by 1948 and abandoned its operations by 1950. Columbia Records, another major label that had cultivated a strong base in "race" music, followed a similar trajectory.[41] As a result, blues recording after 1950 was conducted by a number of small businessmen, record-shop owners, and independent record labels with close ties to local black communities.[42]

This shift in the organization of blues recording was tied to the changing tastes of black urban audiences, which evolved as migrant workers moved to the cities. The fluctuating market first had the effect of creating opportunities for small recording companies. An influx of young, unsigned talent hit cities like Chicago in search of musical outlets, and for many the opportunity to record was in itself more important than forging an association with an established label. The major concerns like Bluebird were rather set in their ways by the 1940s. Though Lester Melrose continued to look for new talent, the aforementioned "Bluebird sound" had lost much of its appeal, and was imposed upon young performers with little regard for their own musical strengths. The smaller local concerns proved themselves more willing and, in some cases, better able to respond to the new "sounds of the city." Although most such labels met with rapid financial failure, a few like Aristocrat had the combined good fortune and good judgment to latch onto the sounds and the performers that would shape Chicago music for the next two decades.

Arnold Shaw has discussed another factor in his account of the rise of rhythm and blues, *Honkers and Shouters*—the changing racial politics of the Chicago music scene. Specifically, Shaw describes a contrast between the relative openness of the Chicago club scene during the wartime years and the renewed enforcement of segregation patterns in the years following the war. In wartime, a number of black musical groups found steady work in clubs and lounges patronized by whites, particularly in areas like Chicago that served as centers of defense production. Willie Dixon, for one, regularly played for white customers in the downtown clubs of Chicago with his band, the Big Three Trio, favoring a musical style that owed more to vocal groups like the Mills Brothers and the Ink Spots than to the blues styles with which he would later become identified.[43] Such opportunities were not open to all black groups; the more "down-home" varieties of African-American music were kept rather squarely in the ghetto.[44] Nonetheless, both black musicians and black audiences were freer to travel outside the ghetto during the war than after, when the attempt to re-establish domestic order brought about a retrenchment of civil rights initiatives. Thus did Arnold Shaw state that "the Negro was being forced back into his own world for entertainment—black bars, taverns, clubs, saloons, and lounges—and when he was too tired or too broke, his home record-player."[45] According to Shaw, such conditions did much to distinguish African-American music in the postwar years, as performers oriented their music to the immediate conditions of black urban life.

While African-American musical activity may have assumed a distinctively internal focus during this time, many if not most of the institutions set up to record, distribute, and present black music remained under white ownership. So it was with Aristocrat/Chess. Neither Leonard or Phil Chess were eminently knowledgeable about either blues music or the music business, but they owned a string of bars that presented black performers. Unlike other blues or rhythm and blues entrepreneurs like Ahmet Ertegun and Jerry Wexler at Atlantic Records, they were not serious aficionados of African-American music. But they took their endeavors seriously, and worked hard to understand the nature of the appeal of blues, while developing a certain feel for the music itself.

Gaining an understanding of the quality of the relationships between the Chess brothers and the African-American musicians who recorded for Chess is no small challenge. Many associated with the company have described the uneasy camaraderie that characterized Chess recording sessions, with Leonard and Phil trading verbal jousts and profanity with the musicians. The epithets thrown around in the Chess studios were not explicitly racial, but rather centered around the racially neutral though sexually charged "motherfucker," a favorite bit of ghetto slang.[46] However playful these exchanges may have been, the undertone of aggression informing such interactions at times escalated into full-fledged violence, especially when money was concerned. The most notorious incident at Chess involved singer and pianist Willie Mabon, who came looking for Leonard Chess with a gun after feeling that he had been cheated out of royalties for a song. According to another pianist, Eddie Boyd, both he and Mabon had never been adequately promoted by Chess due to their unwillingness to play by the company's rules. Boyd offered some scathing and insightful comments on race relations at Chess in a 1977 interview, several years after he left the United States to settle and perform in Europe:

> Leonard Chess is the man who REALLY killed me in this country. He never did like me. At first when he first saw me he thought I was just like all these other BOYS, you understand . . . it was lot of cats [at Chess], used to do

things that was shameful. You know, when an artist is a artist, you don't have to do so many low things and tom and all this kind of thing, man, to get along with a record company, because one thing for sure: I tried to always tell these people, a artist CAN make it without a record company, but a record company cannot make it without artists . . . So you don't have to go around and do all those NIGGER things. That's what I call niggers—it's somebody who can be used as a tool. And Leonard found out I wasn't one of those kind of fellows and he didn't like me, man.[47]

Boyd does not name specific musicians who fell into the "tomming" roles he describes, and it would be unfair to speculate. However, one does not have to look hard to find evidence of a sort of paternalism that governed the economic relations at Chess. Muddy Waters, for instance, stayed with the company almost thirty years without ever signing a formal contract. In exchange for his loyalty, he was assured that Chess would always work on his behalf to promote his records (assurance that Boyd asserts he was never given) and that, when his records were not selling so well (as happened during the late 1950s), he could still depend on the company for a certain amount of financial remuneration. To an extent such an arrangement was an outgrowth of the family-style management procedures favored by the Chess brothers during most of the company's history, a style that depended upon a series of close informal relationships for its success. Muddy Waters himself often expressed his satisfaction at being part of the Chess family, and only severed his ties with the company after the death of Leonard Chess, when a more corporate style of management came to the fore. Yet anyone versed in the history of American race relations knows that the family metaphor has a troubling set of connotations, and that paternalism has historically been one of the primary means of justifying black dependency. Waters may have rightly judged that his situation at Chess was as good as he could hope for given the context of the times, but his satisfaction should not be used to legitimate the company's economic practices.[48]

The hierarchy that structured racial and economic relations at Chess assumed a different cast in the recording studio. Here, too, Leonard Chess was known to wield a heavy hand at times, but the musicians had more freedom to fight back and disagree; extremes like the conflict with Willie Mabon gave way to a more regular, day-to-day clash of wills and values. The end result was a sonic collaboration that was very much a studio product, not simply a recording of sounds already existing on the streets and in the clubs of Chicago. Chess, for his part, was one of the key pioneers of blues recording techniques such as the use of echo. His son, Marshall, recalled that Leonard and Phil crafted a lot of the sounds produced in the studio: "They were talking about . . . the *sound* of the guitar, how they wanted to get the distortion."[49] Malcolm Chisholm, a recording engineer who joined Chess in 1955, remembered working with Willie Dixon in similar terms, and gave the songwriter and bassist a good amount of credit for striking the proper balance in the sonic mix of Chess recordings:

> Will would tell me if he wanted to hear more guitar, which is not just a matter of turning up the guitar . . . Blues is a very dynamic medium, and for an engineer, highly dynamic music is much more difficult to handle. Will told me what the fixed balance of blues should be—that is, you carry far too much guitar and far too much voice because they need to be heard and the fill instruments are carried a little lower than one might ordinarily expect.[50]

Chisholm's comments offer a good bit of insight into the values that governed pop music recording at the time. In referring to the blues as a dynamic medium, he seems to be highlighting the preference of blues musicians for tones and volume levels that were at odds with the standard recording practices of the day. One of the qualities that contributed to the success of Chess was the willingness of Leonard Chess and Willie Dixon to accommodate their production methods to the boosted sound levels of amplified blues. Dixon further supports such a view with his reflections on the recording of electric guitars at the Bluebird studios: "Melrose and them had electric instruments but were keeping 'em turned down to sound acoustic-style."[51] By contrast, even on Waters's earliest Aristocrat releases like "I Can't Be Satisfied," the presence of the electric guitar was clearly audible, conferring a brightness and resonance to Waters's guitar sound that would not have been achievable to the same degree on an acoustic instrument.

While the site of the recording studio and the process of recording were crucial to the shaping of the electric blues sound, much of the work that went into the making of this sound still happened with the individual guitarist and his amplifier. Over the course of the 1950s, blues guitarists would employ increasingly coarse, distorted tones, extending the expressive palette of the electric guitar in new directions. The creation of these sounds was generally the result of a fairly simple process of playing amplifying equipment past its limits and taking advantage of the tones that emerged. How this process worked technically is a somewhat more complicated matter, but one worth exploring.

Every amplification system has a built-in limit on the output strength of the signal produced. Typically, this limit is reached at less than maximum volume. The middle range of an amplifier's volume level is the range at which a player can achieve the best balance of loudness and clarity of sound. Maximum volume, then, often pushes the amplifying system beyond its signal capacity, and this is when distortion occurs. Under ordinary circumstances, the amplifier multiplies the strength of the signal delivered from the guitar by a consistent measure, called the gain. Yet when the system is overloaded, the relationship between input and output signal loses its consistency and the amplifier begins to clip, or cut off, the signal at its point of maximum strength. It is this clipping of the output signal that produces distortion by generating an overflow of harmonic resonances in addition to the main frequency of the note being played. Feedback, another favored effect, involves an oscillation between the source of the incoming signal (the guitar) and the source of the output (the amplifier). When the gain of the system is sufficiently high, and the signal transmitted by the amplifier is in phase with that of the guitar, then feedback occurs and a note that begins from the vibration of a string seems to take on a life of its own, sustaining as long as the system is left undisturbed.[52]

Among the guitarists who inhabited the Chicago clubs and recording studios of the period, perhaps no figure used these sounds to greater effect than Buddy Guy. Yet Guy's experience also illustrates some of the constraints placed upon the desire to pursue sonic innovation within the Chess studio system. Along with his flamboyant performing style, Guy began experimenting with feedback and distortion during his club performances, using the excess of sound made available by his guitar and amplifier to increase the sustain of individual notes. According to Guy, he came upon such techniques by accident while on a break from one of his sets: "Once I took a break and forgot to cut my guitar off, and this lady passed by with a wide skirt. The jukebox was going with a tune that I liked—I had punched it—and her dress tail hit the G string [of Guy's guitar], and this guitar just stayed there, humming in G, the whole time that record was going. I got the idea from that to just hold this sustained note."[53] Building upon this chance moment, Guy continued to test and extend the potential of amplification in his live playing. In subsequent years, when guitarists like Jimi Hendrix used feedback to open a range of new expressive avenues, they looked to Guy as a model. In the 1950s, Guy's alternately playful and intense use of feedback was banned from the recording studio. In 1987, Guy bemoaned the course of his recording career, stating that "in person I've always been Buddy Guy; in the studio I never has been Buddy Guy," and recounting his experiences at Chess with frustration: "they'd always tell me to turn that amplifier down, don't play that, that's *noise*. And I'd say, Man, this is my blood, this is *me*."[54] Guy's comments reflect the tendency of blues performers to consider their sound to be the basis of their musical identity. Unable to record that sound, Guy spent the first decade of his recording career working primarily as a sideman to many of the city's leading lights, eventually leaving Chess in 1967 to record for Vanguard under the auspices of Sam Charters, blues scholar and producer.

More generally, Guy's example highlights some of the conflicts that arose in transferring a sound and style of music developed within the performing conditions of the Chicago clubs onto tape and converting that sound into a saleable commodity that bore repeated listening. To a certain extent, we find in this process some of the imperatives of repetition discussed by Jacques Attali. Analyzing the "new aesthetic of performance" that has taken hold in recording studios during the past several decades, when producers and engineers have exerted increased control over the sound of music via electronic means, Attali claims that the new procedures produce "information free of noise."[55] The capability of the musician to create sounds that signify a critical difference from the mass of musical product has, according to Attali, been curtailed in favor of the demand to produce music according to the dictates of a technologically determined sonic order. At issue in this conflict is not only the proper sound of music, but also the proper role of the body engaged in musical performance. Attali's remark that "the production of repetition requires a new kind of performer, a virtuoso of the short phrase capable of infinitely redoing takes that are perfectible with sound effects,"[56] finds substantiation in guitarist Jimmy Rogers's discussion of the work rhythm that often characterized Chess recording sessions. Said Rogers in a 1973 interview:

> Only time it'd be a rerun would be somethin' Chess would want to change, and that would be the end of a good record. When he changed it, he'd take all the soul and everything from it. And that happened quite a few times . . . I figure the best way to do a blues tune, catch it as you play 'em as you feel it. Whatever you feel, play it that way and forget about it, you know. Because you keep turnin' it around, you's gonna start findin' fault, and then once you start findin' faults, it's dead . . .
>
> It'd take you three days to do a session which you've supposed to have done in two hours or three hours, well, you get the same money that you was gonna get if you'd have did it in an hour . . . And what [Chess] is tellin' me to do, I don't like it, see. I don't feel it and I really don't like it, so that gets you to the place you don't care then whether you record or not. You supposed to go in the studio happy and come out happy, man. You don't supposed to go in there like you're goin' in a steel mill.[57]

On one level, Rogers draws upon a set of rather commonplace assumptions that portray the blues as a music particularly driven by spontaneous expression or emotional authenticity; Rogers can only mean a performance if he feels it in a given way, and that feeling is best achieved by foregoing intensive scrutiny and allowing the song to proceed apace. Yet the overall tenor of Rogers's insights is far from commonplace; what he describes is a situation strikingly similar to that discussed by Attali, in which the structure of recording imposes upon the musician a mode of practice and of (re)production at odds with the methods that the musicians have learned and developed over time. Central to this conflict, as Rogers suggests, is the nature of musical work, or more specifically, the degree to which that work is pleasurable for the musicians involved, and the extent to which it allows for the creation of sounds and of songs in which the musicians can recognize the stamp of their own performance. The repeated takes demanded by Leonard Chess interrupted what seemed to musicians like Rogers to be the natural flow of a song. Furthermore, such procedures were predicated upon the pursuit of an abstract sound ideal removed from the aesthetic of performance that has governed so much of African-American musical activity.[58]

Assessing the dynamics of Chess recording sessions, Pete Golkin put the matter most succinctly. "Though the early Chess recordings sound to the listener like spontaneous works of musical luck and inspiration," observed Golkin, "the making of such records stemmed from slow and methodical trial and error as the tension between performer and producer built with each take."[59] One might say that Chess sought to make records that sounded good, while for many of the musicians who recorded at the studio the main goal was to capture a good performance on record. We need to be careful, though, not to exaggerate the amount of opposition between these objectives. Despite Attali's claims about the search for abstract perfection in the production of music under a repetitive economy, Leonard Chess and his associates in the studio did not so thoroughly subordinate the recording process to such demands. Indeed, Willie Dixon stressed the value of imperfection to the making of effective records. Explained Dixon,

> It wasn't actually the policy of a mistake—it was the policy of a sound. The majority of the public today don't know right from wrong in recording. It's only the people that ain't gonna buy any music, the musicians and critics, that pay any attention to the little mistakes . . .
>
> If it was what you considered a perfect record, it never sold. But if it had a good feeling and good time, even when some of the words couldn't be understood, it would be better to go with that than one that's so perfect the people don't enjoy it.[60]

As an African-American musician with a grounding in the blues, Dixon undoubtedly brought many of his own values to bear upon his work as a producer, values that may not have fully coincided with those of his employers. However, even if Leonard and Phil Chess followed a regime of musical production at odds with the wishes and practices of many Chess musicians, their idea of a good blues record was largely shaped by their work with those musicians. The Chess brothers maintained ultimate authority over the workings of the studio and over the nature and quality of the records being released, but the Chess "sound" was nonetheless the product of a unique collaboration sparked by equal amounts of cooperation and conflict.

*   *   *

Muddy Waters enjoyed a more cooperative relationship with Chess than most, in no small part because he was responsible for so many of the company's early successes. As "I Can't Be Satisfied" found quick local sales and helped to set Aristocrat on a secure footing, so did Waters's 1950 recording "Rollin' Stone" serve as the first official release of the renamed Chess Records and the first record put out by the Chess brothers to achieve significant national sales. Where "I Can't Be Satisfied" filled out Waters's performance with "Big" Crawford's string bass, "Rollin' Stone" featured Waters in a true solo performance. The overall sound is spare, but Waters's guitar sounds far more coarse than in the earlier performance, with an edge of distortion that contributes to the menacing tone. Eschewing the bottleneck slide, Waters spends the bulk of the song working the key of E, insistently pumping the guitar's lowest string while striking the musical figure that drives the song: an off-pitch bend on the middle A, pulled off to open G and then hammered onto the E at the second fret of the fourth string. Harmonically there is no progression to speak of—the end of each verse is marked by a slight quickening of the rhythm and several repetitions of the figure described as Waters moans the fatalistic phrases "Oh Lord" and "Oh well." Perhaps no song better demonstrates Waters's musical prioritization of tone and rhythm over melody and harmony. Meanwhile, the lyrics celebrate a form of virile manhood that became a common theme in Waters's recordings, and that played no small part in their later popularity with young white male blues aficionados.

> Well I wish I was a catfish
> Swimming in the whole deep blue sea
> I would have all you good looking women (fishes)
> Swimming after me . . .

"Rollin' Stone" was a tough, effective urban blues performance that lyrically pointed the way to much of Waters's subsequent output. However, it was another 1950 recording that first captured some of the intensity of Waters's club performances with his bandmates. Waters, Little Walter, and Baby Face Leroy recorded the two-part "Rollin' and Tumblin'" for the Parkway label, a newly established company that signed

Walter and Leroy to their own contracts. The song was released under Leroy's name; Waters's presence on the track is indicative of the fluidity with which musicians moved between labels in these early days of the postwar boom in Chicago recording activity, and can also be taken as a sign of the guitarist's dissatisfaction with Leonard Chess's unwillingness to record him with full accompaniment.[61]

The sound of "Rollin' and Tumblin'" was not yet up to the fully amplified ensemble sound that Waters's bands would eventually achieve; Walter's harmonica is amplified rather straightforwardly with a microphone, lacking the echo and volume of his later work, and Foster's drumming is heard as a steady tapping that has fairly little presence within the overall mix. But the instrumental interplay between Waters and Walter combined with the alternately moaned and shouted vocals of Foster and Waters (and perhaps Jimmy Rogers as well) to create a small-scale maelstrom that stood in marked contrast to the spareness of "Rollin' Stone," recorded only a month later. Moreover, on "Rollin' and Tumblin'" Waters exploited the tone of his electric guitar with new force, moving his bottleneck slide up and down the neck with a rare sense of abandon. Said Ry Cooder of Waters's performance on the song, "that track's an example of somebody who transcends anything we think we know about the guitar . . . I mean, that could've been a one-string there, it could've been a post with a string, it could've been any of my guitars—it wouldn't have made any difference." Cooder continued:

> What's great about when guys play like that is you don't feel frets and six strings and scale length. It's beyond construction and principles. Muddy's playing where he knows those notes are, and they are locking into this spirit thing of playing the movement of the song. And he goes past the note—the note isn't just there at the fret, because there are degrees of the note. It's like Turkish music in some ways—there are 5,000 notes . . . There are nuances—no phrases come down the same. When you need a lift you go sharp, and when you need to sour it up and make it feel a little darker, you go flat. But you don't think about it. You just do it.[62]

Cooder's explanation offers a striking portrait of the microtonal dimensions of Waters's guitar playing. Throughout "Rollin' and Tumblin'" Waters plays notes and combinations of notes that fall between the values of the tempered European scale. Despite Cooder's cross-cultural comparison, the techniques he describes are firmly rooted in African-American musical culture. What Cooder's analysis does capture, though, is the way that Waters's playing on "Rollin' and Tumblin'" pushes those techniques to their limits.

Writing a historical overview of the slide guitar for *Living Blues* magazine, Lawrence Hoffman noted that "Muddy Waters took slide guitar out of the black ghetto and into the larger musical marketplace."[63] Leonard Chess, for one, recognized the trademark value of Waters's slide playing. Not only did he strongly reprimand Waters for having displayed his talents on another label, but he had the guitarist record another version of "Rollin' and Tumblin'" at the same session that produced "Rollin' Stone," to be released by Chess under Waters's name. The Chess "Rollin' and Tumblin'" lacked the overall energy of the Parkway release, as Waters was fit back into the standard format of himself on guitar and vocals accompanied by "Big" Crawford on bass. However, Chess may well have been motivated by the strong sound of Waters's Parkway effort to finally record the guitarist with a full band.

On his next session in October of 1950, Waters was joined in the studio not only by Crawford but by Little Walter on harmonica and Elgin Evans on washboard. This collaboration resulted in "Louisiana Blues," considered by many blues scholars to be a landmark in the history of Chicago blues. Lyrically, the song introduced another theme that would recur throughout Waters's career, that of the power of hoodoo. Waters sang of "goin' down to New Orleans/Get me a mojo hand."[64] Musically, "Louisiana Blues" may have lacked some of the adventure of the Parkway "Rollin' and Tumblin'," but it presented a more balanced musical setting marked by a solid integration of the different instrumental parts and sounds. Waters's high whining slide opens the piece, only to be quickly joined by the full ensemble. As the song moves along, the guitarist alternates between a low rhythmic pulse that blends with Crawford's bass and high-pitched melodic elaborations that complement and occasionally coincide with Walter's harmonica. Completing the second verse, Waters invites his bandmates to "go back down to New Orleans," and the musicians engage in a fine bit of instrumental interplay that brings the performance to a close, rounding out what Robert Palmer called "the first really successful recording of the new, heavily amplified Delta blues."[65]

With "Louisiana Blues," Waters set the musical pattern that would

4.1. Muddy Waters with a version of his mid-1950s electric band. Waters is on the far left, fellow guitarist Jimmy Rogers is on the far right. Sitting at the piano is Otis Spann. Courtesy of the Val Wilmer Collection.

characterize the remainder of his recording career. Over the next few years his regular collaborators in the clubs began to play a more pronounced role in the studio. During 1951 Waters made his first record with Jimmy Rogers, "Honey Bee," a song that showcased the pair's unique division of responsibility, with Waters's slide guitar set against Rogers's steady low-end groove. Later that year came the first record on which Little Walter's harmonica was amplified to full effect, "She Moves Me," which also featured Leonard Chess pounding on a bass drum.

Only in 1952 did the different elements of Waters's live band fully come together in a single studio performance. "Standing Around Crying," a slow blues lament about romantic and sexual frustration, included Waters alongside Rogers, Walter, and Evans. Also listed on the song's credits was the newest addition to Waters's performing band, pianist Otis Spann, though Spann can be heard to better effect on the following year's "I Want You to Love Me." Both songs find Waters and his band cultivating a self-consciously big sound built upon the creative use of amplification and the dense layering of instruments. Interviewed by James Rooney, Waters discussed his decision to bring Spann into the band in terms of the possibilities opened by the incorporation of the piano: "If you get that piano in there you get a whole full bed of background music. Before they had pianos and guitars together like Leroy Carr and Scrapper Blackwell, but that wasn't a big sound. I developed that. I kept that backbeat on the drums plus full action on the guitar and harmonica and the piano in the back, then you've got a big sound."[66] Here, in a nutshell, was Waters's mature philosophy of music making, with all the instruments in "full action" to produce a heavy sound based upon the alternation between tight synchronization and free-ranging improvisation. Spann's piano filled out the band's sound, adding an extra layer of harmonic and rhythmic texture. Meanwhile, amplification remained crucial to the overall effect, lending percussiveness to the attack of the guitars and allowing the harmonica to float over and around the steady pulse as it took liberties with the melody.

"I Want You to Love Me," on which Big Walter Horton replaced Little Walter on harmonica,[67] introduced another Waters trademark: the stop-time rhythm, a musical structure that showed off the band's new format and demonstrated Waters's claims about bringing a "heavy beat" to down home blues. In the stop-time rhythm, all the instruments joined in for the main rhythmic and melodic figure (some variation on the now-familiar "da-DA-da-da"), followed by a pause filled by Waters's vocal and instrumental fills by the harmonica, piano, guitar, or some combination thereof. A series of repetitions (four or eight, depending on the song) would lead into the turnaround and the chorus, where all the instruments would combine in a more loose and flowing fashion only to return to the strict start-and-stop motif of the verse. Stop-time provided the basis for a number of Waters's later recordings—including a string of Willie Dixon compositions such as "Hoochie Coochie Man," "I Just Want to Make Love to You," and "I'm Ready,"—that were among the singer's biggest commercial hits. As a musical device it marked a crystallization of Waters's development as a bandleader. He had assembled a group of musicians who could follow his concept of the blues while inserting their own creativity, working together to produce a big, integrated sound that depended upon amplification for much of its power.

In this setting, the electric guitar played a central role, though less for its value as a lead instrument than for the ways in which it contributed to the overall sound. Indeed, comparing his music to that of a more celebrated lead guitarist, B. B. King, Waters expounded on the vast difference in approach between the two musicians:

B. B.'s got that squeezing sound. Man, that's a different country from me. My sound and his sound is the same as two different countries. 'Cause I'm not a squeeze man. That's what I try to keep my guitar players down with. Don't put too much B. B. on me. It don't mix. I'd rather for you to play big-four chords, you know. But if I give you a solo then you can go wild, you can do what you want to do. But behind me, don't put too much squeeze behind me.[68]

King's sound and style would, of course, exert a considerable influence of its own, maybe even greater than that of Waters. By the end of the 1950s, for instance, a young generation of King-influenced guitarists, including Buddy Guy, would find their way into the Chicago scene, working the higher registers of their guitars to create single-note solos of impressive facility. This "West Side Sound," as it came to be known, became popular among young white guitarists in England and the United States who "discovered" the blues in the late 1950s and early 1960s, and would go on to shape the subsequent history of the electric guitar. Muddy Waters's use of the electric guitar, however, draws attention to aspects of the instrument that are easily overlooked. Too often those who write about the electric guitar and its primary exponents emphasize the ways in which amplification allows the guitar to stand out as a solo instrument. Waters's music shows how the electric guitar, and how amplification more generally, could be used not simply to accentuate the role of the individual musician but to create new combinations among musicians. Both King and Waters, though, along with Buddy Guy, Louis Myers, and a number of others, can be taken as examples of the ways in which African-American musicians worked to expand the tonal range of the electric guitar during the 1950s, generating sounds that went against the established norms of amplification and creating the basis for a new set of sonoric values through the manipulation of volume, distortion, and other electronic effects.

Roll Over

Chuck Berry got his first electric guitar some time in late 1950 or early 1951, bought from a guitarist at the St. Louis radio station where Berry worked as a janitor. He had already been playing guitar for some time, taking lessons from a local jazzman, Ira Harris, whose brother cut the hair of most of the men in Berry's neighborhood. More recently Berry had started auditioning at bars—white bars, he is sure to note in his autobiography—and playing parties for friends with his four-string tenor guitar. Berry purchased an electric guitar, it seems, to replace his four-string with a more common six-string instrument; that it was an electric instrument was incidental at first. Soon, however, he "found it much easier to finger the frets of an electric guitar, plus it could be heard anywhere in the area with an amplifier." Berry noted that "it was my first really good-looking instrument to have and hold. From the inspiration of it, I began really searching at every chance I got for opportunities to play music."[69] What stands out in Berry's account, considered against the stories of other guitarists, is how relatively little the electric guitar upset Berry's approach to music, and how little effort he put into electrifying his sound. Unlike Les Paul or Chet Atkins, Berry did not spend his time experimenting with strategies for more effectively amplifying his instrument; unlike Muddy Waters, he saw amplification as neither an economic necessity nor as a break from an already-established sound. Berry grew up listening to the music of Charlie Christian (to whose music he had been introduced by Ira Harris) and T-Bone Walker, both early exponents of the electric guitar. Perhaps because of his early influences, perhaps also because of his upbringing in St. Louis, an urban area where amplified instruments were readily available, acquiring an electric guitar did not require enormous effort.

Only months after purchasing his electric guitar, Berry purchased another piece of musical technology: a reel-to-reel magnetic wire recorder, which he bought from a friend. In his autobiography, Berry recalled being "completely fascinated" by the reproduction qualities of his new device, and described it as a further bit of inspiration in his path to becoming a professional musician.[70] It was the recorder, as much as the electric guitar itself, that spurred Berry on to a new commitment to his guitar playing. "With the recorder, I started hanging around more with Ira Harris. I picked up a lot of new swing riffs and ideas from Ira's playing, which was similar to the style of Charlie Christian's . . . I buckled down and started taking seriously the task of learning to play the guitar."[71] That Berry developed his abilities on the guitar with a tape recorder at his side is perhaps evidence of what Theodore Gracyk has called "record consciousness," a mode of experiencing music in which the recorded sound becomes the measure of musical reality and the standard against which a good performance is judged.[72] More important for my purposes, though, is the observation that for Berry, as for Les Paul and Chet Atkins, technologies of sound production such as the electric guitar were often closely allied with technologies of sound reproduction like the magnetic tape recorder. Both modes of technology were crucial for musicians as they worked to develop a distinctive style and a professional sound. Berry's access to the tape recorder in particular was a mark of his privilege relative to other African-American musicians like Muddy Waters, who had neither the resources to afford such devices early in their career nor the experience to have made use of them. At the same time, one can detect the limits upon that privilege by noting that Berry did not move to a position of control within the recording studio as did his white counterparts. With very few exceptions (such as Willie Dixon), such opportunities were simply not open to black musicians of the time.

Despite these limits upon what Berry could achieve within the existing structure of the music industry, the guitarist stands as a useful reminder that popular access to, and interest in, technology has not been the domain of white males only. Historians of technology have usually characterized technological enthusiasm as a white male pastime. Berry was not an enthusiast on the order of Paul or Atkins, but his acquisition of the means to record himself and his professed fascination with these means certainly demonstrates a high level of interest in ways of shaping sound through electric technology. Moreover, Berry's familiarity with technology offers a key bit of insight into why and how he was able to assimilate the demands and desires of young white listeners more effectively than all but a few of his African-American counterparts. I do not mean to suggest by this statement that recording technology had a homogenizing influence on the sound of popular music, or at least I do not mean to suggest this in any simple way. Rather, electric technologies of sound production and reproduction were becoming an integral part of the pop music process and of the expectations that listeners brought to popular music, and musicians, black or white, who had access to these technologies were in a powerful position in the rapidly changing musical market. From this perspective, Michael Lydon's statement that it was the "niggers" who "got" electricity assumes a materialist quality grounded in the recognition that electricity was not simply there for the taking, and that its acquisition had as much to do with issues of access and of interest in new sound technologies as it did with the cultural factors that he chose to emphasize.

Berry's rock 'n' roll peer at Chess, Bo Diddley, provides an even better example of an African-American musician whose interest in technology shaped his musical approach in ways beyond the purchase of a guitar and amplifier. Diddley was a bona-fide electronic tinkerer whose favorite pastime besides playing music was scouring the junkyards surrounding his Chicago home for parts he might use in his various projects. Parts of Diddley's biography have striking parallels to the experiences of Les Paul where electronics are concerned. Like Paul, for instance, Diddley first amplified his guitar with parts from the family radio and record player:

> When I was still at school, I used to go in the back of my mother's big old radio when she wasn't around, an' I figured out that it had to be some way that the sound was comin' through that radio . . . I got me two wires and touched two of the pins, an' kept on till I found the two that the thing came through. That's how I electrified my guitar: I played it through the radio.
>
> The pick-up I had was made out of an old Victrola record-player cartridge—you know them old Victrolas? I didn't *buy* me no electric guitar; shit, man, I had to figure out a way to *make* me one![73]

As a young man growing up on Chicago's South Side, Diddley likely could not afford an electric guitar of his own, and his mother was at the time encouraging him to pursue the violin. Yet the young musician was already making his first moves onto the city's lively music scene, and fast realized that amplification was a virtual necessity for holding an audience's attention in the bars and on the streets.

Having pieced together his first electric guitar, Diddley continued to acquire knowledge of electronics, experimenting with different means of amplifying his guitar. His former bandmate, harmonica player Billy Boy Arnold, remembered Diddley as an "electronics freak" who built his own amplifiers.[74] Diddley himself downplayed his efforts in this regard, stating that he never built an amplifier from scratch but did often remove and exchange parts in an effort to derive a cleaner sound. "I spent *twelve* years tryin' to develop a good clean sound because I *hate* distortion," claimed Diddley, who continued, "You know what happened? Some guy built a *fuzz-pedal!* [Laughs] Busted my bubble!"[75] Diddley's desire to eliminate distortion from his sound echoes Les Paul's desire for a "pure" tone, a surprising goal for a guitarist whose sound was so predicated upon the use of loud amplification as Diddley's was. Over time Diddley would devote himself more to looking for ways to alter the tone of his guitar away from any kind of sonic purity. Perhaps his favorite effect was the tremolo that was featured on many of his most successful recordings, including his first Chess single, "Bo Diddley." Tremolo involved an oscillation of the electronic signal transmitted from the guitar to the amplifier so that the volume level would fluctuate at regular intervals between extreme loudness and virtual silence. Diddley built a tremolo device for himself out of an old clock: "I found you could bend one part of the clock to get a slow sound and bend it again to get a faster sound."[76] Varying the speed of the effect, Diddley essentially added a second layer of timekeeping to his guitar playing, setting the tremolo against the pace struck by his right hand to create the dense electronic polyrhythms that characterized his most famous musical device, the Bo Diddley beat.

Along with his experiments in sound and amplification, Diddley also played with different ideas of electric guitar design. Throughout his career he favored an assortment of oddly-shaped electric guitars that demonstrated the extent to which the solid-body concept had liberated the shape of the guitar from the sound it produced. That guitar manufacturers had not fully exploited this quality of the solid-body was a mark of their desire to assimilate the new instrument into the existing aesthetics of guitar design to a greater or lesser degree. Even Leo Fender's Stratocaster, issued in 1954 and described by Tom Wheeler as akin to a "rocket ship" with its contoured body and double-cutaway horns, was comparatively tame next to the guitars that Diddley built for himself.[77] One of Diddley's guitars was made in the shape of a Cadillac tail-fin, while another replaced the standard curves of the guitar with a square body. In later years Diddley would have his guitars custom built by the Gretsch company, but it was Diddley himself who did much to promote recognition that in performance, or on record covers, the electric guitar was not simply an instrument but a valuable prop that had an entertainment value of its own.

Chuck Berry did not expend as much effort as Diddley upon the technological elements of his instrument, but he certainly exhibited a similar awareness of the electric guitar's visual appeal. In his first film appearance, performing the song "You Can't Catch Me" in the 1956 rock 'n' roll exploitation film *Rock, Rock, Rock!*, Berry appeared alone with his guitar on an otherwise empty screen. Lip-synching the song's lyrics, Berry strutted and pranced through his performance with guitar firmly in tow, strumming on the instrument despite the clearly visible fact that it was not plugged into any system of amplification. No matter; Berry's guitar may have been silent, but he used it to convey the spirit of the song through his gestures. At a point in the song when Berry told his lover to cuddle up close, he drew the instrument toward his face, affecting a look of devotion as he planted a kiss firmly on the neck of the guitar. The end of the song finds Berry going into his "duck-walk," bending his knees to bring his body toward the ground and pacing back and forth across the stage, his head butting forwards and back while his guitar pointed out from his body in a position that was phallic but arguably more playful than aggressive.

The duck-walk was one of Berry's more characteristic moves. Though used here to bolster a performance in which Berry simulates his guitar playing, he more commonly used it while playing to audiences, typically in the midst of a solo (even in "You Can't Catch Me," Berry goes into the walk during the brief solo section at the end). As such he was invoking, deliberately or not, earlier African-American performers like T-Bone Walker and Guitar Slim who had introduced a significant element of demonstrative physical display into their performances. The electric guitar served to heighten the attention drawn to the performer's body. With guitar in hand, performers like Walker and Slim assumed positions that emphasized the flexibility of the body and the ability of the guitarist to maintain concentration upon his playing even as his body was set in a way to make playing difficult. Such practices, the outgrowth of the guitar battles often held in black urban clubs, were more generally tied to the

4.2.   Chuck Berry in his famous duck walk pose. Courtesy of the Michael Ochs Archives, Venice, California.

intense competitiveness of the market for black popular music, within which performers who could not hold the attention of an audience were subject to being quickly replaced by performers who could. More than economic determinism was at work in this scenario, though. The stages of ghetto clubs were spaces where black performers, and male performers in particular, could enact forms of physical assertion unavailable in their everyday lives away from the stage. Viewed from this perspective, the electric guitar orchestrated the performance with a noise of its own that played into the disturbance of everyday norms and restrictions.

Chuck Berry enacted some of these same impulses, but in a markedly different setting where his body was on display more to whites than to other blacks. The degree of risk involved was consequently greater and required a different set of strategies for positioning the body relative to the audience. Just how great the risks could be for black performers in this situation was articulated by DeFord Bailey, an African-American harmonica player who was for years the only black musician regularly featured on the Grand Ole Opry. Interviewed by David Morton, Bailey discussed how he had felt compelled during his career (which lasted from the 1920s to the 1940s) to conceal many of the physical tricks he could do while playing his harmonica so as not to upset the expectations of his white audience. "I could do things, me walking, laying on the floor, turning over, turning somersaults, and still blowing the train . . . Well, back in that time [they would have said], 'Well he's too smart . . . He does too much.'"[78] Bailey's desire for physical display was thus held in check by the audience's demand for bodily reserve, boundaries imposed upon the black male body by white onlookers. That Berry could get away with antics similar to those described by Bailey can be taken as a mark of the changing expectations of white audiences, and also undoubtedly says something about the different kinds of audiences to which the two performers played. Those differences only extended so far, though, and many an early rock 'n' roll show was broken up by police because of the perceived moral and physical threat that the music presented to the white youth in attendance.

Of course there was another set of expectations surrounding African-American entertainers that basked in the very physicality others sought to contain. As Eric Lott and Robert Cantwell have argued, such expectations and desires were at the heart of blackface minstrelsy, and continued to exert an enormous pressure upon black performers in this century.[79] When increasing numbers of African-American performers moved into minstrelsy during the second half of the nineteenth century, they were expected to play to the types and caricatures already established by white performers like T. D. Rice and Dan Emmett, types constructed out of a blend of genuine sympathy for African Americans and a racist preoccupation with the supposed sexual virility of black men. Over time black performers learned to manipulate the confining standards of the minstrel mask, introducing elements of veiled critique and gradually carving out space for the articulation of a more autonomous set of performance norms and practices. Charlie Christian was one musician who adopted a strategy of what Houston Baker called the "deformation of mastery," a social and artistic way of asserting his mastery over the values of the dominant culture and at the same time interjecting practices and values rooted in African-American vernacular culture.[80] Christian never resolved the conflict between musical self-determination and the demands of white listeners and onlookers. Rather, that conflict structured his career and informed his music, which was itself split between the tight-knit interplay of the Benny Goodman sextet and the more challenging improvisational forms taking shape at Minton's nightclub.

Berry's career was structured by these same tensions, but on the surface at least he demonstrated a greater desire to please and entertain his audience, and was thus closer to the playful, at times minstrel-like postures of musicians such as Louis Armstrong and Louis Jordan than the respectable jazz musicians like Christian. Indeed the element of play was a central component of Berry's music and persona, one most often noted by the few writers who have considered his career in any depth. Robert Christgau's remarks on Berry and the subject of play or "fun" are both characteristic and insightful. According to Christgau, Berry managed to write effective songs for a white teen audience because he so strongly valued fun. Fun, Christgau continues,

> was what adolescent revolt had to be about—inebriated affluence versus the hangover of the work ethic . . . Because black music had always thrived on exuberance . . . it turned into the perfect vehicle for generational convulsion. Black musicians, however, had rarely achieved an optimism that was cultural as well as personal—those few who did, like Louis Armstrong, left themselves open to charges of Tomming. Chuck Berry never Tommed. The trouble he'd seen just made his sly, bad boy voice and the splits and waddles of his stage show that much more credible.[81]

For Christgau, Berry's prioritization of fun was neither a mark of the musician's lack of seriousness nor a sign of his overzealous desire to appease white onlookers. Instead, Berry sang about fun, and enacted it through his onstage moves, in a way that was at root ideological, celebrating the abundance of pleasures made available by a thriving consumerist economy while decrying the rigid work schedule (or school schedule, as the case may have been for Berry's songs) that kept people from being able to fully pursue those pleasures. In such a way could Berry forge an interracial link between himself and his fans while maintaining his self-possession and avoiding the reproduction of racial caricatures.

There is much that I find persuasive in Christgau's argument, but I want to posit another dimension to Berry's emphasis upon fun and playfulness. While Berry may have largely avoided the performance of simple racial stereotypes, I think his playfulness, and the particular brand of fun he promoted, was also a key means of deflecting some of the anxieties surrounding the black male body. Specifically, the youth-based, adolescent mode of fun that dominated most of Berry's best-known songs undercut the fact that these songs were performed by a full-grown, African-American man. While "Brown-Eyed Handsome Man" may have been, as Christgau suggests, Berry's most emphatic (though still veiled) declaration of racial pride, more characteristic was "Almost Grown," a briskly sung narrative of the everyday pleasures of the adolescent world sung from the point of view of a young (almost) man. This "almost" quality with regard to adulthood and, by extension, to manhood set Berry apart from many of his black musical peers like Muddy Waters and Bo Diddley who sang of their manhood in far less qualified terms. Rock critic Charles Shaar Murray claimed in connection to Waters and Diddley that when the two performers sang "I'm a Man," as each would do in recordings from 1955, the subtext was one of racial and sexual self-assertion: "don't *ever* call me a boy."[82] Such a stance was, I think, a key reason why neither performer achieved the same level of crossover success as did Berry; not only because their music—even Diddley's music—remained too rooted in the ghetto, as some have suggested, but because their music presented too unflinching a portrait of African-American masculinity, in contrast to the less full-bodied characters that populated Berry's songs.[83]

What we find in this comparison among Chuck Berry, Muddy Waters, and Bo Diddley is an important instantiation and variation of Paul Gilroy's remark that "gender is the modality in which race is lived."[84] The phenomenon of crossover had, and has, as much to do with strategies for performing gender as it does with styles of racial presentation. This is not to say that there is any simple formula at work, that the right blend of veiled racial assertion and tempered masculine bravado is the key to crossover success. Indeed, Jimi Hendrix's exaggerated performance of male potency was very much a part of his crossover appeal. However, if Hendrix stands as a counterexample to singer Terence Trent D'Arby's assertion that "any black act in the States who has been [a] massive quote-unquote crossover success has had to emasculate himself to some degree," Berry can be taken as evidence for D'Arby's claim, though with qualifications.[85] Emasculation is, I think, too strong a term for the image that Berry put forth, and furthermore contains an implicit valuation of an idealized manhood that is itself problematic, even when the problems faced by black men are taken into account.[86] In the context of U.S. race relations, the perceived hypersexuality of African-American men is alternately enticing or distressing, and often both at once. Black performers like Chuck Berry, who have worked specifically to cultivate a white audience, have had to carefully measure their enactment of masculinity or else run risks greater than a lack of commercial success.

*   *   *

In a telling scene from the film documentary of his career and his sixtieth birthday concert, *Hail! Hail! Rock and Roll* (1987), Berry walks through the old Fox Theater in St. Louis, Missouri, the town of his birth, and where his career began. When he was a boy, Berry recalls, the theater was a monument to elegance and class. It was also closed to himself and the other black inhabitants of the city. But that night, it was to provide the setting for his birthday concert, a star-studded event organized by one of Berry's most famous fans and musical disciples, Keith Richards. "This theater was the Great White Way in St. Louis," said Berry, "But whatever it be, because of my music, I will generate the feeling that we had back in our neighborhood. Because that's one thing about rock 'n' roll. It's freedom." Later in the film, Berry expounds more fully on the connection between the music of his neighborhood and the world outside, and how that connection shaped his career goals:

> I was trying to shoot for the entire population instead of, shall we say, the neighborhood. Muddy Waters, I knew he was dynamite in our neighborhood, he's dynamite with me . . . but working with my father in the white

neighborhoods, I never heard Muddy Waters, I never heard Elmore James, Howling Wolf, I never heard 'em. I heard Frank Sinatra, I heard Pat Boone, you know Pat Boone doing Muddy Waters or whoever's number . . . And I said now can I do as Pat Boone does and play good music for the white people and sell as well there as I could in the neighborhood. And that's what I shot for.

One can dwell on the historical inaccuracies: Pat Boone never recorded a Muddy Waters song (and no white musician would until the 1960s), and Boone's success came well after Berry's own crossover moves had begun. Rhetorically, though, Berry's comment reveals much about his approach to music and to race. On the one hand fully recognizing the effects of segregation—Berry's choice of words for discussing black listeners, "the neighborhood," is especially telling—and on the other hand suggesting that those effects could be flaunted by sheer willfulness or by the communicative power of music, Berry makes plain the hopes that resided in early rock 'n' roll and the contradictory nature of the freedoms set forth by the music. He further lays bare the commercial impulses that drove this notion of freedom, demonstrating how rock 'n' roll did not so much break racial barriers as expand the potential listening base.

During the early 1950s, when establishments like the Fox Theater were closed to African Americans, Berry made his reputation playing at a more modest St. Louis establishment that served as the center of the city's lively music scene. According to Cub Koda, the Cosmopolitan Club was where Berry's crossover strategy crystallized "through hit-and-miss, drop-this/add-that, night-after-night experimentation."[87] Berry began playing the Cosmo as part of pianist Johnnie Johnson's combo. Initially an instrumental trio featuring piano, saxophone, and drums, the band began moving in a different direction with Berry on vocals and guitar, though Johnson's piano style provided a key element of continuity, with his syncopated boogie-influenced rhythms complementing and contributing to Berry's own swing- and blues-inspired approach. By all accounts, however, what set the band apart from other black acts was their decision, driven by Berry, to begin featuring covers of popular country music songs in their sets. Berry explained the decision: "The music played most around St. Louis was country-western, which was usually called hillbilly music, and swing. Curiosity provoked me to lay a lot of country stuff on our predominantly black audience and some of the clubgoers started whispering, 'Who is that black hillbilly at the Cosmo?'"[88] As with so many of Berry's remarks, the tone here is somewhat disingenuous; what Berry describes as curiosity was more likely a calculated effort to push his music beyond the standard fare of the black clubs, with the hopes of attracting white patrons. Berry himself supports such an interpretation by stating that when playing hillbilly songs, "I stressed my diction so that it was harder and whiter. All in all it was my intention to hold both the black and white clientele by voicing the different kinds of songs in their customary tongues."[89] Sure enough, the ratio of white to black clubgoers at the Cosmo increased considerably during the early run of Berry and the Johnson band, and by 1955 the group's steady success led Berry to make a move toward a recording career by traveling to Chicago.

The image of Berry as a black hillbilly has exerted a powerful hold over those who have chronicled his career and his music. Writing in *Guitar Player,* Tom Wheeler perhaps best summed up this view, calling Berry the "flip side of the Presley coin, the black man who broke character, who was steeped in blues and swing and yet loved country and western."[90] Berry's performances at the Cosmopolitan certainly had novelty appeal, but they also confused whites who, only having heard his music over the radio or on the jukebox, had assumed that the singer and guitarist was white as well. Berry recounts one such episode in his autobiography, telling of a time he was booked to play a club in Knoxville, Tennessee, only to be turned away at the door when he showed up for the engagement. Upon producing his contract, Berry was met with the response that "It's a country dance and we had no idea that 'Maybellene' [Berry's first single for Chess] was recorded by a niggra man."[91] Berry's racial ventriloquism demonstrates just how intimate an association had developed between race and musical category in the expectations of many listeners.

Berry's black hillbilly music had its precedents, however, not only in the efforts of DeFord Bailey but more generally in the musical marketplace of the 1940s and 1950s. Most notable was King Records of Cincinnati, another of the independent record labels to have emerged in the postwar era. King was one of a small number of labels that focused equal amounts of attention upon both white country and black rhythm and blues, and further worked to promote a brand of crossover between the two musics by having a performer in one style record a song by a performer in the other who was also signed to the label. Henry Glover, an African-American musician who organized and supervised much of the recording activity at King, recalled:

> Sam Phillips has received great recognition because he did the novel thing of recording R&B with white country boys. He deserves credit . . . But the fact is that King Records was covering R&B with country singers almost from the beginning of my work with Syd Nathan [the company's founder] . . . We were more successful in doing the reverse—covering C&W hits with R&B singers . . . I'll confess that we didn't think we were doing anything remarkable. It's just that we had both types of artists, and when a song happened in one field, Syd Nathan wanted it moved into the other.
>
> You see it was a matter of Cincinnati's population. You couldn't sell Wynonie Harris to country folk, and black folk weren't buying Hank Penny. But black folk might buy Wynonie Harris doing a country tune.[92]

Berry's inclusion of country music elements in his music, then, was in some ways as much a culmination of existing trends as it was an innovation. He was performing these songs for white patrons, however, rather than following the more segregated policy outlined by Glover's comments.

"Maybellene," Berry's first Chess single, was a clear outgrowth of the country/blues hybrid the guitarist had been working toward in his performances at the Cosmo. According to Berry, the song was based on an old country song titled "Ida Red"; the initial title for Berry's song was "Ida May," but he changed it on the advice of Leonard Chess to avoid confusion with the earlier track.[93] Opening with a brief, distorted guitar figure, Berry and band jump into a steady 2/4 beat that had a markedly different bounce than other blues or rhythm and blues tracks released by Chess at the time. Over that beat, Berry rapidly laid out with his "hardened" diction the tale of a car chase in colorful detail:

> As I was motorvatin' over the hill
> I saw Maybellene in a Coupe de Ville . . .
> Cadillac doin' about ninety-five
> Bumper to bumper, rolling side to side.

Along with his display of verbal dexterity, Berry inserted into the song a crisply-played solo on his electric guitar, exploiting the raw tone with a series of blues-oriented bent notes syncopated against the rhythm, followed by a series of chord fills and double stops that demonstrate the guitarist's capable grasp of blues harmony. In all, "Maybellene" exemplified Berry's "mathematical" approach to music, as he described in an interview in 1971: "Music is so much mathematics, it's pathetic. Anything off-beat has to get back on the beat, or the whole thing is going to be out. So, with most of my music I keep the basics on 4/4 time, and *I* take the deviations."[94] The time of "Maybellene" may have been different, but it was no less regular, and Berry's solo showed him taking those "deviations" with characteristic aplomb.

Released in May 1955, "Maybellene" achieved almost immediate crossover success. As Philip Ennis points out in his study of the emergence of rock 'n' roll, Berry's song was one of only three released in 1955 to move into the top ten on all three major *Billboard* charts: pop, rhythm and blues, and country.[95] Following closely on the heels of Bo Diddley's earlier crossover success with his eponymous first single, "Maybellene" set a new course for Chess records. The company shifted its attention from developing local talent for success on the rhythm and blues charts to courting performers with potentially broader appeal, a path that left many of the company's established blues performers hanging in the balance. Having had three records in the top ten of the rhythm and blues charts in 1954, for instance, Muddy Waters would never have another song place so high on the charts. Jimmy Rogers, long an outspoken critic of Chess, charged that after Berry, the company more or less stopped promoting its blues performers with the same energy as it had before.[96] Not that Chess completely ceased to record the blues; Waters continued to record steadily throughout the 1950s, as did Howlin' Wolf, Sonny Boy Williamson (who came north to record for the label in 1955), and others. But the style of urban electric blues associated with Chess was largely submerged in the changing musical market of the mid- to late 1950s, and would have to wait until the next decade to find a new, enthusiastic (and largely white) audience.

Meanwhile, Berry would go on to achieve a level of stardom and public visibility that, among African-American musicians, had previously been reserved for jazz figures like Louis Armstrong and Duke Ellington. Featured in a number of films as well as on television—he was a regular presence on Dick Clark's *American Bandstand*—and appearing in music halls across the country in a series of rock 'n' roll "package tours," Berry not only promoted his own image but also that of the electric guitar. I have already discussed how the guitar figured into Berry's performing style. The visual centerpiece of his act, the electric guitar was also the musical centerpiece of Berry's songs. Cub Koda has rightly pointed out that Berry's guitar style is often understood in its most reductive manner, that his most famous riffs are taken to represent the whole of his sound. In fact, Berry's recordings reveal a mix of sounds and styles, including the occasional use of a pedal steel guitar and the incorporation of Latin-influenced melodies to supplement his more pronounced blues and swing tendencies.[97] The role of the electric guitar in Berry's music, however, is perhaps best understood not simply as a musical device or a visual prop, or some combination thereof, but as an aspect of the narratives that structured Berry's songs.

The storytelling qualities of Berry's lyrical style are often interpreted as part of his connection to country music, which tends to concentrate more on linear narrative than blues. Almost no attention has been paid to the ways in which Berry's music complemented these narratives, and indeed can be seen as having a narrative quality of its own. One might start with the simple observation that almost all of Berry's best-known recordings (the songs contained on the compilation *The Great Twenty-Eight*) begin with an unaccompanied electric guitar. Sometimes Berry merely strums a chord, as with the introduction to "Rock and Roll Music," but often the figures he used were more elaborate, as in "Roll Over Beethoven" and "Johnny B. Goode." In either case, Berry establishes the electric guitar as his lead instrument with this songwriting convention. The instrument organized Berry's songs through an alternation of chord-based rhythms, melodic fills between lines of the verses, and the regular inclusion of the guitar solo, usually somewhere in the middle or last third of the song. Moreover, given the preponderance of Berry lyrics that were devoted to rock 'n' roll music itself, the electric guitar was the embodiment of rock 'n' roll in his songs.

Of all Berry's songs, "Johnny B. Goode," recorded in 1957, perhaps best demonstrates how Berry effectively uses the electric guitar as a narrative device in his music and in rock 'n' roll more generally. The song opens with what has certainly become the archetypal Chuck Berry guitar lick, one of the most copied riffs in the recent history of popular music. A three-note lead-in moves to a series of quickly stroked double-stops[98] at the sixth fret of the first and second strings (the key of B♭), followed by a blues-based descending pattern that settles on another set of double-stops at the eighth fret of strings four and five (the same B♭ chord, but played two octaves lower). Another brief blues figure resolves on E♭ (the IV of the standard I-IV-V progression), at which point the band joins in while Berry continues to solo on his guitar for several more bars before beginning his vocal. The first verse establishes the story of Johnny B. Goode, a "country boy" from Louisiana "who never ever learned to read and write so well/but he could play that guitar just like a-ringing a bell." As Berry moves into the chorus, his shouts of "Go" to Johnny ("Go! Go Johnny Go!") are met at each turn with the sound of the electric guitar, with Berry standing in for the hero of his song. Real proof that the song dramatizes the force of the electric guitar as much as it dramatizes the rags-to-riches tale of the fictional Johnny comes during the solo section after the second verse and chorus. The band pauses while Berry plays variations on the opening theme, his characteristic double-stops met at the end of the first bar with a brief rhythmic surge by the band, which then falls back into silence, and then met at the end of the second bar with a propulsive set of accents that brings the full band back into the fold. Lafayette Leake's piano provides especially lively support for Berry's swift solo. The pattern repeats a second time, further rupturing the flow of the song and building the tension for yet another display of Berry's guitar playing, which in turn sets the stage for the final verse, in which Johnny's mother forecasts his ascent to stardom: "Maybe someday your name will be in lights/Saying 'Johnny B. Goode tonight.'"

*   *   *

In one of the few academic essays to consider Berry's music, Timothy Taylor discusses the three myths that pervade the lyrics of "Johnny B. Goode," myths indicative of "the choices and problems Berry faced in his career as an African-American musician in the 1950s and 60s."[99] These myths, distinct but closely connected in the song's narrative, are of genius (Johnny's natural talent), of the notion that such talent will prevail over adversity, and of assured financial success, or the distinctively American rags-to-riches story.[100] Setting these myths alongside the conflicts experienced by Berry during his career, Taylor notes that when originally composing the song, Berry had described Johnny as a "colored boy," only later changing the phrase to "country boy" to make it more accessible to white listeners.[101] In his autobiography, Berry continues his discussion of the song's meaning by further stressing the racial dimensions of the song's story of success, drawing the connection to his own success and the role that "Johnny B. Goode" played in it. Declaring his appreciation for the many people who have enjoyed his music, Berry states,

> I imagine most black people naturally realize but I feel safe in stating that NO white person can conceive the feeling of obtaining Caucasian respect in the wake of a world of dark denial, simply because it is impossible to view the dark side when faced with brilliance. "Johnny B. Goode" was created as all other things, and brought out of a modern dark age. With encouragement he chose to practice, shading himself along the roadside but seen by the brilliance of his guitar playing. Chances are you have talent. But will the name and the light come to you? No! You have to "Go!"[102]

Berry's observations blend a determined recognition of racism with an equally determined faith in the ability of talent combined with drive to overcome oppression and social indignity. That Berry acknowledged the ways in which racism shaped his success speaks to the complexity of his outlook. His own career has been interrupted by a series of arrests and criminal charges, suggesting that, however "acceptable" Berry might have become, he still remained a threatening presence as an upwardly mobile, intensely visible African-American male.

If Berry's career has not borne out the myths articulated in his most famous song, those myths have nonetheless continued to exert a strong influence upon American popular culture in general and rock 'n' roll in particular. And by no accident, the electric guitar figures prominently in the song's narrative of achievement, as it has in many careers in rock 'n' roll itself. In "Johnny B. Goode," Chuck Berry invests the electric guitar with considerable symbolic value, making it as much a signifier of the song's themes as Johnny himself. Not only do the hero's guitar-playing abilities figure as the source of his potential fame, but Berry's guitar playing itself propels the song forward and takes center stage for much of the performance. More than a showcase for Berry's instrumental skills, "Johnny B. Goode" constructed and popularized a myth about the electric guitar as an instrument of uncommon musical and financial value, a myth that resonates with all the racial and sexual ambivalence that resided within Berry's career.

Tracks

As it happens, "Johnny B. Goode" was also the first Chess release to feature overdubbed guitar tracks, and maybe the first such song recorded by an African-American guitarist.[103] The overdubbing was not nearly as involved as Les Paul's multi-track experiments—Berry recorded the guitar intro and his rhythm parts with the full band, and overdubbed his fills and the solo that takes up the middle of the song onto another track—but nonetheless represented a crucial innovation in the recording of music by black performers, who had previously been subject to the "one mike" theory of recording. Whether Berry was himself responsible for the decision to use multi-track techniques is an open question, but as I have noted earlier, the guitarist brought at least a basic familiarity with recording equipment into the studio for his first Chess session, and paid close attention to the recording process. Less than a year later Berry would overdub all the parts, including bass and drums, for the recording of his song, "Memphis."[104]

Berry's efforts support the notion that African-American as well as white guitarists used the electric guitar as a portal to a broader engagement with technologies of sound production and reproduction. In noting this parallel between the activities of white and black musicians, though, we also have to note the disparities. While Les Paul and Chet Atkins worked as producers of their own material, not only in the act of recording, but in the position they occupied within the record industry, African-American musicians were rarely if ever accorded such positions of control. Those who did oversee recording sessions, like Willie Dixon, have at times been cast as "company men" whose work was in the service of the whites who employed them. Meanwhile, Chuck Berry, for all his acquaintance with the technological means of (re)production, occupied a position at Chess roughly similar to that of Muddy Waters. Both musicians were, in their ways, privileged within the company, yet neither had ultimate control over the release of their music or over the distribution of profits that their music produced. Berry, with his greater education, was more equipped than Waters to watch over his financial relationship with the company, but even he was led to split the royalties for his first release, "Maybellene," with two men who had no part in the writing of the song, disk jockey Alan Freed and an unknown person named Russ Fratto who was likely a cover for Leonard Chess's attempt to get in on the publishing rights to the song.

Despite these constraints, Chess proved a fruitful site for the production of sounds that moved the electric guitar, and American popular music, in new directions. The Chess sound was created out of the alternately cooperative and conflicting relationships between the Chess brothers, especially Leonard, and the musicians who worked with the company. In this relationship, Chess did not simply record the sounds that musicians brought with them to the studio, but worked to actively shape those sounds, adding echo and other sonic effects and using microphones to get the right balance between instruments, a balance that was itself influenced by the musicians' use of amplification. By the same token, the sounds of the city that Chess promoted were not exclusively studio creations, but had many of their origins in the clubs around Chicago and other urban centers of black popular music. Chuck Berry forged his unique blend of country music with blues, swing, and R&B at the Cosmopolitan club in St. Louis, and Muddy Waters built the sound of his fully amplified blues ensemble at clubs like the 708 in Chicago years before that sound was committed to record. More generally, African-American guitarists in clubs and in the studio expanded the range of the electric guitar through their experiments with amplification. In the next decade, these sounds and methods would capture the imagination of a new generation of guitarists, mostly white, who were as much intrigued with the African-American sources of the new sounds as with the sounds themselves. Amid this new wave of electric guitar activity, though, it was another African-American musician who would push the use of amplification to its furthest extremes and, in so doing, would dramatically enact the complex interaction between sound, race, and sexuality that took shape around the electric guitar during the 1960s.

Chapter 5

Black Sound, Black Body

Jimi Hendrix, the Electric Guitar, and the Meanings of Blackness

A World of Sound

During the last year of his life, Jimi Hendrix opened a world of sound. Electric Lady, it was called, a state of the art thirty-two track recording studio where the guitarist could pursue all the sounds running through his head. And they were plentiful, those sounds, maybe too much for one guitarist to handle: "Most of the time I can't get it on the guitar, you know? Most of the time I'm just laying around day-dreaming and hearing all this music. And you can't, if you go to the guitar and try to play it, it spoils the whole thing, you know?—I just can't play guitar that well, to *get* all this music together."[1] Over the course of his brief career, recording studios assumed a special significance for Hendrix as the sites where he could enact his wildest fantasies of sound, and where he could work to exert the greatest amount of control over the sounds he produced with his guitar. By the accounts of his ex-bandmates, his attention to detail in the studio verged on obsessive, laboring for hours over a single effect, manipulating the various technologies at his disposal past their limits, exploring every parameter until he found the sound that was just right for the song, or the song that was just right for the sound.[2]

Electric Lady was Hendrix's effort to move his control over sound one step further, to actually own the means of musical (re)production. It was also his attempt to create a "total environment" in which physical design and visual appearance segued into the overarching purpose of making music. According to Curtis Knight, a musician and Hendrix biographer, Electric Lady was "designed to give an atmosphere of being in space," and featured "every electronic innovation that could be conceived."[3] Another biographer, David Henderson, provides a more detailed portrait of the setting: "The carpeted stairway led to an underground reception area that was shaped like a flying saucer. A low, round cubicled mini-office was encircled by a soft, low couch. Passageways led to the first studio and, curving around a bend, to the second. Curving passageways disappear in muted lights, spacey spectrum colors gave the effect of endlessness. A sound-buffered, upholstered, cozy underground lab."[4] Henderson goes on to point out that the construction of Electric Lady was testament to the willfulness of Hendrix, who saw the project through to its completion despite a range of hassles, financial and otherwise.[5] With the opening of the studio in 1970, Hendrix had achieved a degree of artistic control inaccessible to most African-American musicians of the time, including the many players who populated the Chess studios in Chicago. At the same time, though, this physical embodiment of Hendrix's desires was as much a product of the mounting pressures on the artist as it was a result of his musical vision. The sound-buffered underground laboratory of Electric Lady studios was also a sanctuary where Hendrix could escape the burdens of performing according to a set of expectations that he had helped to foster and yet had no ability to manage, expectations that came with the position of being a black hipster artist playing amid the predominantly white counterculture of the late 1960s.

> History arrives only when we don't know what has happened. Only when we forget. Only when people disagree on what has happened. That is why a theory of history must always come into being at the same time as history itself.
>
> —*Samuel Delany (1993), p. 494.*

> The Jimi Hendrix Experience happened fast, so fast that we didn't really know what was going on. As a result, Jimi-the-myth is hard to separate from James Marshall Hendrix/Jimmy James/Jimi Hendrix.
>
> —*Noel Redding (1996), p. 25.*

It might seem a bit perverse to begin a study of Jimi Hendrix, a musician widely remembered as one of the most compelling live performers in the recent history of popular music, with an evocation of his attachment to the recording studio. Setting aside quibbles about the problematic opposition between live and mediated performance in popular music, however,

I want to posit Electric Lady, and the recording studio more generally, as a crucial supplement to the more spectacular, better-documented dimensions of Hendrix's performing identity. If Hendrix on stage was a near-mythic presence who both drew upon and signified a complex history of racial representations, Hendrix in the studio was someone else, an almost insular figure who could lose himself in the seemingly endless sound possibilities afforded by electric technology. In neither case do we find a more authentic Hendrix, but rather in the sum of the two we find a story of the contradictions he embodied. The most public of African-American performers, he surrounded himself with a world of sound, which seemed more and more an attempt to escape the trap of his celebrity.

Certain truths about Hendrix have slipped beneath the surface of collective memory. In particular, I am concerned with Hendrix's relationship to blackness as a category of representation. When Jimi Hendrix stepped onstage or into a recording studio, when he sang and played his guitar in ways unlike any guitarist who preceded him, he put forth not simply a demonstration of his own talent but a particular conception of blackness embodied in his own person. What did this mean to his audience? What did it mean to him? And finally, what might it mean to us now?

To answer these questions, I will first consider the question of authenticity surrounding African-American music in general, and Hendrix's music in particular. Paul Gilroy has written astutely of the ways in which Hendrix's performance style and his peculiar brand of musical creativity exposed a conflict "between the contending definitions of authenticity which are appropriate to black cultural creation on its passage into international pop commodification."[6] Following Gilroy's observation, I will examine how Hendrix negotiated, through music, his status as a crossover artist, and how his creative strategies compared with the ideals of musical blackness constructed by African-American intellectuals during the 1960s, a time when such ideals were being voiced with new force. In the second half of this chapter, I will focus upon intersections of race and gender in Hendrix's public image and his performance style, with particular attention devoted to the guitarist's overtly phallic use of his instrument. The issue of crossover reappears in the analysis of how Hendrix used his body and his guitar in the framework of white perceptions surrounding African-American masculinity.

Both sections consider the relationships among music, race, and technology. Like his blues-playing forebears Muddy Waters and Buddy Guy, but perhaps to an even greater degree, Hendrix seemed to derive a significant amount of inspiration from the technological potential of his instrument. His musical innovations were largely predicated upon the new vocabulary of electronic sounds offered by the electric guitar. Moreover, in interviews he often enunciated the view that the music generated by such sounds might have the power to transcend racial and other differences. Indeed, there seems to have been a genuine mysticism underlying many of Hendrix's beliefs about electric technologies. In a 1969 interview with *Life* magazine, Hendrix stated:

> Atmospheres are going to come through music because music is a spiritual thing of its own . . . It's constantly moving all the time. It is the biggest thing electrifying the earth. Music and motion are all part of the race of man . . .
>
> I can explain everything better through music. You hypnotize people to where they go right back to their natural state which is pure positive—like in childhood when you got natural highs. And when you get people at that weakest point, you can preach into the subconscious what we want to say. That's why the name "electric church" flashes in and out.[7]

The concept of the "electric church" is one that appears consistently in interviews with Hendrix, and has occupied the attention of several of Hendrix's biographers and critics.[8] I prefer to leave the full implications of Hendrix's mysticism to others, while calling attention to his more basic, but no less essential, belief in the power of electronic sound.

Shades of Noise

> It's time for a new national anthem. America is divided into two definite divisions . . . The easy thing to cop out with is sayin' black and white. You can see a black person. But now to get down to the nitty-gritty, it's gettin' to be old and young—not the age, but the way of thinking. Old and new, actually . . . because there's so many even older people that took half their lives to reach a certain point that little kids understand now.
>
> —*Jimi Hendrix, quoted in Hall and Clark (1970), p. 25.*

"O say can you see . . ." Or rather can you hear that this version of the "Star-Spangled Banner" has no words. Only melody—coupled with some of the most jolting noise one could ever hope to hear, all produced by a single electric guitar. Jimi Hendrix performed the "Star-Spangled Banner" on several occasions, including one tempestuous evening at the Los Angeles Forum in 1969.[9] Amid a teeming crowd made angry by police harassment of those nearest the stage, Hendrix plinks the opening notes of the anthem, and then announces, "Here's a song we were all brainwashed with." The melody moves through once, then twice, the guitar still at a quiet volume that defuses the song of any grandeur. As Hendrix completes the second melodic couplet, he interjects a single word: "Bullshit." And then the sparks begin. "And the rockets' red glare"—volume up, distortion overwhelms the melody as the guitarist deforms the song through the radical use of his Stratocaster's tremolo bar, shifting between high-pitched screams and dive-bomber bursts of low-end crunch. The rest of the song continues at this pitch of volume and intensity, with notes descending into electronic feedback shrieks and another fit of cacophony after the penultimate line ("O'er the land of the free") that forestalls resolution and disrupts progress toward the closing "home of the brave."

Of course, Hendrix's most famous rendition of the national anthem came later that year during his performance at Woodstock, and the contrasts between the two versions of the song are notable. Whereas the L.A. Forum version was largely parodic of the song's intent, at Woodstock Hendrix played the "Star-Spangled Banner" with a greater recognition of the anthem's symbolic force.[10] Gone are the verbal interjections; the Woodstock version was strictly an instrumental statement. Hendrix's guitar enters here not quietly, but at full volume, thus investing the melody with considerably more weight than in the earlier performance. Consequently, when the guitarist pushes the song in the direction of electronic noise, as he does once again on "rockets' red glare," the effect is less of a departure from the original melody than an extension of it, albeit a severely disorienting extension. Moreover, the intrusions of noise play a much larger part in this rendition. Another immaculate sheet of sound follows the line, "the bombs bursting in air," with Hendrix crafting the sound of his guitar into all manner of permutations through a combination of physical and electronic effects, his hands striking the guitar at various points along the neck and body to achieve multiple shades of noise. Hendrix's use of feedback in the last lines of the song evokes the earlier performance, but again the sounds here seem to flow from the melody even as they disrupt it, so that by the time the guitarist converts the single note of "free" into a shrill bit of feedback that descends into a miasma of sound, one has the sense of having heard not just a rendition of the national anthem but a full-fledged reinvention of it, such that the original can never be heard quite the same way again.

When asked his opinion of D. W. Griffith's inflammatory film, *Birth of a Nation,* President Woodrow Wilson declared that the film was nothing less than "history written with lightning." The Woodstock version of the "Star-Spangled Banner" is also history written with lightning, but of a sort that neither Wilson nor Griffith could scarcely have imagined, an "Unbirth of a Nation" rooted not in the power of images but in mastery of sound. Charles Shaar Murray, the most astute of Hendrix's many critics and biographers, called the performance "probably the most complex and powerful work of American art to deal with the Vietnam war and its corrupting, distorting effect on successive generations of the American psyche."[11] Hendrix translated the fractiousness of the war at home and abroad and the damage it did to American patriotism into a war between music and noise that was at once a supreme act of defamiliarization and a stunning political critique. Meanwhile, Samuel Floyd offers another reading of the Woodstock "Banner," one that lays less emphasis upon the explicitly political dimensions of the performance, and instead highlights the extent to which Hendrix's musical approach remains embedded in the "core" practices of African-American culture. According to Floyd, Hendrix's juxtaposition of identifiable melody and sonoric excess stands as a classic example of call and response, with the guitarist "Signifyin(g)" upon the call of the original tune with responses that echo the methods of African callers and early bluesmen in their preoccupation with timbral distortion.[12] As the "Star-Spangled Banner" breaks with a particular tradition of nationalist sentiment, then, it retains strong connections to a distinct tradition of African and African-American musical performance.

Or does it? For Floyd's assertions regarding Hendrix are part of a broad and contentious discourse on the nature of black music, a debate that extends back several decades and that reached a crescendo in the years surrounding Hendrix's career. Within this discourse, Hendrix exists as a threshold figure who marks the point at which black music comes into contact with other forms, other traditions, and other audiences to the extent that it risks losing its status as a singularly or identifiably black phenomenon.[13] Considered from this perspective, Floyd's analysis of Hendrix and the "Star-Spangled Banner" works on at least two levels. First, it functions as a means of reclaiming Hendrix as a black performer, which in turn allows Floyd to assert the priority of African-American musical influences upon the rock music of the 1960s. Second, it revises received notions of black music and black culture in order to admit a greater recognition of the value of cultural exchange. There is much in this framework that I find convincing, and also much that seems to me sympathetic with Hendrix's own revisionist tendencies where African-American music was concerned. Before assenting to Floyd's interpretation of Hendrix and the black musical tradition, though, we would do well to examine the terms of the discourse on black music more closely in order to understand why it is such contested terrain. To do so, I want to look back to Hendrix's contemporaries, the adherents of the Black Aesthetic movement, whose efforts to define a separate black cultural identity continue to resonate within contemporary culture and politics.

*   *   *

Perhaps the fundamental recognition of the artists and intellectuals who made up the diverse constituency of the Black Aesthetic movement was that what we know as black music is no simple matter of sonority, just as black art more generally cannot be defined purely by reference to aesthetic codes any more than it can by reference to the color of an artist's skin. The Black Aesthetic was the cultural movement that paralleled the drive toward political autonomy expressed by Black Power. Adhering to the black aesthetic involved accepting the maxim "black is beautiful" as the first step toward breaking away from white European aesthetic standards that had so long associated blackness with ugliness, depravity, and evil. Aesthetics were transfigured into a battleground in which black and white artists struggled over control of the images that shaped the collective racial consciousness. Larry Neal offered a striking articulation of this sensibility in his essay on the Black Arts Movement.

> The motive behind the black aesthetic is the destruction of the white thing, the destruction of white ideas, and white ways of looking at the world. The new aesthetic is mostly predicated on an Ethics which asks the question:

whose vision of the world is finally more meaningful, ours or the white oppressors? What is truth? Or, more precisely, whose truth shall we express, that of the oppressed or of the oppressors? . . . It is clear that the question of human survival is at the core of contemporary experience. The Black artist must address himself to this reality in the strongest terms possible . . . The Black Arts Movement believes that your ethics and your aesthetics are one . . .

[The black aesthetic] comes to stand for the collective conscious and unconscious of Black America—the real impulse in back of the Black Power movement, which is the will toward self-determination and nationhood, a radical reordering of the nature and function of both art and the artist.[14]

Programmatic as Neal's assertions regarding the social and political function of art might seem, the Black Aesthetic movement as a whole did not simply seek to subordinate aesthetic imperatives to political ones. Rather, it sought to create a space in which the avant garde tendencies that were so pronounced in black art of the 1960s would become relevant to the African-American community at large. Nowhere was the tension between cultural avant-gardism and sociopolitical populism more pronounced than in the movement's attitude toward "Black Music" (the title of one of Amiri Baraka's key critical works during the period). As Don Lee put it in an essay on black poetry, "Those black artists that are active and hip would gladly agree, I'm sure, that black music is our most advanced form of black art."[15]

Black music was seen to be most advanced in large part because it was the mode of expression that had best weathered the middle passage, and had provided the basis for cultural survival in a setting where language, art, and other cultural forms had been severely repressed. Amiri Baraka's groundbreaking study of African-American music, *Blues People* (1963), cast a shadow over the subsequent florescence of black artistic and critical activity with its argument that the black experience in the United States could be best understood through music, and more specifically through blues and jazz, the quintessential African-American forms.

I cite the beginning of the blues as one beginning of American Negroes. Or, let me say, the reaction and subsequent relation of the Negro's experience in this country in *his* English is one beginning of the Negro's *conscious* appearance on the American scene . . . There were no formal stories about the Negro's existence in America passed down in any pure African tongue. The stories, myths, moral examples, etc., given in African were *about* Africa. When America became important enough to the African to be passed on, in those *formal* renditions, to the young, those renditions were in some kind of Afro-American language. And finally, when a man looked up in some anonymous field and shouted, "Oh, Ahm tired a dis mess/Oh, yes, Ahm so tired a dis mess," you can be sure he was an American.[16]

Baraka's argument in this passage is by no means uncomplicated in its association of the blues with blackness. His argument is very much rooted in social and historical experience; he understands the blues to have arisen out of the specific set of social relationships in which Africans found themselves upon their displacement to America rather than out of an essential black cultural identity. Nonetheless, his location of the origin of a specifically African-American consciousness in the rise of the blues placed black music at the center of the African-American historical experience in such a way that music became *the* constitutive element of black American cultural identity.

Complementing this sense of the historical significance of African-American music, both in Baraka's text and in the Black Aesthetic movement more generally, was a sense of the specific relevance of contemporary black musical forms, especially jazz. Since the late 1950s, Ornette Coleman and a small but significant cadre of other musicians had been striving to break down the formal barriers of jazz, to turn the music into a forum for unfettered collective improvisation in which individual artistic freedom would be at once enhanced and balanced by the group-oriented nature of musical performance. This innovative trend, which came to be called free jazz after Coleman's album of the same name, struck many African-American intellectuals as the height of a specifically black artistic impulse. It was a music that, as jazz, maintained its ties to history, but at the same time was very much of the moment, a product of the artist's response to the immediate conditions of his existence. Such a conception of free jazz led critic Ron Wellburn to assert that

The black musician is ahead of everyone in the expression of true black sensibility. For him, negritude or soul or blackness has never been a matter for soapbox articulation . . . More than any other kind of black artist, the musician creates his own and his people's soul essence, his own negritude. He can also do more damage to the oppressor's image of himself than heavily armed urban guerillas . . . Black musicians do not really *think about* the aesthetic; they simply project it. Soul is a manner of dancing, walking, speaking, interpreting life as we see and know it . . . We should all, then, re-establish ourselves as musicians: every black American can at least become a drummer or learn to play on a simple reed flute, just as every black person can dance.[17]

The competing strains of thought running through this passage—avant-gardism, populism, racial essentialism—combine to form a rather stunning manifesto on the place of music in African-American culture. For Wellburn, music was at once a vanguard product played by a highly select group of black male performers (in keeping with the gender bias of 1960s cultural nationalism) and a form of expression accessible to all black people. Blackness in this context took shape as a set of natural qualities held by all black people, a "soul essence" that bridged the gap between the artist's free jazz experiments and the experience of ordinary black Americans. Music for Wellburn provided the common language for a unified and undifferentiated African-American consciousness liberated from the "oppressor's image" of negative black identity.

The essentialism that undergirds Wellburn's analysis assumes an added dimension as he outlines in bold relief the contrast between jazz (black music) and rock (white music). In opposition to the vitality of jazz, he describes rock as a decadent musical form reflective of the "spiritual, creative, and sociological weaknesses of white America."[18] White rock fed like a vampire upon African-American musical forms, according to Wellburn, using black music to satiate "white American psychosexual illusions."[19] Moreover, Wellburn asserted that rock music reflected the subordination of spirituality to science and technology so characteristic of Euro-American culture:

White rock is a technology, not a real music. It is an affectation, not a felt experience. It is parasitic, not symbiotic, to black culture and lifestyles . . . Electronic music can make the black man blind from the sight of money and the white man rich on his deathbed, laughing absurdly at having fooled the niggers this last go-round. Black musicians should re-evaluate the technological intrusions now threatening our music; times may come when that technology will be useless. Our music is our key to survival.[20]

Wellburn's criticism concerning the exploitation of black music and musicians in a music industry run by whites certainly has more than a grain of truth to it. Yet truthfulness by any objective measure is not the issue. Wellburn, along with Baraka, Neal, and a host of other African-American artists and intellectuals, sought through the construction of a black aesthetic to create a myth of blackness that transcended social and historical specificity, that cut to the very soul of every black person. Within this movement, music was valorized because it possessed several qualities perceived to reflect the true meaning of blackness: orality, physicality, emotionalism, spirituality, and improvisation as a style of creativity that was derived not from rational calculation but from immediate lived experience. In black music, the past, present, and future of African-American life were perceived to intersect. It retained a connection to the past as it pointed the way toward the future.

* * *

Within such a conception of blackness, Jimi Hendrix would seem to have little place. Writing after Hendrix's death, Paul Carter Harrison made explicit the guitarist's separation from black modes of expression in terms similar to Wellburn. "Jimi Hendrix was a profoundly gifted blues guitarist," observed Harrison, who immediately qualified his praise of the guitarist by noting Hendrix's technological innovations, which he saw as "concessions to the American counter-culture mode . . . Those who listened attentively could hear the lingering intimations of traditional ethos," Harrison observed, "yet it could not penetrate the excessive electronic manipulations which obscured the subtlety of intonation which emanates from a black experience."[21] Like Wellburn, Harrison portrays technology as a threat to the purity of African-American cultural life. Hendrix, for his part, embraced those same sounds and technologies with his concept of the "electric church," envisioning not the assertion of difference but its transcendence through the overpowering influence of electronic sound. On a less grandiose level, Hendrix's decision to play rock music as opposed to a "blacker" style such as jazz, soul, or even straight electric blues clearly contradicted the presiding notions of musical authenticity held by adherents to the black aesthetic.

Hendrix's music, his performance style, and his career all force a reconsideration of the meaning of cultural tradition as defined within the Black Aesthetic movement. Samuel Floyd gestured toward such a shift in his analysis of Hendrix's "Star-Spangled Banner." Taking this line of analysis one step further, Paul Gilroy, considering "Black Atlantic" music, inquired, "How are we to think critically about artistic products and aesthetic codes which, though they may be traceable back to one distinct location, have been changed either by the passage of time or by their displacement, relocation, or dissemination through networks of communication and cultural exchange?"[22] Gilroy's question points not toward the complete deconstruction of cultural tradition, but toward the acknowledgment that it is subject to change, break, and rupture even as it retains traces of a distinct cultural or historical past. He further rejects the attempt to draw strict lines between "racial identity and racial non-identity" so characteristic of the work of African-American critics of the 1960s, preferring a notion of culture rooted in the recognition of hybridity rather a longing for racial or cultural purity.[23] His theorization of black culture is ultimately more useful for understanding the implications of Hendrix's aesthetic achievements.

Yet the Black Aesthetic movement remains crucial to my study on at least two levels. First, as a movement contemporaneous with Hendrix's career, it provides a cultural context for Hendrix's decision to play rock music, a decision linked to his refusal to describe his music in race-specific terms. Second, the impulse behind the black aesthetic toward strict racial definitions, an impulse that arose out of a sense of struggle against the hegemonic influence of whiteness, offers critical insight into what the stakes were and are in defining a racial image. What did it mean that Hendrix did not share this sense of struggle? What are the implications for claiming him as a symbol of the positive value of cultural hybridity when the positive value of an autonomous black, or African-American, culture remains largely unrecognized? The tensions between an essentializing cultural nationalism and an acknowledgment of the disruptive and discontinuous nature of racial and cultural identity will perhaps always remain unresolved. Figures like Hendrix, who refuse to contain themselves within a single cultural tradition, force us to reexamine the value of racial (and sexual and aesthetic) boundaries, and to understand what might be gained through their erasure as well as what might be lost.

*   *   *

Of course, to suggest that a single artist might have the power to effect such an erasure of differences would be absurd. It is quite another thing, however, to examine how an artist might envision this sort of erasure. Take, for instance, the following interview with Hendrix by Jay Ruby in 1968:

> *Hendrix:* You can have your own blues. It doesn't necessarily mean that folk blues is the only type of blues in the world. I heard some Irish folk songs that were so funky—the words were so together and the feel. That was a great scene. We have our own type of blues scene. We do this blues one on the last track of the LP (*Axis: Bold as Love*), on the first side. It's called "If Six Were Nine." That's what you call a great feeling of blues. We don't even try to give it a name. Everybody has some kind of blues to offer, you know.
>
> *Ruby:* What about the white/black scene. Is white blues really the blues?
>
> *Hendrix:* Well, I'll tell you. The Bloomfield band is really out of sight and you can feel what they're doing no matter what color the eyes or armpits might be. Because I can really feel it, I want it. I say, "O.K., they've got this white cat down in the Village playing harmonica, really funky." So we all go down to the Village and then, wow, he turned me on so much, I said, "Look at that." He was really deep into it and nobody could touch him there because he was in his own little scene. He was really so happy. I don't care like I said before, it all depends on how your ears are together and how your mind is and where your ears are.[24]

Blues, the expressive form said by Amiri Baraka to signify the origin of a distinctly African-American consciousness, for Hendrix had little to do with race; indeed, one might say his conception of blues had little to do with "the blues," strictly defined. Whereas for Baraka the blues emerged out of a specific set of social and historical relationships, out of the lived experience of African Americans, for Hendrix the blues seem almost to have a life of their own removed from any specific context (although the example of Ireland in the above passage is intriguing, perhaps a recognition by Hendrix of Irish people's status as the "niggers" of the British Isles). Hendrix's notion of the blues centered upon the degree of genuine emotional content; it was concerned less with where singers came from and more with their psychic and spiritual states. Thus could Irish folk songs be as funky and together as any "real" (read: black) folk blues.

Thus, moreover, could white musicians play the blues as authentically as blacks in Hendrix's perception. Hendrix's take on race is curious, not so much in his acknowledgment of the validity of white blues, but in the way he tries to all but discount the significance of race as a social factor. "No matter what color the eyes or armpits might be": Hendrix's language pokes fun at the notion that color might have anything to do with the quality of music, and in so doing casually elides the troubling issues of cultural appropriation and exploitation raised, however implicitly, by the interviewer's question concerning the authenticity of white blues.

Moving from these insights, I want to posit two hypotheses about Hendrix's attitude toward music and race, ideas that I do not plan to prove in any standard academic fashion but rather would like to assert as provisional truths according to which we might understand Hendrix's interpretation of the blues. First, Hendrix's understanding of race, at least insofar as it was expressed through his statements in interviews like the one above, cannot be separated from his understanding of music. Both musical and racial boundaries (which intersect in the division, say, between "real" blues and "white" blues, or between blues and rock) appeared to Hendrix to be similarly artificial constructs that served to limit the free play of the imagination as well as the ability of individuals to play freely with one another. Second, Hendrix's ideas about musical freedom (and by implication, racial freedom), the innovative impulse that underlay his music, cannot be understood apart from his exploitation of electronic technology.

That the electric guitar stood for Hendrix as the literal and symbolic instrument by which he could transgress musical and racial boundaries can be discerned from the guitarist's articulation, in a separate interview, of a "wish [that] they'd had electric guitars in cotton fields back in the good old days. A whole lot of things would have been straightened out."[25] Hendrix's strange wish may shed little light on the nature of slavery, but it says much about the great symbolic weight he invested in his favored instrument. The electric guitar was to exert a transformative effect upon the contemporary social landscape, and on a smaller scale, was to allow Hendrix to escape the restrictions normally imposed upon African-American performers within the music industry. Whether and to what extent he actually did escape those restrictions is still a matter for debate. I am convinced, though, that this was in large part what he sought to achieve, that he sought the freedom to experiment with musical ideas along with the power to reach a mass audience (a set of desires not so far removed from the avant-garde populism of the Black Aesthetic movement), twin desires that Hendrix articulated through his innovative use of the electric guitar.

*   *   *

Question [posed by Albert Goldman]: What is the difference between the old blues and the new?

Answer [by Hendrix]: Electricity.
—*Albert Goldman (1992), p. 87.*

Question and answer in the form of a riddle: Hendrix's answer mocks the notion that there is any significant difference between blues old and new. The music is the same, his one-word response seems to imply, it only sounds different. Yet as I stated earlier, for Hendrix and for 1960s rock in general, that sound had significant transformative power in itself. Discussing the experience of playing at "little funky clubs," for instance, Hendrix observed that "Everything is sweating. It seemed like the more it got sweaty, the funkier it got and the groovier. Everybody melted together, I guess! And the sound was kickin' 'em all in the chest. I dig that! Water and electricity!"[26] Here the physical atmosphere of the club blends with the physicality of the sound to create a realm of intense sensation that, in Hendrix's mind, worked to bring people together. This notion of the extreme materiality of amplified sound was also put forth by Frank Zappa in a 1968 essay on "the new rock," in which Zappa raised the following series of provocative questions:

Why does the sound of Eric Clapton's guitar give one girl a sensation which she describes as "Bone Conduction"? Would she still experience Bone Conduction if Eric, using the same extremely loud thick tone, played nothing but Hawaiian music? Which is more important: the timbre (color-texture) of a sound, the succession of intervals which make up the melody, the harmonic support (chords) which tells your ear "what the melody means" (Is it major or minor or neutral or what), the volume at which the sound is heard, the volume at which the sound is produced, the distance from source to ear, the density of the sound, the number of sounds per second or fraction thereof . . . and so on?[27]

5.1. Disfiguring virtuosity in action: Jimi Hendrix in performance at Woburn Abbey, tweaking the tremolo bar of his Fender Stratocaster. Courtesy of the Experience Music Project.

Zappa's questions remain unanswerable in the present context, but his emphasis upon the significance of sound, as well as its multidimensionality, points to the ways in which the sound of 1960s rock changed the experience of music as it changed the music itself. The "sound" became all-encompassing, and the experience of music became a jolting activity—the body a conductor of electric energy transmitted through amplified sound.

Can electricity be the basis of difference? It is a strange concept, and definitely leans too far to the side of technological determinism. Nonetheless, to understand Hendrix's simple answer to the question of the difference between the old blues and new is perhaps to understand at once how far he had come from the old blues and how much he remained rooted in its language. Hendrix's use of electronic sound significantly expanded the musical vocabulary of rock. Indeed, his array of bent, distorted notes teetering over the edge of tonality and feedback shrieks struggling to avoid the inevitability of sonic decay introduced sounds that had really never been heard before in any musical setting. In doing so, he took advantage of two key sets of technological innovations that came about during the 1960s. First, in amplifier design, a British drummer and music shop owner named Jim Marshall and his partner, electronic engineer Ken Bran, responded to the demand among young British guitarists for adequate amplification with an amplifier that was inspired by the popular Fender Bassman (favored by many electric blues performers), but made with some significant changes in electronic components. Marshall amplifiers soon set a new standard for rock guitar amplifiers, with greater gain and more output power than their American counterparts, as well as a tone rich in harmonic frequencies. Hendrix took to visiting the shop regularly during his tenure in London, and had Marshall design for him some custom amplifiers with added gain so that he could more readily reach his equipment's output limit and move into the distortion- and feedback-filled realm of the clipped signal.[28]

To further facilitate his use of an overdriven electric sound and his general desire to expand the sonoric range of his instrument, Hendrix also drew upon a range of sonic effect devices that began to appear during the 1960s. Often referred to colloquially as "stompboxes,"[29] these were small metal boxes containing transistor circuits that, when connected between the line that ran from guitar to amplifier, altered the electronic signal delivered to the amp, changing the sound. The most common such device was the distortion-inducing fuzzbox, a staple of Hendrix's sound. Also prominent were the Octavia (which generated octaves of the note being played at higher frequencies, to give added dimension to the sound) and the wah-wah pedal (named for the way it abruptly shifted the tone of the guitar from low to high, creating a "wah"-like quiver in the sound). For many of his effects, Hendrix turned to another British electronics specialist, Roger Mayer, who custom-designed effects boxes for many of the leading guitarists on the British scene. Mayer shared with Hendrix a fascination with the many faces of distortion and sound modification, and once described his work as "an exercise in knowing what to do wrong . . . Once you deviate from a perfect amplifier, which, in essence, does nothing except make the signal larger, you are doing something incorrect in terms of theory. Designing electronic sound devices . . . becomes an exercise in knowing exactly what to do wrong, because when you design a circuit and something is incorrect about it, there are an awful lot of complex changes that occur."[30] With Mayer's effects pedals in tow, Hendrix could more readily enact his own willful deviations from the norms of electronic sound design and capitalize upon the accidents made possible by amplification to push the sound of his guitar in new directions.

However innovative the *sound* of Hendrix's music may have been, its form typically stayed close to standard blues models. Moreover, the sounds themselves had their roots in the playing of earlier blues guitarists like Buddy Guy and Muddy Waters. Although he had more resources at his disposal, many of the effects that Hendrix sought to achieve, and that electronic engineers like Jim Marshall and Roger Mayer incorporated into their products, were extensions of the effects achieved a decade earlier by blues guitarists who were testing the limits of their own equipment. Thus did Hendrix recall in a 1968 interview that "the first guitarist I was aware of was Muddy Waters. I heard one of his old records when I was a little boy and it scared me to death, because I heard all of those sounds. Wow, what is that all about? It was great."[31] Hendrix himself sought to tap into a similar strain of musical expression, defamiliarizing standard song forms through the power of electric sound combined with his own disfiguring brand of virtuosity. With respect to Hendrix's interpretation of the blues, this combination of innovative style applied to traditional form was perhaps nowhere more apparent than in his recording of the song "Voodoo Child (Slight Return)," the final cut from his 1968 double album, *Electric Ladyland*.

"Voodoo Child (Slight Return)" was itself a revision of another track called "Voodoo Chile" that appeared on side one of the same album. The first "Voodoo Chile" is a long (about fifteen minutes) slow blues jam recorded "live" in the studio, which features guest musicians Stevie Winwood of Traffic on organ and Jack Casady of Jefferson Airplane on bass. Beginning with some spare vamping by Hendrix, who enters with the proclamation, "I'm a Voodoo Chile, Lord know I'm a Voodoo Chile," the song builds to a loping groove as the other band members join the guitarist. Hendrix's lyrics draw heavily upon the well-worn blues themes of masculine braggadocio framed by mysticism and black magic (the same combination of themes that made up many of Muddy Waters's best-known recordings), which he updates with his own obscure brand of psychedelia:

> Well I'll make love to you in your sleep
> And God knows you'll feel no pain
> 'Cause I'm a million miles away
> And at the same time I'm right here in your picture frame
> 'Cause I'm a Voodoo Chile
> Lord knows I'm a Voodoo Chile

Each line is punctuated by Hendrix's bluesy guitar fills, and with his final vocal assertion the music surges forth, building in volume and density while Hendrix launches into an extended solo that at times turns into a musical dialogue with Winwood's organ. The guitarist's playing stays rather close to blues conventions throughout, and the tone of his guitar, deep and fluid, blends with the other instruments as often as it sets itself apart.

In "Voodoo Child (Slight Return)," by contrast, Hendrix's guitar *is* the song; the accompaniment by drummer Mitch Mitchell and bassist Noel Redding, however frenetic, is all but submerged beneath the presence of the guitarist's electrifying performance. Once again, the song begins with Hendrix's lone guitar. However, whereas in the earlier piece the opening strains were loose and almost casual, here the introduction is highly rhythmic. At first there are no notes, only the sound of Hendrix picking at his muted strings, a sound altered by a wah-wah pedal, which he uses to alter the timbre and place rhythmic accents. After a brief melodic statement also inflected by the wah-wah, the bass and drums enter the song while Hendrix's guitar assumes a harsh distorted tone that slashes and burns its way through the other instruments.

The basic musical figure of "Voodoo Child (Slight Return)" is a rather simple assemblage of bent notes and a droning E note bass string (actually an E♭, as Hendrix tended to tune his guitar down half a step). Between virtually every repetition of the figure, Hendrix plays some high-pitched improvisatory variation that transfigures the basic structure into something very different. The lyrics are closely tied to the first version of the song, continuing the singer's exploration of surrealistic blues imagery.

Well I stand up next to a mountain
Chop it down with the edge of my hand
I pick up all the pieces and make an island
Might even raise a little sand.

Having once again declared his cosmic power, Hendrix plays a searing solo on the upper registers of his instrument, his guitar shrieking and crying like a witch burning at the stake. Long sustained notes melt into rapid runs that verge on chromaticism, while the sound of his guitar is electronically processed to shift in and out of earshot, composing a rhythmic alternation of sound and silence. The solo ends, the song quiets, and Hendrix sings a cryptic verse in which he bends the limits of space and time and envisions some sort of otherworldly reconciliation: "I won't see you no more in this world/I'll meet you in the next one—So don't be late." Another restatement of the chorus is followed by an apocalyptic guitar solo in which Hendrix's guitar emits sheets of sheer electronic noise, once again alternating between excess and virtual silence until, with a last fleet tremolo-bent trip across the fretboard, the song fades away to its end.

*   *   *

About the two versions of "Voodoo Chile," Charles Shaar Murray has written that Hendrix's identification as the Voodoo Chile functions as his statement of black identity: "a staking of claim to turf that no white bluesman . . . could even hope to explore, let alone annex. Whether Hendrix intended 'Voodoo Chile' as an explicit challenge to the hegemony of Western rationalism and black American Christian culture is ultimately not the point. That Hendrix was announcing, explicitly and unambiguously, who he thought he was, is."[32] Murray goes on to call Hendrix "the first and last of the space-age bluesmen" whose distinctly modern blues style posed a challenge that subsequent musicians have failed to meet.[33] According to Murray, Hendrix stretched the blues well beyond its limits while still retaining its spirit; he updated the tradition without entirely removing himself from its confines. Greg Tate, an African-American writer, offers a similar judgment of Hendrix in his description of the influence of Hendrix and other black rock innovators upon Miles Davis:

What Miles heard in the musics of P-Funk progenitors, James Brown, Jimi Hendrix, and Sly Stone, was the blues impulse transferred, masked, and retooled for the Space Age through a low-down act of *possession* . . . Where J. B. and especially Jimi and Sly took music isn't something that can be summed up in a few quotidian riffs any more than a Marquez novel can be experienced through synopses. It's at once a thought process, a textural language, and a way of reordering tradition and myth unto itself.[34]

Like Paul Gilroy, Murray and Tate are concerned with tradition not as a static entity but as a historical phenomenon subject to varying degrees of transformation. Both Murray and Tate locate in Hendrix the most radically revisionist of tendencies, and at the same time value him because even in his most innovative moments, Hendrix maintained a strong sense of musical roots. Perhaps Murray is right that the coupling of "Voodoo Chile" and "Voodoo Child (Slight Return)" stands as Hendrix's foremost articulation of blackness, that the songs stand as a sort of space-age blues in which the tradition gains strength even as it is denaturalized and tech-nologized. I want to suggest, however, that Hendrix's articulation of blackness in these songs can also be read as a disarticulation, that the savage guitar rites of "Voodoo Child (Slight Return)" disfigure the more conventional blues sounds of the earlier version to such an extent that blackness itself is left as an empty category. Hendrix may indeed be assert-ing his blackness, but only if he can live it according to his own rules; and blackness therefore becomes a matter of individuality rather than a social condition. Hendrix proclaims he is a "Voodoo Chile," and one can only wonder what these lines might have meant to his audience; for Hendrix, the space-age bluesman, played his innovations to a mass of star-gazing white children.

Bodily Sights/Bodily Sites

On June 18, 1967, at the Monterey Pop Festival, Jimi Hendrix enacted one of rock's most visceral moments with his performance of "Wild Thing." After playing the first half of the song relatively straight, the guitarist brings it to a prolonged, intense climax. "Wild Thing" descends into a fit of electronic noise as Hendrix turns away from the crowd to simulate intercourse with his guitar and amplifier, aggressively thrusting his hips at his "equipment." He then moves back toward the audience and, after straddling his guitar for a moment, retrieves a can of lighter fluid from the back of the stage, which he proceeds to "ejaculate" onto his instrument. And next comes a match—the guitar is on fire at the foot of the stage, and Hendrix, kneeling over it, flicks his tongue and motions with his hands to conjure the flames higher. Picking up the tortured, still-burning instrument, he smashes it to pieces, and proceeds to fling its scorched bits into the crowd before stomping off the stage, amplifiers still squealing with feedback.[35]

Add to this scene a still image of Hendrix in the most obviously phallic of poses: his body arched slightly backwards as he plays the guitar behind his back, the neck of his instrument protruding through his legs like a surrogate penis, surrounded by his large black fist. In such instances, which were by no means isolated within the context of Hendrix's career, he specifically and intentionally manipulated his guitar so that it took shape as a technological extension of his body, a "technophallus." The electric guitar as technophallus represents a fusion of man and machine, an electronic appendage that allowed Hendrix to display his instrumental and, more symbolically, his sexual prowess. Through the medium of the electric guitar, Hendrix was able to transcend human potential in both musical and sexual terms. The dimension of exaggerated phallic display was complemented by the array of new sonic possibilities offered by the instrument, possibilities he deployed with aggressive creativity. Hendrix's achievement therefore rested upon a combination of talent and technology in which the electric guitar allowed him to construct a superhuman persona founded upon the display of musical and sexual mastery.

Hendrix's overtly phallic style of performance was just as crucial to his rock persona as his sound. Yet to say that Hendrix's appeal was sexual as well as musical is only to begin to understand the meaning of his sexuality for his audience. The bodily gestures that constituted Hendrix's performance style, and the ways in which those gestures were perceived, can only be understood when judged within the broad set of cultural meanings and discourses surrounding black male sexuality. Hendrix's music cannot be considered as separate from his physicality: his style of virtuosity was itself highly phallocentric, and his combination of musical and bodily flamboyance was perceived by many of his white guitar-playing peers to offer a unique challenge to their own talent and, by implication,

5.2. The electric guitar as technophallus: Jimi Hendrix. Courtesy of the Michael Ochs Archive, Venice, California.

their masculinity. But did Hendrix's performance style pose a similar challenge to stereotypes of black male potency and hypersexuality? Or did it simply represent his success in tailoring a "caricature" to fit the "mythic standards" of his audience (as Robert Christgau suggested in his review of the Monterey Pop Festival)?[36]

*   *   *

Perhaps no one has addressed the troubled white perception of black male sexuality more forcefully or more poignantly than Frantz Fanon. In his book, *Black Skin, White Masks,* written over forty years ago, Fanon described the damaging effects of what he termed the "epidermalization" of blackness under colonial relationships of power.[37] Epidermalization refers to the reduction of blackness to a matter of surface, a bodily effect that produces a thoroughly negative consciousness in the black individual. When Fanon recounts his own experience of race, the sight of blackness becomes all-important as he learns to view himself through white eyes.

> "Look, a Negro!" It was an external stimulus that flicked over me as I passed by. I made a tight smile.
>
> "Look, a Negro!" It was true. It amused me.
>
> "Look, a Negro!" The circle was drawing a bit tighter. I made no secret of my amusement.
>
> "Mama, see the Negro! I'm frightened!" Frightened! Frightened! Now they were beginning to be afraid of me. I had made up my mind to laugh myself to tears, but laughter had become impossible.
>
> . . . Assailed at various points, the corporeal schema crumbled, its place taken by a racial epidermal schema . . . I discovered my blackness, my ethnic characteristics; and I was battered down by tom-toms, cannibalism, intellectual deficiency, fetishism (sic), racial defects, slave-ships, and above all else, above all: "Sho' good eatin'."[38]

This final lapse into dialect conveys the full degradation of colonial black identity. As Fanon details his personal recognition of difference, his body becomes a trap "drawn tight" around his subjectivity. The sight of his own blackness in the eyes of (an)Other reduces him to an epidermal projection of essential blackness. Tamed into submission by a child's fear, he is compelled to forsake his individuality, and to assume his place in the white colonial imagination.

Difference, for Fanon, is born out of white anxiety. For the colonial black subject, consciousness of difference arises out of the confrontation with whiteness. For whites, on the other hand, the black as Other is a constitutive element of personality. Fanon invokes Jacques Lacan to assert that "only for the white man The Other is perceived on the level of the body image, absolutely as the not-self—that is, the unidentifiable, the inassimilable. For the black man . . . historical and economic realities come into the picture."[39] The recognition of difference affirms white sovereignty, but also raises the threat that whiteness can never be wholly unified. Anxiety is born out of this desire for wholeness, which leads to the reification and fetishization of blackness as a mark of *absolute* difference. The white fear of difference is therefore simultaneously a fear that difference may not be complete, that blackness might bear some similarity to the white self.

More than a desire for wholeness is at issue for Fanon, however, in his discussion of the white personality. As blackness is experienced as a negative body-image for the white man, so the black man is correspondingly reduced in the white imagination to a purely biological being. Fanon portrays this disturbing brand of objectification in a fascinating passage that begins with the question, "Can the white man behave healthily toward the black man and can the black man behave healthily toward the white man? A pseudo-question, some will say," Fanon continues. "But when we assert that European culture has an *imago* of the Negro which is responsible for all the conflicts that may arise, we do not go beyond reality." Fanon goes on to quote French author Michel Cournot on the matter of the threat presented by the black man's body as it is imagined by white men. Cournot's remarks are worth quoting at length, as is Fanon's response, which combines visceral anger with critical insight.

"The black man's sword is a sword. When he has thrust it into your wife, she has really felt something. It is a revelation. In the chasm that it has left, your little toy is lost. Pump away until the room is awash with your sweat, you might as well just be singing. This is *good-by* . . . Four Negroes with their penises exposed would fill a cathedral. They would be unable to leave the building until their erections had subsided; and in such close quarters that would not be a simple matter . . ."

When one reads this passage a dozen times and lets oneself go—that is, when one abandons oneself to the movement of its images—one is no longer aware of the Negro but only of a penis. He *is* a penis . . . The white man is convinced that the Negro is a beast; if it is not the length of the penis, then it is the sexual potency that impresses him. Face to face with this man who is "different from himself," he needs to defend himself. In other words, to personify the Other. The Other will become the mainstay of his preoccupations and his desire.[40]

According to Fanon, then, black masculinity occurs in the white male imagination as a threat; the black man's penis becomes a "sword," a weapon of assault always poised to strike, and to sever white corporeality. Fanon, through the words of Cournot, here portrays racial anxiety to be a fear of being penetrated by difference, as the ultimate boundary between self and other, the body, becomes the potential site of attack. He further suggests that behind such fears lay equally potent desires. Fetishization of black male potency and hypersexuality show the extent to which the black man has become the "mainstay" of the white man's "preoccupations and desires." White men wish to possess such qualities themselves even though they have been taught to associate such bodily excess with "Other"-ness. The desire for the black man must be opaque, beyond easy recognition, so it is turned into fear or otherwise displaced, but the desire persists.

*   *   *

To begin to understand how this field of racialized desire affected the career of Jimi Hendrix, I turn again to Frank Zappa, rock 'n' roll pundit. In an essay that attempts to explain "The Jimi Hendrix Phenomenon" to the readers of *Life* magazine, Zappa describes Hendrix's sound as "very symbolic" with its "orgasmic grunts, tortured squeals, lascivious moans . . . and innumerable audial curiosities . . . delivered to the sense mechanisms of the audience at an extremely high decibel level."[41] Ultimately, though, the source of Hendrix's appeal lay elsewhere. Despite the intensity of his sound and manner of performance, suggests Zappa,

the female audience thinks of Hendrix as being beautiful (maybe just a little scary), but mainly very sexy. The male audience thinks of him as a phenomenal guitarist and singer . . .

The boys seem to enjoy the fact that their girl friends are turned on to Hendrix sexually; very few resent his appeal and show envy. They seem to give up and say: "He's got it, I ain't got it, I don't know if I'll ever get it . . . but if I do, I wanna be just like him, because he's really got it." They settle for vicarious participation and/or buy a Fender Stratocaster, an Arbiter Fuzz Face, a Vox Wah-Wah Pedal, and four Marshall amplifiers.[42]

Zappa creates a dichotomy between Hendrix's sexual appeal and his musical appeal: girls like him because he is sexy, and boys like him because he is a great musician. Yet as his description proceeds the categories begin to collapse. The boys actually "enjoy" the fact of their girlfriends' excited response to Hendrix, they acknowledge their own deficiency at the same time as they long to approximate Hendrix's unique blend of musical and sexual prowess. Hendrix becomes an object of desire for the boys as well as the girls, an object "maybe just a little scary" in his ability to cross over both race and gender lines in his appeal.

Zappa displaces the suggestion of homoeroticism only to tacitly readmit the possibility of white male desire for black male sexuality. Hendrix's appeal is not simply a product of his flamboyance, but is intrinsically tied to cultural perceptions of black masculinity, as articulated by Fanon. But Zappa's words, along with Cournot's, should also force us to deal with what is generally absent from Fanon's account: the problematic role of white women's sexuality in this scenario. (Black women are strikingly and distressingly absent from all accounts.) For Fanon the colonial relationship was at its root homosocial, being a relationship between men. Thus did he all but overlook the ways in which the white female body, as the primary object of white male desire, became the screen upon which were projected the various fears and desires associated with black masculinity. Zappa's description of the white male fascination with their girl friends' excited response to Hendrix echoes Cournot's line about the "black man's sword": "When he has thrust it into your wife, she has really felt something." In both instances the white man is reduced to a voyeur forced to recognize his own impotence—unless he is somehow able to possess the black man's tools, as Zappa's boys seek to do with their purchase of Hendrix-related merchandise. Commodification as castration? Perhaps. Just as significant, though, is the way in which white women's imagined sexual gratification is taken as the true measure of black male potency.

A photo essay from the same June 1968 issue of *Life* magazine that

5.3. Hendrix with fellow "Experience" bandmates, drummer Mitch Mitchell *(left)* and bassist Noel Redding *(right)*. Note the dueling afros of Hendrix and Redding. The look of the band played upon racial difference and similarity. Courtesy of the Experience Music Project.

contained Zappa's article further illustrates this point. The piece portrays "The flailing, wailing freakout of the Hendrix Experience" with a large photograph of Hendrix and his white bassist Noel Redding. The two are obviously caught in the act of performing. Redding, his afro as big as that of Hendrix, grimaces while his arm and bass are both blurs of motion. Hendrix strikes a similar pose, his guitar strapped securely across his body, his arm poised in the air as though he has just struck a massive flurry of notes and is now allowing the sound to play itself. Accompanying the image is a slyly suggestive text: "The Jimi Hendrix Experience is a fusion of shock, squealing static, earthy songs, erotic gestures. Hendrix . . . is an American Negro who plays with two white English sidemen (with him here is guitarist [sic] Noel Redding). The Experience is rock's miscegenation of black and white, of Beatles and soul, of taunting challenge and (next page)—response."[43] One turns the page to find that the "freakout" of the Hendrix Experience "whips flesh as well as soul"; and the flesh in question belongs to a young, blond white woman. The position of her body suggests that she is dancing: arms stretched into the air above her, head raised, hair tossed to one side, eyes closed as though she is in some sort of ecstatic trance, "whipped" by the monumental sound of Hendrix's music. Once again, it is the white woman's response that matters, her ecstasy that authenticates the power of Hendrix's "Experience."

These photos, like Zappa's descriptions, are largely played for fun. They are there primarily to amuse rather than to edify the reader. Yet the photo caption belies any notion of simple playfulness. Hendrix stands as a symbol of miscegenation, as the embodiment of desires at once threatening and titillating. Moreover, this implication of racial mixing is doubly signified in the images. While the text draws attention to the response of the white woman, the visual presence of white bassist Noel Redding provides further testimony to the supposed disruption of racial boundaries represented by Hendrix and his group. Indeed, Redding's physical similarity here is notable, making one wonder how accidental was the mistaken identification of him as a guitarist. Furthermore, Redding and Hendrix are positioned on the page as virtual mirror-images of one another, so that one need only flip the page in half to almost perfectly overlay one image onto the other. If we accept that the white female body serves as the mirror reflecting and displacing white male desire for black masculinity, we might add to this that the white male may himself mirror the black male (for Hendrix is certainly the controlling figure here), that he might incorporate onto his body the various artifacts (guitar, afro, style of dress, a set of bodily gestures) that outwardly signify the black man's own perceived prowess.

If this scenario has a ring of familiarity, which I hope it does, it is because I have tried to describe a situation that is essentially a form of minstrelsy. Gone, perhaps, is the blackface, but so many symbols of black masculinity, and specifically of Hendrix's masculinity, are visible on Redding's body that the process of literally "blacking up" is no longer necessary.[44] I would further suggest that this particular example is indicative of a much broader trend during the 1960s. Scores of white guitarists in the United States and Great Britain became infatuated with the blues, many of whom had only come into contact with black music through recordings, and they found in Hendrix a living model for their own attempt to transgress racial boundaries. Hendrix's presence on the white blues-rock scene had a double-edged effect: on the one hand he lent white musicians an air of legitimacy; on the other hand, he threatened their own claims to authenticity. The threat posed by Hendrix was both sexual and musical, and on each count took shape on the contested terrain where race and masculinity intersect.

*   *   *

Written accounts of Hendrix have ranged from the explicit reduction of Hendrix to his penis to grudging envy to enthusiastic praise for his bluesman heritage. The following four quotations express this range, reimagining what Hendrix's audience might have perceived when they watched him perform. The first, drawn from David Henderson's biography of Hendrix, *'Scuse Me While I Kiss the Sky,* recounts the guitarist's encounter with infamous groupies the Plaster Casters, a pair of young Chicago women who made plaster casts of rock star genitals. The story of Hendrix's meeting with the women has been told and retold in various books about him, and has thus acquired mythic status. The latter three quotes are drawn from three white blues guitarists: Eric Clapton, Michael Bloomfield, and John Hammond, who recount their impressions of watching Hendrix perform.

> We needed a ratio of 28:28 and found this barely sufficient. He has got just about the biggest rig [penis] I've ever seen! We needed to plunge him through the entire depth of the vase. In view of all these dodgy precedents, we got a BEAUTIFUL mold. He even kept his hard for the entire minute. He got stuck, however, for about fifteen minutes (his hair did) but he was an excellent sport—didn't panic . . . he actually enjoyed it and balled the impression after it had set. In fact, I believe the reason we couldn't get his rig out was that it wouldn't GET SOFT!
>
> —*From the diary of the Plaster Casters, quoted in Henderson (1983), pp. 180–181.*

> Everybody and his brother in England still sort of think that spades have big dicks. And Jimi came over and exploited that to the limit,

the fucking tee. Everybody fell for it. Shit. I fell for it. After a while I began to suspect it. Having gotten to know him, I found out that's not where he's at, not at all. The stuff he does onstage, when he does that he's testing his audience. He'll do a lot of things, like fool around with his tongue and play his guitar behind his back and rub it up and down his crotch. And he'll look at the audience, and if they're digging it, he won't like the audience . . . If they don't like dig it, he'll play straight 'cause he knows he has to.

—*Eric Clapton, quoted in Fong-Torres (1981), p. 28.*

You couldn't even tell what Hendrix was doing with his body. He moved with all those tricks that black guitarists had been using since T-Bone Walker and Guitar Slim—playing behind his head and with his teeth. He took exhibitionism to a new degree. He used to crash his guitar against his hip. It was a bold gesture, and he would get a roaring, fuzzy, feedback sound. His body motion was so integrated with his playing that you couldn't tell where one started and the other left off.

—*Michael Bloomfield (1975), pp. 56–57.*

[Hendrix] was playing a Fender Stratocaster upside down and left-handed—one of those things that just boggles your mind. I just could not believe it—playing with his teeth, and doing all those really slick techniques that I had seen in Chicago on the south side on wild nights. But here was this guy doing it, and he was fantastic playing blues. He really dug me, and I really dug him.

—*John Paul Hammond (1975), p. 20.*

For Hammond and Bloomfield, Hendrix was a real bluesman whose set of techniques—musical as well as bodily—evoked the history of black music, or the atmosphere of South Side Chicago. Michael Bloomfield went on in the same interview to assert that "Jimi was the blackest guitarist I ever heard. His music was deeply rooted in pre-blues, the oldest musical forms, like field hollers and gospel melodies. From what I can garner, there was no form of black music that he hadn't listened to or studied, but he especially loved the real old black music forms, and they just pored out of his playing."[45] This remark becomes all the more striking when one considers how far removed it seems from the notions of blackness put forth by the Black Aesthetic movement. Whereas Hendrix went against the grain of musical authenticity as it was conceived by advocates of 1960s-era cultural nationalism, to Bloomfield, himself something of a fetishist on issues of musical purity, he is the "blackest" of musicians.

How can one account for such a disparity of perception? Perhaps by recognizing that Bloomfield, and other white musicians like him, themselves had something at stake in claiming Hendrix's blackness, maybe even more at stake in some ways than Hendrix himself. Acknowledgment of Hendrix's authenticity can also be read as a strategy of self-authentication, a point borne out by the closing line of Hammond's statement: "He really dug me, and I really dug him." Hammond was a regular performer in the Greenwich Village clubs where Hendrix was "discovered," and at one point even employed Hendrix as his guitarist. As he reminisced about Hendrix in *Guitar Player* magazine, Hammond pushed this strategy to almost absurd limits. Describing his first meeting with Hendrix, Hammond recalled:

> He knew me and had my albums, and he was just knocked out that I was there. See, I had all these Muddy Waters and Howlin' Wolf tunes on the *So Many Roads* album, and he had gotten them from my record—at least, this is what he told me. He was hanging out in the Village where I was very popular at that time, and he had been turned on to my album, and he went from there. I'm sure as he got more and more well known, I became less important to his reality, and he had to say, "Oh, I got this thing from Muddy Waters and Howlin' Wolf" which I can understand. But Robbie Robertson's guitar playing on that album is what really inspired him.[46]

Hammond rather remarkably constructs a history of Hendrix's musical life centered around himself. For just a moment he expresses a well-founded doubt about this scenario—"at least, this is what he told me"—but this doubt quickly recedes, and he is left suggesting that Hendrix really did not understand the blues until he moved to the Village and learned about it from white bluesmen like Hammond. There is some truth to the observation that the bohemian setting of the Village gave Hendrix a sense of artistic freedom he had not experienced earlier in his career.[47] Yet Hammond's narrative has much broader implications that ultimately have far less to do with the facts of Hendrix's biography—which do not bear out Hammond's story—than with the ways in which he was viewed by the white musicians who were at once his audience and his peers.

Eric Clapton takes us a bit deeper into the problem of Hendrix's reception. Here is a response, not to the actual sight of Hendrix's penis, but to the sight of his performance, which according to Clapton was overshadowed in the minds of the British public by the idea of his penis. Ample evidence for such an assessment can be found in the depiction of Hendrix among the British press, where, as Charles Shaar Murray recounts, "the national daily tabloids treated him like a freakshow, dubbed him the 'Wild Man of Pop,' and generally trotted out the would-you-let-your-sister-marry-this-man ritual greeting with which new pop phenomena have traditionally been welcomed since the invention of Elvis Presley in the fifties."[48] The mainstream American press was also no harbinger of moderation in its response to Hendrix. Along with the aforementioned responses from *Life* magazine (the photo essay and article by Zappa), there was *Newsweek*'s description of the Hendrix Experience as a "nasty looking trio with its triptych of smirking simian faces;"[49] another *Life* article that made reference to "the Helenic [sic] sculpture of [Hendrix's] trousers;"[50] and, most colorfully, a *Time* magazine review that recounted how Hendrix "slung the guitar low over swiveling hips, or raised it to pick the strings with his teeth; he thrust it between his legs and did a bump and grind, crooning: 'Oh, baby, come on now, sock it to me!' Lest anybody miss his message, he looked at a girl in the front row, cried, 'I want you, you, you!' and stuck his tongue out at her."[51]

Clapton's remark concerning how Hendrix played to the public's idea that "spades have big dicks" is well-documented by such reactions from the popular press. However, his comments push in other, more ambivalent directions. Clapton's suspicions and revelations about the extent to which Hendrix was "putting on" his audience tapped into a broad discourse among 1960s musicians and critics concerning the relative value of putting on a show. For Clapton, Hendrix's way of catering to certain racial stereotypes was part of the guitarist's extreme flamboyance and physicality, which distracted audiences from his exceptional musicianship.[52]

Whether such demonstrative behavior added to or detracted from the value of a given performance was one of the great unsettled issues of the

1960s rock subculture. Those like Clapton who were concerned above all with maintaining a certain authenticity felt that the showiness of a figure like Hendrix rubbed against the grain of a good performance. Others were less sanguine in their judgments. Michael Rosenbaum, for instance, put the matter in some perspective in an article in 1968, "Jimi Hendrix and Live Things." He deciphered two sorts of act styles among 1960s rock performers: the "internal," which involved "spontaneous emotional movement by a performer or group"; and the "external," which was essentially "theater set apart from the music."[53] Rosenbaum perceived Hendrix to embody a fusion of these different styles, but also noted the tendency of many in the rock audience to get upset by the "external" mode, to which the writer offered the counter, "You are what you pretend to be . . . it's sometimes hard to decide if something is natural or not."[54]

Both Clapton and Rosenbaum viewed Hendrix as acting unnaturally, although they drew different conclusions from their perceptions. Many others in the blues-centered counterculture of the 1960s saw no pretense in Hendrix's performing style at all, however. Recall, once again, the impressions of Hammond and Bloomfield: though neither described Hendrix in especially phallic terms, both highlighted the role of the guitarist's bodily gestures in conveying what they perceived to be Hendrix's authenticity. For Bloomfield in particular, Hendrix's sound was inseparable from his body. Considering the highly coded nature of the black male body, Bloomfield's observations carry far more weight than (I assume) he intended.

Michael Bloomfield also gave voice to the sense that Hendrix's presence posed a challenge, if not an outright threat, to the legitimacy of the white male guitarists who were so caught up in playing the blues. For a time in the mid-1960s, Bloomfield was considered to be *the* hot young American blues guitarist, a figure who had absorbed the lessons of black Chicago blues and successfully moved them into a new expressive context. According to Bloomfield, all of that changed when he came upon Hendrix performing at Greenwich Village's Cafe Wha? in 1966.

The first time I saw Jimi play he was Jimmy James with the Blue Flames. I was performing with Paul Butterfield, and I was the hot shot guitarist on the block—I thought I was *it.* . . . Hendrix knew who I was, and that day, in front of my eyes, he burned me to death. I didn't even get my guitar out.

H bombs were going off, guided missiles were flying—I can't tell you the sounds he was getting out of his instrument. He was getting every sound I was ever to hear him get right there in that room with a Stratocaster, a Twin (amplifier), a Maestro fuzz tone, and that was all—he was doing it mainly through extreme volume. How he did this, I wish I understood. He just got right up in my face with that axe, and I didn't even want to pick up a guitar for the next year.[55]

Bloomfield, himself a talented guitarist, was almost shamed by his own claims to virtuosity after seeing and hearing Hendrix perform. He was awed by Hendrix's talent, and by the amazing array of sounds Hendrix produced. Perhaps he responded as much to what he perceived to be Hendrix's overwhelming blackness and masculinity as he did to his music. Whatever Bloomfield may have felt, his story gives evidence of the way in which the electric guitar became both the instrument and the symbol for a highly gendered and racialized form of virtuosity in which the individual player asserted his masculinity as he demonstrated his talent. As a white bluesman who had strong ideas about both musical and racial authenticity, Bloomfield could not conceive of matching Hendrix's "in your face" performance.

Bloomfield's feelings of humiliation were echoed by Pete Townshend, guitarist for yet another British blues/R&B influenced band, The Who. Indeed, it is in Townshend's story that the convergence of Hendrix's musical and sexual effects gain their clearest articulation. In a 1989 interview with *Guitar Player* magazine, Townshend recounted his earliest experiences with Hendrix, when he and his friend Eric Clapton would go to see the guitarist perform.

I suppose like a lot of people, like Eric, for a while there I think we gave up [after having first seen Hendrix play], and then we started again and realized . . . it was very strange for Eric and me. We went and watched Jimi at about 10 London shows together, and he [Clapton] wasn't with a girl at the time, so it was just me, my wife-to-be Karen, and Eric, going to see this monstrous man. It got to the point where Eric would go up to pay his respects every night, and one day I got up to pay my respects, and he was hugging Eric, but not me—he was kind of giving me a limp handshake—just because Eric was capable of making the right kind of approach to him. It was a difficult time. You have to remember the other thing about him, that he was astonishingly sexual, and I was there with my *wife,* you know, the girl I loved. And you could just sense this whole thing in the room where every woman would just [claps] at a snap of a finger.[56]

Townshend's story describes something very different from mere musical humility. For Townshend, Hendrix was a "monstrous" man whose presence threatened the integrity of his relationship with "the woman he loved." Townshend's anxieties hinge upon the possibility that his wife may be violated, or maybe even worse, that she might simply succumb to Hendrix's overpowering sexual aura. Either way, Townshend feels as though he has suffered a blow to his masculinity (note the "limp handshake" offered by Hendrix), a blow that is built out of a combined sense of musical and sexual inadequacy.

Despite this perceived sexual threat, or perhaps even because of it, Townshend, like the other musicians cited, remained fascinated with Hendrix. He, too, could not escape the perception that Hendrix, as a black performer, was true to the music in a way that neither he nor any of his white counterparts could ever be:

> [Hendrix had] been in the black milieu as the sideman for this musician and that musician and this was his chance to not only draw himself out of the mire of mediocrity but also to do something for the black cause . . . there was a tremendous sense of him choosing to play in the white arena, that he was coming along and saying, "You've taken this, Eric Clapton, and Mr. Townshend, you think you're a showman. This is how *we* do it. This is how we can do it when we take back what you've borrowed, if not stolen. I've put it back together and *this* is what it's all about, and you can't live without it, can you." And the terrible truth is that we *couldn't* live without it. There was a real *vengeance* that we *couldn't* live without.[57]

Townshend gives dramatic expression to the sense in which Hendrix's decision to play rock was perceived as a deliberate act of reappropriation, a vengeful attempt to beat the white guitarists by reasserting African-American ownership of the symbols from which rock performers drew their power. Even more telling, though, is Townshend's suggestion that he and his peers "couldn't live without" what Hendrix had to offer, that they needed his enactment of blackness not simply to justify their endeavors but to remind themselves of what they lacked. Townshend thus forcefully articulates a version of Fanon's insights concerning the constitutive role of black masculinity within the construction of white manhood, a relationship that was central to the rock counterculture of the 1960s. White rock musicians in particular sought to replicate a certain style of blackness that bolstered their masculinity while it shaped their musicianship. Hendrix's move to join their ranks, in turn, gave them a figure onto whom they projected received notions of racial and musical authenticity. In the words of Hendrix biographers Caesar Glebbeek and Harry Shapiro, then, "Jimi Hendrix was treated as superhuman and subhuman, but rarely just human."[58]

* * *

While the preceding analysis says much about how Hendrix was perceived by others, it offers only the vaguest of clues as to how Hendrix understood himself. Although all answers to such a question are hypothetical, the effect he had upon his audience was surely at least partly intentional. Certainly, Hendrix specifically and intentionally manipulated his guitar to create an air of phallic potency. In interviews, he tended to characterize his more flamboyant gestures, such as burning his guitar, as a simple and natural outgrowth of the musical moment: "We just get excited by the music, and carried away."[59] Such a casual attitude is belied, though, by his stylized movements on stage. Perhaps he experienced each performance as a unique, spontaneous act, but the repetition of gestures over time suggests a more conscious and more complicated process. Hendrix's body language fills the silence left by his words.

Of course, Hendrix's bodily motions were never a thing unto themselves, but were always tied to musical effects. With this confluence of the musical and the bodily, Hendrix enacted a rather sophisticated version of what Henry Louis Gates has called "Signifyin(g)." Focusing upon African-American literature, Gates suggests that "whereas black writers most certainly revise texts in the Western tradition, they often seek to do so 'authentically,' with a black difference, a compelling sense of difference based on the black vernacular."[60] According to Gates, black writers construct their difference by "Signifyin(g)" upon both white and black texts. As opposed to white ways of signifying, of representing an object or idea through signs, "Signifyin(g)" within the African-American tradition is based upon a constant play of signs that focuses attention upon the sound of a text rather than its literal meaning.[61] Literary "Signifyin(g)" employs principles of repetition and difference, which Gates links to jazz improvisation: preexisting texts (novels or songs) serve as the starting point for the artist (writer or musician) to display his own mastery of language by interrupting or transforming the original source through the devices of his own creativity.[62] The practice of "Signifyin(g)" as defined by Gates therefore stands as a crucial strategy by which African-American artists can challenge culturally dominant aesthetic forms at the same time as they might choose to participate in dominant modes of artistic production.

Whether Hendrix ever did anything authentically is, of course, highly questionable, as is Gates's own move to authenticate certain elements of African-American expressivity. Nonetheless, there is much in his framework that can help us to understand Hendrix's achievements. As a crossover artist who opted to play in a predominantly white medium, Hendrix carved a distinct space for himself through a combination of bodily flamboyance and musical innovation. His "Signifyin(g)" gesture was thus twofold. With his body, he "Signified" upon the preexisting text of black male potency and hypersexuality, and with his music, he "Signified" upon the various traditions that contributed to his own style.

One can see these processes at work in Hendrix's performance of "Wild Thing" at the Monterey Pop Festival. He disfigures and defamiliarizes a song his audience would have recognized through his use of excessive feedback. Even more striking, though, is the bodily dimension of his performance, and particularly his final sacrificial act, when he destroys the very symbol of his own prowess, perhaps only to further assert that he has nothing left to prove. Hendrix's act was nothing if not contradictory, but I think it is a mistake to say that he was simply playing to the expectations of his audience. He was also playing upon those expectations, using preexisting material to demonstrate his own creativity and virtuosity.

Hendrix's performance of "Johnny B. Goode," taken from a 1969 show at the Berkeley Community Theater, is another example of his "Signifyin(g)" style, in which both the sound and the image of the electric guitar disrupt one of the founding songs of rock 'n' roll. Musically, Hendrix repeats Chuck Berry's original melody, but also transforms it through distortion and sheer volume. Meanwhile, the song's guitar solos show Hendrix employing extended feedback wails and rapid blues lines that virtually abandon the structure of Berry's performance, moving the song into a realm of electronic effects and flamboyant virtuosity that would have been all but impossible to produce ten years earlier. Such musical exhibitionism is complemented by the physical aspects of the performance, in which Hendrix plays the guitar with his teeth and, at one point, swings himself around 180 degrees with his guitar at crotch level while holding a sustained, distorted note, his face grimacing, his guitar protruding like an oversized phallus ejaculating sound onto the audience. That the song was itself originally written and performed by an African-American is not incidental. Rather, his choice of text, combined with the fact of his own blackness, show Hendrix refiguring the rock tradition in the face of its increasing whiteness during the 1960s.

Some have chosen, as I have, to locate some liberatory or deconstructive potential in Hendrix's "Signifyin(g)" style. Hendrix himself, though, ultimately came to feel somewhat trapped in his own definition of blackness. He came to realize, gradually, that it was in many ways a role already defined for him. Toward the latter part of his brief career, he began to deemphasize the bodily dimension of his style and portray himself as a musician first, not a performer:

> As long as people come to listen rather than to see us, then everything will be all right. It's when they come to expect to see you doing certain things on stage that you can get hung up.[63]

> [T]he main thing that used to bug me was that people wanted too many visual things from me.
> I never wanted it to be so much of a visual thing. When I didn't do it, people thought I was being moody, but I can only freak when I really feel like doing so. I can't do it just for the sake of it. I wanted the music to get across, so that people could just sit back and close their eyes, and know exactly what was going on, without caring a damn what we were doing while we were on stage.[64]

For Hendrix, as for Fanon, the sight of blackness in the eyes of others had become oppressive, and so he expresses a desire to heard, not seen; listened to, not watched. The most "visible" of black performers, he yearns for a sort of invisibility. He wants to remove himself from the demands of his public into a realm of pure music where both he and his audience can lose themselves in the power of sound.

Utopia Unfulfilled

> Almost anyone who has the power to keep their minds open listens to our music. Black kids think the music is white now, which it isn't.

The argument is not between black and white now. That's just another game the establishment set up to turn us against one another. But the black kids don't have a chance too much to listen—they're too busy trying to get their own selves together. We want them to realize that our music is just as spiritual as going to church.

—*Jimi Hendrix, quoted in Henderson (1983), p. 206.*

Somewhere amidst the words and the music of Hendrix lies a vision of utopia, an imagined transformation of the world into an "electric church" where all differences would submerge beneath a wave of electronic sound. Somewhere, but not here; someday, but not today: as much as Hendrix might have wanted the black kids to realize the spiritual potential of music, he realized that utopia was far from an achieved state, and that blackness stood to separate people from one another. He was continually striving to push against the boundaries of both music and race, boundaries that were inextricably tied within his outlook. Yet through this process he was also perhaps forced to recognize that certain boundaries can be intransigent, that to imagine alternative realities is not to bring them into being. A tragic lesson, as one can only imagine, for someone who seemed to live through his music. Tragic, but maybe necessary: Had Hendrix lived, would he have moved his art to a whole other level of commitment? This we can never know, but we can continue to draw our own lessons from Hendrix, to keep our own imaginations alive, and realize that to do so can never be enough.

Chapter 6

Kick Out the Jams!

The MC5 and the Politics of Noise

A Riotous Noise

In early 1968, that most momentous of years according to chroniclers of
the 1960s, the MC5 released their second single, "Looking at You," a
mutinous creation said by Chuck Eddy to have been recorded in downtown Detroit "sometime circa the [1967] riots or World Series."[1] Eddy's
comment concerning the circumstances of the song's creation is probably
a half-truth at best, but says much about the myth surrounding the MC5,
in which the band were a group of "rock 'n' roll guerrillas" who both
fomented and embodied disorder with their rousing performances. Moreover, Eddy's association of the song with the riotous Detroit cityscape
speaks to the unrest conveyed by "Looking at You," unrest present in so
much of the band's music. The track tumbles forth like a bull released
from its pen, the bass and drums rolling atop one another while the
guitars issue forth a screeching chaos that threatens to engulf Rob Tyner,
the singer. John Sinclair, long-time manager of the band and producer of
the single, offers a more hands-on account of its recording:

> It was really a non-existent production job, since I "produced" it and didn't
> have any idea of what I was doing. I just knew that the music was killer and
> that we had to get it down, but I didn't know the first thing about mixing,
> and consequently the record was never really mixed, it was just released
> unmixed. I wanted to make sure that all the high sound got in there because
> I had noticed that when records were played on the radio the high sounds
> dropped out, and I loaded them on to *Looking at You* to the point that the
> record was worthless for standard record-player playing.[2]

Thus was the feedback-laden sound put on tape, unmixed and, in Sinclair's description, thoroughly unlike any standard musical product. "Looking at You" was designed not to be a hit, but to let the people of Detroit know "that the band really existed," to attract people to their live gigs at the Grande Ballroom and cultivate a following. Over the subsequent months they accomplished their goal, becoming the main attraction in a burgeoning Detroit/Ann Arbor rock 'n' roll scene. Also during this time, the Five became the musical arm of Sinclair's radical White Panther party, and were the only rock band to perform at the Yippie-organized Festival of Life held during the week of confrontation at the Chicago Democratic Convention in 1968. Norman Mailer was among those who witnessed this performance:

> [A] young white singer with a cherubic face, perhaps eighteen, maybe twenty-eight, his hair in one huge puff ball teased out six to nine inches from his head, was taking off on an interplanetary, then galactic, flight of song, halfway between the space music of Sun Ra and "The Flight of the Bumblebee," the singer's head shaking at the climb like the blur of a buzzing fly, his sound an electric caterwauling of power come out of the wall . . . and the singer not bending it, but whirling it, burning it, flashing it down some arc of consciousness, the sound screaming up to a climax of vibrations like one rocket blasting out of itself . . . it was the roar of the beast in all nihilism, electric bass and drum driving behind out of their own non-stop to the end of mind.[3]

To the end of mind, and the beginning of—what? Mailer could not see beyond the sound, so to speak. He was enveloped by electronic vibrations, at once stimulating and distressing, that heralded the destruction of an old order but offered no discernible substance to put in its place.

For better or worse, this sound was to become the basis of the MC5's politics, which were primarily a politics of affect. The stated goal was to turn the momentary synesthetic pleasures of musical experience into the basis for cultural revolution. These pleasures were the subject of many of the Five's best songs, such as "Looking at You," in which the singer exults in "feeling happy having a good time" at a rock 'n' roll show, whereupon he is struck by desire:

> Danced out into the dancing crowd
> Felt like screaming out loud

I saw you standing there
I saw your long—saw your long hair.

Such lyrics no doubt bear witness to Dave Marsh's claim that the Five's politics had far more to do with pleasure, in the sense of immediate gratification, than with transforming modes of production (and one might add, had more to do with heterosexual male pleasure in particular than with other forms).[4] Yet Marsh, a noted rock journalist and Michigan native who attended many a gig by the MC5, has also attested to the resounding sense of possibility that arose from his experiences with the band.

> So powerfully did the MC5's music unite its listeners that leaving those 1968 and 1969 shows, one literally felt that anything, even that implausible set of White Panther slogans, could come to pass. In that sense, the MC5, with their bacchanalian orgy of high energy sound, was a truer reflection of the positive spirit of the counterculture than the laid-back Apollonians of Haight-Ashbury ever could have been. And from the glimmerings of that confused babble, from the evidence of its hints of success, one could begin to construct an aesthetic and perhaps even a program that proposed how rock culture fit into society as something more significant than a diversion.[5]

Whereas Mailer observed the MC5 as an outsider who felt overwhelmed by their energy, Marsh writes as one who excitedly went along with the band's rise to national attention only to be frustrated, in the end, by their failure and dissolution. What he expresses is not mere nostalgia (though there is much of that), but a search for a usable past, for a fusion of aesthetics and politics that seemed as necessary in 1985, when he wrote his reflections, as it did in 1969 (and as it seems to me today).

The MC5's music affected both the Detroit scene and the broader countercultural movement, and their use of maximum amplification altered the experience of watching and listening to rock 'n' roll. As such, phenomenology and politics joined together in the band's approach. The energy that the Five generated was to break down the barriers between audience and performer, awakening their audience's deadened senses and compelling them to throw off the (mostly sexual) constraints imposed by the culture at large. Such a crude notion of sexual liberation was decidedly pre-feminist if not anti-feminist, as so much rock 'n' roll has been and continues to be, and was further built upon a pronounced fetishization of phallic potency that centered around an idealized notion of black masculinity common among white male radicals of the 1960s. To merely dismiss the MC5 as sexist and racist, though, is to unduly simplify the structures of desire articulated in their music and to gloss over the specific ways in which gender and race shaped their concept of liberation. Moreover, such a stance would overlook the legitimately positive elements of their aesthetic and political program—breaking aesthetic conventions with electronic noise and establishing the basis for an anti-authoritarian community of rock 'n' roll devotees.

The Scene

One band doth not a music scene make, but until the MC5's surge into local notoriety the Detroit/Ann Arbor area housed a scene-in-the-making more than a scene as such, at least with regard to rock 'n' roll. Certainly there was popular music, with Berry Gordy's Motown label issuing forth its stream of hits. Yet for white rock 'n' roll bands, there was a shortage of performance spaces, radio stations that would play their music, and media outlets that would cover their activities. Billy Lee and the Rivieras, a mid-1960s ensemble led by a white soul shouter named Mitch Ryder and identified by Dave Marsh as having laid the groundwork for the scene's later blossoming, spent much of their time playing weddings, bar mitzvahs, and free hops before settling in for a regular gig at the Walled Lake Casino, over thirty miles north of Detroit.[6] The MC5's career followed a similar path, performing in what guitarist Wayne Kramer called the "Downriver Rock and Roll scene" and what John Sinclair called the "hickory rock circuit of fraternity parties, mixers at colleges, and the occasional teen-club job."[7] Making ends meet with a haphazard array of gigs and dead-end jobs was precarious and frustrating to a band with the ambitions of the Five.

Even in their earliest days, the members of the MC5 sought to be something more than just another garage band. Drawn to the hard soul sound of Stax records in Memphis, they were also beginning to experiment with their own version of "avant-rock" which sounded very close to some of the music coming out of England at the time, especially bands like the Yardbirds, the Who, and Them: three-chord rock with a strong blues/soul orientation, but also with an aggressive use of electric instruments that set it apart from the music of most black musicians. The structure was simple but the sound was complex, verging toward a noisiness that, to untrained ears, did not sound much like music at all. Thus the original members of the band, guitarists Wayne Kramer and Fred Smith and singer Rob Tyner, went through a number of musicians before settling on the rhythm section of Michael Davis on bass and Dennis Thompson on drums, losing a bassist and several drummers who could not relate to the band's sound. The band even structured one of its most experimental compositions, "Black to Comm," around drummer Bob Gasper's utter distaste for the piece, as Tyner recounted in a 1969 interview.

> There's a thing that happens in *Black to Comm* that starts out with Fred playing the basic sound of the tune and the drums don't come in for a long time. Dennis waits and lets it build. That came from Bob Gasper's unwillingness to play the song, period. Sometimes the song'd go on for ten minutes with no drums. He'd sit there and sit there and get madder and madder and madder because he hated it so much and he couldn't relate to it at all. We're all flipping out, screaming into the mike, and finally he'd go crazy, and take out all of his frustrations by coming in very strong, maintaining the thing at a very high energy level. We always maneuovered (sic) him into that situation. So there's the Bob Gasper Memorial Wait at the beginning of *Black to Comm*.[8]

Energy born out of anger and frustration is one crucial part of the Five's development and their myth, particularly that part of their myth that connects them to the later rise of punk rock. Anger is only part of their story, though, and the energy that motivated their music was neither so spontaneous nor so undirected as the Gasper story might make it seem. However great a value the Five placed upon the spontaneous outburst, they were a band with at least some outline of a plan, and their plan crystallized upon meeting John Sinclair.

As the band tell it, they were drawn to Sinclair because of his preeminent place within the hip community of Detroit. In 1966 that community was quite small and rather elitist in their attitudes toward rock 'n' roll, according to Sinclair.[9] Marijuana and jazz were the glue that held this enclave together. The goal was to create an alternative lifestyle in which everybody was free, to live a life of art and poetry removed from the strictures of the workaday world. Into this classic bohemian setting the MC5 marched with the presumption that Sinclair and his fellow beatniks might be receptive to their music, and that they might serve as an important bridge into creating a following among the kids of Detroit.[10] What they found in Sinclair was not merely a conduit, but a collaborator and source of creative inspiration. Wayne Kramer described Sinclair as "a great big cat" with "all this energy, you know, and he just turns it on you . . . I had just left home, and here was this older cat who could explain all these things that I didn't understand about the world."[11] What Sinclair explained to the band seems to have had much to do with the beauty and value of free jazz, itself a restless noisy outgrowth of African-American culture, which Sinclair perceived to parallel the Five's own brand of noise. Sinclair eventually signed on as manager and worked tirelessly to publicize the Five's exploits in the various underground channels of the Detroit and Ann Arbor areas.

More than any single person, and probably at least as much as the band themselves, John Sinclair sought to cultivate a self-conscious recognition among Detroit's youth and counterculture that they were a part of a genuine rock 'n' roll scene. In his columns for the underground newspaper the *Fifth Estate,* Sinclair reported in issue after issue about the activities of the MC5 with a commitment that was at once self-serving and enlivening. At the center of the saga he constructed were the band's continual conflicts with authority, which were part of a broader crackdown by police on the mounting youth culture of the Detroit/Ann Arbor region. One incident in particular, which occurred on May 31, 1968, reveals the dynamics at work in the relationships among the MC5, their audience, the police, and the club owners.

The situation begins with a small-scale drug bust: two cops come upon Sinclair and drummer Dennis Thompson as they smoke some marijuana outside the Grosse Point Hideout, where the band was to play that evening. When the police threaten to take everyone down to the station, Sinclair sends word to the rest of the band, who confront the officers while the band's equipment manager announces to the waiting crowd in the club that "the only way they'd get to hear the band would be to surround the cops outside and *make* them give us up."[12] Sinclair continues the story:

When the band, intact once again, returned inside to play the first set, the crowd went into a spontaneous scream scene to welcome them back to reality. And when Tyner kicked off the first tune with "KICK OUT THE JAMS, MOTHERFUCKER!" [the title of one of the band's songs] it was madness all the way, with wild applause and jubilation before and after every jam.

The Hideout's manager was furious by this time, but he was caught in a simple capitalist contradiction: he couldn't move to censure the band because the paying customers were behind us all the way, and they were a lot more than "paying customers" by that time too—they were *ready!* When the chomp shut off the electricity during the closing energy-orgy "Black to Comm" to get the band off the stage, the crowd joined Fred Smith in chanting "Power! Power! Power!" until the juice came back on and the music soared to its natural climax.[13]

Confrontations like this one consolidated the Five's audience, and the broader rock audience of Detroit, into something approximating a self-conscious collectivity. When performing music and going to shows became contested activities, both the crowds and the band were compelled to take sides if they were to hold on to "their" culture in the face of police and club owners fearful of disorder. The actions of the police cemented the solidarity between the MC5 and its audience, and also contributed significantly to the band's politicization.

In clashes with the police, amplification was a useful weapon. As much as the illegal substances and the unlawful cries of "MOTHERFUCKER," electricity itself became a source of contestation. More than a way to turn on a crowd, volume (or its lack) became a symbol of control, wonderfully signified in the crowd's chant of "Power! Power! Power!" The authoritarian impulse toward silence was countered by the restless noise of youth, which was in turn amplified by the band's sonic excess—all leading toward a restoration of "juice" (electric and otherwise) and a natural climax made possible by technology.

*   *   *

If rock 'n' roll is loud, heavy metal rock 'n' roll is loudest and then some . . . the genre's practitioners have been obsessed—even more blatantly than the rest of us—with the technological phallus, with sheer decibel volume and the size and quantity of their "equipment."

But *loudest* is not only the best and most important part of the heavy metal style, *loudest* is also why this style was so suited to the cavernous, sound-devouring arena and so to the economy of scale that would be the linchpin of mass production rock 'n' roll, just as it had been the linchpin of Henry Ford's Detroit. And it's not coincidence that in the opinion of many rock 'n' rollers the city of Detroit is the heavy metal capital of the world.

—*Robert Duncan (1984), p. 39.*

The only real hope [for truly vital rock 'n' roll] is Detroit, where the kids take a lot of downs and dig down bands but at LEAST there's no folkie scene and lots of people still care about getdown gutbucket rock 'n' roll passionately because it takes the intolerableness of Detroit life and channels it into a form of strength and survival with humor and much of the energy claimed.

—*Lester Bangs (1987), p. 69.*

Lester Bangs and Robert Duncan had two very different views of Detroit rock 'n' roll. Duncan's association of volume with a particular economy of scale refers to a situation that the MC5 did not survive to see: the rise of "arena rock" that occurred during the 1970s, in which heavy metal music was central to the corporatization of loud sounds. The Five never gained the sort of popularity that would have filled arenas, except perhaps in their native Detroit, but their use of extreme volume certainly set the stage for the later incorporation of "loudestness" described by Duncan. Moreover, Duncan's association of the fetishization of technology in heavy metal and the industrial landscape of Detroit is directly relevant to the MC5's sound.

Lester Bangs, by contrast, locates resistance to that same cityscape not in the sound itself so much as in its reception. Among the youth of Detroit he witnesses an energy and passion that could not be contained by the "intolerableness of Detroit life." What Bangs means by this intolerableness is elaborated upon in a 1970 piece from the Detroit rock magazine *Creem.*

The alternative culture in the Detroit/Ann Arbor community is first and foremost a rock 'n' roll culture. Whatever movement we have here grew out of rock 'n' roll. It was rock 'n' roll music which first drew us out of our intellectual covens and suburban shells. We got excited by and about the music and started relating to each other on the high plane of energy that has come to be associated with our community; it is around the music that the community has grown and it is the music which holds the community together.

The reason is simple: there isn't anything else here . . . Life in Detroit is profoundly anti-intellectual. If you live in San Francisco or New York, the traditions are there, and even if you reject them wholly you've been shaped by them. Detroit is completely lacking in climate; our institutions are industrial and businesslike, not cultural or intellectual.[14]

Here the sterile industrialization described by Duncan is fused with the more hopeful observations of Bangs. Life in Detroit is pervaded by an overarching boredom solved only by devotion to rock 'n' roll; and that boredom is made even more unsettling by the specter of Fordism, which threatens to foreclose any alternatives to its totalizing presence. Particularly for the young white men who made up the core of the MC5's audience, Fordism represented both a legacy and a future without promise. John Sinclair powerfully expressed this sentiment in his response to the harsh criticisms put forth by Detroit Black Panther member William Leach. When Leach counseled white radicals to go work in the factories to get to know the workers, Sinclair countered, "our fucking parents have been working in those factories . . . for years and years so we won't have to do that anymore," and went on to assert that "we know all about the white working class, and the white lower, middle class and white middle class because that's where we come from. That's why we're the way we are, because we won't have anything to do with that bullshit. The way to change a system like this is to stop supporting it with your life, not to join the machine."[15]

Sinclair gives voice here to the divided class identity that motivated the Five's music and gave force to the band's relationship with its audience. While this may have been a music born out of Fordism, and out of a white male working-class sensibility, it was also founded upon a rejection of working-class life insofar as that life was perceived to be crippling in its lack of opportunity. Thus the MC5's music, along with the music of other Detroit bands like the Stooges, may be judged as an outgrowth of that moment in history when the significance of Fordism shifted from representing the American Dream to standing for the failure of that dream. Jerry Herron has argued that the history of Detroit is also a history of humiliations; it is a history as humiliation. What I mean by this is summed up in the famous dictum attributed to Henry Ford . . . : "History is bunk." He may or may not have uttered the famous words; nevertheless, making bunk out of history was surely what "Fordism" was all about, and it's what the town that became synonymous with Ford's inventions came to be about: the creation of a material plenitude so vast that people would quit worrying about the past, and history would cease to matter. Detroit's humiliation of history seemed an exhilarating idea, so long as the good times lasted, but when they ran out, it left both the city and the people in it painfully undefended and up for grabs.[16]

Whereas the counterculture has been widely interpreted by historians to have arisen out of the abundance of the postwar period, in Detroit we get a different story.[17] Not simply the result of heightened expectations, Detroit's rock 'n' roll counterculture also takes shape out of a fear that those expectations might never be met within the city's industrial economy, and a sense of futility at even harboring expectations of advancement.

The intense, almost distressing energy of the music that came out of the Detroit scene was at least in part a product of this ambivalent network of expectations and desires, which gave the music a character not found in the more middle-class countercultural environs of San Francisco. The music of the MC5 and other Detroit bands like the Stooges did not simply reproduce the logic of repetition and standardization that undergirded Fordism, but rather stood as an attempt to turn that logic against itself. The production of a disorderly electronic noise in this context indicated a contradictory stance toward technology, a willful move to master the tools of standardization which at the same moment threatened to drown out the human presence with the force of the machine. The repetitive sounds and lyrics in the Five's music signified the boredom and sameness of everyday life, but also counteracted this boredom by producing a disorienting noise that brought listeners to an ecstatic pitch, as in the following account of one of the Five's shows written by Pam Brent for the first issue of *Creem*.

The temperature soon becomes unbearable, and as the Five mount the stage, the place is literally an inferno. Rob Tyner invites us to remove any extraneous clothing, and in response, shirts, ties, scarves, etc. are removed. The music begins. The wall of sound assaults every cell in these close quarters . . . Bold, exalting tones rip through the heat and set fire to the very air, as sweat drips down the backs and brows of all present.

The roaring vibrations and now-language combine to put the audience in an indescribable and frenzied mood. The voice of the Five resounds all that is the youth of today. An aura of all our sought-after goals; love, peace, freedom, and f—king in the streets—they are echoes, and incarnation of our will. We receive them with appropriate joy and rapture.[18]

While Brent's description can only begin to do justice to the heat of the musical moment, she records a wave of synesthetic impressions very much like that articulated in the Five's lyrics: visual, aural, and tactile pleasures all blend together into a mood of "appropriate joy and rapture." Just as significant, though, is the political language of Brent's passage, the "sought-after goals" of youth that formed the basis of the MC5's political program.

Rock 'n' Roll, Dope, and Fucking in the Streets

John Sinclair issued his "White Panther Statement," the official declaration of the formation of the White Panther party, in the November 14–27, 1968 issue of the *Fifth Estate*. Drawing his inspiration from the combined influences of the Black Panthers and the Yippies, he outlined a movement of "visionary maniac white mother country dope fiend rock 'n' roll freeks" who were to parallel the Black Power movement in African-American politics with their own brand of cultural revolution.[19] Stating the party's opposition to "the white honkie culture that has been handed to us on a silver plastic platter," he especially emphasized the centrality of rock 'n' roll music to the group's platform. "Rock and roll music is the spearhead of our attack because it's so effective and so much fun," proclaimed Sinclair, who further cited the MC5 as the best example of the "organic high-energy guerrilla bands who are infiltrating the popular culture and destroying millions of minds in the process."[20] To conclude the statement, he called attention to the absolute centrality of black politics and black music in the formation of the White Panther program.

The actions of the Black Panthers in America have inspired us and given us strength, as has the music of black America, and we are moving to reflect that strength in our daily activity just as our music contains and extends the

6.1. Wayne Kramer, guitarist for the MC5, in a revolutionary pose, facing the American flag with guitar and rifle on his back. Photo © Leni Sinclair.

power and feeling of the black magic music that originally informed our bodies and told us that we could be free.

I might mention Brother James Brown in this connection, as well as John Coltrane and Archie Shepp, Sun-Ra, LeRoi Jones, Malcolm X, Huey P. Newton, Bobby Seale, Eldridge Cleaver, these are magic names to us. These are men in America. And we're as crazy as they are, and as pure. We're bad.[21]

This reverence for African-American masculinity was essential to the White Panther program, and also to the music of the Five. A program from an MC5 concert dated May 10–11, 1968 betrays the pervasive presence of "black magic music" referred to by Sinclair. Among the fourteen songs on the program, six are covers of songs by black performers, while one is an original jazz piece dedicated to Archie Shepp, one of Sinclair's "men in America" and a saxophonist who was part of the Black Power movement.[22] The six covers are themselves interesting for the way they are distributed among different styles of African-American music: "Upper Egypt," originally by Pharoah Sanders, and "Tungi," by John Coltrane, drawn from the same free jazz terrain that Shepp occupied; "Stormy Monday Blues," by T-Bone Walker, and "Bad Sign (Born Under a . . .)," by Albert King, which were blues numbers; "I Put a Spell on You," by Screaming Jay Hawkins, and "I Believe It to My Soul," by Ray Charles, soul or rhythm and blues pieces. What linked these disparate styles for the Five was their high energy, and a sensibility that represented to the band a subversion of the "white honkie culture" and an affirmation of a new aesthetic and political order founded upon the celebration of bodily pleasure.

That this return to the body was to be led by "pure" black men and that one of its goals was to reconstruct white men as sexually charged "rock 'n' roll guerrillas" does not speak well for the Five's revolutionary vision. Indeed, it betrays the sort of primitivization of blackness, and of black masculinity in particular, that has characterized so many of the attempts by white European and American men to escape or transcend the constrictions of "their" culture. Frantz Fanon has described how black maleness has been reduced historically not only to a body but to a penis, which is in turn amplified to superhuman proportions. Marianna Torgovnick, in turn, has discussed the ways in which "the idiom 'going primitive' is in fact congruent in many ways to the idiom 'getting physical.'" Fascination with the primitive "other" works to overcome "alienation from the body, restoring the body, and hence the self, to a relation of full and easy harmony with nature or the cosmos, as they have been variously conceived."[23] In this relationship, white men colonize the body of the "other" to resolve the split between mind and body that has been enforced by the civilizing process.[24]

Indeed, Sinclair and the MC5 seemed to believe that it was only through the appropriation of black masculinity that white men could become any kind of men at all. The Five's attitude paralleled that branch of 1960s radicalism that claimed the consumer-driven technocratic order had emasculated American manhood. Although Barbara Ehrenreich, among others, has called attention to the "androgynous drift" of countercultural masculinity,[25] Todd Gitlin has discussed the strong masculinist impulse that underlay so much of the New Left and the counterculture. Describing a 1967 SDS meeting that was crashed by members of San

Francisco's anarchistic Diggers, Gitlin recalls the confrontational display enacted by Digger Emmett Grogan:

> He leaped down, kicked over the table, smashed down a chair. He knocked down a woman and slapped around some others, or went through the stage motions—accounts disagree. "Faggots! Fags! Take off your ties, they are chains around your necks. You haven't got the balls to go mad. You're gonna make a revolution?—you'll piss in your pants when the violence erupts. You, spade—you're a nigger, what are you doing here? Your people need you . . ." Grogan unrolled a scroll of wrapping paper, declaimed a poem by Gary Snyder called "A Curse on the Men in the Pentagon, Washington, D.C.," including the line, "I hunt the white man down/in my heart."[26]

The masculinist program of action performed by Grogan strongly parallels that of the MC5 with its denigration of passive, tie-wearing men, who came to stand for white masculinity in general. Gitlin goes on to explain how, as the movement turned toward a "revolutionary vision," the Black Panthers ascended to models of action for white men in the movement.

> If revolution was imminent, the black underclass, rioting in the streets, were the plausible cadres. Who seemed to represent those specters better than Huey Newton, Bobby Seale, and Eldridge Cleaver, these intelligent brothers in black leather jackets, James Dean and Frantz Fanon rolled into one, the very image of indigenous revolutionary leadership risen from the underclass and certified in prison?[27]

Where Gitlin provides substance for noting the connections between the MC5's fascination with black manhood and that of the political and countercultural movement at large, his allusion to the specter of the rioting black underclass should also force us back into a recognition of the specificity of this fascination within the context of Detroit. The Detroit riot of July 1967 was among the deadliest of the 1960s, with a death toll of over forty. Local authorities witnessed the event with fear, but radicals like John Sinclair adopted a far different perspective. Writing in the *Fifth Estate* during the immediate aftermath of the "Rebellion," Sinclair described the action as a ritual of purification, and went on to assert: "No, baby, it's not a 'race riot,' or anything as simple as that. People just got tired of being hassled by police and cheated by businessmen and got out their equalizers and went to town . . . Oh it was Robin Hood Day in merry olde Detroit, the first annual city-wide all-free fire sale, and the people without got their hands on the goodies."[28] Sinclair's imagination was clearly stoked by the spectacle of unrest, yet his rejection of the simple classification "race riot" was likely more than a rhetorical flourish; Gitlin provides corroborating evidence that the events in Detroit were an integrated affair.[29] Furthermore, Eric Ehrmann, in profiling the MC5 for *Rolling Stone,* described a pact between the city's white and black militants "to stick up for each other," a pact that Sinclair himself was instrumental in engineering.[30] Given the aforementioned dispute between Sinclair and Black Panther William Leach, one hesitates to conclude that there was a secure alliance between Detroit's countercultural enclave and the black community. If nothing else, though, what we can locate in Sinclair's words is a desire for a connection to exist between the two communities, a desire that became in the "White Panther Statement" a longing to participate in the black revolution itself, and to follow an aesthetic and political path that black men had already charted.

Given the political context of the time, Chuck Eddy's "half-truthful" association of the MC5's music with a riotous Detroit gains in symbolic truth-value what it might lack as a statement of fact. If the Five's music was not literally produced during the riots, it certainly gained much of its definition from the racial unrest that characterized Detroit during the mid- to late 1960s. The MC5's music certainly can be taken as a response to the political imperative felt by Gitlin, Sinclair, and other white activists during the 1960s in the face of black political activity, an imperative articulated by Gitlin with the simple question: "What does Whitey do?"[31] Yet this perspective only takes us so far in understanding their music, which arose out of a broader mix of influences than any reference to the riots can explain. Furthermore, the band's and Sinclair's attraction to black music predated the riots, and was rooted in patterns of racial and sexual desire that extend well beyond the 1960s.

Insight into these patterns can be gleaned from Eric Lott's study of minstrelsy, *Love and Theft.* Seeking to move beyond the notion that blackface minstrelsy arose solely out of twin white impulses to denigrate blackness and capitalize upon that denigration, Lott locates in the form evidence of a "profound white investment in black culture" that cannot be explained as mere racism.[32] More specifically, Lott identifies in minstrelsy "a gendered pattern of exchange, a kind of commerce between men" motivated by a "complex dynamic" in which white performers' tendency to dominate black maleness "coexisted with or indeed depended on a self-conscious attraction to the black men it was the job of these performers to mimic."[33] The putting on of blackface also involved putting on a particular style of masculinity, one in which the qualities thought to belong to black men—"cool, virility, humility, abandon, or *gaité de coeur*"—were transferred.[34] According to Lott, the sexual envy that motivated this homosocial exchange betrayed a sort of homoerotic desire on the part of white men; the desire to have the black man's qualities slid easily if uncomfortably into the desire to have the black man, with the ambivalence between economic and sexual possession residing in the word "have."

Although Lott's analysis is centered upon minstrelsy as an antebellum form, he makes a convincing case that these modes of homosocial exchange laid the foundation for the subsequent history of relations between white bohemians and African-American culture. The MC5 and the many legions of other white musicians who drew from African-American culture no longer literalized the putting on of blackness through the application of blackface, but did adopt other signifiers to mark the exchange (especially hair, in the case of the Five).[35] However, I would argue that it was primarily by strapping on electric guitars, and in their use of technology more generally, that groups like the Five most clearly reproduced the logic of blackface.

Here we have to mediate between two sets of dichotomies, both of which revolve around technology, and both of which speak to a powerful contradiction in the race/gender dynamic at work in this process of appropriation. First is the opposition between black nature and white technology, an opposition that lies at the very heart of primitivist desires. Blackness gains its potency from its closeness to nature in this paradigm of racial thought. It is the embodiment of a primal essence that connotes a sort of purity. Technology, by contrast, is an outgrowth of white rationality indicative of the alienation of mind from body. It amplifies certain bodily effects and functions to compensate for white bodily deficiency. Ron Wellburn's characterization of white rock as a "technology" in the previous chapter is an example of this view. He suggests that rock is not a music, which stands as an affectation rather than something that is authentically "felt" (in physical and emotional terms). That Wellburn writes from a black nationalist position demonstrates the power of these associations across racial lines, and gives evidence of the ways in which the "primitivization" of blackness was appropriated by black men during the 1960s as the basis for a critique of white masculinity.

However, within another set of oppositions, that between female nature and male technology, what is configured as a symbol of lack becomes itself a sign of mastery. Woman as nature connotes the passivity of an existence ruled by external forces. Men wield technology to display their transcendence of nature, and their power to order the world according to their will. It is out of this second, gendered set of associations that Susan Hiwatt, a feminist critic of rock music, exclaimed:

> It blew my mind the first time I heard about a woman playing an electric guitar. Partly because of the whole idea we have that women can't understand anything about electronics (and we're not even supposed to want to), and also because women are supposed to be composed, gentle, play soft songs. A guy once told my sister when she picked up his electric guitar that women were meant to play only folk guitar, like Joan Baez or Judy Collins, that electric guitars were unfeminine.[36]

Technology in Hiwatt's account is clearly gendered in such a way as to reinforce associations of masculinity with knowledge as opposed to ignorance, force as opposed to gentleness, and loudness as opposed to the songs that women are supposed to play. Moreover, Hiwatt offers a rare moment of insight into the way in which men guard their privileged access to technology as a means of policing the boundary that separates maleness from femaleness.

In the MC5's approach to technology, these two paradigms—the racialized and gendered configurations of technology—are brought into an uneasy alliance. The electric guitar as an instrument of mastery amplifies the masculinity of the band's performers. Even Rob Tyner gains force from the sheer volume of sound around him. Yet this use of the electric guitar threatens to call attention to the artificiality of this performance of masculinity. To borrow a phrase from Marjorie Garber, the guitar "artifactualizes" the male body, insofar as it shows that masculinity can only be achieved by putting on certain appurtenances.[37] This is where the recourse to racial discourse becomes so instrumental; for if white men take black masculinity as their model, they also aspire toward the "naturalness" that blackness signifies. The threat of artifice is therefore contained by the putting on of black manhood, which renaturalizes the virility of the male body.

Such a paradoxical mating of race, gender, and technology can be heard to great effect in the MC5's song "Rocket Reducer No. 62 (Rama Lama Fa Fa Fa)," the closing cut on side one of their first album, the "live" *Kick Out the Jams*. The very title of the song is indicative of the multiple levels of meaning at play in the Five's music: the rocket as technological signifier of potency coupled with the nonsense syllables so common to soul, rock 'n' roll, and other musical forms derived from African-American traditions. Similarly, the song itself couples a one-chord soul-blues vamp with the sort of maximum amplification that gave the Five's music its distinction. That this is a song about the power of the electric guitar becomes clear during the introduction, when Rob Tyner exclaims, "This song starts out with Brother Wayne Kramer, Brother Wayne Kramer," who proceeds to hammer out the main musical figure over a wave of feedback generated by fellow guitarist Fred "Sonic" Smith. As the entire band joins into the repetitive groove, Tyner sings insistently about his status as a "natural man." "I've got to keep it up 'cause I'm a natural man" is his constant refrain, leading to the reassertion of his masculinity in the chorus: "I'm the man for you baby/Yes I am for you baby." The climax of the song, though, comes at the end, when the two guitarists take off on an orgasmic solo flight, pursuing each other on their respective fretboards while the rest of the band lays silent. A full minute of rapid distorted runs is capped by a final bluesy bend, and when the rest of the band rejoins for a final crash of chords, the rocket is reduced to a state of detumescence in the ensuing silence as both the song and the album's side come to an end.

With this orgasmic outburst closing a rather explicit celebration of natural manhood, "Rocket Reducer" would seem to correspond to Susan McClary's analysis of the phallocentric narrative that has defined Western classical and popular musics during the past three centuries. Upon closer inspection, though, the song, and the Five's music in general, does not conform so easily to McClary's observations. For McClary, tonal music, that music which makes the most sense to Western ears, is organized according to a teleology in which the dominant musical mode states its control over other keys in a way that signifies both the assertion and the achievement of phallic mastery.[38] She further explains that this narrative depends upon a song's departure from the tonic or dominant mode, so that the music performs

> an adventure in which other key areas are visited . . . and in which the certainty of tonal identity is at least temporarily suspended. Otherwise there is no plot . . . To the extent that "Other" keys stand in the way of unitary identity, they must finally be subdued for the sake of narrative closure. They serve as moments both of desire (because without the apparent longing to approach these other keys, there is only stagnation) and of dread (because they threaten identity).[39]

However phallocentric the Five's music might seem, this plot, with its emphasis upon the visitation and conquest of other musical areas, is absent in much of their music, including "Rocket Reducer No. 62." Until the final guitar tirade, the song is most notable for its lack of narrative content, as the same chord and musical figure are struck again and again, establishing a tonic against which no other is defined. Moreover, when the guitars take off at the end of the song, it is not into a climactic tonal flourish but into atonality. The instruments abandon the relentlessly dominant mode of the song for a freer type of playing that disobeys any sense of proper musical form.

My analysis is not meant to deny the distinctly masculine bias of the MC5's music, but to show how they did not simply reproduce standard musical narratives of phallic achievement. Rather, the orgasmic imperative articulated in "Rocket Reducer No. 62," which I would argue was in many ways the driving force behind the Five's music in general, was divided in its motivation: while on the one hand offered as the supreme affirmation of the (white male) self, on the other hand this imperative pointed toward the obliteration of the boundaries between self and other. Thus, in his original liner notes for *Kick Out the Jams,* John Sinclair outlined a philosophy based upon the principle "Separation Is Doom," in which he stressed the Five's status as a "*whole thing:*"

> There is no way to get at the music without taking in the whole context of the music too—*there is no separation.* We say the MC5 is the solution to the problem of separation, because they are *so together.* The MC5 is totally committed to the revolution, as the revolution is totally committed to driving people out of their separate shells and into each other's arms.

6.2.   Guitarists Wayne Kramer and Fred "Sonic" Smith show what it means to "come together." Courtesy of the Michael Ochs Archive, Venice, California.

I'm talking about *unity,* brothers and sisters, because we have to *get it together.* We *are* the solution to the problem, if we will just *be* that. If we can *feel* it, LeRoi Jones said, "Feeling Predicts Intelligence." The MC5 will make you feel it, or leave the room. The MC5 will drive you crazy out of your head into your body. The MC5 *is* rock and roll. Rock and roll *is* the music of our bodies, of our whole lives—the "resensifier," Rob Tyner calls it. We have to *come together,* people, "build to a gathering," or else. Or else we are dead, and gone.[40]

Consider alongside this statement of purpose the MC5 song "Come Together," alluded to by Sinclair. Bearing no resemblance to the Beatles song of the same name (which was, in any case, released over a year later), "Come Together" was an explicit expression of the band's program of union through the musical enactment of orgasm. As with "Rocket Reducer No. 62," the song is characterized above all by an excess of volume and noise and by its unchanging harmonic structure: a single note struck for several beats, followed by two massive power chords, repeat throughout the course of the song without interruption. No guitar solos here; the band operates as a "whole thing" while Rob Tyner intermittently shouts vocals punctuated by the line "Together in the darkness," a line multiply inflected by the sexual and political command of the song's title. Any sense of variation comes from subtle shifts in the level of loudness; the thunderous density of the band's attack eases as Tyner announces that "it's getting closer . . . God it's so close now" with a voice that sounds pained with anticipation. The volume rises once again while the song rushes into its concluding gasp toward togetherness, ending with a progression of chords that ascends and then lunges back downward while becoming increasingly out of tune, the blur of the drums and the whirr of the feedback further contributing to the heightened disorder that immediately precedes the song's finish.

The prioritization of volume in this song, the way in which loudness was to provoke bodily excitement and changes in the level of noise provided the friction, if you will, that was to bring this excitement to its climax, lead us further into the MC5's aesthetic and political program. More specifically, it is here that we come to the Five's principles of high energy music as a tool of cultural revolution. For the band, the revolutionary potential of their music lay in its presumed ability to drive people "into their bodies," to provoke what Rob Tyner called "purification and resensification on all levels. Resensify you back to your meat, because that's the way you take it in. Your meat is your senses, because your senses are made out of meat. And if you don't keep in contact with your meat . . . that's why all these straight people are so fucked up, man, 'cause they let their meat loaf—and it just rots, it rots."[41] Rock 'n' roll as an assault upon straight society might seem like the most naive sort of sixties idealism, yet there is also in Tyner's statement a powerful recognition of civilization and its discontents. Here the primitivism that underlay the band's reverence for black manhood comes back into play: if straight, civilized society required the dissociation of mind and body and the sublimation of physical pleasure, the Five would counter this system with a sonic assault on the senses that would, ideally, rid the body of its civilized trappings and return it to a purity of sensation that had long been lost.

Bodily pleasure, then, was not an end in itself for the MC5. Instead, the band's music was motivated by an impulse very similar to that described by Norman Mailer in his notorious essay, "The White Negro." According to Mailer, the white negro, or hipster, is a sort of psychopath seeking to resolve "those mutually contradictory inhibitions upon violence and love which civilization has exacted of us."[42] Refusing the negative associations of psychopathy, Mailer finds the hipster/psychopath especially adapted to the tensions of modern life, and defines the project of the hipster in terms that foreshadow the Five's own brand of sensual politics:

> What characterizes almost every psychopath and part-psychopath [and thus every hipster, according to Mailer's logic] is that they are trying to create a new nervous system for themselves. Generally we are obliged to act with a nervous system which has been formed from infancy, and which carries in the style of its circuits the very contradictions of our parents and our early milieu. Therefore, we are obliged, most of us, to meet the tempo of the present and the future with reflexes and rhythms which come from the past. It is not only the "dead weight of the institutions of the past" but indeed the inefficient and often antiquated nervous circuits of the past which strangle our potentiality for responding to new possibilities which might be exciting for our individual growth.[43]

Like Mailer's hipster, the MC5 sought to escape the reflexes and rhythms of the past for a new mode of response. The desire to restore the body to a condition of purity, then, was not only a longing for primal return but also a vision of new possibilities for the future. Blackness, meanwhile, is crucial to this scenario; for both Mailer and the Five located the model for these potentials of bodily experience in the "super-sensuality" of black men.[44]

* * *

Mailer claimed, "The language of Hip is a language of energy, how it is found, how it is lost."[45] Energy was the keyword within the Five's program—an energy born from sound, an energy that reorganized the senses. Indeed, as described by Rob Tyner, the effect upon the body was immediate and transformative:

> Pure sound energizes. The more energy in the sound, the bigger the sound that gets to you, the more intense the experience is, and the more intense the experience is, the more intense reality is—your metabolic reality at that moment, you know, an intensive feeling of your metabolism—that's where you find your reality. And music is equated on that level too, because it does make metabolic changes. Like on the stage, I notice metabolic changes at every instant. So fast—your heart beat and your respiration and everything, because you're using your body 100 per cent—that's what music is supposed to make you do.[46]

Tyner's words are echoed by John Sinclair, who in a letter written after his break with the band offered his own articulation of their high-energy music:

> [The MC5's stage show] was a beautiful demonstration of the principles of high-energy performance: as the performer puts out more the energy level of the audience is raised and they give back more energy to the performers, who are moved onto a higher energy level which is transmitted to the audience and sent back, etc., until everything is totally frenzied. This process makes changes in the people's bodies that are molecular and cellular and which transform them irrevocably just as LSD or any other strong high-energy agents do.[47]

Sinclair brings us back to the collective basis of the Five's emphasis upon sound, energy, and the body. Energy in these passages represents the ways in which sound acts upon the body, or more precisely, the ways in which sound and body act upon each other, and the process through which the sensual experience of a single individual and a single body might be communicated to other individuals and other bodies. Thus was music not only to resensify but to spread that resensification, and to drive people "out of their separate shells, and into each other's arms."

Such a goal was utopian, to be sure, and what part of the band's audience shared this communal ecstasy is all but impossible to measure.[48] Nonetheless, the MC5 sought to translate the powerful sensations they felt from their own experience of amplified music into a mass rock 'n' roll movement. In other words, their politics cannot be understood apart from their use of amplification, which opened for them levels of sensory experience that seemed fundamentally new.

The Five's aesthetic and political program, as an attempt to come to terms with the possibilities offered by new technologies, can be better understood in the context of 1960s social philosophy such as that of Marshall McLuhan. McLuhan believed his society was marked by a shift from the mechanical technologies that had dominated the age of industrialization toward a new electronic universe in which separation of all kinds was being overthrown. "The medium, or process, of our time—electric technology—is reshaping and restructuring patterns of social interdependence and every aspect of our personal life . . . Electric circuitry has overthrown the regime of 'time' and 'space' and pours upon us instantly the concerns of all other men . . . Its message is Total Change, ending psychic, social, economic, and political parochialism."[49] Where Sinclair understood the Five's music as a "whole thing," McLuhan similarly believed that electric media would abolish the boundaries that separated time and space, which in turn enforced the difference between self and "other." Electronic media would upset the relation between the center and the margins, converting the urbanized spaces of the imperializing West into nodes within a global village. McLuhan further claimed that electronic media would transform our sensorium, and would move us away from the objectifying emphasis upon vision and visuality that had been born with the Enlightenment toward a new prioritization of sound: "The ear favors no particular 'point of view.' We are enveloped by sound. It forms a seamless web around us. We say, 'Music shall fill the air.' We never say, 'Music shall fill a particular segment of the air' . . . Where a visual space is an organized continuum of a uniformed connected kind, the ear world is a world of simultaneous relationships."[50] The reorganization of the nervous system, then, was already underway in McLuhan's conceptualization of electronic technology. Linearity and fragmentation were to give way to simultaneity and unification, all of which were to be embodied in the new sound relationships that people had with one another.

This sense of imminent possibility that McLuhan located within electricity was in many ways also the crux of the MC5's music early in the band's career. One does not have to look hard to find traces of McLuhan's rhetoric, for instance, in Sinclair's writings on the band and on rock 'n' roll in general. "Rock and roll kicked off the 21st century almost fifty years ahead of time," proclaimed Sinclair in the introduction to his book, *Guitar Army,* "it made the leap from the mechanical to the electronic age in the space of three minutes, 45 revolutions per minute."[51] McLuhan's idea that "the medium is the message" found its way into Sinclair's discussion of the style with which the Five incorporated amplification into their music:

> The power of the amplifiers was built into the [MC5's] songs and arrangements of other people's songs they used, they were not separable from it, and in that sense the MC-5 made what can best be described as a "post-Western" music, in the same sense that Archie Shepp's or John Coltrane's or Cecil Taylor's or Sun Ra's music can only be called post-Western. That is, these musics destroy separation on every level, and separation is the basis of all Western musics up to and including most of rock and roll expression.[52]

McLuhan's categories not only justified the prioritization of the medium in the Five's music, but also are used here by Sinclair to situate the band within a global process of musical production. McLuhan suggested that "Electric circuitry is Orientalizing the West,"[53] and Sinclair holds a similar faith in electricity's power to break free from Western traditions.

Underlying both versions of this faith is yet another idealization of the primitive as described by Marianna Torgovnick, one less concerned with getting physical than with going home. "Going primitive is trying to 'go home' to a place that feels comfortable and balanced . . . Whatever form the primitive's homeliness takes, its strangeness salves our estrangement from ourselves and our culture."[54] So it is that the Orient, or blackness, symbolizes both the extent to which electronic technology breaks with the conventions of the West and remains continuous with broader patterns of human existence. Electricity takes us beyond ourselves only to restore us to our original state, a state from which "others" (the East, blacks) never strayed so far: such is the trope through which technology was imagined to be both radically different and comfortably familiar in the writings of McLuhan and Sinclair, and in the music of the MC5.

*   *   *

It was not technology as a thing in itself, but technology in its capacity to generate noise that the MC5 found so full of possibilities. In their use of amplified sound, the Five embody many of the ideas put forth by Jacques Attali in his musicological tract, *Noise: The Political Economy of Music* (1985). Attali locates in music a strong prophetic tendency, and asserts that the forms and structures that organize music are not determined by social forces, but instead predict the future shape those forces will take. Sound, noise, and music are all fundamental to Attali's concept of the social order, and like McLuhan but with greater intellectual rigor, he seeks a theoretical language that will overturn the hegemony of sight within the sensory hierarchy.

> More than colors and forms, it is sounds and their arrangements that fash-ion societies. With noise is born disorder and its opposite: the world. With music is born power and its opposite: subversion. In noise can be read the codes of life, the relations among men. Clamor, Melody, Dissonance, Har-mony; when it is fashioned by man with specific tools, when it invades man's time, when it becomes sound, noise is the source of purpose and power, of the dream—Music. It is at the heart of the progressive rationalization of aesthetics, and it is a refuge for residual irrationality; it is a means of power and a form of entertainment.[55]

Thus does Attali build an argument for the political centrality of music. Modern societies have been predicated upon the organization of noise into assimilable forms: The harmonious, rationalized tones of the Western musical canon convey a sense of the unity and order of all things, and at the same time urge us to forget the chaos of sounds that pervade our everyday life. With the move toward a consumer-driven musical economy, that chaos becomes normalized through processes of what Attali terms "repetition." A greater diversity of sounds is present in such repetition, but these sounds still operate to divert our desires into established chan-nels. "Repetition produces information free of noise," writes Attali, it creates a "silence in sound, the innocuous chatter of recuperable cries."[56] Attali locates the exercise of power in music, but he also identifies possibilities for subversion through an emergent mode of musical production he names "Composition." "Composition," he notes, "calls into question the distinction between worker and consumer, between doing and destroying, a fundamental division of roles in all societies in which usage is defined by a code; to compose is to take pleasure in the instruments, the tools of communication."[57] In Composition, music is no longer oriented toward demands outside itself. Best exemplified by the efforts of free jazz musicians, the musical worker uses his instrument to create his own musical code in which noise no longer signifies an unwanted dissonance but rather demarcates the autonomy of desire.

Attali's imagined utopia of musical practice resonates strongly with the MC5's own utopian goals. The Five were about nothing if not taking pleasure in the instruments of communication, and with those instruments they similarly strove to establish a realm of autonomous desire in which the distinction between worker and consumer, or between audience and performer, was abolished. Of course, in the case of the Five, their utopia went unrealized—after an initial burst of public notoriety, they were relegated by 1972 to drifting around Europe, having lost the solid base of local support that had driven their early career. Nonetheless, in their short-lived prime the MC5 injected rock 'n' roll with a level of hopefulness that continues to exert a significant influence upon both the music's practitioners and its critics. Thus, twenty years after the band's demise, Chuck Eddy described the Five's first album in the following terms:

> Not merely the only live debut album that's ever mattered (damn few have ever even *not mattered!*), this is one of the livest *anythings* ever . . . a toast to civilization and its discontents, pinkos-in-training defending armed love atop insurrectionarily inflamed National Guard jeeps on Murder City's East Side, dredging up hoodoo demons from the darkness . . . The MC5 were as American as apple pie, red-bleeding white-skinned blues-belters no matter how black they wanted to be.[58]

Where Eddy want to recuperate the Five's whiteness in the face of their desire to be black, I would assert that the Five's whiteness cannot be understood apart from their fascination with black manhood, and that their utopianism could not have existed apart from this fascination. In light of the recurrent privileging of "other" cultures in the revolutionary and utopian ideals that have pervaded this chapter (Gitlin, Mailer, McLuhan, as well as the Five), one finally has to wonder whether white males of the late twentieth century can imagine a utopia that is not founded upon the absorption of the other. Certainly during the 1960s, the use of primitivist rhetoric as a means of cultural critique was a fundamental part of the counterculture to which the MC5 contributed. It is specifically in music, moreover, that we gain the clearest access to a complex range of desires that made up this countercultural moment. Race, gender, and technology were all mythicized through the MC5's music in ways that reproduced conventional hierarchies even as the band sought the abolition of those hierarchies. By the same token, their music was marked by a restless exuberance that cannot be entirely explained by or reduced to standard academic categories. Thus does Chuck Eddy conclude his review of *Kick Out the Jams*: "And there's Sonic Smith's and Wayne Kramer's riffs dueling their way into the spontaneous simplicity of a Sun Ra cover where everything unravels in unropable feedback-jazz and where every last little honky sings and every last little honky plays whatever he motherfucking feels. Like wow man, it's anarchy."[59]

Coda: An Exhortation

In early 1969, at the crest of the MC5's popularity, *Creem* magazine ran a fake advice column called "Contact Truss," a spoof on local music impresario Russ Gibb. Gibb owned the Grande Ballroom, where the Five had made their reputation as the world's most notorious guerrilla rock 'n' roll band and recorded their cataclysmic first album. Among the parodic letters to "Truss" was the following naive question: "Dear Uncle Truss, What does 'Kick out the jams' mean?" which "Truss" (actually writer Peter McWilliams) answered as follows:

> Well, as you might know, for maximum comfort of all attendees, we limit the ticket sales at the Ball Room to 100 per concert. This allows for lots of room for all. However, about 1000 people per performance SNEAK IN and make the place jam packed. These people are called The Jams, in Ballroom vernacular. When a band is playing and they feel the atmosphere is too confined, they yell "Kick out the jams, please" which means the hired police officers check for ticket stubs and throw out any unauthorized concert goers. I hope that answers your question.[60]

Intended as a satire of the growing dedication to the profit-margin among Detroit's club owners (invoking paranoia that people might actually sneak in to see music without paying), this passage also perfectly inverts the spirit in which the MC5 meant "Kick out the jams." Rob Tyner provides a better description more in keeping with the band's intentions in a 1970 interview:

> We used to do all kinds of things to wake the audience up. We'd turn on the house lights and start a tape which said "Important . . . come to the stage . . . come to the stage . . ." and all the kids would cluster round while we'd sit down and stare at them. Then the tape would say "Look at all those people . . . why are they standing there? . . . what are they doing? . . ." and it was like slapping them in the face. We'd jump on the chicks in the audience, all kinds of things, and after a while the kids got to really dig it.[61]

Far from exhibiting the concern with the maximization of comfort and personal space expressed by faux rock 'n' roll capitalist "Truss," the MC5 cultivated crowds in order to facilitate their war on separation. "Kick out the jams" was the band's rallying cry, a call to "break everything loose and free everybody from their very real and imaginary prisons."[62] Never was it followed by the polite "please" of Truss's description; instead, the cry in its fullness was a paean to impoliteness: "KICK OUT THE JAMS, MOTHERFUCKER!" Flaunting Michigan's obscenity laws, the MC5 did not appeal to the police for assistance, but rather called them into action, much as they had in the earlier clash over the right to amplification.

> [Guitarist Wayne] Kramer kicked off the second set with "Ramblin' Rose," and when it came time for the magic moment Tyner strolled onstage and told the kids he needed some help. Everybody knows what comes next, he said, and we need your help in calling off the tune because we've been hearing all kinds of weird stuff about it. Everybody knows it's all right, don't you now (YEAH!!), so I'll just count three and then we can get this old tune started. But everybody's gotta do it together, or else it won't be any good.
>   Tyner counted to three—the whole band counted—and then the place exploded: "KICK OUT THE JAMS MOTHERFUCKER!!" 400 deranged teen-age freeks screamed in unison, and the band *got down*. The pigs were infuriated, but they would've had to've arrested everybody in the place on the phony rap to get anyone. And after that it was freedom all the way.[63]

More than a simple exhortation, "Kick out the jams" created a collective euphoria. Both the band and the kids basked in breaking the rules of public decorum. Yet however much the phrase itself exerted a symbolic power over the events of the MC5's performances, it was ultimately the band's music that carried the proceedings. The phrase itself would not have raised the audience to such a fever pitch had the song not followed. Beginning with two crashing power chords that segue into feedback over the pulse of the drums, "Kick Out the Jams" was a musical statement full of both fury and joy. The four musicians—Fred Smith and Wayne Kramer on guitar, Michael Davis on bass, and Dennis Thompson on drum set— locked into a fully amplified three-chord electric crush-groove while Rob Tyner sang in a voice that was alternately soulful and manic of the pleasures of experiencing just the sort of music the band was playing: "Well I feel pretty good and I guess that I could get crazy now baby . . . Yes I'm starting to sweat and now my shirt's all wet but I'm feeling" (in the background one of the band members laughs exuberantly). After Kramer's screaming spastic guitar solo, full of high-pitched notes repeated to the point of delirium, the song lunges toward its final chorus, a celebration of sound and self in which rock 'n' roll is the key to liberation:

> The wailing guitars and the crash of the drums
> Make you want to keep a rockin' till the morning comes
> Let me be who I am
> And let me kick out the jams—Yes!
> Kick out the jaaaaaaaams
> I done kicked 'em out.

Chapter 7

Heavy Music

Cock Rock, Colonialism, and the Music of Led Zeppelin

(Meta)Physical Graffiti

A series of photos, laid out on a single page, tells a story about the status of the electric guitarist in 1970s rock. "The Led Zeppelin Story," the article is titled, a brief history of the band's career published by London rock journal *Melody Maker* in 1975, in anticipation of Zeppelin's first British concerts in two years.[1] Stretched sideways across two newspaper-length pages, the article is arranged in a way that offers an uncharacteristic degree of vertical space. At the foot of these two pages that appear as one, three photographs rest side by side. On the left corner is a picture of John Paul Jones, with electric bass in hand, peering into the distance; on the right, John "Bonzo" Bonham, attacking a cymbal of his surrounding drum set. Between the two stands singer Robert Plant, head tilted back, eyes shut, mouth open to direct a shout at the microphone held toward it. Each of these photos is cropped at the waist, and the three musicians are all squarely contained within the borders of their respective pictures, the only protruding object being Plant's microphone, which juts upward to break through the dark space that surrounds his body.

The minor transgression of visual space occasioned by Plant's technologically extended physical presence is amplified by the accompanying photograph of guitarist Jimmy Page, which towers over those of his bandmates. Page's figure stretches across the expanse of the layout; rather than being encased in a clearly bounded photographic space, the shape of his body dictates the visual arrangement of the article. His legs move down to the pictures of his fellow musicians, who appear at/as his missing feet. Plant's well-placed microphone resides where Page's left foot would otherwise be, and directs our gaze upwards toward the guitarist's crotch, where his instrument is poised. With his left hand, Page frets a chord at the bottom of the guitar's neck, while with his right, he wields a violin bow that he rubs against the strings. Meanwhile, his bearded face is directed downwards at his instrument in a look of intense concentration. Beside him is the simple caption, "Jimmy Page: guitarist extraordinaire."

Led Zeppelin was one of the most commercially successful bands of the 1970s, and also among the most powerful, in terms of both their influence and their reputed effect upon audiences. In 1975, they were at the peak of their success. Their new double album, *Physical Graffiti,* rushed to the top of the sales charts upon its release, and the band embarked upon one of its trademark massive tours, all of which served to strengthen the epic sense of grandiosity surrounding the band. Chris Welch, for instance, testified, "It says much for the power and imagination [Led Zeppelin] pack into their playing, that somehow the very name of the band conjures something vast and heroic."[2] These sentiments were echoed throughout the rock press during the 1970s, and in the many retrospective articles written since the band's demise in 1980.[3] By most accounts, Jimmy Page was the source of much of the band's power. As much as Led Zeppelin was a band, Page was regularly acknowledged to be the group's presiding figure, the brains behind Zeppelin's sonic brawn. In part this was due to his role in founding the band, yet the sort of attention Page garnered can be attributed to more than historical fact. If Led Zeppelin as a whole was something of a heroic entity to many fans and critics, Page himself exemplified a distinct version of heroism, one that can be traced back to the 1960s or perhaps even earlier, but that flourished during the 1970s: the guitar hero.

Jimi Hendrix was in many ways the archetype of the modern guitar hero, using the technology of the electric guitar to mediate among the racial and sexual tensions that have governed the production of popular music. Understanding Jimmy Page's and Led Zeppelin's version of the guitar hero presents a unique set of challenges. Widely hailed as progenitors of the musical sub-genre heavy metal (despite the band members' protestations to the contrary), the influence of Zeppelin looms large in the recent history of rock, and the band figures prominently in a number of key debates concerning the music. Most notably, Led Zeppelin has been understood by many as the quintessential purveyors of "cock rock," that brand of guitar-driven music that most clearly articulates a male-oriented regime of power and pleasure. In his role as lead guitarist, Page sheds light upon the ways in which the electric guitar might be said to signify the "cock" of cock rock.

. . . Or the "rock," for that matter. As the 1960s mutated into the 1970s in the imaginations of musicians and critics, the purpose of rock itself was uncertain. The hopes held by the MC5 and many others in the counter-culture that loud electronic rock music would effect a cultural revolution lost much of their credibility by 1970. Before the new decade had even officially begun, the gatherings at Woodstock and Altamont had been mythologized into the triumph and immediate downfall of rock 'n' roll's imagined utopia.[4] In the crisis of definition that followed, the constituent elements of what had been considered the rock community began to diverge. For some, the heavy sounds that had dominated rock music during the 1960s represented an exhausted form. This segment of the audience opted for quieter, more introspective music, such as that pur-veyed by singer-songwriters or by the new wave of country-influenced rock musicians. Others still preferred loud rock dominated by the electric guitar, and it was for this segment of the audience that Led Zeppelin stood as heroes. Yet as Zeppelin became standard-bearers of heavy music, they also continually modified their sound to incorporate more acoustic (as opposed to electric) elements, and mediated between the polarization of rock into quiet and loud camps. At a time when rock's definition was subject to serious debate, Zeppelin strove to place itself not on one or the other side of the musical divide, but on both sides at once, to present an image of the band that resisted easy categorization.

The acoustic/electric divide was only one of the boundaries Led Zep-pelin worked to transgress. Just as significant was the band's continual manipulation of cultural and racial boundaries, its incorporation of ele-ments drawn not only from African-American music but also from what Jimmy Page has referred to as the "C.I.A." influence—Celtic, Indian, and Arabic musical elements that were taken up with little regard for ethno-logical propriety.[5] Page's ability to synthesize disparate musical styles has drawn much comment, often from writers critical of his appropriative tendencies, yet few have sought to place his international eclecticism within a framework that recognizes the significance of colonialist and

Orientalist ideologies in the music of Led Zeppelin. Within the musical logic of the band, acoustic sounds were regularly used to signify exotic musical styles, and the far-ranging soundscape was to conjure an expansive imaginary landscape in which the two leaders, Page and Robert Plant, enacted a fantasy of exploration rooted in colonialist desires.

*   *   *

Page's violin bow, a curious detail of the opening photograph, takes us one step further into this array of themes. An incongruous object within the context of rock performance, the bow was quite familiar to any committed fan of Led Zeppelin, having been a regular part of Page's onstage repertoire since the band's origin in 1968, and even before that when he was a member of the Yardbirds. When asked about his use of the bow, Page asserted that it was not just a gimmick, and that he used it because "some great sounds come out. You can employ legitimate bowing techniques and gain new scope and depth. The only drawback is that a guitar has a flat neck, opposed to a violin's curved neck, which is a bit limiting."[6] Two ideas emerge from this statement that bear upon Page's status as guitar hero. First, Page, like Hendrix before him, is concerned with using the electric guitar to expand the sonic palette of rock, and is further interested in increasing the possible sounds derived from the guitar itself. His bowing segment recorded in the Zeppelin concert film, *The Song Remains the Same,* finds him generating a range of unusual sonic effects organized into a free-floating structure, sans accompaniment, that gives the guitarist maximum room for experimentation. Second, Page's recourse to a language of proper musical technique makes plain the central role of virtuosity to his persona, and to the guitar hero in general. The guitar hero is a master of his instrument, possessing the technique necessary to play musical passages outside the reach of other musicians. While Page was often rather humble with regard to his own technique, his concern with such matters shows him playing to type nonetheless.

Technical capabilities alone do not explain the impact of the guitar hero, however. Whatever Page might say about "legitimate bowing techniques," the use of a violin bow to play an electric guitar is a decidedly illegitimate practice. It was the very incongruity of the bow that made it such an effective symbol, connoting a style of virtuosity not typically associated with rock. Thus did Chris Welch deem the guitarist the

7.1. Jimmy Page, guitar hero, in classic virtuoso pose, playing his Gibson Les Paul with a violin bow. Courtesy of the Michael Ochs Archive, Venice, California.

"Paganini of the Seventies, who makes audiences scream by scraping a violin bow across screeching guitar strings."[7] Here Page's musical authority is put on par with one of the most noted of classical virtuosos in a manner that suggests the transhistorical power of musical prowess.[8] However, as the writer elaborates upon this comparison, other, stranger dimensions appear. Welch reminds us that "as a young man, the violinist [Paganini] wore tight trousers, hypnotised women and made them faint, while men said he must be possessed by the Devil, such was the effect of his playing."[9] The same analogy between Page and Paganini is made by Stephen Davis in his biography of Led Zeppelin, *Hammer of the Gods,* which recounts in greater detail the story of Paganini's reputed deal with the Devil, and asserts that "there has always been something about music and the lives of virtuoso musicians that carries with it the whiff of brimstone."[10]

These supernatural overtones are further reinforced by the film version of Page's bowed guitar solo. Beginning as a rather straightforward documentation of the performance, the visual track of the scene mutates into a fantasy sequence featuring the guitarist as an archetypal seeker, climbing a mountain in search, one assumes, of eternal truth. When he reaches the top, he is met by the sight of an ancient man bearing a light and a staff. The camera zooms onto the man's face, which undergoes a transformation backwards in time, tracing the various ages of man. As layers of old age (and makeup) are peeled from the face, it becomes recognizable as Page's own; he is positioned as both seeker and source of wisdom. While the bow-induced guitar pyrotechnics create a maelstrom of sound on the audio track, the old man Page continues his transfiguration, his face shifting from adolescence to infancy to the fetal stage, and then reversing the process of aging to become an old man once again. At this point, the aged figure whips his staff over his head, weaving a trail of multicolored impressions in the air above him, and then fades from sight as Page the guitarist reassumes the screen, bow no longer in hand, to whip into the guitar solo section of the Zeppelin track "Dazed and Confused" with the rest of the band back in tow.

Often taken as an example of Page's pretentiousness and tendency to take himself too seriously,[11] the preceding scene nonetheless offers compelling evidence of the extent to which Page's capabilities as a guitarist were regularly framed in terms of power and mystery. The former of these qualities was common to all "guitar heroes"; the latter was more specific to Page, whose widely noted interest in the occult played into his image as an explorer of obscure or unknown musical territories.[12] In a dialogue between rock writers John Swenson and Bruce Malamut concerning Zeppelin, one of the principals speaks of the band's music as "Devil music," and goes on to declare that Page "has this whole idea of how to play that is so unique, so dissonant, so out of step with the norm that he develops a new language."[13] Even for those less concerned with the demonic underpinnings of his music, Page stood as a musician who pushed listeners in unexpected directions. In a review of one of Zeppelin's concerts, critic Roy Hollingsworth described Page's virtuosity in such terms: "when technical ability might just swamp feeling, Page finds a dirty dischord, and lets it cut ugly and messy through the tapestry. It sort of jerks your body and throws you, and then he finds a true line again, and weaves on in a straight, sharp direction."[14] These representations of Page share the idea of the guitarist as an unsettling performer who pushes his audience past the comfort zone yet manages to satisfy them nonetheless.

One can detect in these comments strong hints of a romantic conception of the artist as a heroic individual whose freedom of imagination permits him to transgress or transcend the constraints of everyday life.[15] From this perspective, the critical preoccupation with Page's interest in the occult can be interpreted as an example of the historical romantic association between art, and especially music, and the forces of unreason.[16] More intriguing, though, is Page's correspondence to what musicologist Lawrence Kramer has termed the "impossible object" of the virtuoso performer. Kramer describes the "impossible object" as an excessive figure that arouses both desire and repulsion, and locates this structure of desire most firmly in the manner of "bravura performance" employed by virtuoso musicians. "The esthetics of bravura reduces music to sound production. What the audience sees is a theatrical icon of the inspired musician; what it hears is a highly charged extension of the performer's touch, breath, rhythm."[17] With the virtuoso, the sound of music becomes inseparable from the spectacle of the performer, whose technical flamboyance disrupts any effort to perceive music as a self-contained structure. Every note takes explicit shape as a physical manifestation of the performing musician; and this intense physicality is often transmitted to those in the audience, as Roy Hollingsworth's assessment of Page makes clear. In rock music of the 1970s, moreover, this tendency of the guitar hero to exceed the normal boundaries of musical practice was often indistinguishable from the electric guitar's role in defining those boundaries, particularly with regard to the gendered nature of rock performance.

Every Inch of My Love

Of course, the association of the electric guitar with excessive male physicality is a familiar theme. As I have already argued, the electric guitar as "technophallus" was built out of a highly charged relationship between white and black men, within which white men sought to appropriate what they perceived to be the potency of black men. The electric guitar mediated this relationship in at least two ways. Visually, it was used to accentuate the phallic dimensions of the performing male body. Aurally, the volume and distortion generated by the instrument had a similar effect, amplifying the physical presence of the performer.

The London music scene of the 1960s, out of which Led Zeppelin emerged, was perhaps the main crucible of activity for this style of guitar performance. It was no accident that Jimi Hendrix achieved a degree of success in London that had eluded him in the United States. By the time of Hendrix's arrival in London in 1967, a significant cult of the electric guitarist had already developed, largely around a trio of musicians who played, at one time or another, in a single band, The Yardbirds: Eric Clapton, Jeff Beck, and Jimmy Page. Part of the British "beat music" movement that arose in the middle of the decade, the Yardbirds in their early period were considered counterparts of the Rolling Stones, insofar as both groups exhibited the influence of African-American music without the melodic, pop-oriented trappings of the Beatles.[18] When the band began to move toward a more well-produced sound in keeping with standards of pop success, their guitarist, Clapton, opted to quit rather than compromise his commitment to a blues-based authenticity. As the story goes, Jimmy Page, then a noted London session guitarist, was asked to replace Clapton, but refused, and recommended his friend Jeff Beck instead. Page himself joined the band in the middle of 1966, originally to replace bassist Paul Samwell-Smith; but eventually he shifted to guitar, his native instrument. For a time the Yardbirds featured Page and Beck as dual lead guitarists, but personality conflicts led to Beck's departure, and Page occupied the lead guitar position by himself until the breakup of the band in 1968.

This continual shifting of personnel led long-time Yardbirds producer Giorgio Gomelsky to label the group a "laboratory for lead guitar players."[19] Particularly after Beck joined, the band's "experimental" impulses were widely championed in the London rock press. Along with Pete Townshend of the Who, Beck was one of the first British guitarists to play with the possibilities of electronic sound, crafting feedback into his solos in a way that trod the line between controlled and uncontrolled expression. Indeed, this ability to impose control upon the potential sonic chaos of the electric guitar contributed greatly to the perception of the guitarist as a heroic figure.[20] Meanwhile, Clapton more thoroughly represented the other side of the guitar hero equation, the mastery of the guitar as a solo instrument through the acquisition of a blues-based virtuosity. As art-school students in the early 1960s, Clapton, Beck, and Page all participated in the bohemian networks of exchange that developed at these schools, networks focused upon the shared appreciation of American blues and rock 'n' roll.[21] Whereas Beck and Page never lost their early attachment to rock 'n' roll guitarists like Cliff Gallup and James Burton, Clapton has described how his tastes shifted significantly during his tenure with the Yardbirds: "At first I played exactly like Chuck Berry for six or seven months . . . Then I got into the older bluesmen . . . I just finally got completely overwhelmed in this brand-new world. I studied it and listened to it and went right down in it and came back up in it."[22]

Clapton's immersion in the blues, and his willingness to quit one of London's most popular groups rather than compromise his musical principles, led to his virtual deification among a core of rock enthusiasts; the stories of "Clapton Is God" graffiti appearing on London streets during his tenure with John Mayall's Bluesbreakers have become part of the popular mythology of rock. More relevant to my purposes here, though, is the way in which first rock 'n' roll and then the blues signified a "brand new world" for Clapton and his fellow musicians, a world made exotic by its association with two terms of otherness, "black" and "American," which together formed the basis of an alternative teen identity among British youth.[23] The electric guitar, in turn, became one of the primary symbols of this identity, conferring an aura of coolness upon anyone lucky enough to own one, let alone be able to play it. Clapton has related his attachment to the guitar to his youthful fantasies about "being a Chicago bluesman, driving around in a Cadillac and living the life," a notion of black existence that he now acknowledges was born out of ignorance of the real circumstances of African American life.[24] The general enthusiasm for the guitar is more elaborately conveyed by Jeff Beck in his detailed account of his efforts to build his first electric instrument.

> The first one I made was out of a piece of cigar box, and then I progressed on that . . . And I had so little money, and that was the thing I wanted to do so much. I'd go down to the shop and wait 'till the place was pretty packed out and I whipped one of these pickups right out of the shop . . . Oh boy, I couldn't have cared if I'd got thrown in jail for six months, I had my pickup. And there was a little hole cut in the guitar that had been waiting for that pickup for about eight months. And it fitted perfectly because I had already got the dimensions from a plan, and it just slipped in there with two screws and, boy, I was the king! I used to deliberately carry my guitar around without a case so everyone could see what it looked like . . . the expressions on people's faces when they saw this weird guitar, that was something. It wasn't something boring like a violin or a sax in a very stock-looking case. It was bright yellow with these wires and knobs on it; people just freaked out.[25]

The strangeness of the electric guitar made it an ideal symbol of rebellion and prestige for young men like Beck and his schoolboy chum Jimmy Page who disdained the norms of bourgeois life—"boring" instruments like the violin or saxophone. In contrast to those "stock-looking" instruments, Beck's guitar was a product of his own endeavors and a statement of his personality. Thus was the electric guitar in these early years linked to a version of expressive authenticity seen to be opposed to the standardization of everyday life. As Page stated, "The good thing about the guitar . . . was that they *didn't* teach it in school . . . I know that Jeff Beck and I enjoyed pure music because we didn't *have* to."[26]

Even more provocative is Beck's language in describing his placement of the pickup, a perfect example of the ways in which the ideal of masculine achievement contained within the guitar hero ("boy, I was the king!") hinges in part (or in parts) upon the eroticization of technology. The pickup, without which the guitar could not be amplified, stands in Beck's narrative as the part which makes the electric guitar into a whole. This tension between the whole and its parts is, according to Judith Butler, a central dynamic in the construction of the phallus as a privileged signifier. In her essay, "The Lesbian Phallus and the Morphological Imaginary," Butler deconstructs the opposition between physical and imagined bodies to raise the problem of "determining what constitutes a body part at all, and . . . what constitutes an erotogenic body part in particular."[27] Her goal is to upset the persistent assumption that the penis is the dominant "part" in the production of sexual pleasure. Thus does she enact a complex argument about the relationship between the penis, as that part of the male body taken to be most essentially masculine, and the phallus, as the imaginary signifier that functions to organize the various parts of the male body into a unified whole, and to mask the extent to which that unity gains its significance from a single part.[28] She goes on to assert that the phallus bears no necessary relationship to the penis, or to the physical male body, that insofar as it represents an imaginary relationship it can be appropriated by any active sexual subject regardless of biological attributes, and moreover can be appropriated in ways that do not merely reproduce or imitate masculinist modes of pleasure and power.

The full implications of Butler's critique of the phallus lead us beyond the scope of this chapter, but her argument remains very much relevant to my purpose of analyzing the gendered dimensions of the electric guitar. Much as the pickup stood for Jeff Beck as the part that ensured his instrument's wholeness, the electric guitar itself can be interpreted as the part that ensures the integrity of the performing male body, a body whose very dependence upon technology threatens its unity in ways discussed in the previous chapter. This is the main importance of the electric guitar as technophallus: as a phallus clearly dissociated from the penis, it produces the appearance of male potency even as it threatens to denaturalize that appearance, to reduce masculinity to its constituent parts.

All of which brings us to the matter of cock rock. Though often used as a generic descriptive term to denote the masculinist orientation of rock, cock rock has also been defined in more specific terms by Simon Frith and Angela McRobbie to refer to the male-centered exhibitionism of hard rock performance.[29] For Frith and McRobbie, cock rock is "explicitly about male sexual performance," and as such stands as a distinctly homosocial activity that holds little attraction for girls who "are educated into understanding sex as something nice, soft, loving, and private."[30] In cock rock performance, mikes and guitars are phallic symbols, and "cock rockers' musical skills become synonymous with their sexual skills (hence Jimi Hendrix's simultaneous status as stud and guitar hero)."[31] The culmination of such practices for the two writers was "the heavy metal macho style of Led Zeppelin," which represented the consolidation of "mass youth music . . . as a male form of expression," and therefore repudiates the idea held by many that rock offers a liberated version of sexuality.[32]

There is much in the cock rock framework built by Frith and McRobbie that is sympathetic with my own argument. Yet, as Frith himself acknowledged in a later essay, there is also much that is crude and reductionist in the cock rock formulation, particularly regarding the failure of the two writers to clearly define the relationship between sex and gender or to decide whether cock rock merely reinforced existing gender relations or worked to produce these relationships.[33] My reasons for addressing it despite these reservations voiced by one of the authors are twofold: first, the term "cock rock," and the conceptual framework it implies, remains influential in rock criticism, specifically with regard to Led Zeppelin; and second, there are flaws in the critical notion of cock rock beyond those Frith has already recognized.

*   *   *

The quintessential cock rock song, by almost unanimous critical decision, is Zeppelin's "Whole Lotta Love," the lead track from their second album, *Led Zeppelin II*, released late in 1969. Structured around a three-note riff jerked into motion by Page's distorted guitar, the song's musical insistence—guitar, bass, and drums locked into a repetitive groove that stutters toward resolution with every measure—was reinforced by Robert Plant's vocals, which mediated between blues shout and high-pitched scream in a manner befitting the coarse sentiments of the lyrics:

> Way, way down inside
> I'm gonna give you my love
> I'm gonna give you every inch of my love
> Gonna give you my love

After two verse-chorus sequences, Plant's voice and Page's sliding guitar descend into a midsection that shifts radically from the song's main riff. John Bonham's quickly tapped cymbal supports an assemblage of seemingly formless, unsettling sonic effects generated by Page's tape experiments and his use of the theremin, an unusual instrument that allows for the manipulation of sound by waving a hand around an antenna attached to an electronic oscillator.[34] Over these sounds that alternately crash and flow in waves, Plant's voice emits various groans and heaving pants that are similarly processed by electronic technology. Out of this morass, a sustained, middle-ranged hum induced by Page's guitar is punctuated by Bonham's now-pounding drum, which gives way to a stunning series of virtuosic episodes by Page, notable for their brevity: sharp-toned high-pitched bent notes interrupted at every measure by two severely loud power chords. The sixth such episode brings us to another verse-chorus statement that speeds along into a second instance of dissolution. As the instruments fall silent, Plant's voice bursts forth,

> Waaaaaaay down inside
> Woman
> You need

(Guitar, bass and drums issue two massive power chords, from E, the song's dominant, to A, and then lapse back into silence.)

> Loooooooooooooove

The descending pitch of Plant's last, extremely protracted syllable gives way to yet another fit of Bonham's drums, and as the main riff reasserts itself one last time Plant's guttural vocal gestures echo a Howlin' Wolf blues: "Shake for me girl/I wanna be your back door man."

In his discussion of "Whole Lotta Love," Charles Shaar Murray stresses the tune's crude paraphrase of blues sexuality, using the song to illustrate how this particular strain of the blues "gradually mutated into the penile dementia of heavy-metal rock."[35] Whereas the clearest precedent for the song, Muddy Waters's "You Need Love," is described by Murray as "intimate, relaxed, utterly sensual," Led Zeppelin's version is likened to "thermonuclear gang rape" within which the woman addressed in the song is reduced to a "mere receptacle."[36] Like Frith and McRobbie, Murray stresses the extent to which such a style of performance is ultimately intended for other men, serving as a ritual that validates masculine prowess. He goes on to assert that the "Love" of the title "is a euphemism for something measurable with a ruler; when Plant howls, 'I'm gonna give you every inch of MAH LURVE,' the term 'imply' is too mild for the intensity he brings to the suggestion that his love is, quite literally, his penis."[37]

That Led Zeppelin, in a song like "Whole Lotta Love," work to elide any separation of penis and phallus in a way that upholds a phallocentric regime of power and pleasure is, for all intents and purposes, inarguable. What I find problematic in the observations of Murray, Frith, and McRobbie is the extent to which their criticisms, however well articulated, leave this operation intact, and how the term "cock rock" reifies the very process it seeks to break down. "Whole Lotta Love" presents a less unified version of masculinity than critics would admit. The interruption of the throbbing, single-minded riff by the quagmire of the middle section enacts a crisis in the representation of phallic potency;[38] and even the resuscitation performed by Page on his guitar is a rigidly contained musical statement, his virtuosity hemmed in by the wall of sound produced by the band as a whole. Thus, while Page's guitar and Plant's microphone do indeed work to produce an effect of phallic mastery, they do so in a way that makes plain how that mastery is not a given, but must be achieved, and further signify that masculine integrity, as Judith Butler suggests, continually threatens to break down into its parts.

The relationship between Page and Plant alluded to above warrants further attention, for they present an important example of the sorts of relationships that were established between men in hard rock performance. Reviewers of the band's shows regularly discussed the interplay between the two, examples of which can also be seen in *The Song Remains the Same:* singer and guitarist seeking to echo and imitate one another "as both get inside each other's phrases to twist, expand and blow them up," Plant exploiting the possibilities of electronic sound every bit as much as his counterpart Page.[39] Such exercises did not only work to reinforce a sense of fraternal bonding and camaraderie among the musicians, however. As characterized by Robert Plant, the interaction between himself and Page was at once tense and playful: "Jimmy was a vicious bastard . . . [During the climax of the song "You Shook Me"] we used to lean forward and look at each other. He would go higher and higher up the frets until he was somewhere around top E. I could see his fingers going further and further up, and I'd be going, 'No, don't do this to me!'"[40] Much as "Whole Lotta Love" presented sexual and musical

7.2. Page and singer Robert Plant—a pair whose combination of competition and camaraderie set the tone for onstage relationships between the men of 1970s hard rock. Courtesy of the Michael Ochs Archive, Venice, California.

prowess to be ridden with conflict, the interplay between Page and Plant was marked by both cooperation and competition.[41] Together they disturbed the boundary between voice and guitar, and the manner in which Plant's voice is effectively denaturalized in descriptions of the band in performance emphasizes how the singer used his voice as "another instrument . . . geared along the lead guitar's screaming highs."[42] Electronic technology was the medium through which Page and Plant negotiated for space within their band, complementing and clashing with one another as they worked to strike a balance of power between their respective instruments.

In the rock world of the 1960s and 1970s, a similarly competitive dynamic existed among lead guitarists. Indeed, one of the main results of the apotheosis of the guitarist was precisely this highly gendered element of competition to see who could outplay whom. Jimmy Page often spoke in such terms when describing his experience with the Yardbirds: "The whole group was a guitar precedent. Everybody was just into doing what's now known as jamming on stage. Eric [Clapton] began the precedent, and when he left Jeff [Beck] felt that he had to be better than Eric, and when I was left, I felt I had to try hard too."[43] Meanwhile, Yardbirds' bassist Chris Dreja spoke of the tension that often arose onstage during the brief period when Page and Beck were together in the band: "I personally don't think Jimmy ever went out on stage with the intention of trying to blow Jeff off the stage. But with Jeff I think it got to be a 'my-balls-are-bigger-than-yours' sort of thing."[44] Intergroup tensions reflected the broader mood of the rock scene; by the 1970s, guitarists interviewed by *Guitar Player* magazine regularly bemoaned the emphasis upon technique that turned music into a contest to see who could play the fastest, loudest, or most precisely.[45] Jimmy Page, for his part, complained that "people shouldn't . . . expect to see the epitome of what they consider to be the best rock guitar . . . There's nobody who's the best—nobody's the best."[46] Yet the process of heroization was already well underway, and a new hierarchy of masculine achievement was created, continually reinforced by magazine polls that ranked guitarists according to their abilities. Guitarists, Page included, were expected to combine virtuosic display, bodily flamboyance, and mastery of the ability to control and manipulate technology.

*   *   *

The people most attracted to the ideal of the hard, hairy, virile hunk
of male are, in fact, other men.

—*Sheryl Garratt, in Frith and Goodwin (1990), p. 402.*

This remark by Sheryl Garratt articulates what seems to have become the
conventional wisdom regarding the guitar-oriented style of hard rock
performance purveyed by Led Zeppelin. It certainly restates the assumptions of Murray, Frith, and McRobbie regarding cock rock as a sort of
homoerotic spectacle oriented toward the affirmation of male prowess.
While there is a significant degree of truth in this interpretation, I think
we might do well, once again, to investigate this claim further. Eve Sedgwick reminds us in *Between Men* that the line between homosociality and
homosexuality is one of the most strenuously guarded in the last several
hundred years of Euro-American culture. "What *counts* as the sexual is
. . . variable and itself political," she declares, and goes on to assert that
while homosociality has been central to the operation of patriarchy, it has
tended to exist alongside a virulent homophobia.[47] One can easily apply
such notions to the study of rock sexuality; for as the electric guitar as
technophallus works to affirm a phallocentric, male-dominated sexual
order, it works with equal vigor to produce the appearance that this order
is unquestionably heterosexual. Thus did Susan Hiwatt argue that despite
the relative marginalization of women within rock, "The whole rock
scene (as opposed to rock music) depends on our being there. Women are
necessary at these places of worship so that, in between sets, the real
audience (men) can be assured of getting that woman they're supposed to
like."[48] However eroticized the relationships between men might seem in
hard rock performance, then, we stress their homoerotic content at the
risk of reducing their complexity and their full political significance.

Where Led Zeppelin is concerned, women tend to assume one of two
roles in the narratives spun around the band's career: wife or groupie. The
wives are the most thoroughly marginalized characters in books like
Stephen Davis's *Hammer of the Gods* and Richard Cole's *Stairway to
Heaven*. When they are mentioned, it is usually in the context of trying to
keep them ignorant of the band's sexual antics while on tour. Which, of

course, is where the groupies come into the story. Tales of Zeppelin's sexual excesses have assumed mythical proportions, which members of the band have done nothing to deny. Robert Plant's nostalgic reminiscence of "shoving the Plaster Casters' cast of Jimi Hendrix's penis up one of the girls in Detroit" as an instance of "free love" might be read as disingenuous, but no interpretation can overcome the connotations of rape contained within the scene.[49] The specter of female violation that hovered around the Zeppelin entourage was powerfully conveyed by Ellen Sander, one of the relatively few women who wrote regularly about rock during the 1960s and 1970s. After traveling with the band for weeks to report on their 1969 U.S. tour for *Life* magazine, Sander

> stopped in to say good-bye and godspeed. Two members of the group attacked me, shrieking and grabbing at my clothes, totally over the edge. I fought them off until [Zeppelin manager] Peter Grant rescued me, but not before they managed to tear my dress down the back. My young man of the evening took me home in a limousine borrowed from an agent friend and I trembled in exhaustion, anger, and bitterness all the way. Over the next week I tried to write the story. It was not about to happen. It took a whole year just to get back to my notes again with any kind of objectivity.
>
> If you walk inside the cages of the zoo you get to see the animals close up, stroke the captive pelts, and mingle with the energy behind the mystique. You also get to smell the shit firsthand.[50]

Sander's is a rare female voice that managed to articulate the trauma that many women who participated in the rock scene undoubtedly shared. Her example stands as evidence that the deployment of sexuality by the members of Led Zeppelin had very little to do with "free love," or with any notion of sexuality that was to provide for either female pleasure or female agency.

That such behavior was effectively normalized in the context of 1970s rock is borne out by another tour report filed by a female rock journalist, Jaan Uhelszki. More subtle in tone and detail, Uhelszki recounts a conversation with an evasive Plant concerning the band's activities. She notes how guarded Zeppelin try to be about their offstage antics, and then teases her reader by asking, "But wouldn't you be disappointed it there weren't *any*? I know I'd be aghast if I heard Zeppelin had cleaned up their offstage act."[51] Later in the article, Uhelszki pauses to "wonder if part of their popularity is due to the fact that they're the last of an era of cock rockers who play dirty and, if you'll excuse the expression, 'chauvinistic' rock 'n' roll."[52] Uhelszki's critical voice rears its head, but defensively, for she knows both her audience and her subjects too well. Rock stars of Zeppelin's stature were expected to play dirty, and part of the privilege that went along with being a male rock star was the power to do so with impunity, even when the stakes involved something on the order of rape.

Important as it is to recognize the reality of sexual violence in this context, though, it would be a mistake to conclude that violence was the only outcome for women drawn to Zeppelin, or that rock sexuality offers no satisfying outlet for female heterosexual desires. The memoir of Pamela Des Barres, who for years was the reigning groupie on the Hollywood rock scene, offers a fascinating account of a woman who was clearly coveted as a prize by male rock stars, yet who in having sex with those rock stars also enacted her own version of sexual fantasy. Her discussion of her sexual coming of age, which occurred amidst her shifting allegiance from the Beatles to the Rolling Stones, is especially suggestive:

> My brief sexual encounters with [my boyfriend] Bob had opened new vistas of turgid, twisting thoughts, and Mick Jagger *personified* a penis. I took my new records and my glossy photographs into my rock and roll room, where I scaled new heights of tortuous teen abandon . . . With my precious Paul [McCartney], I never really got past the hoping stage, but now I dared to imagine Mick with his widewale corduroy trousers down around his ankles.[53]

Out of such youthful desires, Des Barres formed her ideal of "hanging on to the hand of an English rock star," which she fulfilled many times with figures like Jagger and, in perhaps her most reputed affair, Jimmy Page. For Des Barres, Page and Led Zeppelin epitomized "The Glorious English Pop Star to perfection," with their long hair and satin outfits.[54] She recounts the aura of danger that hovered around the band, and particularly Page, who had already earned something of a reputation among the groupies on the scene. Yet when she is invited to accompany the guitarist on tour, she exclaims, "I was exactly what I had always aspired to be: the girlfriend of the lead guitar player in the world's biggest and best rock and roll band."[55]

Des Barres's experiences cannot be taken as wholly typical. As perhaps the most coveted groupie on the rock scene, she occupied a clear position of privilege that exempted her from the mistreatment that many other women faced. Yet her account of the pleasures to be derived from a fascination with hard rock stars should not be judged as a simple anomaly. In a 1969 interview with Germaine Greer, for instance, a groupie by the name of Dr. G asserted that "the great thing about starfucking is that every time you play a record, or just dig his thing again, it's all there, like he was there."[56] Greer has offered a more hands-off analysis of the appeal of rock stars for women. Contrasting rock musicians with the proliferation of nude male pin-ups produced during the 1970s that were supposed to turn on women sexually, Greer declares that the musicians "celebrate phallic energy" rather than "exposing passive flesh." "The way the singer moves, the pulse and boom of the music, the guitarist's affair with his instrument, the exhibitionism of the drummer, all demonstrate the power of libido" in a manner that Greer herself found quite arousing.[57] Regarding Led Zeppelin, similar sentiments were put forth by Susan Whitall in a 1979 article in *Creem,* in which the writer remembers listening to "Jimmy's tarty guitar on 'You Shook Me'—a few bars and my lower torso would become 17-year-old rice pudding. Which brings me," Whitall continues, "to my pet Heavy Metal theory—girl fans only go (went?) for the bands who sell sex along with their consciousness-destroying power chords. And nobody can peddle below-the-belt heaving and moaning as prettily as the Zep boys."[58] Zeppelin's brand of phallic display was indeed male-oriented, and the band's practices sometimes had violent effects that were not merely imaginary, but neither of these points foreclosed the possibility of active female desires within which the "boys" figured as coveted objects.

Along these lines, perhaps the most provocative statement was made by the mysteriously named Emily XYZ. Writing for a recent *Village Voice* retrospective on Led Zeppelin, Emily XYZ reiterates Susan Whitall's observations concerning the sexual content of Zeppelin's music, but in more exaggerated terms:

If ever a band generated SEX on a grand, gothic scale, it was Zeppelin. So high was their net efficiency that by 1979 it was determined they had added something like 40 per cent to the world's proven reserves of Uncontrollable and Insatiable Lust. In fact, there is nothing in their music *but* sex, all of it unequivocally male. Jimmy Page's insistent guitar is the voice of a man bent on seduction, whose goal is not pleasure but absolute domination . . . And Plant is his flip side: regular guy as victim of coldhearted sorceress, kicked in the balls by the little schoolgirl he worships . . . in a word, PUSSY-WHIPPED. Makes my cock hard just to think about it, and I don't even have a cock.[59]

Cock rock here assumes a new fluidity rooted in the sort of lack of sexual fixity gestured toward by Judith Butler in her discussion of the lesbian phallus. Emily XYZ appropriates through language the cock that others have assumed was only for male use, and proceeds to proclaim that "Jimmy Page the two-timing fuck and Robert Plant the pathetic dweeb made soundtracks for the edification of young women everywhere, all with the same moral: sex is power. Love may be democracy, but sex is autocracy, maybe even dictatorship."[60]

Critics of cock rock have decried the gender/power dynamic enacted in Led Zeppelin's music, but Emily XYZ celebrates its exaltation of potency. Her comments do not overturn the cock rock argument so much as they present a model of desire that existing criticisms of rock sexuality have rarely taken into account. Which is to say that although desire and power often reinforce one another in the context of rock performance, and although both generally work to uphold patterns of male domination, desire is nonetheless not determined by these relations in any simple correlative manner. Moreover, phallocentrism does not stand in absolute opposition to a pure, nonhierarchical feminine desire, as some critics have suggested, but exists as a powerful, at times brutal tendency that opens certain possibilities for pleasure and closes others.[61] This may not be the sort of liberated sexuality that many had desired from rock during the 1960s, but neither was it a bleak, repressive sexual dystopia that only served the gratification of some mythic cock.

Heavy

In the summer of 1971, British pop newspaper *New Musical Express* published an article indicative of the mood of the times in rock. "Ear Bashers Are Out," read the headline, and the writer, John Stirn, began by proclaiming rather matter-of-factly that "rock music is dead. Not the term rock music," clarified Stirn, "but the music known as rock has become a ghost and the remains are gentle, reflective and calm."[62] Gone was the sense of impending youth revolution that had driven so much sixties rock; according to Stirn, the moment when rock might have acted as a force for change had slipped by, and perhaps was never more than an illusion anyway. "Rock music has come to mean a lot of things. So when it is stated that rock is dead it means that superamplified music associated with the Beatles [?], Jefferson Airplane, Canned Heat, Cream and the Stones is gone. And so are most of the groups that played it. For clarity, call this music acid rock."[63] For Stirn, acid rock was a music in which excessive volume precluded any potential for subtlety and sophistication, and lack of discipline led not to freedom but to exhaustion or even death, in the cases of Janis Joplin and Jimi Hendrix (or in the case of rock itself, as Stirn would have it). The future rested in musicians like James Taylor, whose more quiet and introspective songs were easier to listen to and were premised upon a sensitivity that eschewed the anger of sixties rebellion in favor of a more positive, contemplative outlook.

Stirn's pronouncement reverberated throughout the pages of *New Musical Express* in the ensuing months, and nowhere more so than in discussions of Led Zeppelin. Recounting a confrontation between police and several thousand Zeppelin fans who were refused admission to a sold-out concert at a Vancouver hockey arena, Jim Smith offered that "soft music may, like everyone's saying, be the current rage. But someone forgot to tell all those hard-rock fans that times have changed. Unless Led Zeppelin is a soft-rock group."[64] Only a few weeks later, in a review of a Zeppelin concert in Toronto, Ritchie Yorke voiced an almost identical sentiment: "Despite the oft-heralded downfall of hard rock, Led Zeppelin is living, loving proof that although James Taylor is doing fine, he has quite a way to go before reaching the superstar success level of the Zepp or their U.S. counterparts, Grand Funk Railroad."[65]

Perhaps the most interesting response to Stirn's comments, though, was a letter to the editor by one David Brown, from Newcastle-upon-Tyne, who stated that "All this talk about heavy rock music going out of style is in my opinion totally unfounded."[66] Unlike his journalistic counterparts, Brown refused to draw strict lines between soft and heavy music, but instead insisted that "when a new style of music comes along it should exist alongside of what has gone before," and went on to point to Led Zeppelin as a band that had "the right balance . . . of hard rock and softer numbers."[67] Indeed, Zeppelin's position within the debate over the relative value of hard versus soft rock was somewhat ambiguous, though most commentators opted to place them squarely on the hard rock divide, a point that endlessly frustrated Jimmy Page. By 1971, the band's music had moved toward something of a synthesis of these different sounds. *Led Zeppelin III,* released in 1970, featured a whole side of acoustic songs, and the untitled follow-up album, issued a year later, continued the efforts at sonic variety. In the pages of *New Musical Express,* Jimmy Page declared his relative ignorance of the new wave of bands like Grand Funk Railroad who had been grouped under the hard or heavy rock label, and expressed a wish, very similar to that articulated by *NME* reader Brown, to move away from the sort of rock scene in which styles and sounds were pitted against one another:

> The sort of scene I'd like to see is where all the different facets of the arts in the musical sphere are accepted readily by the media and the public.
>
> As it stands at the moment, and it's because of the press, there has to be one particular thing in vogue at any one time. As soon as that one thing becomes really popular, that's it; you've got to find something else, something new.[68]

Page's comments here are colored by his enduring antagonism with the press, but also give voice to a curious brand of musical ecumenicalism that stood in opposition to the more general tendency to categorize and polarize the varieties of rock music. Moreover, they are reflective of Page's general disengagement from arguments about the meaning of rock, and his lack of interest in framing Zeppelin's music in any concrete social and political terms. For Page it was the music that mattered; in interviews, he regularly fell back on a language of aesthetic autonomy, discussing rock in terms of its growing structural complexity in a way that virtually collapsed the distinction between high and popular musical forms.[69] These impulses were manifested most explicitly in the release of the band's fourth album. Disappointed by the critical response to *Led Zeppelin III,* Page led the group's decision to release the next album in an unusual package, with a cover that bore no title, no logos, and no mention of the band's name. Explaining the rationale behind this move, he asked,

> What does Led Zeppelin mean? It doesn't mean a thing. What matters is our music. If we weren't playing good music, nobody would care what we call ourselves. If the music was good, we could call ourselves cabbages and still get across to our audience . . . the record company told us we were committing professional suicide [in releasing an album so unconventionally packaged]. We said we just wanted to rely *purely* on our music.[70]

Page's yearning to move Led Zeppelin away from having a fixed public image, to have the band judged solely on the merits of its music, seems to have been a result of an almost obsessive desire to control how the band was received and understood. To work as "Led Zeppelin" meant always having to play to expectations that fans and critics brought to each album and each performance, a situation that for Page limited the possibilities for the band's creativity. Yet for all Page's desire not to have his music tied to a single term or a single sound, Led Zeppelin remained a hard rock band, probably the preeminent hard rock band of its time, and as such figured prominently in debates over the music's significance and direction.

*   *   *

The most controversial band of the moment in 1971 was Grand Funk Railroad, aforementioned "American counterparts" to Led Zeppelin, and purveyors of a more crudely heavy sound than Zeppelin practiced. For their crudeness they were reviled by most rock critics, who perceived them to be playing to the lowest common denominator of rock taste. Yet they also proved to be wildly popular during the first years of the new decade, and the disparity between critical opinion and popular appeal led to them becoming a sort of cultural phenomenon, as writers continually puzzled over what fans could appreciate in their music. Of the many articles written about the band, the most provocative was by Richard Goldstein, whose assessment of Grand Funk contains many of the same points as John Stirn's discussion of hard rock, but more sympathetically and with a sharper eye toward the politics of popular culture.

Where Stirn had presented the "death of rock" as something desirable, an event that allowed more mature and thoughtful musical forms to flourish, it was this very move toward maturity that Goldstein viewed critically. "Rock has developed an etiquette," bemoaned Goldstein. It had become polite, even sophisticated, and in the process had "eschewed the gluttony it once celebrated, the kind of no-stakes, no-use energy, and the freedom that kind of force incurs."[71] In effect, rock music risked losing touch with its core audience, the only audience that really mattered as far as rock was concerned: the young, or more specifically, lower middle-class youth. "To be a rock 'n' roller requires that one occupy a certain position in life," stated Goldstein, "that one hunger after distinction, the joy of exhibition, and the gratification of ritual love"; and such hungers were to be found most clearly in "the lower reaches of the rock hierarchy, below the level of the current tapedeck saints . . . where a kid sits hunched over his amp, ready to enact again the mythic hustle that is rock 'n' roll."[72]

It was precisely at this level that Goldstein saw the appeal of a band like Grand Funk Railroad, and it was because they appealed to this strata of the rock audience that he perceived them to be of great significance to the current state of rock music. Rather than cater to those who associated the "progress" of rock with confessional lyrics and refined musicianship, Grand Funk presented for Goldstein a more populist alternative. Quoting the band's manager, Terry Knight, Goldstein presents an image of Mark Farner, Grand Funk singer and guitarist, as "a symbol of freedom." "He takes that guitar and he holds it, and he says, 'See this, brothers and sisters, this is how I broke the mold. I found one thing and I stayed at it. This is the power that put me here. This is the symbol that the establishment picks apart. This is what every music critic in the world said I can't play, but this is what brought us together, brothers and sisters.'"[73] One might recognize the rhetoric here as being very close to that of the MC5 (and Grand Funk were also a Michigan band, though from Flint rather than Detroit), but in this instance the emphasis on solidarity is less incendiary, even where the "establishment" is invoked critically. More to the point, hard rock is figured here as an outlet for a particular sort of freedom, not the revolutionary freedom the MC5 had gestured toward, but an almost defensive freedom, a freedom to pursue basic, immediate pleasures in the face of the pressure to strive for a more elevated sense of purpose. The electric guitar is posited here as the ultimate symbol of this freedom, perhaps even its source.

That this is a decidedly ambivalent sort of freedom, one born from limited opportunities and that on some fundamental level accepts those limitations rather than challenging them, is acknowledged by Goldstein when he describes a Grand Funk concert. Performing in the massive Shea Stadium in New York, Grand Funk produce what Goldstein calls a distinctly "mechanical" sound with the "power of an engine," a sound with "no virtuosity, no variety, no shading in volume or in mood, only the propulsive competence of a clean machine."[74] Indeed, for Goldstein, Grand Funk stand as the ultimate example of "the performer as cyborg," for whom the tools of technology are so foregrounded as to erase the appearance of human activity.[75] The encompassing power of the electric guitar and its attendant technologies gives release to a force and energy that has the capacity to move thousands. This form of release, Goldstein reiterates, belonged squarely to the young, to that new generation of teens for whom the revolutionary hopes of the 1960s were old news.

At this point, we might pause to consider the disparity between the version of hard rock put forth by Grand Funk and that put forth by Led Zeppelin. While Goldstein describes Grand Funk as lacking variety and virtuosity, Zeppelin lacked neither; where Grand Funk presented a version of rock in which human performers seemed mechanical and technology seemed the true hero, Jimmy Page's guitar heroics presented a more complicated relationship between performer and technology, one in which musical virtuosity signified the ability to manipulate technology to one's own ends. Despite these differences, though, Goldstein's comments, and the broader narrative of rock's development of which they are a part, are of considerable relevance to understanding Zeppelin's historical position and importance. The terms of Goldstein's analysis, which were also the terms of the debate surrounding hard rock in the early 1970s, continue to resonate in contemporary discussions of rock, of popular music, and of popular culture more generally. They are also the terms that have framed the evaluation of Led Zeppelin's music, and the genre with which the band is most often associated, heavy metal. What we see in these debates of 1971 is an articulation of the historical conflicts and tensions that contributed to the formation of heavy metal as an identifiable musical category, and evidence that heavy metal was never merely a matter of sound (the distinction between acid rock, hard rock, and heavy metal can at some point never be more than tenuous), but also an ideological category created to signify one outgrowth of these tensions.

*   *   *

Led Zeppelin live in 1969 was an event unparalleled in musical history. They played longer and harder than any group ever had, totally
changing the concept of rock concerts. They flailed around like der-
vishes, making so much sound that the air was heavy with metal.

—*Pamela Des Barres (1988), p. 134.*

For those concerned with origins, Led Zeppelin's second album, recorded during their 1969 U.S. tour and released at the end of that year,
has often been considered the musical starting point for heavy metal.
Rolling Stone, for instance, canonized the album as one of the hundred
most influential records of the previous twenty years in 1987, and began
its review with the assertion that "heavy metal doesn't get any heavier
than this." The article continued, "*Led Zeppelin II* was like the Book of
Revelation scored for an electric boogie quartet, a vision of high-decibel
holocaust that combined the torrid, animalistic raunch of old Chess and
Sun records with the futuristic scream of rock's latest technology pushed
to the brink."[76] Such apocalyptic imagery is meant to convey the force of
the band's sonic assault, yet given the narrative established around hard
rock, I would also suggest that these metaphors can be taken to stand for
the ways in which Zeppelin's sound symbolically laid waste to the peace-
loving idealism of the 1960s, an interpretation reinforced by Stephen
Davis's like-minded account of *Led Zeppelin II* in his biography of the
band, *Hammer of the Gods.* Writing about the album's lead song, the
previously discussed "Whole Lotta Love," Davis states that it was

> an emergency telegram to a new generation. In its frenzy of sex, chaos, and
> destruction, it seemed to conjure all the chilling anxieties of the dying
> decade . . . Ironically, the song (and Led Zeppelin) didn't much appeal to
> the kids of the sixties . . . But their younger siblings, the high school kids,
> were *determined* to have more fun. Led Zeppelin was really their band. For
> the next decade Led Zeppelin would be the unchallenged monarchs of high
> school parking lots all over America.[77]

Davis goes on to suggest that "Whole Lotta Love," and *Led Zeppelin II,*
put forth a new sound that required a new term, and thus heavy metal was
born out of the terminological confusion that included "hard rock,"
"heavy music," "acid rock," and even "white blues."[78] Moreover, the kids

who made Zeppelin their heroes, by Davis's account, were not ready to settle into the softer sounds dictated by the exhaustion of sixties idealism, but rather latched onto Zeppelin as a means of asserting their own version of rock 'n' roll festivity.

One could point to any number of other examples to demonstrate the extent to which the origins of heavy metal are thoroughly entrenched in the narrative of 1960s decline, and are further caught up in the politics of youth culture. It would be easy enough to deconstruct the sense of historical rupture contained within this framework, and to argue that the tendencies in heavy metal taken to represent a break with the 1960s were in fact an outgrowth of that period, that bands like the MC5 and even Led Zeppelin emerged during the 1960s as counter-tendencies to the prevailing idealism of the Beatles or the San Francisco bands.[79] Yet such an easy dismissal does not adequately reckon with either the continuing power of the myth of the 1960s or the mythic dimensions of heavy metal, for at issue are not simply questions of historiographical propriety but the ideas and narratives we have developed to explain recent history and popular culture. At this level, the interlocking themes of the rise of heavy metal, the decline of the 1960s, and the capacity of rock's young audience to continually renew its sense of purpose are of great significance, for they give us insight into the changing conception of artistic and political possibility surrounding rock music during the past three decades.

Exactly what those possibilities might be remains very much a matter of debate, however. The optimistic accounts of Goldstein and Davis, for whom the kids listening to bands like Led Zeppelin and Grand Funk Railroad figure as the ultimate heroes of rock history, have been counterbalanced by critics who fear that Zeppelin, and heavy metal more generally, cultivated a new passivity among rock audiences. Of these, the most compelling is Robert Duncan, author of perhaps the best book on 1970s rock, *The Noise.* Duncan's analysis of heavy metal is steeped in the conventions already displayed; he rehearses the argument about the end of the 1960s (albeit in more sophisticated form than any of his peers), and assigns Led Zeppelin a position of primacy in his discussion of the genre. Where he departs from those cited earlier is in the sense he makes of metal's fascination with volume. As the loudest of rock styles, heavy metal took the 1960s exploitation of electronic technology, and specifically of the electric guitar, to an extreme. Duncan explains that "rock 'n' roll had always liked *loud* . . . because *loud* meant passion, *loud* meant the pent up anger of the age, and loud rock 'n' roll thus became an acting out of that anger and so some sort of return to the senses in the time of the rational, the technological."[80] In virtually the same breath, though, he issues a warning that "getting loud also meant getting technology, louder, even more"; the expansion of rock's technological base paralleled its expanding economic base, its growth into arena rock, where kids would pay escalated prices to see their favorite bands play from a football field away. Building upon this connection, Duncan argues that

> If *loud* meant passion and acting out, there was a line it crossed and a balance it tipped as it coursed the circuits and tubes of the Marshall amp stacks, and when the loud*est*ness of heavy metal came out the other end, into the arena, it was a series of sonic body blows, true violence and trauma, and finally something quite the opposite of passion. In fact, the loud*est*ness of heavy metal was a deadening of passion, a deadening of the senses . . . With heavy metal there was no acting *out,* just the being acted *upon.*[81]

By foregrounding technology in his discussion of the paradoxical effects of heavy metal "loudness," Duncan parallels the cautionary injunctions of Jacques Attali. While Attali postulated that the musical instrument could provide the basis for a utopian reconceptualization of musical order, he also drew attention to the negative effects that resulted from the undue prioritization of technology in musical performance. The underside of "taking pleasure in the instruments, the tools of communication" was for Attali the "radical inversion of the innovator and the machine," within which musicians worked to produce "what technology makes possible, instead of creating the technology for what one wishes to produce."[82] Attali elaborates upon the limitations of technology in his discussion of "Composition," the most potentially liberating musical practice: "Inducing people to compose using predefined instruments cannot lead to a mode of production different from that authorized by those instruments. That is the trap."[83] For Attali, then, as for Duncan, the issue of technology comes back to the matter of political economy. The electric guitar, and the manipulation of electronic noise, may have opened new creative spaces for musical production during the 1960s, but those spaces were rapidly commodified, so that what had seemed an instrument of revolutionary possibility had become a necessary component of the expanding economic base of rock music. Led Zeppelin broke concert attendance records throughout the 1970s, and worked to foster an image of grandeur that could only be contained within large arenas. And the electric guitar stood at the center of these developments, with Jimmy Page taking up vast amounts of musical space with the sound of his instrument, issuing forth guitar solos that, however breathtaking in their virtuosity, were in keeping with the new conventions of rock performance.

Judged from this perspective, the guitar hero serves a crucial ideological function, offering the appearance of individual achievement and mastery in the face of the growing crowds that occupied the spaces of rock performance. Yet we should be careful in assuming, as Duncan does, that the audience for such figures was so thoroughly pacified by the increased scale of sound and spectacle. The difficulty of determining the effects of Led Zeppelin's music can be gathered from a reminiscence by a fan of the band, Martin Millar. Discussing his years as an adolescent in Glasgow, Scotland, Millar describes how he and his friends "used to walk around the playground carrying [Zeppelin's] albums despite the fact that there was nowhere in school to play them. It was just good to have them around, and be seen with them. I spent a fair part of my early youth walking back and forth clutching *Led Zeppelin Two,* singing the riff to 'Whole Lotta Love' and conscientiously imitating all the guitar solos."[84] Millar's near-obsessive enthusiasm for Led Zeppelin reached new heights of excitement when he went to see the band perform in concert. "I loved every second of it," remembers Millar, "When Jimmy Page played his guitar with a violin bow I quite possibly wept for joy."[85] His experiences are affirmed among his friends at school. "'We are awestruck,' we said, walking around the playground carrying our Led Zeppelin albums. 'Completely awestruck.' And it was true."[86]

Millar's account certainly provides evidence for the claim that Zeppelin cultivated a sort of passivity among its fans. Though clearly intended to be comical, the image Millar presents of fans so engrossed in their appreciation of Zeppelin as to wander aimlessly around the playground, carrying albums they could not even listen to, evinces an almost crippling version of consumerism. At the same time, though, the sheer joy that Millar derived from Zeppelin ("Seeing Led Zeppelin was probably a more satisfying fulfilment of a dream than any that was to follow") is not reducible to a capitalist or technocratic deadening of the senses. Rather, Millar's response evokes the paradoxical nature of pleasure within the sphere of capitalist cultural production, a sort of pleasure described in Ann Powers's assessment of Led Zeppelin's appeal in the *Village Voice*. "Jimmy Page and Robert Plant didn't become the world's foremost monster rockers on dumb luck—these two have a knack for making music big enough for any number of fans to live inside at once . . . This is why people hated them: they took up so much space. And it's why people loved them: that space could swallow you up, take you in."[87] Here the size of Zeppelin's impact, the volume of the musical presence, is set in a new light, one that remains connected to the economic sphere but retains the capacity to exceed the mandates of capitalist accumulation. Led Zeppelin, more effectively than any band of the 1970s, negotiated between economic and artistic imperatives. The divided critical response to the band is indicative of the extent to which Zeppelin managed to foster a sense of expansive artistic possibilities even as they participated in the standardization of rock music as a cultural product.

Whereas Duncan links the size of heavy metal's impact to its unmitigated prioritization of technology as a means of producing "loud*est*ness," Led Zeppelin produced the illusion of vastness not merely through volume but through a complex alternation of acoustic and electric, or soft and loud, sounds.[88] To gain some perspective on the significance of this matter, it should be pointed out that during the whole of his career, Jimi Hendrix recorded only one song with acoustic guitar, a song that was never released on any of his official albums, but did appear in a film documentary. Hendrix was very much an electric guitarist, whose musical achievements cannot be separated from his mastery of technology. Jimmy Page has been similarly lauded as a sound technologist, but in contrast to Hendrix had a long-standing fascination with the acoustic guitar that complemented his attraction to its electric counterpart. As far back as 1967, during his days with the Yardbirds, Page recorded an instrumental piece called "White Summer" that laid the blueprint for his later work on acoustic guitar with Led Zeppelin. Sounding very much like a bit of ethnic kitsch, the song features Page playing in an open D tuning working to emulate certain tonalities of East Indian music, with a spare accompaniment of bongo drums and a horn that mimics and simplifies the melody of the guitar line.

Though not a particularly interesting track in itself, the recorded version of "White Summer" set the pattern whereby the acoustic guitar was used by Page to evoke exotic musical traditions and locations. At Led Zeppelin concerts, "White Summer" was extended into a sprawling musical segment that stood as the centerpiece of the "acoustic" part of the band's show, when the members would all move to the front of the stage, sit on stools, and perform some of the quieter songs from their albums. Such was one of the ways in which, both in concert and on record, Zeppelin tried to create the sense of taking its audience on a journey through different musical spaces. Page as acoustic guitar virtuoso exploited the instrument's mutability, exploring different tunings that were each intended to convey a distinct mood or impression that, in turn, was often linked to a distinct if imaginary location. Discussing "White Summer" in a 1990 interview, the guitarist explained the piece to be an outgrowth of his "Celtic, Indian and Arabic influences," many of which were manifested in his use of the "DADGAD" guitar tuning.[89] Pursuing the question of his involvement with Indian music, Page recounts how he "got fascinated with the whole science of it," the division of notes into semitones that occurred in spaces between the notes on the Western musical scale. The guitarist continues:

> But the main thing that I did get from the ragas was the timings: They do things in sort of sevens and elevens. However, I can't discount the allap— I'm talking about sitar basically here. The allap is the first movement. It's quite an emotional thing and I could equate blues, bending and everything to that. Whether I should or I shouldn't have, that's the way I tended to receive it and I guess that all went into the melting pot.[90]

Page displays an involvement with Indian music that is more than casual, and no small degree of understanding of the music's particularity. Nonetheless, his tendency to incorporate Indian musical practices into his own version of a melting pot is what stands out in his comments and in Zeppelin's music. This tendency can be taken as an example of Page's resourcefulness as a musician, but I think is more indicative of the guitarist's participation in processes of appropriation and cultural colonization. The key element is not merely the use of exotic musical elements in Zeppelin's music, but their decontextualization, a quality that has drawn comment from some of the more attentive critics of the band, though such comments have rarely considered the political import of these practices. Writing in *Guitar Player,* for instance, Joe Gore observed that Jimmy Page integrated non-Western modalities into his music "more convincingly than any of his peers," and went on to state that "Page's modalism has less to do with ethnomusicological authenticity than with crafting trippy melodies."[91] In a similar vein, British journalist Nick Coleman mused on the matter of "Zeppanthropology," his term for the band's proclivity for drawing the musics of the distant British and Irish past and the Orient into an unlikely but surprisingly effective alliance. According to Coleman, "the first principle of Zeppanthropology holds that whatever it is you're after, you'll find it in the grooves."[92] Relating to cultural systems of music making primarily, if not exclusively, in terms of sound allowed Page and his bandmates to assimilate aspects of those systems without worrying over matters of ownership and propriety, a quintessentially appropriative move. As Steven Feld has noted, "Appropriation means that the question 'Whose music?' is submerged, supplanted, and subverted by the assertion 'Our/my music.'"[93]

That Page and Plant enacted their fascination with the East in a series of travels to India and North Africa for the explicit purpose of absorbing local musical practices only adds substance to these insights. By 1976, when Zeppelin were still at the peak of their popularity, the two bandmates had already gone to Morocco, and had planned more extensive trips before Plant was involved in a car accident that left him and his family badly injured and placed the band's career in limbo. As Page explained in a 1977 interview,

> [We] had planned to go to Japan and Australia and then work our way back slowly through the East. And we wanted to record in Bangkok, Delhi and Cairo, and soak up the vibes, as we had in Morocco.
> We didn't want to sound like a half-baked imitation but to use the acoustic qualities of their music. It was an interesting challenge to attempt. That would have been a milestone in our career.[94]

More travels were to happen after Plant's recovery, but such a milestone was not to occur during the regular course of Zeppelin's career. The death of Plant's son in 1977 upset the band's equilibrium once again, and drummer John Bonham died only a year after the group renewed itself for another album in 1979, leading to the eventual breakup in 1980. Yet in 1994, Page and Plant reunited to record a segment for the MTV show

Unplugged, and the result, titled *No Quarter* after one of Zeppelin's more cryptic mid-1970's songs, bears the distinct impression of the colonialist designs hinted at by Page some seventeen years earlier. The unplugged format, in which bands are invited to remake their catalog by playing acoustic versions of songs typically recorded with electric instruments in their original form, is itself suggestive given Zeppelin's already-noted proclivity for managing the difference between acoustic and electric sounds. Stubborn veterans that they are, Page and Plant did not adhere strictly to the unplugged mandate, but deployed electric instruments on several cuts during the ninety-minute production, and even on the acoustic tracks used a significant amount of electronic processing to alter the sound and create uncanny musical effects.

More to the point, the video production of *No Quarter* finds Page and Plant performing with a corps of young musicians on location in Wales, and with a troop of local musicians in Marrakech, displaying their "C.I.A." influences to the fullest in both musical and visual terms. The opening montage juxtaposes bird's-eye panoramas of the lush Welsh landscape with street scenes from their Moroccan journey over the reverb-soaked strains of Page's acoustic guitar and Plant's voice as the duo convert the song "No Quarter" into a brooding modal piece with Middle Eastern overtones. The traveling camera settles on an idyllic riverside location, and glimpses of water lead us to the musicians, who sit on chairs amidst the lush greenery, evoking a pastoral ideal that had been a part of the Zeppelin repertoire since the recording of *Led Zeppelin III* in 1970.[95] Upon the conclusion of the song, the viewer is transported to a theater where many of the performances in the video take place. The juxtaposition of locations is a running theme. From the theater, we move back to Wales, this time with the band (Page, Plant, and several younger musicians playing banjo, mandolin, stand-up bass, and hurdy gurdy, along with a more usual drum kit) perched upon a dramatic mountain of rocks, where they perform a rustic version of "Nobody's Fault But Mine." Zeppelin's original version of the tune, recorded in 1977, was itself a remake of an old Blind Willie Johnson blues, which the band hyped up in characteristic fashion with a bevy of distortion and a supremely heavy riff. In the new version, by contrast, the Celtic influence predominates, and the song becomes a sort of reel, building from a slow drone to an energetic climax.

From Wales the viewer is projected head first into Marrakech, where

Page and Plant hold court on the street, playing a cranked-up, thoroughly electric groove called "Yallah" over a taped drum loop in front of a large, enthusiastic crowd of local citizens. Shots of the two musicians in close-up, with Page tweaking at the controls of his sound system to create some twisted electronic effects, are continually intercut with images of the surrounding audience, clapping along or even, in one instance, playing air guitar; and with occasional street scenes dissociated from the moment of performance, serving the purpose, one assumes, of providing some local color.[96] This boisterous performance gives way to a more cloistered outdoor setting in which our musical guides play with local musicians on a piece called "City Don't Cry."[97] Page's acoustic guitar is here joined by a Moroccan string instrument and three drums, and Plant shares the vocal spotlight with the Arabic players, while the visual track creates a sense of intimacy that explodes at the end of the performance, when the musicians are transposed onto another lively street scene where the song concludes amid an even larger audience than for the earlier amplified piece.

The remainder of the video finds the duo back in the theater, working to a climax in which Page, Plant, and the rock unit—electric bass and drums—of their young troop of musicians perform three of Zeppelin's most far-flung musical travelogues: the North African–tinged "Four Sticks," and the Indian-influenced "Friends"[98] and "Kashmir," all of which are reinvented by the presence of two separate orchestras, one apparently a classical orchestra of strings and horns, the other an Egyptian orchestra of strings and percussion. "Kashmir," the closing song, is an especially striking performance. The piece opens with the droning strings of the Egyptian orchestra underpinning Page's flanged chordal manipulations in his favored DADGAD tuning, while Plant voices the opening lines, articulating the impulse toward exploration that has pervaded the preceding hour-plus of music and video footage:

> O let the sun beat down upon my face
> Stars to fill my dreams
> I am a traveler of both time and space
> To be where I have been

Plant engages in some vocal genuflections, dipping his voice during the next line in a variation of Arabic tonality; as he completes the verse, the band and both orchestras kick into a harmonic flourish familiar from the original version of the tune.[99] At this point, the song proceeds according to the pattern established by the original, with the main ascending chromatic riff in D giving way to a G-A power chord progression made elaborate by the melodic variations of the strings, while Plant continues in his role as traveler: "And my eyes filled with sand/As I scan this wasted land." Plant's wailing voice leads to a reiteration of the droning calm that began the song, over which a violin improvises some microtonal scale patterns. A beating Egyptian drum punctuates the calm, which is further unsettled by a sonic deluge from Page's guitar. Plant sings in between further deluges, bringing us again to the main riff and another repetition of the G-A progression, which in turn spills into a storm of percussion and a Page-led set of changes that transforms into the most conventionally rock-like segment of the performance, a brief outburst that at one point musically paraphrases the twenty-five-year-old Zeppelin heavy-boogie number "Black Dog." Page's power chords and Plant's shouts build to a singular point of tension, after which the duo make their farewell bows and leave the Egyptian players onstage to finish the song in a wave of drums and strings.

Discussing the making of *No Quarter* in the British rock magazine *Mojo,* Page and Plant described their desire from the start to deviate from the standard "unplugged" format, in which the artists sit in a nice atmospheric space playing acoustic songs. "We could have done it!" asserted Page, "But this was far more of a challenge to try and go over the horizons again." The horizon of which he speaks would seem to be the electric/acoustic divide that typically defines the show's content, yet as Plant expands on Page's comment, it becomes clear that other boundaries are just as much at issue.

> The whole idea of being able to brandish the Arab link was so important to me, and really crucial because, outside of Rai music and the whole WOMAD politeness, there's something round the corner that we're just touching on now and we're going to expand on, where if you bring these two musics, these two cultures, these two—well, I don't know about our side—aesthetics, on the Arab/Berber/Gnaoua thing, and you don't modify it, you don't present it in hushed tones in the Royal Festival Hall—you mix it with the way we are, a pair of questionable characters of ill-repute, you make a totally different form.[100]

Plant condemns the well-mannered politesse that so often characterizes the fusion of musical cultures. He and Page are working toward something that is, in his perception, far more radical and more satisfying as an artistic statement, and moreover something already present in native styles of musical performance: "Do you know Dimi Mint Abba, a Mauretanian singer? She's amazing. Her band has just started using electric guitars and stuff. It's so reckless!"[101]

Such recklessness is precisely the effect Page and Plant have striven for in their own music as members of Led Zeppelin and, so many years later, as rock veterans reinterpreting their own history. The question that arises here is why do they feel compelled to journey so far afield to achieve their desired effects? What complex of desires motivates such exploratory impulses? A clue might be gathered from Plant's coy description of himself and Page above as characters of ill-repute, a sentiment he had also expressed some years earlier while talking to *Rolling Stone:* "We can't be considered anthropologists or anything like that, but we knew of a few good brothels in the Far East . . ."[102] Such remarks conjure a vision of an intensely libidinized foreign space where white male travelers satiate their sexual appetites, the sort of conjunction of geographical and imaginary landscapes that Anne McClintock has termed "porno-tropics"—"a fantastic magic lantern of the mind onto which Europe projected its forbidden sexual desires and fears."[103] While McClintock's subject is the European colonization of Africa, her ideas can be applied equally well to the East, which has a similar history as an object of white male fantasy. In either instance, though, one must make a crucial qualification: Page and Plant's travels are occurring in a changed imperial setting within which England's status as a colonial power has all but dissolved. They function not as representatives of state power in the traditional sense but of a new kind of global (dare one say post-colonial) commodification of culture, and their presence begs the question of whether this new order might allow for new patterns of cultural exchange along the lines envisioned by Plant, or whether this is merely a recasting of the same historical processes of imperialist appropriation in a new guise.

My own sense is that there is more evidence for the latter of these two conclusions. To cite Steven Feld once again, in relationships between international pop stars and the musicians of foreign locations with whom they perform, the "boundary line between participation and collaboration" is drawn over the issue of ownership.[104] Without knowing all the details of the economic arrangements of *No Quarter,* it is clear from the video document that however much Page and Plant might want to participate with local musicians, in the end the product is presented as "their" music, and they are the ones who reap praise and rewards for their adventurousness. Moreover, the "totally different form" gestured toward by Plant seems in many ways congruent with the patterns of Orientalist knowledge discussed by Edward Said some twenty years ago, patterns within which the Orient figures as a site of excess that contains the potential for upsetting Western norms.[105] Such, I would argue, was one of the key notions underlying Jimmy Page's long-standing (but rarely analyzed) interest in magic and the occult. Although discussion of Page's magical preoccupations has concentrated upon his interest in Anglo-Irish occultist Aleister Crowley, nobody has taken the trouble to observe that Crowley was himself an Orientalist of epic proportions, having spent much of his life journeying through India and the Middle East, and having expressed an abiding faith in the special spiritual qualities of "Oriental" peoples.[106] That Page, as something of a devotee of Crowley, should have shared these assumptions is thus not especially surprising.

What remains fascinating, though, is the way in which the various magical and Orientalist preoccupations of Page and Plant were mapped onto the sound of their music; or, to put it differently, the ways in which sound worked to signify and mediate these preoccupations. Though Page has typically been a rather cryptic interview subject, his interests in sound, magic, and the Orient come together in one of the strangest documents of 1970s cultural history, an interview between Page and William Burroughs. Titled "Rock Magic," the first part of the article features Burroughs offering his own impressions of a Led Zeppelin concert. Having spent many years in Morocco, Burroughs perceives a clear connection between Zeppelin's musical effects and those produced by Moroccan musicians:

> The essential ingredient for any successful rock group is energy—the ability to give out energy, to receive energy from the audience, and to give it back to the audience. A rock concert is in fact a rite involving the evocation and transmutation of energy.
> . . . The Led Zeppelin show depends heavily on volume, repetition, and drums. It bears some resemblance to the trance music found in Morocco,

which is magical in origin and purpose—that is, concerned with the evocation and control of spiritual forces.[107]

When Burroughs broaches the idea of this connection to Page, the guitarist assents cautiously—he had not yet been to Morocco, but was definitely aware of the concentrated energies produced during one of the band's concerts, energies that might spill in any number of directions. Later in the interview, in a more explicit discussion of the potential effects of sound upon an audience, Page refers to the "rhythms within the audience," and suggests that "music which involves riffs . . . will have a trance-like effect, and it's really like a mantra . . . And we've been attacked for that."[108] Here the violent promotion of passivity criticized by Robert Duncan becomes something else, a channeling of energy based upon Eastern practices of disorienting the relationship between mind and body through the manipulation of sound.

Without offering anything to suggest that this is the effect that Led Zeppelin achieved in their music, I do want to offer this explanation on the part of Page and Burroughs as a significant variation on the efforts to make sense of the social value of amplified sound that had been a part of rock discourse since the late 1960s. Page's flights of Orientalist fantasy occupy a similar imaginary space to Jimi Hendrix's Electric Church, or the MC5's hope that electronic noise would provoke something akin to cultural revolution. Though each of these visions points in different, albeit related, directions, what they share is a belief that amplified sound has significant transformative potential, and that the electric guitar in particular could serve to activate that potential through its creation of levels of noise and forms of sound previously inaccessible, if not unimaginable. That Page's, and Led Zeppelin's, version of this scenario was less politicized than those of the earlier musicians tells us something about the ways in which the ideals of the 1960s counterculture were transmuted during the 1970s. Yet we should be careful not to draw too strict a line between these different manifestations of rock 'n' roll utopia, for many of the racial and sexual elements we might find most objectionable in the practices of a band like Led Zeppelin, and a form like heavy metal, were already present in the music of Hendrix and the MC5, and in the way their music was received. Indeed, I think that what we find here is a continuum of ideas and practices within which the electric guitar stands at the center of an effort to negotiate between patterns of racial and sexual identity that seek to incorporate the sensory excitement of the new electronic noise yet remain rooted in notions of race, gender, and sexuality that have a longer, and less liberatory, history.

Stairway

[T]he moment at which the stairway to heaven becomes something actually *possible* for the audience would also be the moment of greatest danger.

—*William Burroughs (1975), p. 37*

That moment of ascent, building to a climax that provokes sensations at once familiar and otherworldly, was perhaps the key to Led Zeppelin's appeal—giving the audience what it already desired, but defamiliarizing the object of desire in the process. Such was the importance of the band's recourse to tropes of exoticism, the cultivation of musical "strangeness" that unsettled fans accustomed to guitar heroics. The manipulation of acoustic and electric sounds seemed to bridge the poles of rock's sonoric landscape at a time when those poles were often represented as being, literally or figuratively, worlds apart. Which brings me at last to that most archetypal of Zeppelin's songs, "Stairway to Heaven," centerpiece of what at least one critic has called the greatest heavy metal album of all time, Led Zeppelin's untitled fourth album.[109] From the opening arpeggios plucked by Page on acoustic guitar to the unobtrusive entrance of an electric twelve-string after the second verse, to the smack of John Bonham's drums that introduces the fifth verse, to the crunch of distortion and the transcendent guitar solo that drives the piece to its final passage, "Stairway to Heaven" follows a logic best described by Chuck Eddy: "It's constructed *as* a stairway, with four steps; on every subsequent one, the music gets louder, and you can either turn the volume higher or turn the radio off. If you vote 'yeah,' to reach the top step, the altar, you will do anything."[110] Perhaps this is the moment of danger to which William Burroughs refers, or maybe these are two different experiences linked by similar metaphors. In either case, it is this moment, this potential of music to transport us away from the immediate context of our everyday lives toward something grander, if painfully temporary, that we least understand. It is this knowledge, above all, that will perhaps have to remain "in the grooves."

Conclusion

Time Machine

In February of 1993, the editors of *Musician* magazine published a list, "The 100 Greatest Guitarists of the 20th Century." The impulse to rank and classify musicians in such a way was hardly new—*Down Beat* and other jazz publications instituted similar practices as far back as the 1930s (Charlie Christian was a three-time winner as best jazz guitarist from 1939–41), and *Guitar Player* began its readers' poll of the year's best guitarists in 1970 (Jimi Hendrix won as best rock guitarist, and Chet Atkins as best country guitarist). Yet the scope of the *Musician* list was clearly of a different order. This was no mere annual reader's poll, but a broad list intended to stand as something of a guitar canon. And with so much at stake, things apparently got a bit ugly.

According to the editors, the idea to put together such a list met with general indifference when broached. Or rather, apparent indifference, for the next day found the names of guitarists beginning to fill the office blackboard. Before long, the process became contentious: "How can you possibly call Johnny Ramone a great guitarist?" "He changed the way 10,000 guitarists play—which is more than I can say for your boy—Randy Rhoads!" "What? Why you . . ."[1] So did the battle begin, as the editors fought among each other to support their favorite choices, struggling in the meantime to define the measure of value by which to judge a guitarist's greatness. At one point, two of the editors were caught erasing names from the final list, replacing "folkies" with "heavy metal players who had been defeated in the general balloting."[2] At another point, in the midst of "a particularly violent debate about the worthiness of Bo Diddley," one of those same editors, Charles Young, proposed the "Green Bay Packer rule" to govern the selection process: "If the 1992 49ers got in a time machine and played the 1965 Green Bay Packers, the 49ers would kill them—but that doesn't mean the '65 Packers weren't a great team. You must judge people in the context of their time."[3] Young's rule in turn set the stage for the more general editorial statement of the terms for inclusion on the list: "To the inevitable question (at least it was inevitable around here), 'How the hell could you say Mother Maybelle Carter was a better guitarist than Roy Clark?' understand that Maybelle got points for inventing and popularizing a simple style that was then copied by every country guitarist for 50 years, while Roy was deemed to be fast as light, but neither *the* fastest nor terribly influential."[4]

When judged against the weight of history, then, a guitarist's greatness was deemed to be more a matter of influence and originality than of sheer technique, and was to be measured against the context of the player's career rather than according to some absolute ideal of musical ability. Yet this resolution regarding the criteria for inclusion on the list seems to leave much unresolved. How, for instance, is one to measure originality or influence? Why should a guitarist's speed matter? And perhaps the most important question: Why make such a list in the first place? On this last point the editors suggest that the process of compiling the list was also its primary justification: "As editors started feuding, fighting and throwing telephones at each other it occurred to us that if critics could get this upset over which guitar players were and were not worthy of posterity, normal human beings might be really interested, too."[5] Indeed, Simon Frith has recently suggested that "normal human beings" are far more engaged in such issues than critics and scholars have been willing to acknowledge. In the introduction to his book, *Performing Rites,* Frith asserts that making judgments about aesthetic value is central to "popular cultural practice," and that "there is no reason to believe a priori that such judgments work differently in different cultural spheres."[6] For those concerned with the guitar, the question of whether Maybelle Carter is a greater guitarist than Roy Clark is no less pressing than the question of whether Picasso was a greater exponent of Cubism than Braque is for those concerned with twentieth-century art. This is not a matter of elevating popular music to the level of high art (such elevation is beside the point), but of suggesting, as Frith does, that similar processes of judgment and evaluation operate among audiences for a wide range of cultural materials, and that these processes are a key part of the way that artistic and cultural products move from being isolated objects to being socially embedded works.

There is still more to this story. While the general significance of such a list as the one created by the editors of *Musician* is that it resonates with many of the ways in which audiences make meaning out of popular music, the particular significance of the list with regard to the history of the guitar, or the electric guitar, is something quite different. Surveying the contents of the list, one finds that although the list pretends to be inclusive regarding the range of guitar performance, the overwhelming majority of players represented are electric guitarists—by my count, eighty-two of the hundred players listed played the electric guitar as their primary instrument. Such is the conflation of "electric guitar" with "guitar" that there is a separate sub-category of guitarists included on the list as "Acoustic," a set of seven musicians whose adherence to unamplified instruments is considered to be a key aspect of their virtuosity. Viewed from this perspective, then, the *Musician* list demonstrates the extent to which the "electric" guitar has become such a general part of the popular music landscape as to have lost something of its specificity. The electric guitar is now simply "the" guitar, it is the normal presence of the guitar in popular music, while unamplified instruments have been displaced as the province of traditionalists or individualists who want to assert their separation from mainstream tastes. At the same time, according to the logic of the list, the electric guitar remains a primary medium for the expression of individuality. It is electric guitarists who are most readily identifiable, and who have made the most innovative contributions to the history of popular music. Electric guitarists, in other words, are the true guitar heroes; for the values embedded in the figure of the guitar hero—virtuosity, bodily flamboyance, an aesthetics of excess in which the sonoric and physical presence of the guitarist spills over the boundaries of the pop song format—are in a sense dependent upon the literal and metaphoric amplification of the guitarist's role brought about by the incorporation of the electric guitar.

How the electric guitar has come to signify these values has been one of the principal questions governing my own inquiry into the significance of the instrument. My concern for this question is as much a result of my personal investment in the electric guitar as of my academic interest in the instrument. I began playing the guitar at age nine, and though my first instrument was a small, inexpensive acoustic guitar, I aspired to sound like the electric guitarists who populated my favorite bands—Ace Frehley of Kiss, Ted Nugent, Joe Perry of Aerosmith, and especially Jimmy Page of Led Zeppelin. I was coming of age during the era of arena rock, when the guitar hero played a crucial role in making four or five small figures on a stage seem to be equivalent to an epic festival of sound and spectacle. Moreover, I was encouraged by the few older musicians in my neighborhood (and by older, I mean they were already in their teens) to admire these guitarists, to consider them to be the height of musical achievement. As I grew older and acquired greater facility as a musician, the range of my tastes in music and in guitarists expanded—at the tender age of eleven I first encountered Jimi Hendrix, while in my teens I was drawn to the fleet-fingered virtuosity of heavy metal musicians such as Eddie Van Halen and Yngwie Malmsteen. I began to read more about music history in magazines such as *Rolling Stone* and *Guitar Player,* and was led by these sources to inspect the history of the guitar in greater detail. Over time I began to listen to blues and jazz as well as rock and heavy metal, and to appreciate the different styles of musicianship that were available. My playing bore the evidence of my changing tastes, and I sifted through selections on the radio and my own growing record collection for new ideas and ways of approaching music, training my ear and my fingers by playing along with anything that captured my imagination. Through all these changes, I maintained a general adherence to the notion that the guitar was the most expressive of instruments, and that certain guitarists stood as models whose playing was to be emulated and perhaps appropriated for my own musical ends. And even though I finally got a quality acoustic guitar for my eighteenth birthday, my electric guitar (which I first got at age thirteen) remained my instrument of choice.

I present this brief autobiography to give a sense of why *Instruments of Desire* assumed the shape that it did, why I have chosen to concentrate upon individual musicians rather than broad trends, and why I have devoted more energy to analyzing what I perceive to have been dominant trends in the history of the electric guitar rather than covering less familiar territory. There have been times in composing this narrative when I have felt as though I were writing little more than a glorified sort of list along the lines of the *Musician* article, a much briefer list in terms of the number of musicians covered, but one that similarly set the terms according to which the history of the electric guitar was to be judged and understood. Questions from fellow guitarists about whether I had included this or that notable figure whenever I tried to describe my project only accentuated this feeling, and as I considered who might ultimately read this book I gave great consideration to just how representative my chosen subjects were. As it turns out, I think they are quite representative, for better or worse—representative of the social, political, and aesthetic limits that have defined the electric guitar's use as well as the sense of open possibilities that has driven so much of the instrument's history. The history of the electric guitar is in many ways a history of the limits of popular music—the limits of noise and technology, of racial cooperation and sexual liberation—and I have tried to write a history that acknowledges the power of those limits while exploring some of the ways in which musicians have sought to move past them.

Of course the electric guitar itself is only so representative of popular music. In recent years it has come to be identified with some of the more retrograde tendencies in popular music, the most blatant sort of white male heterosexism that has (somewhat, but not entirely unfairly) come to be synonymous with hard rock and heavy metal. My argument concerning the problem of cock rock can stand as my primary statement on this matter but by no means exhausts the subject; for part of the repercussion of this movement in the history of the electric guitar is that the rejection of the instrument and its ideological trappings has often played a part in the creation of alternative musical spaces and styles. From punk rock's disdain for virtuosity and musical heroics to the celebration of synthesized repetition in disco and later techno and electronica to the large scale abandonment of traditional pop instrumentation in rap, the electric guitar has arguably been as notable for its negative impact upon popular music of the past two decades as for its positive role. Martin Price of the Manchester house band 808 State put the matter succinctly in denying any affinity between his music and punk rock: "If somebody say 'techno's like punk' to my face, I'll fucking smash 'em in the teeth. This is about machines, punk was about arm power. Nobody wants to see a load of idiots torturing themselves onstage with guitars anymore. The muscles and sinews in dance music are when you're sweating your bollocks off on the dance floor."[7]

At issue for Price is the way in which the guitar becomes a focus of energy and attention, leading the audience to concentrate upon the musician rather than the music, and to become spectators rather than participants in the musical process. In Price's conception of techno, the machinery of sampling and synthesized beats displaces the physical center of music making in a manner fundamentally at odds with the tendency of the electric guitar to accentuate the bodily presence of the performer. With its visual traces all but effaced, musical performance comes to seem almost effortless, while the audience conversely works the beat.

Simon Reynolds presents a similar, but much richer, view of the contemporary musical landscape in his recent book, *Generation Ecstasy* (in which Price is quoted). Reynolds introduces his survey of the proliferation and popularization of electronic dance music over the past decade with a brief discussion of his own budding interest in the music and the British rave scene. Discussing his desire during the 1980s for a "resurrected psychedelia," Reynolds proclaims that "little did I realize that just around the corner loomed a *psychedelic dance* culture, that the instruments and time-space coordinates of the neopsychedelic resurgence would not be wah-wah pedals and Detroit 1969, but Roland 303 bass machines and Detroit/Chicago 1987."[8] Invoking one of the primary scenes of the present study, late 1960s Detroit, Reynolds declares that cultural moment and its principal tools to have been definitively replaced as the way toward musical revitalization. Repudiating his original "rockist" take on dance music, Reynolds goes on to celebrate the sounds of "sampladelia," which he describes as a means of making music that "breaks with traditional ideas of 'musicality'" by substituting the arrangement of sounds via electronic means for the "ideals of real-time interactive playing and natural acoustic space that still govern most music making."[9] For Reynolds, then, "sampladelia" has displaced rock, and electronic samplers have displaced electric guitars, as the principal musical signifiers of the late twentieth century. The real-time virtuosity of the electric guitarist has given way to the assemblage of sounds through an electronic virtuosity that has, in turn, opened the way for a dance-based, participatory musical culture.

All of this is not to say that the electric guitar has receded from popular music. One hardly has to argue for the instrument's continued popularity and prominence. Rather, the narrative of decline surrounding the electric guitar in current musical discourse has more to do with the question of whether the electric guitar has become so normalized, so entrenched in the mainstream of popular music, that it now fulfills a principally redundant musical and social role, promoting the continual reenactment of the moves and sounds that initially brought it to such a position of centrality. These concerns have even motivated *Guitar Player* magazine to pose the question, "Who Killed Rock Guitar?" in bold-faced white letters against the stark black background of its cover. In the accompanying article, features editor James Rotondi scans the contemporary pop music scene with an alternately despondent and optimistic eye where the future of the guitar is concerned.[10] According to Rotondi, the ostensible threat to the position of the guitar is the proliferation of electronic approaches to making music like those described by Price and Reynolds, approaches that rely more on reworking prerecorded sounds than on generating live sounds. Yet the greater threat is that the guitar itself may be exhausted as an expressive medium, at least within the context of rock. In all, the tone of the article is decidedly ambivalent, and ends with a call for rethinking the first principles of rock guitar performance by Sonic Youth guitarist Lee Ranaldo: "Rock and guitar will always go hand in hand—it's just people's notions of what 'rock music' is that must be updated."[11]

I offer no prognostications as to the future of the electric guitar or of rock music. However, it is worth noting that I am writing this book at a time when a considerable amount of energy is being put into mining the electric guitar's past. The *Musician* list of great guitarists, for example, is only one of several such lists to have been published in the past few years; *Guitar Player, Guitar World, Spin,* and *Mojo* are among the other publications that have featured surveys of "The Greatest Guitar Players of All Time," "The Fifty Greatest Rock Guitar Records," or the twenty-five guitarists who have mattered most over the past thirty years. Meanwhile, a rapidly swelling wave of guitar-related books has emerged as well, some of which are little more than extended lists, others of which are focused on the electric guitar itself as a material object, and which offer intensely detailed accounts of the history of particular brands of guitars—Gibson, Fender, Gretsch—which have themselves been deemed worthy of posterity. Paralleling this latter trend has been the demand within the guitar market for vintage instruments, typically instruments made during the decades from the 1930s to the 1960s which are perceived to embody the

height of guitar craftsmanship and to convey some of the aura that surrounded the electric guitar in decades past. Even new guitars are often
designed to match the specifications of vintage instruments, with the
Gibson Les Paul and Fender Stratocaster, two design concepts from the
1950s, providing the basic blueprint for the vast majority of guitars cur-
rently produced.[12]

We are confronted in these various examples with the historicity of the
electric guitar—historicity as defined by Frederic Jameson to denote "a
perception of the present as history . . . a process of reification whereby
we draw back from our immersion in the here and now . . . and grasp it as
a kind of thing."[13] As Jameson remarks with regard to historical time in
general, so it is with the current perception of the electric guitar in time
that the instrument seems to gain meaning from its association with certain predefined historical moments that ultimately have less to do with
history as such than with some version of cultural fantasy about what the
past represents. The operation at work is markedly different from the
approach to the past informing the work of some of the musicians covered in this volume, figures such as Jimi Hendrix and Muddy Waters who
mined past sources for material and inspiration while enacting a version
of transformative ritual on those materials (say, the basic blues form)
designed to reconcile past and present. With a phenomenon like the
vintage guitar movement (a movement with its own publications, formal
organizations, and a considerable amount of economic power), we find a
desire to restore the past "as it was," an acceptance of an idealized past
devoid of the conflict and complexity that marks history. The vintage
guitar offers the fantasy that at least a narrow aspect of history has been
frozen, objectified, reified, and thus preserved intact; and the past itself,
as much as the guitar, is made available for consumption.

If popular culture is a sphere of contestation over the politics of history
and memory, as historian George Lipsitz has suggested,[14] then we need to
attend to which version of history, which memory of the past, holds
power. With regard to the electric guitar, one version of the "dominant"
narrative can be witnessed in the film *Back to the Future,* a blockbuster hit
from the mid-1980s and one of the largest-grossing films in history. A
time-travel fantasy revolving around the Oedipal relations between a
young man and his parents, *Back to the Future* fits Frederic Jameson's
definition of the "nostalgia film," a film that mobilizes "a vision of the

past, or a certain moment in the past," in some new allegorical way.[15] For Jameson the primary allegorical thrust of such films is in terms of class; and indeed there is a strong element of class fantasy in *Back to the Future*. The hero, Marty McFly, returns to the present after his encounter with the past of his parents' teenage years (the 1950s) to find that the lower middle-class status of his family has been elevated to a more comfortable and happy upper middle-class level (signified primarily by the increased autonomy and self-confidence of the father figure, George). As pronounced as these class-based elements are in the narrative of *Back to the Future*, however, there are also strong currents of racial and gender instability in the film, and it is at this level that the electric guitar plays a crucial role to the telling of the film's story.

The opening scene of *Back to the Future* draws upon the long-standing white middle-class male enthusiasm for technical gadgetry that also informed the careers of Les Paul and Chet Atkins. Shots of various strange devices move us through what comes to appear as a mechanized morning routine, but the visual cues—burnt toast coming up from the automatically-wired toaster, for instance—lead the viewer to sense that something is awry. Into this scene enters Marty McFly, who after surveying the minor wreckage moves directly to plug in his instrument, a hot yellow electric guitar. The camera leads us through each step of the process as he prepares to play, and dwells on the dials of the oversized amplifier to let us know that everything is turned up to ten, the maximum setting. Finally ready, Marty strikes a power chord that overwhelms him; he is sent flying several feet backwards onto his rear while the amplifier goes up in smoke, to which he simply responds, "Whoa—Rock 'n' Roll."

Within the context of the film, Marty's interest in the electric guitar helps to define him as a rebel—a mischievous teenager whose taste for heavy metal guitar solos goes part and parcel with his tendency to show up late to school and get into spats with the school principal. At the same time, the electric guitar stands as the symbol of Marty's aspirations. He wants more than anything to be a musician, and responds with genuine hurt when his band is rejected for an audition to play the school dance (because, the judge announces, they are "just too loud"). After the audition, Marty announces his frustration to his girlfriend, claiming that his greatest fear is that he will try to make it as a musician only to find that people do not like him. This classic teenage conundrum—the fear of rejection—is given a broader context when Marty travels back in time. Upon encountering his teenaged father, he learns that the young George held similar creative aspirations, not as a musician but as a writer, and that George is similarly shy about his writing and afraid of rejection. Furthermore, Marty knows from his experience in the future that George gave up his writing to settle into a job as a menial white-collar worker. So does *Back to the Future* inject into its generational narrative a critique of the fate of white middle-class males, who are led by a lack of institutional approval to forsake their most noble dreams in favor of following the path of least resistance. It is this tendency to forsake one's dreams that Marty seeks to combat by tampering with the destiny of his father, so that both young men can reach their full potential rather than become caught in the stagnation of middle-class underachievement.

Following the audition scene, the electric guitar largely fades from view as the film concentrates upon the time travel experiment—made possible by a transformed DeLorean automobile crafted by Marty's good friend, Dr. Brown—and Marty's travails with his parents after he finds himself back in 1955. After Marty finds himself back in time, *Back to the Future* revolves around two interrelated subplots. First, how will Marty return to his own present, the 1980s, given that he has run out of fuel for the time machine? Second, how will Marty be able to restore the relationship between his parents, given that his teenaged mother, Lorraine, has developed a major crush on him? These plots become intertwined as Marty and Dr. Brown formulate a time-dependent solution to the problem of returning Marty to the future that, as it happens, has to be enacted on the night of the school dance at which George and Lorraine first danced together and kissed. Yet a problem arises when Lorraine asks Marty to be her date to the dance. Marty therefore has to determine a way to get George and Lorraine together by the night of the dance, or else his own future will be erased; for as the film would have it, if Marty does in fact displace George as the object of Lorraine's desire, not only would it be a breech of Oedipal conduct but it would mean that Marty would never have been born, and that he would have no future.

The dance scene is in many ways the crux of *Back to the Future,* and functions as the climax of the film's romantic narrative; and it is in this scene that the electric guitar re-enters the story. The scene introduces a further element into the nostalgic fantasy that drives the film: a fantasy of racial cooperation.[16] Through a series of convoluted machinations, Marty engineers the restoration of his parents' relationship. Crucial to the young protagonist's achievement is the presence of an African-American rhythm-and-blues band, Marvin Berry and the Starlighters. The band's performance at the dance is interrupted by an episode in which they help Marty to overcome the school bully, Biff, who yearns to supplant George (and Marty) as the object of Lorraine's affection. While the band members brawl with Biff's henchmen over the use of racial epithets, George bravely knocks Biff cold with a single punch, and thus asserts a new-found sense of power and self-confidence that immediately allows him to gain the attention of his future wife.

From here, the film moves back into the dance, where an injury to Marvin in the battle outside allows Marty to assume the role of the Star-lighters' lead guitarist. Marty stays largely in the background musically while the band plays the romantic nugget, "Earth Angel," a song that serves as the soundtrack for George and Lorraine's first kiss. With the order of his family's future intact, Marty reluctantly agrees to play another song, and after giving the band some brief directions introduces the song as an "oldie"—"Well, it's an oldie where I come from." The song turns out to be "Johnny B. Goode," and as Marty tears into the performance, throwing now-familiar Chuck Berry–style riffs at the dancing crowd, Marvin gets on the phone to his cousin, Chuck, to announce, "You know that new sound you're looking for. Well listen to this . . ." Marty shows himself to have the Chuck Berry style down pat, including the (now) famous duckwalk; but as he moves into his solo, his playing takes on a sense of abandon that removes the music farther and farther from the context of the 1950s. In the next few seconds, Marty performs a capsule history of the electric guitar as processed by a white suburban teenage male, moving from Pete Townshend–style power chords to Eddie Van Halen–style finger-taps to a Steve Vai–like rapid run across the fretboard. The rest of the band grinds to a halt as Marty spins out of control, and as the guitarist falls to his knees to strike a final fleet-fingered run, he opens his eyes to find the teenaged crowd staring back in stunned silence. "Guess you guys aren't ready for that yet," he declares from the stage, "but your kids are going to love it."

Marty's fit of guitar pyrotechnics comes across as something of a digres-sion within the film's narrative, bridging as it does the coupling of his parents and his return to the future/present. Yet the scene completes another subsidiary strand of the story concerning Marty's egoistic need for artistic self-fulfillment. Having been denied the opportunity to play at his own high school dance, Marty exacts his revenge upon the institution (the school is the same one that he attended thirty years later) through his demonstrative display. More important, though, is the historicized nature of the performance. Alongside the personal gratification that he achieves, Marty is shown to affect the entire history of rock guitar. Having traveled back in time, he displaces the African-American "founder" of rock 'n' roll guitar playing, and in so doing both rewrites and plays back the subsequent history of the electric guitar (or at least one strand of it) in his own image. That the scene is presented for laughs, and that it culminates in a somewhat ineffectual loss of control on the part of Marty as guitarist, does not undermine the significance of the historical displacement at work. *Back to the Future* at once acknowledges and effaces the African-American influence upon American popular music, and presents a fantasy of racial cooperation that ultimately upholds and reinforces the priority of the white male self. Meanwhile, the role played by the electric guitar in this scenario, and in the fulfillment of Marty's character, indicates the symbolic weight invested in the instrument within the structure of the film and, arguably, within American popular culture more generally.

Like the vintage guitar movement, *Back to the Future* demonstrates the extent to which the electric guitar can serve as a conduit of history, projecting through its sound and image certain ideas about the past of popular music. Throughout this study I have used the electric guitar similarly, as a time machine that allows one entry into some of the most crucial and definitive moments in pop music history. *Back to the Future* shows how one such moment, the originating instance of rock 'n' roll, has entered into a broader cultural mythology, and how the electric guitar has come to signify some of the potency of that moment in history. At the same time, the film exhibits how readily history can be put in the service of cultural mythology, and how the representation of the past involves simultaneous processes of remembrance and forgetting, recognition and repression.

Concerning the electric guitar, the repression enacted by *Back to the Future* is also an act of silencing alternative histories from that presented in the film. The silence that greets Marty upon the completion of his performance is telling in this regard, and striking in its contrast to the escalating levels of loudness generated by the young guitarist during his moment in the spotlight. I say "loudness," not "noise," because it is precisely the noise of the electric guitar's political and sonoric presence that the film seeks to repress.[17] Rather than disturbing the stolid, conformist veneer of this suburban high school scene, Marty and his electric guitar leave the existing order of things intact while holding out the promise that such unbridled display will be normalized with the passage of time.

Of course, the electric guitar has become significantly normalized over time. The movement from the MC5 to Led Zeppelin, discussed in chapters six and seven, demonstrates that sounds and strategies that were at first oriented toward the construction of musical and political alternatives quickly became part of the expanding industrial framework of 1970s popular music. Moreover, this historical movement was no simple matter of cooptation, of alternative strategies being absorbed into the existing system of musical production. Instead, it was the development of innovative approaches to the use of electric sound in the way of volume, distortion, and other effects that laid the groundwork for the expansion and refashioning of rock music's economic base, represented by the emergence of large-scale arena rock.

This historical trajectory marked the culmination of the history of the guitar hero, the point at which the electric guitar and its players ascended to positions of relative dominance within some prominent strains of recent popular music (especially, though not exclusively, hard rock and heavy metal). Yet as I have tried to suggest throughout *Instruments of Desire,* this result was neither inevitable when viewed within the broader contours of the instrument's history nor unambiguous in its effects. The electric guitar opened a world of new sonoric possibilities within the popular music of the twentieth century. The instrument was part of the broader "rethinking of timbre" that occurred within twentieth-century music, and that entailed a parallel "redefinition of noise," according to Michael Chanan.[18] In the context of popular music, however, this did not bring a full-scale reconceptualization of music as such. Even rock 'n' roll cannot be said to be a result of the introduction of the electric guitar into popular music. If the electric guitar has not revolutionized the form of popular music, it has significantly affected the practice of pop music performance and production, making sound itself subject to new strategies of manipulation that have in turn recast what Jacques Attali has called "the political economy of music."

The general trend of these movements in the electric guitar's history has been more toward the consolidation of capital than the increased autonomy of musical workers, and the breakdown of musical consumers and producers, gestured toward by Attali in the last section of *Noise*. Yet the interplay between these possibilities, between the deconcentration of music through the prioritization of noise and the reconcentration of music through strategies of sonoric containment, is in many ways the legacy of the electric guitar to popular music. One can see variations on these dynamics in the careers of all of the musicians covered in this volume, whether it be those like Les Paul and Chet Atkins who sought to place their music within the mainstream of popular tastes, or those like Charlie Christian and Jimi Hendrix whose relationship to the musical mainstream was fraught with tension. My point in containing all of these musicians in one volume has not been to set up an opposition between those whose innovations have been deemed safe (who have made "music") against those who have played with a more transgressive set of aesthetic rules (who have made "noise"). Rather, I have sought to understand how the boundary between norm and transgression, between music and noise, has been continually renegotiated in the recent history of popular music, and how the negotiation of these boundaries has been thoroughly entangled with a range of social and political tensions that continue to define popular music.

Instruments of Desire is therefore built around an overarching emphasis upon the aesthetics of sound and the politics of sonority, and this emphasis is, to my mind, of key methodological importance. A growing number of popular music scholars have acknowledged the need to address the sonoric aspects of music in conjunction with the assessment of music's social and cultural effects.[19] Simon Reynolds, for instance, makes a useful move in this analytical direction in *Generation Ecstasy*. Considering the difficulty of writing about a musical style and subculture that prioritizes nonverbal, often intensely physical forms of experience, Reynolds observes that

Unlike rock music, rave isn't built around lyrics. For the critic this requires a shift of emphasis, so that you no longer ask what the music "means" but how it *works*. What is the affective charge of a certain kind of bass sound, of a particular rhythm? Rave music represents a fundamental break with rock, or at least the dominant English Lit and socialist realist paradigms of rock criticism, which focus on songs and storytelling. Where rock relates an experience (autobiographical or imaginary), rave *constructs* an experience. Bypassing interpretation, the listener is hurled into a vortex of heightened sensations, abstract emotions, and artificial energies.[20]

The prioritization of musical experience, of the sensations and stimulations that make music not only something to which one listens but also something that one feels, did not begin with rave. Reynolds constructs an opposition between rave culture and rock that is grounded in an unfortunate conflation of the critical discourse on rock with the substance of the music. Nonetheless, his observations constitute a vital proposal for a method of musical analysis that is less concerned with sense than sensation, and that recognizes the place of sound, as music and as noise, in structuring the varieties of musical experience.

This critical turn toward aurality is driven by the conviction, well articulated by Reynolds, that it is in its aural aspects that music works upon its listeners most immediately and, arguably, most powerfully. Aurality is also the level at which music works most directly to forge relationships among its various participants, between musicians and audiences. Christopher Small has captured some of special meaning of this approach to music with his term "musicking," a term he coined to promote the conceptualization of music as an active process rather than a fixed object.[21] According to Small, musicking is grounded in two sets of relationships: "first, those which are created between the sounds . . . and, secondly, those which are created among the participants."[22] These realms of music are, for Small, distinct but significantly intertwined, such that "relationships between sounds in music . . . mirror relationships between people."[23] Musical sounds are produced through the combined application of form and technique among musicians; and those sounds, as produced, establish a listening environment that affects how musicians relate to one another, how musicians relate to their audience, and how the audience members stand in relation to each other as well. So the exploration of musical practice through the medium of sound becomes a way to make sense of the social and political roles that music might fulfill, and of the work done by music, musicians, and audiences to structure relationships of difference and similarity through a politics of affect.

The theoretical concerns of Reynolds and Small echo a number of the voices that have run through *Instruments of Desire*. One need only recall Les Paul discussing the value of intimate sound, a sonoric ideal complementing the domestic image that he and Mary Ford put forth; or, in marked contrast, Louis Myers recounting the power of amplified sound in the Chicago nightclubs, with the sound "hittin' the walls and bouncing back to us," creating an effect that put larger, horn-laden bands in their place. To these we could add Frank Zappa's musings on the phenomenon of "Bone Conduction" in relation to the sound of Eric Clapton's guitar; or Rob Tyner describing the energy and physicality of heavily amplified sound, and the "metabolic" changes that arise from exposure to such music. Taken together, these examples testify to the amount of effort that musicians have directed toward experimenting with electricity and playing with sound. They also reveal an ongoing discourse among musicians and critics about the ways in which sound, and specifically amplified sound, shapes the experience of music that foreshadows the theoretical approaches put forth by Reynolds, Small, and Attali, among others.

If sound has been a crucial area of concern in this book, it has been so out of a desire to understand the nature of the electric guitar as an instrument and how that instrument has stimulated shifts in the performance and understanding of music. Indeed, along with the synthesizer and digital sampling devices, the electric guitar has problematized the fundamental criterion of any musical instrument: that it produce sounds useful for the making of music. By making sound less dependent upon the inherent physical qualities of the instrument, the electric guitar expanded both the range of available sounds and the range of techniques used for accessing and shaping those sounds. In other words, the electric guitar has engendered at various points in its history a sort of re-disciplining of the body in musical performance similar to that described by John Corbett in his discussion of free improvisation.[24] From this perspective, the exaggerated gestures of guitarists like Buddy Guy, Jimi Hendrix, or Wayne Kramer, loaded as they are with gendered and racial connotations, might also be read as a bodily coming to terms with a fundamentally new relationship to sound that in turn reorganizes the physical relationship between the musician and the instrument.

An even more extreme, though markedly different, example of this dynamic can be found in the work of experimental guitarist Hans Reichel. Reichel has taken what Corbett calls a "reconstructive" approach to the electric guitar, using the basic design of the instrument as a blueprint for the creation of new instruments that play with the relationships among the strings, the bridge, and the fretboard.[25] A self-taught luthier, Reichel spent years modifying and reassembling standard electric guitars into permutations with multiple necks extending from both ends of the instrument body and different numbers and combinations of strings. His more recent inventions have a single neck, but have continued the earlier inversion of fretboard and body by significantly extending the length of the guitar string onto the "wrong" side of the bridge, often placing frets on that side as well.[26] Reichel's rearrangement of the physical qualities of the guitar has been consistently geared toward opening new sonic effects; his "two-sided" necks allow for the creation of harmonics and overtones that scatter the sound of the guitar in all manner of unpredictable directions and yet often remain strikingly consonant. To access these sounds, Reichel has dramatically reconfigured his playing technique so that his right and left hands are engaged in almost equivalent processes of fretting, plucking, and striking the strings in a manner far removed from the conventional division of labor, in which the left hand plays on the frets while the right hand picks at the strings.[27] Thus does Reichel work toward the simultaneous reconceptualization of the physical dimensions of the instrument and the repositioning of the body in musical performance in a manner that challenges the normalizing functions of standard instrument design and musical technique.

Far-flung as Reichel's experiments might seem, his persistent tinkering and constant desire to play with sound through the alteration of the instrument recall no one so much as Les Paul. The liner notes to Reichel's album, *The Dawn of Dachsman,* make the connection explicit, opening with a reference to Paul's wish to create a sound that his mother could recognize as his own.[28] Such connections, such coincidences, in markedly different musical settings, are the stuff out of which the history of the electric guitar has been made. One might even identify in this congruence of the activities of Reichel and Paul a structure of desire focused upon the electric guitar that has little to do with music, and more to do with the ways in which the electric guitar as material, technological object engenders (and genders) certain modes of interaction.[29] And yet the ends pursued by these two guitarists are so far removed from one another: for Paul, the creation of a new standard of sound and instrument design that would provide the basis for a string of popular hit recordings; for Reichel, the rejection of standardization and the demonstration that the electric guitar and the music it produces are in a continual process of becoming. In their curious mix of similarity and contrast, Paul and Reichel exemplify Paul Théberge's astute observation that "the manner in which you play an instrument can transform both the instrument itself and the nature of the musical sounds produced."[30] The electric guitar has been shaped and defined by many such transformations, and has in turn figured prominently in the desires of musicians and audiences across a range of musical styles. So does the electric guitar take its place at the historical juncture between music and noise, as a device used to explore, challenge, and compose the systems of order and disorder, sameness and difference, that have constituted popular music in this century.

Adventures in Sound

A Guide to Listening

Charlie Christian

Christian's career was in a sense only getting started when he died in 1942. Not that his accomplishments were slight, having joined one of the most popular groups of the swing era, participated in an epochal shift in the making of jazz, and helped to establish the electric guitar as a major solo voice all by the age of twenty-five. Yet as with so many figures in the history of popular music who died young, it is hard not to dwell upon what might have laid in store for Christian had he been able to continue.

As it stands, Christian never had the chance to record as a full-fledged group leader, a circumstance that would likely have changed if he had lived to see the full florescence of bebop. What we have instead are two principal collections of material: the official Christian, performing in the studio with the Benny Goodman Sextet; and the unofficial Christian, a small but significant set of bootleg recordings that document some of the jam sessions of the early 1940s. Add to this various radio transcriptions of the Goodman band and Christian's contributions to the "From Spirituals to Swing" concert of 1939 and one has a fairly complete picture of Christian's recording career.

To appreciate Christian's tenure with Goodman, the Columbia anthology, *The Genius of the Electric Guitar,* is the most accessible starting point. With sixteen tracks, it is by no means exhaustive; the out-of-print anthology, *Solo Flight*, contains a wider selection of cuts and is worth seeking out in used record bins. However, *Genius* does include the principal official releases and features fine playing not only by Christian but also by Goodman, Lionel Hampton, Georgie Auld, and Cootie Williams. The collection also includes several tracks with Count Basie on piano and two with Basie's regular drummer, Jo Jones; tracks that represent the meeting of Southwest and East Coast swing.

One of these, "Breakfast Feud," recorded in January 1941, may be Christian's finest moment as a soloist with the Goodman band (many prefer "Solo Flight," on which Christian played with the full Goodman orchestra; to my ears, though, "Breakfast Feud" and other Christian cuts with the sextet such as "Seven Come Eleven" have more exciting performances). After an opening theme that sets Williams's trumpet against the deeper voices of Auld's saxophone and Goodman's clarinet, a jumpy rhythm lays the foundation for brief solos by Williams, Goodman, and Basie in succession. On the heels of Basie's solo, the horns join together for an ascending set of riffs that puncture the tune, out of which Christian's guitar rushes forth. A quick burst of notes leads Christian into a solo that is clearly inflected by the blues, within which what stands out is Christian's sense of timing, made plain in his sharp pauses and his use of repeated notes and figures that build rhythmic tension and set the stage for his more varied single-note passages. (The Smithsonian Institute's *Collection of Classic Jazz* contains a version of "Breakfast Feud" featuring five separate Christian solos spliced together from various takes of the song.)

Regarding Christian's participation in the budding bebop scene, we have far less material at our disposal. The few recorded tracks that exist are essentially bootlegs with rather poor sound quality. Yet they offer a fascinating window into a key moment in jazz history, and the recent reissue of these recordings on compact disc under the title *Swing to Bop* is to be welcomed (while I was doing my research, my only source for these tracks was a beat-up old vinyl LP titled *The Harlem Jazz Scene, 1941* that I borrowed from a friend).

On tracks such as "Swing to Bop," "Stompin' at the Savoy," and "Up on Teddy's Hill," we hear Christian alongside the young Dizzy Gillespie, Thelonius Monk, and Kenny Clarke, stretching out in a manner that was off limits in his recording sessions with Goodman. "Stompin' at the Savoy" is especially strong. After a pass through the original melody during which Gillespie and Christian play call and response, the song is given over to extended solos by the two young virtuosos, with a brief solo interlude by Monk. Christian's playing on the piece bears witness to

James Moody's observation that the guitarist would "tear it up" over the most difficult passages. While Christian plays with flare over the changes of the verse, he truly takes off during the key changes and modulations that mark the bridge, exhibiting the sort of chromatic "linearity" that led Gunther Schuller to label him as the most advanced of the Minton's group.

Les Paul

Les Paul has had an amazingly long career as a performer. First appearing on radio in the early 1930s, he continues to play weekly gigs in New York. Yet until the past decade, his extensive catalog of recordings was largely consigned to the budget bin reserved for oldies-but-goodies, one-hit (or no-hit) wonders, and easy listening. Indeed, some of his work remains available only in the budget package form. The Laserlight collection of Les Paul Trio recordings (most likely recorded during the 1940s, though no dates are provided), for instance, is one of the few sources for Paul's pre-multiple-track work. Featuring Paul on guitar accompanied by an unidentified pianist and bassist (and occasional female vocalist), the performances tend toward well-played but fairly standard jazz, though Paul's facile guitar technique is much in evidence, especially on the lightning quick piano-guitar unison lines that ride out "Hand Picked."

In 1991, Capitol released the extensive box set, *Les Paul: The Legend and the Legacy,* thus bringing Paul's work out of the budget bin and into the realm of high-end anthology. With four compact discs, each containing over seventy-five minutes of material, *The Legend and the Legacy* is all the Paul that anyone should need to own (the recordings that he and Mary Ford made after moving to Columbia in 1958 were less successful both commercially and artistically), and probably more than the average interested listener would want to hear. For the curious and cost-conscious, Capitol also released a single disc featuring highlights from the larger set.

That said, *The Legend and the Legacy* is quite a listening experience. Working through the exhaustive collection—over 100 singles and previously unreleased tracks, plus episodes of Paul and Ford's radio show and even some commercial spots that the duo recorded—one gets a sense both of the formulaic nature of their music and of the eclecticism that enlivened their musical sensibility. Just skimming through the titles gives some sense of the range of material covered: "Tennessee Waltz," "Jazz Me Blues," "Jingle Bells," "Tiger Rag," "Honolulu Rock-A-Rolla," "Jumpin' at the Zadicoe," "Nuevo Laredo," "Moritat (Theme from "Three Penny Opera)." And yet each of these tracks fits the same two- to three-minute pop record format, features the same basic instrumentation, foregrounds Paul's multiple-track recording techniques, and is characterized by a marked prioritization of the principle melody that works to structure the tune.

More generally, the work of Paul and Ford can be broken down into three basic categories: guitar instrumentals, vocal ballads, and up-tempo vocal numbers. All are handily represented on *The Legend and the Legacy,* and all offer their pleasures. For this listener, though, the ballads tend to be either overly cloying or tiringly maudlin. "Cryin'," the first Paul/Ford recording (released in 1950), sets the pattern here. After a very brief statement by Paul, Ford's overdubbed vocals enter the mix, singing the part of the jilted lover. Her low-toned voice nicely conveys some of the weight of the sentiments, but her unchanging delivery undermines the turnabout that ends the lyric, when she tells her ex-lover that there may come a day when "it may be you who's cryin'." Ford would play this role of the sad lover throughout her vocal career with Paul, and it was a role decidedly lacking in dimension. Meanwhile, Paul's accompaniment on the duo's ballads was generally notable for its understatement—a nice change of pace, perhaps, for a musician often given over to excess (adding track upon track, playing rapid streams of notes accelerated through tape manipulations), but lacking the sonic adventure of the other elements of his repertoire.

The guitar instrumentals are where Paul first perfected his techniques of multiple-track recording, and are often exceptional showcases for the combination of technological savvy and instrumental virtuosity that he brought to bear on his music. "Lover" and "Carioca," two of his more notable such recordings, were discussed in some detail in chapter 2. "Lover" is especially impressive in the complexity of its multi-tracked arrangement, including the extreme tempo shift that occurs at the song's midpoint. Some of the more intriguing and technically sophisticated of Paul's instrumentals reside on disc four of *Legend and the Legacy,* given over to previously unreleased material; check out "Dark Eyes" and

"Cookin'" for some fine guitar work. The main qualification regarding these pieces is that it was in his instrumental mode that Paul veered most closely toward mood music. Those drawn to the sounds of the "lounge revival" will likely find many a cool groove here, but others may be less moved by the eye-winking tenor of the melodies and arrangements.

Despite the spit-and-shine virtuosity of the instrumental tracks, Paul's guitar work is really heard to best effect on the up-tempo vocal music he produced with Ford. The presence of Ford as vocal foil combined with the more determinate song structures of the vocal material gave Paul's playing a focus that was often lacking in the instrumental arrangements. Musically, the breakneck speed of performances like "Tiger Rag" or "Song in Blue" is itself something to behold—both songs whip by the listener in a blur, and Ford's nonsensical "Here Kitty"s and meowing interludes (in counterpoint with Paul's "meowing" guitar) on "Tiger Rag" are among the most genuinely funny moments that the duo put on record. "Song in Blue" is sheer over-the-top Paul, with a wall of multiple, swiftly-picked guitars cascading through the song. Meanwhile, on "The World Is Waiting for the Sunrise" and "How High the Moon," the novel energy of "Song in Blue" is turned down just enough to make room for a more subtle lyricism. As a result, those two songs represent the peak of Paul and Ford's musical achievement.

Chet Atkins

Like Les Paul, Chet Atkins's career has extended through several decades and continues to this day. Unlike Paul, his career has had a remarkable consistency to it, not so much in terms of the quality of his music as in the extent of his public activity. Whereas Paul more or less went into hiatus during the decade following his 1964 divorce from Ford (only to resurface most prominently with a 1976 record he made with Atkins, *Chester and Lester*), Atkins has released new music regularly ever since he first formed his association with RCA in 1947. His output at this point is enormous—he has dozens upon dozens of albums to his name, and that excludes the many more on which he worked as either session guitarist or producer for the likes of the Everly Brothers, Don Gibson, and Elvis Presley, to name but a few. For an extensive list of Atkins's recordings, far more than I can accommodate here, see the discography accompanying

Jim Ohlschmidt's article on Atkins in the January 13, 1989 issue of *Goldmine.*

Perhaps due to the breadth of his recording career, there is no single anthology that adequately covers Atkins's music. *Chet Atkins: The RCA Years,* a double compact disc set, does a fair job of outlining the contours of Atkins's career (and includes some solid liner notes by Paul Kingsbury), but two discs are simply not enough to do him justice. In trying to give a broad sense of the guitarist's music, *The RCA Years* excludes too many of his best early recordings.

This programming choice is especially regrettable since Atkins's earliest work is among his strongest. The ensembles he led with country comedy team Homer and Jethro (Homer Haynes on rhythm guitar, Jethro Burns on mandolin) were the tightest group performances of Atkins's career, and his guitar playing had a spark that was often missing on his later work. A German label, Bear Family Records, has issued an exhaustive collection of Atkins's early work, but at four compact discs and $120 price tag, it is only for the truly committed; even the archive at the Country Music Hall of Fame, the best source for recorded and printed materials on the history of country music, did not see fit to include it in their collections. Somewhat ironically, one of the best sources of these early tracks is a bargain bin anthology, *Pickin' on Country,* which features no liner notes, dates, or lists of musicians, but does have many of Atkins's finer cuts from the days when he released singles rather than albums, including "Galloping on the Guitar," "Main Street Breakdown," "Chinatown, My Chinatown," "Canned Heat," and the original "Country Gentleman," all recorded during the late 1940s and early 1950s.

As Nick Jones, an Atkins discographer, has suggested, after the mid-1950s the guitarist became very much an album-based (rather than a singles-based) performer, a shift that had much to do with RCA's desire to package their musicians in a way that would target older, more "respectable" record buyers. Long-playing albums were generally associated with classical music during the 1950s, and were perceived as a classy form of release that demanded more of the listener's attention than the immediate gratification of the single. Not coincidentally, this was the period when Atkins's recordings began to feature strong doses of classical music, although it would be unfair to the guitarist to suggest that his affinity for classical guitar styles was not genuine. Indeed, given Atkins's growing status at RCA as performer, producer, and A&R (artist and repertoire) man, he no doubt exerted a strong influence on RCA's new direction.

Atkins's albums from the mid- to late 1950s are his most important releases in terms of assessing his historical importance, and set the tone for the rest of his career in their calculated mix of musical approaches. *Chet Atkins in Three Dimensions,* from 1956, was a key release, organizing Atkins's performances into three categories: folk songs such as "Arkansaw Traveler" and "Ochi Chornya (Dark Eyes)"; popular songs such as "Tip-toe Through the Tulips with Me" and "Blues in the Night"; and classics that included two Bach compositions and Chopin's "Minute Waltz." As I suggested in chapter 3, *Finger-Style Guitar,* released the next year, is widely considered to be the classic Atkins solo guitar album. The format is much the same as on *Three Dimensions,* but less self-conscious about the inclusion of such a wide range of material. Unfortunately, these albums and virtually all of Atkins's catalogue of regular album releases (as opposed to anthologies) are out of print; to find them you would have to scour the used record stores in your area or contact a collector of Atkins material. (If you happen to be in Nashville, the Great Escape used record store, near Vanderbilt University and not too far from Music Row, is an excellent source for old country music albums, including an impressively wide assortment of Atkins material.)

Atkins's sound and style has by no means been unchanging in the ensuing decades. Most notably, he began to feature the nylon-string acoustic guitar on an increasing number of his recordings following his 1960 release, *The Other Chet Atkins* (discussed in chapter 3). Indeed, later in his career Atkins even collaborated with the Gibson company—having jumped ship from Gretsch—on the design of an amplified nylon-string instrument, a hybrid object that violated the norms of classical guitar design and yet embodied a desire to retain some of the aura of a classical tone in a manner in keeping with Atkins's paradoxical career. Meanwhile, in the 1980s, after four decades of association with RCA, Atkins switched to Columbia Records, where he has recorded a series of light but solid efforts, graced by guest appearances by a number of admiring fellow guitarists, including Mark Knopfler and George Benson.

Finally, anyone who wants to appreciate the Atkins guitar style has to go back to the principal source, Merle Travis. *Walkin' the Strings* is a Rhino Records reissue of a series of radio transcriptions recorded by

Travis during the 1940s and 1950s, and it contains a wealth of brilliant playing. (A friend of mine, after listening to the opening cut, "Walkin' the Strings," observed that Travis is "the Art Tatum of country music," which seems an appropriate bit of praise.) The collection has a good mix of instrumentals—some of which are less than a minute long—and vocal tracks, and provides evidence of the range of Travis's talents as both a guitarist and songwriter. Travis's songwriting chops are more the focus of *The Best of Merle Travis,* which includes three songs from his out-of-print classic *Folk Songs of the Hills* (1947). "Dark as a Dungeon" and "Sixteen Tons"—which would become a number one hit for Tennessee Ernie Ford in the 1950s—are Travis originals that sound like they have been passed down from generations of Kentucky coal miners. And Travis's collaboration with Atkins, *The Atkins Travis Traveling Show* (1974), is a pleasant, relaxed showcase for the two guitarists built out of their mutual admiration.

Muddy Waters

Waters's recording "career" started in a sense while he was back on Stovall's plantation in Mississippi, well before he began to surface as a significant figure in the mid-century "rhythm and blues" market. Alan Lomax's field recordings of Waters in 1941–1942 were intended for documentary as opposed to commercial use; Lomax was looking to preserve the sounds of musicians who, to his ears, embodied the Delta region's musical traditions. Yet as Waters testified in an interview with Jim and Amy O'Neal (cited in chapter 4), it was that initial contact with Lomax and his tape recorder that made him realize that he could move into a career as a recording musician.

These earliest Waters recordings have been subsequently released in various packages. My source was the imported Document collection, *Muddy Waters (1941–1946), First Recording Sessions in Chronological Order.* Included here are not only the Lomax recordings but a number of unreleased sessions from Waters's first years in Chicago, almost all of which feature Waters on acoustic guitar. As the quasi-academic title suggests, this is music of interest primarily to serious blues collectors and scholars, and not the place to begin if relatively unacquainted with Waters's work. Yet there are some excellent performances. The earliest

Lomax recordings, "Country Blues" and "I Be's Troubled," are strong examples of acoustic country blues, the former hearkening back to Waters's main influences, Son House and Robert Johnson, and the latter foreshadowing Waters's first important amplified single for Chess, "I Can't Be Satisfied." And closing the disc are "Rollin' and Tumblin'," parts one and two, in their original Parkway incarnations. Waters recorded these tracks in 1950 on the sly from Chess Records (as was noted in chapter 4, they were released under the name of Baby Face Leroy, the drummer of the ensemble), and they remain among the rawest electric blues recorded by any Chicago ensemble. Waters's slide guitar quavers vigorously throughout the song's two parts, and the vocals transmute from part one's guttural moans to part two's barely articulate but decidedly spirited shouts.

Waters's career at Chess began in 1947 (the first year of the label's existence, when it was called Aristocrat), but really got under way in 1948 with the release of "I Can't Be Satisfied." That song, and other sides covering the "classic" period of Waters's career from the late 1940s until 1954, are included on *The Best of Muddy Waters*. The album is rather modest in its offerings—only twelve songs, and a total playing time of just over thirty-five minutes. Nonetheless, it is easily the best place to begin to appreciate Waters's musical accomplishments, and also a good source for tracing the changes in his sound and the composition of his band during a crucial phase in his career. The tracks recorded in 1950 and 1951, such as "Rollin' Stone," "Honey Bee" (with Jimmy Rogers on second guitar), "Louisiana Blues" and "She Moves Me" (both with Little Walter on harmonica), find Waters's guitar and voice as the central elements within a shifting set of small ensembles (or in the case of "Rollin' Stone," as the sole presence). Meanwhile, the songs from 1953 and 1954, such as "I Want You to Love Me," "Hoochie Coochie Man," and "I Just Want to Make Love to You," present the performances in which Waters's full electric band first cohered on record.

Supplementing *The Best of Muddy Waters,* and containing many fine performances in its own right, is *The Real Folk Blues*. First released in 1966, *Real Folk Blues* was compiled by Chess out of Waters's recordings over a span from 1947 to 1964; the title was mainly an attempt to capitalize upon the folk music boom, which had revived interest in the music of Waters and other blues performers whose careers had been thrown off course by the emergence of rock 'n' roll in the mid-1950s. Though not as strong a collection as *Best of Muddy Waters* overall, it does contain several good early Waters pieces on which he is accompanied only by "Big" Crawford on bass (notably the Chess version of "Rollin' and Tumblin'" and "Walking Blues," a revision of the Son House/Robert Johnson standard that Waters had recorded as "Country Blues" for Alan Lomax), and also includes the rousing 1955 recording of "Mannish Boy," Waters's adaptation of Bo Diddley's "I'm a Man."

Waters underwent some significant career changes during the middle and later parts of the 1950s. I alluded above to his waning commercial success as rock 'n' roll emerged onto the national scene. Just as important, if not entirely unrelated, were the personnel shifts that occurred within Waters's band. Little Walter was the first to leave; as early as 1952, he forged his association with the Four Aces, and as the decade progressed he was featured on fewer of Waters's recorded sides, to be replaced by either Big Walter Horton or James Cotton. Then, in 1956, Jimmy Rogers moved on to record under his own name, his position taken by former Sun Records stalwart Pat Hare. *Trouble No More, Singles (1955–1959)* collects much of Waters's best work from this transitional period. What is most striking about these recordings is how little Waters's music suffered from the surrounding instability. Though some, like Mike Rowe, have viewed Waters's late 1950s output as a sign of decline and descent into formula, I would agree with Don Snowden, author of the liner notes to *Trouble No More,* that this period is better seen as one in which Waters consolidated his sound and style along the lines established by full band recordings like "I Just Want to Make Love to You." The band sound on these tracks is tight, and "Got My Mojo Working" in particular finds Waters and crew rocking hard. "All Aboard," on the other hand, is a train-based blues that displays a unique instance of Waters performing with two harmonicas (Little Walter scatters melodic lines through the song, while the younger James Cotton handles the more strictly train-derived whistles). Meanwhile, the songs with Pat Hare on guitar, such as "She's Got It" and especially "She's into Something," bring into Waters's band a style of electric lead guitar that he had mostly shunned during the years he performed with Rogers.

The material on the above three albums has recently (1997) been reconfigured by Chess in honor of the company's fiftieth anniversary. *His Best, 1947–1955* and its counterpart volume for the years 1956–1964 bring the bulk of Waters's important work over almost two decades onto two compact discs, with the tracks arranged in chronological order. As such, the new compilations can be considered an improvement on the earlier collections in terms of presenting Waters's material in a coherent framework (as opposed to the rather scattershot contents of *The Real Folk Blues,* for instance), although whether chronology is the most compelling means of presenting musical material of this sort remains debatable in my mind. Also part of the commemorative reissue series is *The Aristocrat of the Blues: The Best of Aristocrat Records,* a two-disc anthology that covers the earliest phase of the Chess brothers' recording endeavors and that situates Waters's earliest work for the label alongside the music of Robert Nighthawk, Sunnyland Slim, and a range of lesser-known figures.

Waters continued to record and perform actively until his death in 1983, and over the years experienced a number of ups and downs. The 1960s found a revival of interest in Waters's music, spurred at different moments by the folk music boom and the fascination with blues that marked so much of late 1960s rock. *Muddy Waters At Newport,* a recording of Waters's 1960 performance at the famous jazz festival, captured the early side of this process as Waters and his band (featuring some energetic guitar work by Pat Hare) put forth a spirited set of music to an audience brimming with enthusiasm. Unfortunately, the renewed interest did not lead Waters to record any works that would be considered among his best; produced out of Marshall Chess's desire to capitalize upon the changing nature of Waters's audience and of the popular music scene in general, albums such as *Electric Mud* and *The London Muddy Waters Sessions* removed Waters from the setting of his own band, and they are albums on which Waters does not sound at home. Such was the state of Waters's recording career until the late 1970s, when albino blues/rock guitarist Johnny Winter forged a working relationship with the older bluesman that led to a series of energetic albums such as *Hard Again* and *King Bee,* on which Waters set new songs alongside reworkings of many of his older tunes, accompanied by a sympathetic band that included James Cotton on harmonica. For an overview of Waters's long career, check out *The Chess Box,* which contains all of the best cuts listed above and more spread over three compact discs.

Chuck Berry

In his drug-addled rock-crit classic, *The Aesthetics of Rock,* Richard Meltzer deemed Chuck Berry the foremost practitioner of repetition in rock 'n' roll history. "All Chuck Berry songs sound exactly alike to both the skilled and the unskilled listeners," proclaimed Meltzer with characteristic exaggeration; and according to Meltzer this knack for "orgasmic monotony" was precisely the strength that made Berry among the most important and the most copied figures in the history of the music. Meltzer's assessment is not entirely fair, by any means—a listen to any of Berry's albums for Chess from the late 1950s and early 1960s, such as *Chuck Berry Is on Top* or *New Juke Box Hits,* uncovers such uncommon fare as the steel guitar–led "Blues for Hawaiians" and the slow blues of "Driftin' Blues" amid the high-energy music for which Berry is most noted. And yet Meltzer is right in a sense, for if Berry was a more eclectic artist than his best-known songs would indicate, his significance lies in the musically compact but lyrically expansive formula that he established as one of the principal models for rock 'n' roll songwriting.

Those wishing for the big picture of Berry's career can dive into *The Chess Box,* which includes many of Berry's lesser-known performances and covers a broad range of his recorded work through the 1970s (including his 1972 number one novelty single, "My Ding-a-Ling"). However, all the *really* essential Berry music, the music that laid the groundwork for the early Beatles and Rolling Stones, as well as countless raggedy garage bands, can be found on a single compact disc, *The Great Twenty-Eight.* A listen through *The Great Twenty-Eight* is like hearing so many variations on a theme; while even his most familiar songs are not as monochromatic as Meltzer would have us believe, there is an incredible consistency of approach that runs through the bulk of these tracks. "Maybellene," "Roll Over Beethoven," "Rock and Roll Music," "Carol," and "Johnny B. Goode," all recorded between 1955 and 1958, are prime examples of the Berry sound (which he achieved, of course, with help from his band, especially pianist Johnny Johnson), and also feature some of Berry's most exciting guitar work, including his trademark guitar-only introductions and his creative use of double-stops. Many of the licks and lines played by Berry may have their roots in the playing of forebears like Charlie Christian, T-Bone Walker, and Carl Hogan (who played with Louis Jordan), all routinely cited by Berry as prime influences, but he gave those licks a new inflection, and set them within a rhythmically dynamic context that complemented the charge surrounding the sound of his electric guitar.

If the above songs are most representative of Berry's strengths, other tracks on *The Great Twenty-Eight* show him moving into unique thematic territory, or dealing with familiar material in distinctive ways. The much-discussed "Brown-Eyed Handsome Man" was a cleverly coded assertion of the charm and appeal of dark (eyed) men, often taken as one of Berry's rare musical statements of racial pride. "Memphis," on the other hand, is one of Berry's most country-inspired tunes, a winding story about a man trying to contact his lost love, who happens to be a three-year-old girl. And one of my favorite Berry moments is "Little Queenie," on which Berry's spoken verses interject a funny but unsettling air of lechery into a song about a young girl whose coming of age occurs in line with her taste for rock 'n' roll.

To gain a sense of how Berry fit into the general flow of Chess offerings, and the extent to which Chess's output was grounded as much in rhythm and blues as in blues itself, conventionally defined, check out another Chess box set, *Chess Rhythm & Roll* (a corresponding set exists for the blues end of the spectrum, titled, appropriately enough, *Chess Blues*). Here some of the most choice offerings of Berry and his best-known rock 'n' roll counterpart at Chess, Bo Diddley (such as "Maybellene," "Johnny B. Goode," and "School Days" for Berry; and "Bo Diddley," "Who Do You Love?" and the signifying classic "Say Man" for Diddley) are interspersed over four compact discs with songs from dozens of other performers. Some of the artists are well known, like Etta James, Little Milton, and the Miracles and the Four Tops in pre-Motown appearances. Most, though, are on the order of The Five Blazes, Paul Gayten, or The Kents, acts that may have enjoyed local celebrity, and perhaps even enjoyed some brief national popularity, but did not have the kind of success that supported sustained activity. The preponderance of doo-wop tracks on *Rhythm & Roll* is particularly notable, though just as impressive is the wide range of material presented on the collection, a good indication of how immersed Chess Records was in the music of the period, and just how willing the label was to fish around for unknown performers in search of a hit.

Jimi Hendrix

The incredible stream of posthumous Hendrix recordings that has been released in the three decades since the guitarist's death has served at once to broaden and to confuse our understanding of Hendrix's significance as a performer. On the one hand, the recordings of live performances in particular represent some key aspects of Hendrix's talent not so accessible through the recordings released during his lifetime, specifically his willingness to play with form and improvise upon basic song structures. On the other hand, much of the studio material that has been released was unfinished material and as such is substandard. While these releases give us another musical artifact, they do not necessarily add to our comprehension of what made Hendrix such an effective musician. As Chuck Eddy wrote in one of his many acerbic comments about Hendrix, "This dead guy puts out three or four concert albs every year, it seems, and if you really expect me to stay awake through all of 'em you better convince Harmony to pay me more than just ten grand." If Eddy's remarks seem ungenerous, they also capture something of the redundancy of the consistent wave of Hendrix releases that have hit the market in recent years.

With such an unruly assortment of offerings to choose from, the best recourse is to start at the beginning. *Are You Experienced?*, *Axis: Bold as Love,* and *Electric Ladyland,* the three studio albums released by Hendrix and the Experience in 1967 and 1968, are three of the most imaginative albums to emerge from rock's psychedelic era. The title song from *Are You Experienced?* features a brilliantly constructed guitar solo pieced together from snatches of backward-masked electric guitar, while "Third Stone from the Sun" is as heady a sonic maelstrom as Hendrix would ever produce in the studio, more engaging in its relative brevity than the later, much longer suite of "1983 . . . (A Merman I Should Turn to Be)" and "Moon Turn the Tides" from *Electric Ladyland.* "Fire" and "Foxey Lady," also from *Experienced,* exhibit signs of Hendrix's grounding in soul and rhythm and blues, elements of his music that would come to the fore more on subsequent releases.

Hendrix's second album, *Axis: Bold as Love,* downplayed the feedback-laced festivities of *Experienced* for a more compact approach that still left significant room for aural experimentation. Generally speaking there is a much funkier vibe to this album than the first; "Ain't No Telling," "You Got Me Floatin'," and "Little Miss Lover" foreshadow the later funk/rock fusion of George Clinton and Funkadelic, while "Little Wing" and "Castles Made of Sand" are softer tunes on which Hendrix exhibits a facility with the finer points of rhythm-and-blues harmony shared only by the likes of Curtis Mayfield. Some of this funk carried over to the next album, *Electric Ladyland,* on such cuts as "House Burning Down" and "Still Raining, Still Dreaming." Over the two records of *Electric Ladyland,* though, Hendrix's funk is mixed with a wide assortment of styles and sounds. From the abstract soundscape of "Moon Turn the Tides" to the versions of "Voodoo Chile" and "Voodoo Child (Slight Return)" discussed in chapter 5, the album finds Hendrix pushing into new territory, expanding and revising his musical approach. On the whole, *Electric Ladyland* may lack some of the consistency of the earlier albums, but it contains some of Hendrix's best music, and side four of the original vinyl release is one of the best sides of music Hendrix ever recorded (in sequence: "Still Raining, Still Dreaming," "House Burning Down," "All Along the Watchtower," and "Voodoo Child").

Not long after the release of *Electric Ladyland,* the Experience started to dissolve as a unit, largely due to the dissatisfaction of bassist Noel Redding. For the last two years of his career Hendrix seemed to be searching for the right cast of bandmates. Billy Cox, a bassist he had met while in the army in the early 1960s, was Hendrix's most regular accomplice during this period. On drums Hendrix forged an association with Buddy Miles, but also continued to rely on Experience drummer Mitch Mitchell for many a gig and recording session.

On New Year's Eve, 1969, Hendrix, Cox, and Miles recorded a performance at the Fillmore East in New York. Released under the name *Band of Gypsies,* the album was taken by many as a sign of Hendrix's growing sensitivity to racial issues; in the midst of the Black Power movement, Hendrix's decision to perform with other African-American musicians and to turn to a more thoroughly soul-based song list seemed a statement of racial solidarity. Yet musically, *Band of Gypsies* was not much of a departure from Hendrix's earlier soul-inflected material; reading the album as Hendrix's "blackest" offering is an all-too-easy judgment. Just as important, the band of Cox, Miles, and Hendrix does not always cohere, especially on the more "straight" soul tracks that comprise the second half of the album. Side one, however, does contain one definitive Hendrix cut: "Machine Gun," twelve minutes of stuttering riffs and some of the guitarist's most incendiary playing. Along with the "Star-Spangled Banner," it is Hendrix's most direct representation of the political violence of the period.

Band of Gypsies was the last Hendrix album released during his lifetime. Shortly thereafter, the wave of posthumous releases began. *Cry of Love,* the first such release, is a strong offering of original material, compiled from tracks that Hendrix had left in a mostly-finished state at the time of his death. Some of the songs here—"Freedom," "Ezy Rider," "Night Bird Flying," and "Angel"—rank among Hendrix's best work, and the album as a whole shows him moving toward soul much more successfully than on *Band of Gypsies.* However, on subsequent 1970s releases like *Crash Landing* and *Midnight Lightnin',* most of which were produced by Alan Douglas, the quality of the material was not as strong, and unfinished tracks were often padded with performances by studio musicians to give them a "finished" quality that did not always fit the song. Two recent releases, *First Rays of the New Rising Sun* and *South Saturn Delta,* repackage much of the best of this material with new mixes by Hendrix's recording engineer, Eddie Kramer, designed to recapture the original intention of the tracks. *First Rays* is especially noteworthy as an effort to reconstruct the album Hendrix had been recording at the time of his death, and does succeed in recombining tracks drawn from a range of posthumous releases into a more coherent sequence than earlier such albums.

More interesting are the albums of live Hendrix material that have circulated in the years since his death. One of the earliest was *Hendrix in the West,* which contains a strong extended version of "Red House," and also includes three songs from the 1969 Berkeley concert that was captured on film as *Jimi Plays Berkeley,* including the rendering of "Johnny B. Goode" discussed in chapter 5. *The Jimi Hendrix Concerts,* issued in 1982, offers a broader range of live material, and features more performances on which Hendrix and company really stretch out, including a ten-minute version of "Stone Free" and the album closer, "Hear My Train a Comin'," another of Hendrix's more blues-based songs. *Live at Winter-*

land, released five years after *Concerts,* is drawn exclusively from the October 10–12, 1968 engagement that provided *Concerts* with more than half its cuts (though there is almost no overlap between the two), and provides a valuable audio snapshot of Hendrix and the Experience holding forth over the course of a single set of shows. And then there is the recently issued (1994) compilation, *Jimi Hendrix: Blues,* a set of previously unreleased studio tracks and live performances that captures some excellent playing while engaging in the ideologically conflicted task of presenting Hendrix as a "bluesman." My feelings about the album are ambivalent—the liner notes by Michael Fairchild are emblematic of some of the worst excesses that surround Hendrix's posthumous canonization—but the collection is redeemed by the music, and especially by the final track, another version of "Hear My Train a Comin'" that pushes into "Machine Gun" territory in the pyrotechnic virtuosity exhibited by the guitarist.

The MC5

One of the more intriguing side effects of the resurgence of punk rock that has occurred in the United States during the 1990s has been the revival of interest in bands considered to be American punk "precursors." The MC5, along with their Detroit counterparts the Stooges, have been among the primary beneficiaries of this turn toward punk's (supposed) past. Following the Five's dissolution in 1972, their small catalogue of recordings was put out of print for most of the remainder of the 1970s, and for the next decade as well. Not that nobody was listening; the Five enjoyed status during these years as a cult band, knowledge of whom was passed along from older fans to younger. It was in this semi-underground guise that the MC5 did indeed become an important influence on the punk movement, though in this phase of the band's "posthumous" career they were probably talked about much more than their albums were heard. But with the success in the early 1990s of Nirvana and other grunge and punk bands who cited the Five as a key influence, the band's original albums were made available once again, now on compact disc, while more recently former manager John Sinclair has taken the opportunity to issue some previously unreleased recordings of live Five material as well.

Of course, live was how the band's recording career effectively got underway. *Kick out the Jams!,* the band's first album, remains a powerful document of a band with energy to burn, playing to an enthusiastic home-town crowd on Halloween 1968. Many of the musical high points are covered in chapter 6 (though one cannot overlook the album's last track, a version of Sun Ra's "Starship"). Also of importance was the controversy surrounding the album, which centered around the infamous introduc-tion to the band's signature song, "Kick out the Jams, Motherfuckers!" One of the Detroit area's main retail outlets, Hudson's, refused to carry the album due to the obscenity. The Five's record company, Elektra, responded to Hudson's and other voices of protest from radio and retail by releasing an alternate version of the album, which overdubbed "motherfuckers" with "brothers and sisters." Meanwhile, the band took out a full-page ad prompting listeners to ignore the protests with the derisive assertion, "Fuck Hudson's." Such impudence led to an irrepara-ble rift between the MC5 and Elektra, and shortly thereafter the band was released from its contract.

For their second album, *Back in the USA,* the MC5 struck a deal with Atlantic Records. The switch of label was by no means the only change that figured into the making of *Back in the USA,* though. In 1969 the band also broke its association with manager and ideological linchpin John Sinclair in a rather acrimonious set of affairs that was only worsened by Sinclair's imprisonment on charges of marijuana possession. In Sinclair's absence, the Five forged an association with perhaps the most influential American rock critic of the time, Jon Landau. *Back in the USA* was Landau's first job as record producer, a role to which he would return some years later with Bruce Springsteen. The results of the collaboration between the MC5 and Landau marked a decided shift in the band's approach; at Landau's urging the songs were all condensed into two- to three-minute blasts of sound, with little room for the stretching out that had been one of the band's trademarks. This is not to say that the album lacks excitement; songs like "Call Me Animal" and a revised version of "Looking At You" almost jump out of the speakers, and the latter fea-tures some dynamic guitar work by Wayne Kramer. "American Ruse" and "Shakin' Street," meanwhile, offer some of the Five's sharpest songwrit-ing, honing the band's politics into a critique of the boredom engendered by coming of age in a world of consumption. Whether the shift marked by *Back in the USA* shows the music of the MC5 assuming a new degree of focus, or whether it shows the band losing its edge, remains a matter of contestation among critics and devotees alike; with hindsight, though, the album hardly seems the failure that many close to the band judged it to be at the time of its release.

Whatever the artistic success *Back in the USA* may have enjoyed, commercially it did not meet the hopes of either Atlantic or the MC5. Both in their native Detroit and in the broader rock scene, the countercultural enthusiasm that had driven the Five's audience was waning, and the band's once-solid base of support withered. *High Time,* the third MC5 album, fared even worse commercially than its predecessor, and was to be the final album by the band. That it was such a strong album makes the band's subsequent demise seem all the more unfortunate. *High Time* finds the MC5 returning to an "extended play" format more akin to *Kick out the Jams* than *Back in the USA.* "Sister Anne," a rollicking seven-minute ode to a nun, sets the pace as the album's opening track: beginning with a single heavy note (a low E) played on guitar and bass, the band jumps into a tight groove energized by the interlocking guitars of Smith and Kramer, and keeps the momentum going straight to the song's coda, played by a Salvation Army band. "Skunk (Sonicly Speaking)," the closing song, is perhaps the closest approximation to the sonic chaos of *Kick out the Jams* that the Five ever produced in the studio, with a full minute of quasi-tribal percussion at the start and a manic trajectory that climaxes in a sequence of horn solos and power chords dissolving into feedback.

For those seeking a quick overview, *Babes in Arms,* issued in 1983 by ROIR Records, is the closest thing to an MC5 anthology, but is far from adequate in covering the band's strengths. The alternate takes of songs such as "Shaking Street" and "Skunk" that comprise the bulk of the album are generally inferior to the cuts included on *Back in the USA* and *High Time,* and the only track from *Kick out the Jams* is the uncensored "motherfucker" version of the title song. Of greater interest are the pieces recorded prior to the release of *Kick out the Jams,* most notably the original recording of "Looking at You" produced by Sinclair in early 1968 and discussed in the opening paragraphs of chapter 6. Sinclair's recent compilations of rare MC5 live material, such as *Power Trip* (1994), are intriguing for their documentary value (*Power Trip* contains an otherwise-unavailable version of the band's notorious "Black to Comm," for instance), but suffer from drastically poor sound quality. Perhaps the most pleasurable event in the many years since the band's final disintegration has been the revived career of guitarist Wayne Kramer, who has released several albums under his own name since 1995, and has resurfaced as an exciting live performer who mixes original songs with extended reinterpretations of MC5 material. *The Hard Stuff,* Kramer's comeback album on L.A. punk label Epitaph, is an especially fresh blast of noise, and reveals the guitarist to be a mature, politically charged songwriter with a poetic edge, as on the sardonic "Junkie Romance" and the "hidden track" tribute to poet and novelist Charles Bukowski.

Led Zeppelin

Did heavy metal begin with Led Zeppelin? Listen to the first two albums by the band and decide for yourself (of course it would help if you also listened to Blue Cheer, the MC5, Steppenwolf, Iron Butterfly, Black Sabbath . . .). Released in 1969, the first, eponymously titled Led Zeppelin album certainly turned up the decibels on late-1960s blues-rock. "You Shook Me" and "I Can't Quit You Babe" are clearly blues-based, but playing the blues "straight" was never really what Led Zeppelin was about. Indeed, in many ways it was their lack of concern with questions of authenticity that set the band apart, and that gave their sound an unpredictability lacking in many of their counterparts (which is not to say that the band was above reproach for their uncredited appropriations of the blues on songs like "The Lemon Song," from *Led Zeppelin II*).

As I noted in chapter 7, the second Led Zeppelin album is the one routinely cited as the founding moment of heavy metal. "Whole Lotta Love," discussed at length in that same chapter, is a large part of the reason why, though "Heartbreaker" is just as potent a piece of rock, with plenty of phallocentric swagger in its own right. The latter song also features one of Jimmy Page's most extroverted guitar solos (from a performer never shy about exhibiting his goods), an unaccompanied flurry of notes that rends the song in half and leads into a churning steamroller of a riff against which Page solos all the more, while the rhythm section of John Paul Jones and John Bonham gives him the solid support that was the great secret to the band's success. Despite its reputation for heaviness, *Led Zeppelin II* is not all of a piece; a soft-hearted ballad ("Thank You") closes side one, and other songs ("Ramble on," "What Is and What Should Never Be") employ more gentle sounds alongside the louder out-bursts, creating the shifts in sonic dynamics that would become one of the band's trademarks.

Led Zeppelin III altered the balance of the band's music. The album is split almost literally in half between predominantly acoustic and princi-pally electric songs. Side one is the heavier side, and contains one of Page's best blues performances on "Since I've Been Loving You." The Eastern-flavored acoustic track "Friends" foreshadows what is to come on side two, on which the band make a move toward a sort of acoustic guitar–driven pastoralism. Elements of Celtic music, country, and blues glide through tracks like "Gallow's Pole" and "That's the Way," while Page throws into the mix not only acoustic guitar but mandolin and pedal steel. Overall, *Led Zeppelin III* represents a successful expansion of the band's musical range, and further shows how Led Zeppelin negotiated the "great divide" between acoustic and electric sounds that was so much at issue in 1970, the year of the album's release.

The next Led Zeppelin album, untitled but often referred to as the "zoso album" because of the symbols reproduced on the record jacket, refined the band's mix of sounds, increasing the quotient of out-and-out rock 'n' roll but still leaving considerable room for the quieter side of the band to emerge. "Black Dog" and "Rock and Roll," the opening cuts on the album, are two of the hardest rocking, most rhythmically propulsive songs the band would ever record. "Battle of Evermore," an odd little piece of acoustic drama, is almost medieval in its tone and temperament, and finds Robert Plant matching vocal chops with former Fairport Con-vention singer Sandy Denny. Then comes the monumental "Stairway to Heaven," described so well by Chuck Eddy in a passage cited in the conclusion to chapter 7. "Stairway to Heaven" is a curious piece of lyrical mysticism framed by a uniquely compelling musical narrative, embodying in its seven-plus minutes the scope of Zeppelin's approach to sound. Side two offers almost a mirror of the first side, with two rockers ("Misty Mountain Hop" and "Four Sticks"), a ballad ("Going to California"), and an epic side-closer ("When the Levee Breaks"). That final epic track, though, offers an apocalyptic vision that contrasts markedly with the "shining white light" of "Stairway." The lumbering, bottom-heavy ar-rangement, driven by John Bonham's massive drumbeats, is occasionally interrupted by an almost utopian-sounding, brightly melodic bridge, only to fall back into the dark morass within which the wailing harmonica and slide guitar are all but subsumed.

These first four Zeppelin albums are the crucial material for understanding the development of the band's sound. Yet the band continued to issue generally strong albums over the next few years. *Houses of the Holy,* released two years after *Untitled,* finds John Paul Jones asserting himself in the band's mix on tracks like "The Rain Song" and "No Quarter" (on both of which he plays keyboards). The former is the lushest ballad Zeppelin would ever record. More on the rocking side of things are the opening and closing tracks: the adventurous and tuneful "The Song Remains the Same," on which Page's solos shine, and the crunching "The Ocean." *Physical Graffiti,* released after another two-year gap, was the only double album that Led Zeppelin would record (excepting the live *Song Remains the Same*). Some consider it to be the band's best work; and tracks like the grandiose "Kashmir" (discussed in chapter 7) and the wonderfully arranged "Ten Years Gone" are certainly among Zeppelin's most fully realized compositions. Yet for all the strong material, there is too much filler on the album (including, to my ears, most of side four), rendering it less cohesive and thus less compelling than the earlier *Untitled.*

The late 1970s found Zeppelin's output growing a bit uneven. *The Song Remains the Same,* released in 1976, was the audio version of the documentary film made during the band's 1973 U.S. tour. Of interest as the band's only official "live" release, it presents some good extended performances of some of the more familiar songs from the band's catalogue, but does not capture the group at their performing peak (and tracks like the twenty-seven minute "Dazed and Confused" can tax one's patience). *Presence* was recorded in the aftermath of an almost fatal car accident involving Robert Plant and his family (Plant would lose his son shortly thereafter to an unrelated illness). "Achilles Last Stand" is another well-orchestrated epic with some dense guitar textures by Page, and "Nobody's Fault but Mine" is a solid, energetic piece in the band's "revisionist blues" mode. However, on the whole the album lacks the dynamic range that marks the group's best work. *In Through the Out Door,* Zeppelin's final release, has a broader range but is somewhat short on focus and energy; only "In the Evening" rocks convincingly, and Page is generally far less present on this album than on any of the band's earlier work. John Paul Jones, by contrast, often seems the controlling presence.

Relative to someone like Jimi Hendrix, little new Led Zeppelin product has been issued since the band's demise in 1980. The reasons are several: the band's (and especially Page's) guardedness about what is released under the Led Zeppelin name; the focused manner in which the band recorded, which meant fewer unheard or unfinished tracks lying about; and the fact that Plant and Page, the two principals, sought to distance themselves from Led Zeppelin and to embark on independent careers, with varying degrees of success. *Coda,* issued in 1982, includes a fairly small selection of unreleased or alternate cuts, and is mostly undistinguished. The more recent *BBC Sessions* captures some exciting performances from early in the band's career, but features some redundant song selections (three versions of "Communication Breakdown," for instance). Plant and Page's recent reunion produced some surprisingly stirring reinterpretations of earlier material on their "Unplugged" performance (released on compact disc as *No Quarter*), but the follow-up, *Walking into Clarksdale,* takes fewer risks despite being composed of original material.

Discography

Selected Recordings

Atkins, Chet. *Chet Atkins in 3 Dimensions*. RCA, 1956.

—— *Finger-Style Guitar*. RCA, 1957.

—— *Mister Guitar*. RCA, 1959.

—— *Chet Atkins at Home*. RCA, 1961.

—— *Down Home*. RCA, 1962.

—— *Teen Scene*. RCA, 1963.

—— *My Favorite Guitars*. RCA, 1965.

—— *Pickin' on Country*. RCA, 1988.

—— *Chet Atkins: The RCA Years* (2 compact discs). RCA, 1992.

Atkins, Chet and Les Paul. *Chester and Lester*. RCA, 1976.

Atkins, Chet and Merle Travis. *The Atkins-Travis Traveling Show*. RCA, 1974.

Atlantic Rhythm and Blues, Vol. 1: 1947–1952. Atlantic, 1985.

Basie, Count. *The Essential Count Basie, Vol. 1*. Columbia, 1987.

Beck, Jeff. *Truth*. Epic, 1968.

Berry, Chuck. *The Great Twenty-Eight*. MCA, 1984.

Blue Cheer. *Vincebus Eruptum*. PolyGram, 1968.

Blues Masters, Vol. One: Urban Blues. Rhino, 1992.

The Butterfield Blues Band. *East-West*. Elektra, 1966.

Chess Blues (4 compact discs). MCA/Chess, 1992.

Chess Rhythm & Roll (4 compact discs). MCA/Chess, 1994.

Christian, Charlie. *The Genius of the Electric Guitar*. Columbia, 1987.

Christian, Charlie and Dizzy Gillespie. *The Harlem Jazz Scene, 1941*. Esoteric.

Christian, Charlie and Benny Goodman. *Solo Flight*. Vintage Jazz Classics, 1991.

Cream. *Best of Cream*. Polydor.

Dale, Dick. *King of the Surf Guitar: The Best of Dick Dale and His Del-Tones*. Rhino, 1989.

Derek and the Dominos. *Layla and Other Assorted Love Songs*. RSO, 1970.

Diddley, Bo. *In The Spotlight*. Chess/MCA, 1987 (original release 1960).

—— *Bo Diddley Is a Gunslinger*. Chess/MCA, 1988 (original release 1963).

The Electric Flag. *A Long Time Comin'*. Columbia, 1968.

From Spirituals to Swing: Carnegie Hall Concerts, 1938/1939. Vanguard, 1987.

Gibson, Don. *18 Greatest Hits*. Curb Records, 1990.

—— *Girls, Guitars and Gibson*. RCA, 1961.

Great Blues Guitarists: String Dazzlers. Columbia, 1991.

Guitar Player Presents: Legends of Guitar—Country, Vol. 1. Rhino, 1990.

Guitar Player Presents: Legends of Guitar—Country, Vol. 2. Rhino, 1991.

Guitar Player Presents: Legends of Guitar—Jazz, Vol. 1. Rhino, 1990.

Guitar Player Presents: Legends of Guitar—Rock: The '50s, Vol. 1. Rhino, 1990.

Guitar Player Presents: Legends of Guitar—Rock: The '50s, Vol. 2. Rhino, 1991.

Guitar Slim. *Sufferin' Mind*. Specialty, 1991.

Guy, Buddy. *A Man and the Blues*. Vanguard, 1987 (original release 1968).

—— *Stone Crazy!* Alligator, 1981.

Hendrix, Jimi. *Are You Experienced?* Reprise, 1967.

—— *Axis: Bold as Love*. Reprise, 1968.

—— *Electric Ladyland*. Reprise, 1968.

—— *Smash Hits*. Reprise, 1969.

—— *Band of Gypsies*. Capitol, 1970.

—— *The Cry of Love*. Polydor, 1971.

—— *Hendrix in the West*. Polydor, 1971.

—— *The Essential Jimi Hendrix, Vol. 1*. Reprise, 1978.

—— *The Essential Jimi Hendrix, Vol. 2*. Reprise, 1979.

—— *Nine to the Universe*. Reprise, 1980.

—— *The Jimi Hendrix Concerts*. Warner Bros., 1982.

—— *Lifelines*. Reprise, 1990.

—— *Blues*. MCA, 1994.

Hooker, John Lee. *The Ultimate Collection: 1948–1990*. Rhino, 1991.

Howlin' Wolf. *Howlin' Wolf*. Chess, 1984 (original release 1958).

—— *The Wolf Is at Your Door*. Charly, 1992.

Jansch, Bert. *The Best of Bert Jansch*. Shanachie, 1992.

Johnson, Robert. *King of the Delta Blues Singers*. Columbia, 1961.

Jordan, Louis. *The Best of Louis Jordan*. MCA, 1975.

King, B. B. *Live at the Regal*. MCA, 1971.

—— *The Best of B. B. King, Vol. 1*. Ace/Virgin, 1985.

Led Zeppelin. *Led Zeppelin*. Atlantic, 1969.

—— *Led Zeppelin II*. Atlantic, 1969.

—— *Led Zeppelin III*. Atlantic, 1970.

—— *Untitled*. Atlantic, 1971.

—— *Houses of the Holy*. Atlantic, 1973.

—— *Physical Graffiti*. Swan Song, 1975.

—— *Presence*. Swan Song, 1976.

—— *The Song Remains the Same.* Swan Song, 1976.

—— *In Through the Out Door.* Swan Song, 1979.

—— *Coda.* Swan Song, 1982.

Little Walter. *Blues with a Feeling.* Charly, 1992.

Mayall, John. *Blues Breakers.* London, 1977 (original release 1965).

MC5. *Kick Out the Jams.* Elektra, 1969.

—— *Back in the USA.* Rhino, 1992 (original release Atlantic, 1970).

—— *High Time.* Rhino, 1992 (original release Atlantic, 1971).

—— *Babes in Arms.* ROIR, 1983.

—— *Power Trip.* Alive, 1994.

Monroe, Bill. *Blue Moon of Kentucky.* Sony, 1993.

1930s Jazz: The Small Combos. Columbia, 1987.

Nuggets: Classics from the Psychedelic Sixties. Rhino, 1986.

Paul, Les. *The Legend and the Legacy* (4 compact discs). Capitol, 1991.

—— *The Les Paul Trio.* LaserLight, 1991.

Presley, Elvis. *The Complete Sun Sessions.* RCA, 1987.

Reichel, Hans. *The Dawn of Dachsman . . . Plus.* Free Music Production, 1994.

Rush, Otis. *His Cobra Recordings, 1956–1958.* Flyright, 1988.

Ryder, Mitch. *Rev Up: The Best of Mitch Ryder and the Detroit Wheels.* Rhino, 1989.

The Stooges. *The Stooges.* Elektra, 1969.

—— *Fun House.* Elektra, 1970.

—— *Raw Power.* Columbia, 1973.

A Sun Blues Collection. Rhino, 1990.

The Sun Story. Rhino, 1987.

Travis, Merle. *Walkin' the Strings.* Capitol, 1996 (original release 1960).

—— *The Best of Merle Travis.* Rhino, 1990.

Tubb, Ernest. *Country Music Hall of Fame Series.* MCA, 1991.

Turner, Ike. *The Best of Ike Turner.* Rhino, 1994.

Walker, T-Bone. *The Complete Imperial Recordings, 1950–1954.* EMI, 1991.

Waters, Muddy. *The Best of Muddy Waters.* MCA/Chess, 1987 (original release 1958).

—— *The Real Folk Blues.* MCA/Chess, 1987 (original release 1966).

—— *Hard Again.* Blue Sky, 1977.

—— *Trouble No More: Singles, 1955–1959.* MCA/Chess, 1989.

—— *First Recording Sessions, 1941–1946.* Document, 1992.

Wells, Junior. *Hoodoo Man Blues.* Delmark, 1966.

West, Speedy and Jimmy Bryant. *Stratosphere Boogie: The Flaming Guitars of Speedy West and Jimmy Bryant.* Razor & Tie, 1995.

The Who. *The Who Sell Out.* Decca, 1967.

—— *Live at Leeds.* MCA, 1970.

———— *Meaty, Beaty, Big and Bouncy.* MCA, 1971.

Williamson, Sonny Boy. *The Real Folk Blues.* MCA/Chess, 1987 (original release 1966).

———— *King Biscuit Time.* Arhoolie, 1989.

Wills, Bob. *The Essential Bob Wills, 1935–1947.* Columbia, 1992.

Woodstock. Cotillion, 1970.

Wray, Link. *Rumble! The Best of Link Wray.* Rhino, 1993.

The Yardbirds. *Having a Rave Up with the Yardbirds.* Epic, 1965.

———— *Roger the Engineer.* Edsel, 1986 (original release 1966).

———— *Little Games Sessions and More.* EMI, 1992.

Notes

Introduction

1. Robert Cantwell, *When We Were Good: The Folk Revival* (Cambridge, Mass.: Harvard University Press, 1996), p. 1.
2. Ibid., pp. 307–308. Other pieces that similarly analyze Dylan's Newport performance in terms of the tensions of the folk movement include Ellen Willis's astute analysis of Dylan's career, contained in her collection, *Beginning to See the Light: Sex, Hope, and Rock-and-Roll* (Hanover, N.H.: Wesleyan University Press, 1992), pp. 3–25; and Geoffrey Stokes's account of Dylan's fusion of rock and folk in a book co-authored with Ed Ward and Ken Tucker, *Rock of Ages: The Rolling Stone History of Rock & Roll* (Englewood Cliffs, N.J.: Rolling Stone Press/Prentice Hall, 1986), pp. 303–314.
3. A. R. Duchossoir, *Gibson Electrics: The Classic Years* (Milwaukee: Hal Leonard, 1994), pp. 53–54.
4. Philip Ennis, *The Seventh Stream: The Emergence of Rocknroll in American Popular Music* (Hanover, N.H.: Wesleyan University Press, 1992), p. 278.
5. Ray Minhinnett and Bob Young, *The Story of the Fender Stratocaster: "Curves, Contours and Body Horns"* (San Francisco: Miller Freeman Books, 1995), p. 37.
6. Ennis, p. 277.
7. "It's Money Music," *Life*, 22 (June 3, 1966), pp. 102–103.
8. Charles Sawyer, *The Arrival of B. B. King* (New York: Da Capo, 1980), p. 99.
9. In fact, the Butterfield Blues Band had its East Coast debut at the same 1965 Newport festival as Dylan's epochal performance. The band caused an uproar of its own that paralleled and perhaps even precipitated the reaction to Dylan's appearance. Alan Lomax, noted folklorist, introduced the Butterfield band by referring disparagingly to their reliance on technol-

ogy, comparing them unfavorably to the old-time African-American acoustic blues performers who preceded the band onstage. After his introduction, Lomax encountered the band's manager, Albert Grossman, at the side of the stage; the two exchanged heated words and were soon on the floor exchanging blows while the band moved into its set. Sawyer, pp. 100–101.

10. Eric Lott, *Love and Theft: Blackface Minstrelsy and the American Working Class* (New York: Oxford University Press, 1993), p. 18.

11. Ibid., p. 49.

12. Paul Gilroy, *The Black Atlantic: Modernity and Double Consciousness* (Cambridge, Mass.: Harvard University Press, 1993), pp. 93–94.

13. Michel Foucault, *Discipline and Punish: The Birth of the Prison,* translated by Alan Sheridan (New York: Vintage Books, 1977); Judith Butler, *Gender Trouble: Feminism and the Subversion of Identity* (New York: Routledge, 1990).

14. Joe Gore, "Jennifer Batten: Storming the Boys' Club," *Guitar Player,* 7 (July 1989), p. 96.

15. Willis, "You Can't Go Down Home Again," *Beginning to See the Light,* p. 27.

16. Ibid.

17. Ibid.

18. Paul Théberge, *Any Sound You Can Imagine: Making Music/Consuming Technology* (Hanover, N.H.: Wesleyan University Press, 1997), p. 185.

19. Ibid., p. 187.

20. Ibid., p. 191.

21. Ibid., p. 2.

22. I am thinking especially of the efforts by editors Thomas Swiss, John Sloop, and Andrew Herman to encourage scholars of popular music to engage with Attali's ideas in their volume *Mapping the Beat: Popular Music and Contemporary Theory* (Malden, Mass.: Blackwell, 1998). They have also assembled a forthcoming issue of *Popular Music and Society* around the work of the French scholar.

23. More commonly called the "vintage guitar" market, this phenomenon is a fascinating instance of the ways in which material culture can serve the ends of nostalgia; the longing for guitars of the 1950s and 1960s has never been so strong, and it is these guitars that are most thoroughly documented in a host of publications dedicated to the history of electric instruments. That these books are oriented toward instrument collectors is clear from the inclusion of details like an explanation of the serial numbers on Gibson Les Paul guitars (see Tony Bacon and Paul Day's *The Gibson Les Paul Book* [San Francisco: Miller Freeman Books, 1993], pp. 91–93). These books

tend to be remarkably well researched with regard to the details of electric guitar production and provide excellent histories of guitar manufacturing. What they generally lack is any concerted effort to tie this history into broader social and cultural processes, and this is where the need for academic scholarship becomes most clear.

24. Robert Walser, *Running with the Devil: Power, Gender, and Madness in Heavy Metal Music* (Hanover, N.H.: Wesleyan University Press, 1993), pp. 57–107.

25. Theodore Gracyk, *Rhythm and Noise: An Aesthetics of Rock* (Durham: Duke University Press, 1996), pp. 99–124; Simon Frith, *Performing Rites: On the Value of Popular Music* (Cambridge, Mass.: Harvard University Press, 1998). Frith gestures toward the sort of multi-dimensional analysis that is needed with regard to the electric guitar, but as with much of *Performing Rites,* he does not pursue it. In his discussion of the importance of performance to the study of popular music, Frith notes, "The particular way in which a guitarist gets a guitar note (whether George Benson or Jimi Hendrix, Mark Knopfler or Johnny Marr, Derek Bailey or Bert Jansch) is at once a musical decision and a gestural one: it is the integration of sound and behavior in performance that gives the note its meaning" (p. 94). The range of guitarists Frith mentions is what I find most suggestive, as well as his implication that by looking at how these different musicians craft their notes, we might see how a single instrument can create a range of meanings depending on the approach of the musician and the genre rules according to which that musician plays.

26. Jacques Attali, *Noise: The Political Economy of Music,* translated by Brian Massumi (Minneapolis: University of Minnesota Press, 1985), p. 5.

27. Ibid., p. 19.

28. Ibid., p. 133.

29. Ibid., p. 4.

30. John Corbett has explored some of the implications of this point in his provocative essay, "Ephemera Underscored: Writing Around Free Improvisation," contained in the collection, *Jazz Among the Discourses,* edited by Krin Gabbard (Durham: Duke University Press, 1995), pp. 217–240. Using Attali as a starting point, Corbett considers the place of the musician's body in musical performance, and the ways in which improvising musicians in particular seek to "re-discipline" the body in ways not instructed by conventional musical technique. The instrument stands within Corbett's analysis as a site of power and knowledge at which the imperative toward reproducing "correct" bodily gestures exists in tension with the impulse toward discovering unfamiliar performative techniques that produce, in turn, unfamiliar musical effects (pp. 226–229).

31. Attali, p. 35.
32. Ibid., p. 135.
33. Ibid., p. 141.

1 Playing with Sound

1. Bill Simon, "Charlie Christian," in Nat Hentoff and Nat Shapiro (eds.), *The Jazz Makers* (London: Peter Davies, 1957), p. 320.
2. On the musical culture of the Southwest, see Charles Townsend, *San Antonio Rose: The Life and Music of Bob Wills* (Urbana: University of Illinois Press, 1976); Ralph Ellison, *Shadow and Act* (New York: Signet, 1964).
3. For an interesting and informative oral history of the southwestern jazz scene, see Nathan Pierson, *Goin' to Kansas City* (Urbana: University of Illinois Press, 1987).
4. Scholarship on the swing era has proliferated since this piece was first written some five years ago. Among the most notable recent titles are David Stowe's *Swing Changes: Big Band Jazz in New Deal America* (Cambridge, Mass.: Harvard University Press, 1994); Scott DeVeaux's *The Birth of Bebop: A Social and Musical History* (Berkeley: University of California Press, 1997), which despite its title is as much about the swing era as it is about swing's musical successor; and Lewis Erenberg's *Swingin' the Dream: Big Band Jazz and the Rebirth of American Culture* (Chicago: University of Chicago Press, 1998). Each of these works is a valuable addition to the historiography of jazz. However, none makes claims that have forced me to reconsider my basic argument. Indeed, the work of Stowe and DeVeaux in particular reinforces one of my own principal points, namely that the boundary between swing and bebop was not so strict, in historical terms, as it has often been made to seem.
5. Amiri Baraka, *Blues People* (New York: William Morrow and Company, 1963); James Lincoln Collier, *The Making of Jazz* (New York: Dell Publishing, 1978).
6. On the confrontational nature of black cultural forms in the years surrounding 1940, see Baraka, *Blues People;* Houston Baker, *Modernism and the Harlem Renaissance* (Chicago: University of Chicago Press, 1987); Lawrence Levine, *Black Culture and Black Consciousness* (New York: Oxford University Press, 1977).
7. Ellison, p. 191.
8. Cecelia Conway, *African Banjo Echoes in Appalachia: A Study of Folk Traditions* (Knoxville: University of Tennessee Press, 1995).
9. Robert Palmer, "The Church of the Sonic Guitar," *Present Tense: Rock &*

Roll and Culture, edited by Anthony DeCurtis (Durham: Duke University Press, 1992), p. 15.

10. The c.d. compilation *Great Blues Guitarists: String Dazzlers* (New York: Columbia/Legacy, 1991) contains a number of early blues performances from the 1920s and 1930s, including such performers as Lonnie Johnson, Tampa Red, and Blind Lemon Jefferson.

11. Ellison, p. 230.

12. Ibid. The Blue Devils were one of the feature orchestras in the Southwest, regularly defeating other bands in public battles during the late 1920s and early 1930s. Eventually, many of the band's members left to join the more financially sound Bennie Moten orchestra, and would later go on to form the Count Basie Orchestra, including Lester Young, Walter Page, and Basie himself.

13. Townsend, p. 61.

14. See James Sallis (ed.), *Jazz Guitars* (New York: Quill, 1984).

15. Donald Brosnac, *The Electric Guitar: Its History and Construction* (London: Omnibus Press, 1975), p. 16; Tom Wheeler, *American Guitars: An Illustrated History* (New York: Harper & Row, 1982), p. 329.

16. Wheeler, p. 331. Such a notion evokes the "mythos" surrounding electricity discussed by James Carey and John Quirk in their essay, "The Mythos of the Electronic Revolution," contained in Carey's collection, *Communication as Culture: Essays on Media and Society* (Boston: Unwin Hyman, 1989), pp. 113–141.

17. Ibid., p. 131.

18. Jas Obrecht and Joel Siegel, "Eddie Durham: Charlie Christian's Mentor, Pioneer of the Amplified Guitar," *Guitar Player,* 8 (August 1979), p. 58.

19. Ibid., p. 55.

20. Jas Obrecht, "Charlie Christian: First Star of the Electric Guitar," *Guitar Player,* 3 (March 1982), p. 48; Obrecht and Siegel, p. 60.

21. Leonard Ferris, "Mary Osborne: A Unique Role in Jazz Guitar History," *Guitar Player,* 2 (February 1974), p. 10; Obrecht, p. 49.

22. Reprinted as Charlie Christian, "Guitarmen, Wake Up and Pluck!" *Guitar Player,* 3 (March 1982), p. 50.

23. Ibid.

24. Frank Driggs and Harris Lewine, *Black Beauty, White Heat: A Pictorial History of Classic Jazz, 1920–1950* (New York: William Morrow and Company, 1982), p. 170.

25. Pearson, p. 92.

26. Ibid., p. 108.

27. Driggs and Lewine, p. 155.

28. For an illuminating and creative discussion of swing as dance music, and

the relation of swing music to its audience, see Albert Murray, *Stomping the Blues* (New York: McGraw-Hill, 1976).

29. Ira Gitler, *Swing to Bop: An Oral History of the Transition in Jazz in the 1940s* (New York: Oxford University Press, 1985), p. 24.

30. Nat Hentoff and Nat Shapiro (eds.), *Hear Me Talkin' to Ya* (New York: Dover, 1955), p. 293.

31. Frank Driggs, "Kansas City and the Southwest," *Jazz,* edited by Nat Hentoff and Albert McCarthy (New York: Rinehart & Company, 1959), p. 192.

32. Gunther Schuller, *The Swing Era: The Development of Jazz, 1930–1945* (New York: Oxford University Press, 1989), p. 548.

33. James Dugan and John Hammond, "An Early Black-Music Concert: From Spirituals to Swing," *The Black Perspective in Music,* 2 (Fall 1974), pp. 194–195.

34. Collier, *Benny Goodman and the Swing Era* (New York: Oxford University Press, 1989), pp. 172–173. Despite such efforts at integration, racial tensions were by no means alleviated during the swing era. While relations between musicians were generally friendly, black musicians often faced considerable adversity, if not outright hostility, when touring. In *Hear Me Talkin' to Ya,* trumpeter Roy Eldridge expressed a common frustration in his description of an encounter he had while trying to check in to a hotel on the road: "The clerk, when he see that I'm the Mr. Eldridge the reservation was made for, suddenly discovers that one of their regular tenants just arrived and took the last available room. I lug that baggage back into the street and start looking around again. By the time that kind of thing has happened night after night, it begins to work on my mind; I can't think right, can't play right . . . Man, when you're on the stage, you're great, but as soon as you come off, you're nothing. It's not worth the glory, not worth the money, not worth anything" (pp. 329–330).

35. Hammond, *John Hammond on Record* (New York: Ridge Press, 1977), pp. 227–228.

36. Hammond, "On Charlie Christian," *Guitar Player,* 3 (March 1982), p. 66.

37. Obrecht, p. 62.

38. Collier, *The Reception of Jazz in America* (New York: Institute for Studies in American Music, 1988), p. 25.

39. Collier, *Benny Goodman,* pp. 289–290.

40. Ellison, p. 234.

41. "Should Negro Musicians Play in White Bands?" *Down Beat,* 11 (October 15, 1939), pp. 1, 10.

42. "Benny Should Be Congratulated for His Courage—Jimmy Dorsey," *Down Beat,* 11 (October 15, 1939), pp. 1, 23.

43. David Stowe makes this point forcefully in *Swing Changes:* "Rather than a

radical departure from swing, bebop is better understood as a variation of swing that emerged at an inopportune historical moment, whose brief cultural trajectory reveals as much as swing's longer ascent and decline" (p. 183).

44. Baker, p. 76.
45. Hentoff and Shapiro, *Hear Me Talkin' to Ya,* p. 338.
46. Ibid., p. 335.
47. Gitler, p. 41.
48. Schuller, p. 577.
49. Ibid.
50. Ellison, p. 201.
51. Baraka, p. 181.
52. Frederic Grunfeld, *The Art and Times of the Guitar: An Illustrated History of Guitars and Guitarists* (New York: Collier Books, 1969), p. 261.

2 Pure Tones and Solid Bodies

1. "Jazzorama," *Jazz Today,* 3 (April 1957), p. 5.
2. Ibid.
3. Chet Flippo, "I Sing the Solid Body Electric," *Rolling Stone,* 180 (February 13, 1975), p. 45.
4. Michael Chanan, *Musica Practica: The Social Practice of Western Music from Gregorian Chant to Postmodernism* (London: Verso, 1994), p. 239.
5. Lynn Spigel, *Make Room for TV: Television and the Family Ideal in Postwar America* (Chicago: The University of Chicago Press, 1992); Keir Keightley, " 'Turn It Down!' She Shrieked: Gender, Domestic Space, and High Fidelity, 1948–1959," *Popular Music,* 2 (May 1996), pp. 149–177.
6. John Rockwell, "Fender the Founder," *Rolling Stone,* 206 (February 12, 1976), p. 59.
7. Thomas Hughes, *American Genesis: A Century of Invention and Technological Enthusiasm, 1870–1970* (New York: Viking, 1989), p. 43.
8. Mr. Bonzai, "Les Paul: The Godfather of Modern Music," *Mix,* 2 (February 1985), p. 122.
9. Mary Shaughnessy, *Les Paul: An American Original* (New York: William Morrow and Company, 1993), pp. 13–14.
10. Susan Douglas, in *Inventing American Broadcasting, 1899–1922* (Baltimore: Johns Hopkins University Press, 1987), pp. 190–191, discusses tinkering as a distinctly masculine form of mastery through the control of technology.
11. Ibid., p. 205.
12. Forrest White, *Fender: The Inside Story* (San Francisco: Miller Freeman Books, 1994), p. 4.

13. Shaughnessy, *Les Paul,* p. 30.

14. Atkins provided a colorful remembrance of his broadcasting adventures with Paul in a 1976 article told to William Ivey, "Jim Atkins: A Life Filled with the Guitar, Chet, and Les," *Guitar Player,* 9 (September 1976), pp. 48, 50. According to Atkins's account, the idea for the Booger Brothers came from Paul's characteristic impulse to disassemble a new record player Atkins had bought. The record player transmitted a signal to a radio speaker without wires, using an oscillator. Noting the principle behind the device, Paul promptly went to a nearby radio shop and asked for "the biggest damn oscillator you got," and fashioned a mechanism that permitted him to send a signal as far as nine miles away.

15. Jon Sievert, "Les Paul," *Guitar Player,* 12 (December 1977), p. 50.

16. Ibid. Determining the date of Paul's inventions can be tricky business; here he cites the construction of the Larson guitar in 1934, but in another interview Paul placed the date at 1937. In either case, this was still early in the electric guitar's history, when it had been taken up by a rather small number of players.

17. The story of the Log has been recounted by Paul in several interviews, and also been retold by numerous guitar historians. Among the best sources are Tom Wheeler, *American Guitars: An Illustrated History* (New York: HarperPerennial, 1992), p. 155; Shaughnessy, *Les Paul,* p. 96; and Flippo, "I Sing the Solid Body Electric," p. 50.

18. Wheeler, *American Guitars,* p. 155.

19. Atkins, "A Life Filled with the Guitar," p. 52.

20. Wheeler, *American Guitars,* p. 61.

21. Ibid.

22. Ray Minhinnett and Bob Young, *The Story of the Fender Stratocaster: "Curves, Contours and Body Horns"* (San Francisco: Miller Freeman Books, 1995), p. 17.

23. Forrest White strongly suggests that Fender did have prior knowledge of existing solid-body designs, and that he (White) himself had built such an instrument as early as 1942, only a year after Paul's Log. Yet White's comments only serve to reinforce the notion that the idea of the solid-body electric was gaining momentum among musicians and instrument makers during the course of the 1940s. White, *Fender: The Inside Story,* pp. 23–46.

24. A. R. Duchossoir, *Gibson Electrics: The Classic Years* (Milwaukee: Hal Leonard, 1994), p. 40.

25. Tony Bacon and Paul Day, *The Gibson Les Paul Book* (San Francisco: GPI Books, 1993), p. 13.

26. Duchossoir, *Gibson Electrics,* p. 42.

27. Bacon and Day, *The Gibson Les Paul Story,* p. 16.

28. Duchossoir, *Gibson Electrics,* p. 41.

29. Ibid., p. 43.

30. Wheeler, *American Guitars,* p. 156.

31. Duchossoir, *Gibson Electrics,* p. 45.

32. Ibid., p. 44.

33. Warren Sirota, "Les Paul: A Celebration of Genius," *Guitar Player,* 1 (January 1989), p. 46.

34. Duchossoir, *Gibson Electrics,* p. 63.

35. Paul Trynka (ed.), *The Electric Guitar: An Illustrated History* (San Francisco: Chronicle Books, 1995), p. 155.

36. Duchossoir, *Gibson Electrics,* p. 66.

37. Les Paul, "Pro's Reply," *Guitar Player,* 2 (March 1971), p. 9.

38. Tom Wheeler, "The Birth of the Les Paul," in *Gibson Guitars: 100 Years of an American Icon,* edited by Walter Carter (Los Angeles: General Publishing Group, 1994), p. 191.

39. Wheeler, "The Electric Guitar as Cultural Icon," *Gibson Guitars,* p. 202.

40. "The Wizard of Waukesha," *Guitar Player,* 1 (February 1970), p. 17.

41. James Kraft, *Stage to Studio: Musicians and the Sound Revolution, 1890–1950* (Baltimore: Johns Hopkins University Press, 1996), p. 100.

42. Ibid., p. 127.

43. Shaughnessy, *Les Paul,* pp. 124–125.

44. Ibid., pp. 139–140.

45. Stephen Peeples, liner notes to *Les Paul: The Legend and the Legacy* (Capitol, 1991), p. 17.

46. Theodore Gracyk develops a suggestive argument concerning "realist" assumptions about the recording process, a set of assumptions that assigns ontological priority to performance over recordings. Gracyk asserts that for much popular music (particularly rock, his main subject), the recorded object is distinct, not merely an effect of the causal act of performance. My suggestion is that the understanding of the recorded musical object Gracyk posits has its roots in the techniques pioneered by Les Paul in his Hollywood garage/studio. Gracyk, *Rhythm and Noise: An Aesthetics of Rock* (Durham: Duke University Press, 1996), pp. 37–53.

47. Peeples, *The Legend and the Legacy,* p. 29.

48. Only a few years earlier, in 1944, Paul had himself participated in a bop-oriented jam with another musician who was soon to take a turn toward a more "pop" direction in his career, Nat King Cole; the two can be heard on the first edition of *Jazz at the Philharmonic,* a series of "live" recordings produced by jazz impresario Norman Granz. Yet Paul decided some time during these years that jazz was no way to make a living, that it had moved away from the tastes of the average listener and was not a suitable forum for the sort of success he envisioned.

49. Shaughnessy, *Les Paul,* p. 142.

50. "Paul's Comeback," *Newsweek,* 10 (September 5, 1949), p. 64; Pat Harris, "No, Them Ain't Hillbillies, It's Les Paul 'N Company," *Down Beat* (September 23, 1949), p. 4.

51. Shaughnessy, *Les Paul,* p. 196.

52. Lucy O'Brien, *She Bop: The Definitive History of Women in Rock, Pop and Soul* (New York: Penguin, 1995), p. 37.

53. Ibid., pp. 42–43. Discussing Peggy Lee, O'Brien asserts that the singer "conformed to a 'Good Girl' standard," and in so doing gained "acceptance into a white mainstream that championed a woman who observed protocol and played ambassador."

54. Les Paul, "I Try to Make Perfect Records," *Down Beat,* 13 (June 30, 1954), p. 81.

55. "Les Paul: I Want Sound as It Really Is," *Metronome,* 5 (May 1957), p. 17.

56. Lynn Spigel, *Make Room for TV,* pp. 110–112. Spigel discusses the ways in which electric technology was invested with the power to purify social space, a key tenet of the ideological underpinnings of postwar suburbia. Spigel's analysis is largely based on the work of James Carey and John Quirk, who elaborate upon the utopian hopes surrounding electricity in their essay, "The Mythos of the Electronic Revolution," contained within Carey's collection, *Communication as Culture: Essays on Media and Society* (Boston: Unwin Hyman, 1989), pp. 113–141.

57. Spigel, *Make Room for TV,* pp. 96, 122.

58. Keightley, " 'Turn It Down!' She Shrieked," p. 149.

59. Ibid., p. 157.

60. Ibid., p. 152.

61. Shaughnessy, *Les Paul,* p. 211.

62. "I Want Sound as It Really Is," p. 19.

63. Ibid.

64. Amy Porter, "The Craziest Music You Ever Heard," *Saturday Evening Post,* 29 (January 17, 1953), p. 98.

65. "Polfuses at Home," *Newsweek,* 4 (July 27, 1953), pp. 68–69.

66. In later years, Paul would invent an actual device called the "Les Paulverizer" that would allow him to reproduce his multi-tracked creations on-stage by triggering different tape recorded parts and then playing over them. For Paul's description, see Sievert, "Les Paul," pp. 60, 62.

67. Simon Frith, *Performing Rites: On the Value of Popular Music* (Cambridge, Mass.: Harvard University Press, 1996), p. 245.

68. Peter Mengaziol, "Going to See the Wizard: Les Paul, the Interview, Part One," *Guitar World,* 2 (March 1983), p. 40.

69. Ibid., p. 45.

70. Don Freeman, "'Want to Get Godfrey Quality in Our Work,' Says Les Paul," *Down Beat,* 12 (June 15, 1951), p. 3.

71. Krin Gabbard, *Jammin' at the Margins: Jazz and the American Cinema* (Chicago: University of Chicago Press, 1996), pp. 26, 28.

72. Shaughnessy, *Les Paul,* p. 206.

73. When Attali declares that "repetition produces information free of noise," and that the most effective performer within a repetitive system of production is "a virtuoso of the short phrase capable of infinitely redoing takes that are perfectible with sound effects," he may as well be writing about Les Paul's efforts to manipulate sound through the mastery of electronic technology. Attali, *Noise,* p. 106.

74. The phrase "south-of-the-border" was used by Paul himself to describe the sound of such tunes. Peeples, p. 46.

75. Shaughnessy, p. 216.

76. Joseph Lanza, *Elevator Music: A Surreal History of Muzak, Easy-Listening, and Other Moodsong* (New York: Picador, 1994), p. 69.

77. Ibid., p. 120.

78. Ibid., p. 124.

79. Mengaziol, "Going to See the Wizard," p. 39.

80. Mengaziol, "The Wizard Speaks to the Young: Les Paul, the Interview, Part Two," *Guitar World,* 3 (May 1983), p. 55.

3 Mister Guitar

1. Thomas Goldsmith, "Country Guitars," in *Classic Guitars of the '50s* (San Francisco: Miller Freeman Books, 1996), p. 35.

2. Charles Wolfe, *Tennessee Strings: The Story of Country Music in Tennessee* (Knoxville: University of Tennessee Press, 1977), p. 100.

3. Rich Kienzle, "The Electric Guitar in Country Music: Its Evolution and Development," *Guitar Player,* 11 (November 1979), p. 34.

4. Chet Atkins with Bill Neely, *Country Gentleman* (Chicago: Henry Regnery Company, 1974), p. 184.

5. John Morthland, "Changing Methods, Changing Sounds: An Overview," *Journal of Country Music,* 2 (1989), p. 4.

6. Ibid., p. 5.

7. Bill Malone, *Country Music U.S.A.* (Austin: University of Texas Press, 1985; rev. ed.), p. 257.

8. Ibid., p. 264.

9. "Genre analysis must be, by aesthetic necessity, narrative analysis": see Simon Frith, *Performing Rites: On the Value of Popular Music* (Cambridge, Mass.: Harvard University Press, 1996), p. 90.

10. Frith says, "It is out of such 'transgressive' performances that genre histo-

ries are written: old genres 'fail' when their rules and rituals come to seem silly and restrictive; new genres are born as the transgressions become systematic." *Performing Rites,* p. 94.

11. Robert Cantwell, *Bluegrass Breakdown: The Making of the Old Southern Sound* (New York: Da Capo Press, 1992), p. 13. Cantwell's declaration here is in accordance with historian Charles Wolfe's account of the early history of the Grand Ole Opry, in which Wolfe notes the conscious decision of Opry ringleader George Hay to emphasize the "folk" aspects of the show. Wolfe recounts: "Soon [Hay] was constructing an image of the show that stressed its rustic, hayseed quality. He asked the musicians to stop wearing their business suits and instead to put on overalls and work shirts; publicity pictures were made of musicians in cornfields, with hound dogs, and jugs of moonshine." Wolfe, *Tennessee Strings,* p. 61.

12. "Hillbilly" was the official marketing term of what is now called country music until the 1940s, when it was supplanted by "country and western." The implications of this shift will be addressed more fully in the course of this chapter.

13. Cantwell, *Bluegrass Breakdown,* p. 191.

14. Robert Cantwell, *When We Were Good: The Folk Revival* (Cambridge, Mass.: Harvard University Press, 1996), p. 82.

15. Chet Atkins, "How Chet Atkins Did It," *Journal of Country Music,* 2 (1989), pp. 11–12.

16. Nick Seitz, "The Hunched-over Chairman of Country Music," *Signature* (April 1971), p. 35.

17. Chet Flippo, "King Picker," *Rolling Stone,* 206 (February 12, 1976), p. 34.

18. Charles Wolfe, *Kentucky Country: Folk and Country Music of Kentucky* (Lexington: University Press of Kentucky, 1996), p. 131.

19. Ibid.

20. Atkins, *Country Gentleman,* p. 121.

21. Chet Atkins, "Chet Atkins, part one," *Guitar Player,* 1 (February 1972), p. 24.

22. Atkins, *Country Gentleman,* p. 160.

23. Debbie Holley, "Billy Byrd: The Jazzman Wore Cowboy Boots," *Journal of Country Music,* 1 (1987), p. 44.

24. Ibid., p. 45.

25. David Halberstam, "New Breed: Jazz-Billy," *Nashville Tennessean* (May 17, 1959). The article was reproduced for inclusion in the "Hank Garland" folder at the Country Music Hall of Fame (hereafter CMHF) archives.

26. Atkins, *Country Gentleman,* p. 213.

27. Red O'Donnell, *Chet Atkins* (Nashville: Athens Music Company, 1967), p. 44.

28. In a sense, the influence of Christian could have manifested itself no other

way among musicians not living in New York, since Christian's work at Minton's was only recorded in bootleg form and went unreleased until the late 1950s. Nonetheless, the point still stands that the style of jazz favored by Nashville musicians was melodically and harmonically conservative when judged against much of the jazz being produced at the time.

29. "Grady Martin," publicity release (Nashville: Monument Records), included in "Grady Martin" folder at the CMHF archives.

30. James Sallis, *The Guitar Players: One Instrument and Its Masters in American Music* (Lincoln: University of Nebraska Press, 1994), pp. 205–206.

31. A. R. Duchossoir, *Gibson Electrics: The Classic Years* (Milwaukee: Hal Leonard, 1994), pp. 56–57.

32. Ray Minhinnett and Bob Young, *The Story of the Fender Stratocaster: Curves, Contours and Body Horns* (San Francisco: Miller Freeman Books, 1995), p. 22; Forrest White, *Fender: The Inside Story* (San Francisco: Miller Freeman Books, 1994), pp. 80–81.

33. In seeking to condense the study of "finger style," I have decided to exclude some intriguing but largely undeveloped sidebars, among which perhaps the most provocative is a comment by rock guitarist Mark Knopfler, another finger-style musician who recorded a couple of albums with Atkins. Discussing the appeal of a finger-style approach, Knopfler declared in a 1990 interview that "the immediacy and the heart and soul of your playing really has to do with the flesh." Though Knopfler does not go on to elaborate his comment, I think it can be taken as an indication of the extent to which finger style has an air of naturalness to it: When finger-style guitarists opt to strike the strings with their flesh rather than with a pick, they have a less mediated relationship with their instruments. Thus finger-style guitar manages to retain a certain folksiness even when its practitioners, such as Atkins, move rather far from the folk sources in which the style is rooted. Gordon Ely, "Chet Atkins and Mark Knopfler: A Couple of Above Below Average Guys . . . Talking Chops," *Guitar Extra,* 3 (Fall 1990), p. 47.

34. Rich Kienzle, "The Evolution of Country Fingerpicking," *Guitar Player,* 5 (May 1984), p. 38.

35. "Head to Come," included in the "Chet Atkins" folder at the CMHF archives. The source of the article is unlisted, though repeated references to radio station KWTO in Springfield, Missouri, where Atkins spent part of his time playing with the Carter Sisters, suggest that it was a publicity release for the station, which would date the piece to sometime around 1949.

36. Wolfe discusses this tradition in the context of a broader investigation of the development of finger-style guitar in Kentucky; see *Kentucky Country,*

pp. 110–114. A somewhat more detailed account of black hillbilly music is contained in a study by Wolfe and David Morton of DeFord Bailey, an African-American harmonica virtuoso. See Charles Wolfe and David Morton, *DeFord Bailey: A Black Star in Early Country Music* (Knoxville: The University of Tennessee Press, 1991). Meanwhile, Cecelia Conway has recently published the first book-length consideration of such patterns in the history of African-American music, *African Banjo Echoes in Appalachia: A Study of Folk Traditions* (Knoxville: The University of Tennessee Press, 1995). Conway's goal is to establish the primacy of African and African-American influence upon Appalachian banjo performance. She identifies a strain of African-American banjo practices that parallel what Wolfe identifies as a black hillbilly tradition.

37. Wolfe, *Kentucky Country*, p. 110.
38. Merle Travis, "Travis," unpublished piece contained in "Merle Travis" folder at CMHF archives, p. 2.
39. Travis recorded the song several times over the course of his career; the version referred to here is taken from a radio transcription recorded around 1949, and included on the album *Walkin' the Strings*, a collection of Travis radio transcriptions from the 1940s and early 1950s first released by Capitol records in 1960, and recently reissued.
40. The story behind this song is told by Archie Green in his classic study, *Only a Miner: Studies in Recorded Coal-Mining Songs* (Urbana: University of Illinois Press, 1972), pp. 294–314.
41. Quoted in Forrest White, *Fender: The Inside Story*, p. 37.
42. Tom Wheeler, *American Guitars: An Illustrated History* (New York: HarperPerennial, 1992), p. 11.
43. Richard Smith, *Fender: The Sound Heard 'Round the World* (Fullerton, Calif.: Garland Publishing Company, 1995), p. 97.
44. Atkins, *Country Gentleman*, p. 54.
45. In a 1995 talk at Vanderbilt University, Atkins spoke of how both his brother and Paul used pseudonyms while playing the National Barn Dance to avoid being identified as hillbilly performers, a designation that would have interfered with their aspirations in the more "respectable" field of jazz and pop. Les Paul and Jim Atkins would eventually move from the Barn Dance to positions with the Fred Waring Orchestra in New York.
46. Cantwell, *Bluegrass Breakdown*, pp. 154–155.
47. Ibid., p. 155.
48. Atkins, *Country Gentleman*, p. 43.
49. Ibid., p. 56.
50. In Chet Flippo's interview with Atkins, the guitarist described in greater detail the process whereby he diverged from his mentor's picking tech-

nique: "I started trying to play like I thought Merle would play and I was playing with a thumb and three fingers. I didn't know he was doing it with a thumb and one finger. And that was luck, see, because if I'd been in Cincinnati and seen him I'da wound up playing *exactly* like him. Later on I met him and he said, how'd you learn to play with three fingers, and I said, hell, I thought that's what *you* were doing." Flippo, "King Picker," p. 32.

51. Ibid., p. 35.

52. Ronnie Pugh, *Ernest Tubb: The Texas Troubadour* (Durham: Duke University Press, 1996), p. 66.

53. A similar sort of transition occurred in African-American blues music, which will be discussed in the next chapter.

54. Referred to briefly in chapter 2, Dunn was among the first musicians of any popular genre to record with an amplified guitar during his tenure in the mid-1930s with the groundbreaking western swing ensemble Milton Brown and His Musical Brownies. Writing about Dunn's career in the *Journal of Country Music,* Kevin Coffey notes the difficulty in determining whether Dunn began employing amplification to be heard over the din of the "crowded, noisy dance halls" or out of a "desire to capture a certain sound." Coffey, "Steel Colossus: The Bob Dunn Story," *Journal of Country Music,* 2 (1995), p. 50.

55. Atkins, *Country Gentleman,* p. 60.

56. Don Menn, "Chet Atkins: Popular Music's Most Influential Fingerstylist," *Guitar Player,* 10 (October 1979), p. 122.

57. Ibid., p. 102.

58. These two tracks have been anthologized on a number of collections. My source for "Galloping on the Guitar" is the compilation, *Legends of Guitar: Country, vol. one,* presented by *Guitar Player* magazine and put together by Rich Kienzle (Santa Monica: Rhino Records, 1990). "Country Gentleman" is included on a budget-priced overview of Atkins's career, *Pickin' on Country,* released in 1988 by BMG music. For a useful critical overview of Atkins's early singles, see Nick Jones, "Chet's Early Career and Singles," in issue 15 of *Mister Guitar,* the official Chet Atkins fan club publication, pp. 4–6.

59. Jones, "Chet's Early Career and Singles," p. 6.

60. Tony Bacon and Paul Day, *The Gretsch Book: A Complete History of Gretsch Electric Guitars* (San Francisco: Miller Freeman Books, 1996), p. 26.

61. Wheeler, *American Guitars,* p. 205.

62. Bacon and Day, *The Gretsch Book,* p. 26.

63. Atkins had in fact urged the company to build a guitar with greater solidity, but never felt that Gretsch achieved an effective solid-body design. For

Atkins's comments on his input into the original Gretsch designs, see Wheeler, *American Guitars,* pp. 213–215.

64. For a discussion of Butts's development of the humbucker, see Bacon and Day, *The Gretsch Book,* p. 41.

65. "Talking Ax with Mr. Guitar," *Guitar Player,* 5 (October 1969), p. 48.

66. Forest Belt, "Guitar Amplification in the Atkins Style," *Radio-Electronics* (November 1966), p. 33; Menn, "Chet Atkins," p. 107.

67. Flippo, "King Picker," p. 30.

68. Atkins, *Country Gentleman,* pp. 66, 78. Ernest Tubb, mentioned earlier as one of the performers who legitimated the electric guitar in country music, was one of the musicians most concerned with disposing of the hillbilly label that had held sway through the years from the 1920s to the 1940s. According to Tubb's biographer, Ronnie Pugh, "To call the music as a whole 'hillbilly' was to Tubb an outrage: too many people used that word as an insult, a putdown. A 'hillbilly' by definition was dirty, ignorant, and isolated, was he not? To call the music by that name was to belittle it, to denigrate." Tubb, like Atkins, saw the shift to country music as a crucial means of elevating the music's stature and broadening its appeal. Pugh, *Ernest Tubb,* pp. 132–134.

69. The line between high and low has of course been one of the favorite subjects of popular culture scholars, with Lawrence Levine's study, *Highbrow/Lowbrow: The Emergence of Cultural Hierarchy in America* (Cambridge, Mass.: Harvard University Press, 1988), being perhaps the most extensive treatment of the subject. Much of the scholarship in this vein has studied the blurring of cultural boundaries, as when figures from popular culture have appropriated highbrow texts or sources to their own ends, questioning the authority of those sources in the process. A more sympathetic critic might read some of these impulses in Atkins's career. However, from what I have learned of Atkins, questioning authority has never been one of his primary goals. Even on the level of unintended effects, his use of highbrow sources such as classical music has done more to reinforce their power as universal repertoire than it has challenged their authority by moving them into less elevated cultural terrain.

70. For a provocative analysis of the gendered dimensions of minstrel performance, see Eric Lott, *Love and Theft* (New York: Oxford University Press, 1993), esp. pp. 38–62.

71. Atkins, *Country Gentleman,* p. 48.

72. Ibid., pp. 18–19.

73. On the wild and often violent nature of southern male recreations, including hunting, see Ted Ownby, *Subduing Satan: Religion, Recreation, and Manhood in the Rural South, 1865–1920* (Chapel Hill: University of North

Carolina Press, 1990). Though Ownby's focus is on the period before Atkins's birth, the narratives surrounding Atkins offer clear indication that his "gentility" was considered to be a break from the conventions of southern manhood, at least as those conventions were popularly understood. An RCA publicity release from the 1960s, for instance, claimed that "it is typical of gentle, unhurried Chet Atkins to have acquired his first guitar by trading an old pistol for it—because the only fireworks Chet wants to produce are musical ones." One only need compare this view of Atkins with the legendary story of the time Opry legend Ernest Tubb brandished a gun at the former director of the show's artist bureau, Jim Denny, to observe how competing ideals of manhood played themselves out in country music. Tubb, for his part, always carried a gun with him on the road. For the Tubb story, see Pugh, *Ernest Tubb,* pp. 222–226.

74. Don Halberstam, liner notes to Chet Atkins, *Mister Guitar* (Nashville: RCA, 1959).

75. John Gabree, "Chet Atkins: Story of a Quiet Man," *Country Music,* 8 (April 1974), p. 28.

76. Noel Digby, "Chet Atkins and His Guitar," liner notes to *Chet Atkins in Three Dimensions* (RCA, 1956).

77. David Halberstam, liner notes to *Chet Atkins' Workshop* (RCA, 1961).

78. Chet Atkins, liner notes to *My Favorite Guitars* (RCA, 1965).

79. "The Guitar Is More Than a Facade," *Billboard* (June 3, 1967), p. CA [for "Chet Atkins"]-13.

80. Cecelia Tichi has discussed the naturalistic impulses underlying so much of country music in her book, *High Lonesome: The American Culture of Country Music* (Chapel Hill: University of North Carolina Press, 1994). There she discusses the ways in which instruments are themselves presented as "living creatures of the natural world," even when they bear the distinct stamp of industrial technology, as in the case of the metal-bodied Dobro guitar (pp. 202–206).

81. Paul Hemphill, *The Nashville Sound: Bright Lights and Country Music* (New York: Simon and Schuster, 1970), p. 50.

4 Racial Distortions

1. On the lineage of this piece, see John Cowley, "Really the 'Walking Blues': Son House, Muddy Waters, Robert Johnson and the Development of a Traditional Blues," *Popular Music* (1981), pp. 57–71. Cowley asserts that it was Son House's influence and not Robert Johnson's that was most significant in the development and transmission of the song, and further dismisses the claim that Lomax's primary purpose in his collecting expedi-

tion was to locate Johnson. For Lomax's own account of his meeting with Waters, see Alan Lomax, *The Land Where the Blues Began* (New York: Delta, 1993), pp. 405–422.

2. Jim and Amy O'Neal, "Muddy Waters," *Living Blues,* 64 (March/April 1985), p. 21.

3. Ibid., pp. 20, 22.

4. Chuck Berry, *Chuck Berry: The Autobiography* (New York: Fireside, 1987), pp. 99–100.

5. Ibid., p. 100.

6. This is Charles Keil's term, borrowed from jazz criticism, for the folk music enthusiasts who deem acoustic country blues to be the only true, authentic blues form, holding all else to be dilution, bastardization, or even emasculation. In jazz criticism of the 1930s and 1940s, "moldy figs" were those who favored old-style Dixieland jazz over the emergent forms of swing and bop. See Keil, *Urban Blues* (Chicago: University of Chicago Press, 1966), pp. 34–38.

7. Robert Palmer, "The Church of the Sonic Guitar," in Anthony DeCurtis (ed.), *Present Tense: Rock & Roll and Culture* (Durham: Duke University Press, 1992), p. 37.

8. In both "Church of the Sonic Guitar" and his earlier blues history, *Deep Blues* (New York: Penguin, 1981), for instance, Palmer refers with relish to Pat Hare's "I'm Gonna Murder My Baby," a vicious yet strangely compelling piece of misogyny mixed with distorted guitar that seems all too prophetic in light of Hare's conviction for the murder of his lover seven years after the recording of the piece.

9. The lionization of Johnson since the 1960s, when he became the patron saint of white guitar heroes like Eric Clapton, raised the ire of more than a few blues aficionados who protested that the single-minded emphasis upon Johnson's skill and influence downplayed the arguably greater achievements and influence of Johnson contemporaries such as Son House; see Paul Garon, "Robert Johnson: Perpetuation of a Myth," *Living Blues,* 5 (Summer 1971), pp. 26–29.

10. Jas Obrecht, "Robert Johnson," in Jas Obrecht (ed.), *Blues Guitar: The Men Who Made the Music* (San Francisco: Miller Freeman Books, 1993), p. 12.

11. Ibid.

12. Michael Lydon, "The Second Coming of Bo Diddley," *Ramparts,* 10 (May 1971), p. 23.

13. Ibid.

14. Ibid.

15. Samuel Floyd, *The Power of Black Music: Interpreting Its History from*

Africa to the United States (New York: Oxford University Press, 1995), p. 28.

16. Palmer, *Deep Blues,* p. 16.

17. Mike Rowe, *Chicago Blues: The City and the Music* (New York: Da Capo, 1975), p. 17.

18. Jas Obrecht, "The Legend of Big Bill Broonzy," *Guitar Player,* 8 (August 1986), p. 70.

19. Paul and Beth Garon, *Woman with Guitar: Memphis Minnie's Blues* (New York: Da Capo Books, 1992), p. 9.

20. Pete Welding, "An Interview with Muddy Waters," *The American Folk Music Occasional,* 2 (1970), p. 7.

21. Dave Peabody, "It's J. R. Time! Jimmy Rogers," *Folk Roots,* 108 (June 1992), p. 21.

22. James Rooney, *Bossmen: Bill Monroe and Muddy Waters* (New York: Dial Press, 1971), p. 112.

23. Bob Rusch, "Jimmy Rogers: Interview," *Cadence,* 9 (June 1979), p. 12; Tom Wheeler, "Waters/Winter Interview," *Guitar Player,* 8 (August 1983), p. 59.

24. Bill Greensmith and Jim O'Neal, "Living Blues Interview: Jimmy Rogers," *Living Blues,* 14 (Autumn 1973), p. 13.

25. Neil Slaven, "Confessin' the Blues: The Story of Little Walter, part one," *Blues Unlimited,* 112 (March/April 1975), pp. 6–8.

26. Andrew Robble, "Junior Wells: Searching for the True Blues Feeling," *Guitar Player,* 11 (November 1994), p. 59.

27. Ibid., p. 60.

28. Ibid.

29. In a different interview, Myers and Walter together described the amplifier that Walter played through, one of the biggest amps owned by anyone on the Chicago scene at the time. Walter commented, "I had an amplifier built. I had four speakers on each side. Amplifier up and one down. If I blew a fuse out of one I just switched my line in the other. I got a terrific sound out of it . . ."

    Myers added, "I ain't never seen but one of them amplifiers. He had one and I saw one guy with one. That was a tough amplifier. It was the speakers, you know. Had long wires. You could hang one so far away. And the other one had the machine in it. Where you plug your wire in and turn it. But he would set the other speakers way away . . . Everywhere he put it that thing sounded. It was powerful, though. It was a damn good amplifier. The best I ever heard a harp on."

    In Bill Lindemann, "Living Blues Interview: Little Walter and Louis Myers," *Living Blues,* 7 (Winter 1971–72), p. 21.

30. Bill Greensmith, "Just Whaling," *Blues Unlimited,* 122 (November/December 1976), p. 10.

31. Greensmith and O'Neal, "Jimmy Rogers," p. 13.

32. Another New Orleans player, Earl King, described Guitar Slim's (literally) colorful manner of performance: "Slim came out with his hair dyed blue, blue suit, blue pair of shoes. He had 350 feet of mike wire connected to his guitar, and a valet carrying him on his shoulders all through the crowd and out into the parking lot. Man, he was stopping cars driving down the highway. No one could outperform Slim. He was the performinest man I've ever seen." Quoted in Jeff Hannusch, "Eddie 'Guitar Slim' Jones," *Blues Guitar,* p. 188.

33. Obrecht, "Buddy Guy," *Blues Guitar,* p. 202.

34. Paul and Beth Garon, pp. 74–75.

35. Greensmith, "Just Whaling," p. 9.

36. Rooney, *Bossmen,* p. 122.

37. Welding, "An Interview with Muddy Waters," p. 7.

38. Tricia Rose, *Black Noise: Rap Music and Black Culture in Contemporary America* (Hanover, N.H.: Wesleyan University Press, 1994), p. 75.

39. On the recorded version, the actual notes are D♭ to A to G♭; I am assuming, though, that G is the intended key of the song, given that open G was one of the most common tunings used among country slide guitarists, and that Waters had his instrument tuned down half a step as well, from G to G♭, another common practice designed to allow for greater resonance in the bass registers and greater ease of bending or vibrating notes due to the loosely wound strings. On the 1948 rerecording of the song that Waters did for Aristocrat records, which will be discussed momentarily, the tune is up a half-step, conforming to the D-B♭-G progression noted above. The 1941 version of the song is featured on the collection, *Muddy Waters: First Recording Sessions, 1941–1946* (Document Records, 1992).

40. Jim and Amy O'Neal, "Muddy Waters," p. 32.

41. Rowe, *Chicago Blues,* p. 76.

42. Ibid., p. 78.

43. Willie Dixon with Don Snowden, *I Am the Blues: The Willie Dixon Story* (New York: Da Capo, 1989), p. 67.

44. Ibid., p. 59.

45. Arnold Shaw, *Honkers and Shouters: The Golden Years of Rhythm & Blues* (New York: Collier Books, 1978), p. 128.

46. Songwriter Cash McCall remembered that at a typical Chess session, "They didn't call you by your name—your name was 'm——-f——' all day long." McCall further observed that "It was kind of a hard play with words there but you could see the camaraderie. They were calling

each other jolly little names." Quoted in Dixon and Snowden, *I Am the Blues,* p. 155.

47. Jim and Amy O'Neal, "Living Blues Interview: Eddie Boyd, part three," *Living Blues,* 37 (March/April 1978), p. 7.

48. Too many commentators have sought ways to justify or apologize for Chess's business practices, often using Leonard Chess's notable philanthropy with regard to Chicago's black community as a means of absolving him from blame with regard to the treatment of his musicians. Pete Golkin, for instance, makes this assumption in an otherwise balanced and insightful article on Chess; see Golkin, "Blacks, Whites and Blues, part two," *Living Blues,* 6 (November/December 1989), pp. 28–29. The issue, however, is not the degree to which Leonard and Phil Chess are subject to accusations of racism on a personal level, but the extent to which Chess business practices were consistent with broader patterns of racial subjugation in the music industry and American society as a whole; and on this latter note Chess is to be held accountable.

49. Randall Grass, "Chess Records: 'Often Imitated, Never Duplicated,'" *Music and Sound Output* (March/April 1983), p. 64.

50. Dixon and Snowden, p. 95.

51. Ibid., p. 62.

52. Mick Davis, "The Many Faces of Feedback," *Guitar Player,* 4 (April 1987), p. 45. Davis wrote a series of articles for *Guitar Player* that together provide an accessible overview of the technical processes behind feedback, distortion and amplification more generally. Also see "Distortion: The Good, the Bad, and the Ugly," *Guitar Player,* 3 (March 1986), pp. 74–78, 96; "Sound and Power," *Guitar Player,* 5 (May 1986), pp. 78–84; and "Sustain: In Search of the Infinite Vibration," *Guitar Player,* 7 (July 1988), pp. 104–108.

53. Obrecht, "Buddy Guy," *Blues Guitar,* p. 205.

54. Gene Santoro, "The Main Man," *Guitar World,* 3 (April 1987), p. 39.

55. Jacques Attali, *Noise: The Political Economy of Music,* translated by Brian Massumi (Minneapolis: University of Minnesota Press, 1985), p. 106.

56. Ibid.

57. Greensmith and O'Neal, "Jimmy Rogers," p. 15.

58. Christopher Small has described this approach to music most eloquently, coining the term "musicking" to refer to the active dimensions of making music, and noting the African and African-American tendency to view the musical work as a process rather than an object. See Small's *Music of the Common Tongue: Survival and Celebration in Afro-American Music* (London: Calder, 1987), esp. pp. 49–79.

59. Golkin, "Blacks, Whites and Blues, part one," *Living Blues,* 5 (September/October 1989), p. 26.

60. Dixon and Snowden, p. 151.

61. Writing in 1992, Robert Palmer suggested that Chess waited to record Waters with his full ensemble until he had developed the facility in the studio to properly capture the full effect of Waters's electric band. Palmer seems in this instance to be giving Chess too much credit, and no other chronicler of Chess history or of Waters's career has offered a similar explanation. More common, and to my mind more convincing, is the suggestion that Chess continued recording Waters solo or with bare accompaniment because that was the mode in which Waters had already made a number of successful records. Palmer, "Church of the Sonic Guitar," p. 22.

62. Obrecht, "Muddy Waters: The Life and Times of the Hoochie Coochie Man," *Guitar Player,* 3 (March 1994), p. 38.

63. Lawrence Hoffman, "The Blues Slide Guitar," *Living Blues,* 105 (September/October 1992), p. 31.

64. The connection between blues and hoodoo has been the object of much comment and speculation, and the source of many powerful myths about the blues, among which perhaps the most famous is the story of Robert Johnson having sold his soul to the devil in exchange for his musical abilities. Robert Palmer plays up this aspect of the blues up in *Deep Blues.* A more detailed examination of the connection between blues and certain currents of African-derived spirituality, among which hoodoo is one variant, is Julio Finn's *The Bluesman: The Musical Heritage of Black Men and Women in the Americas* (New York: Interlink Books, 1991).

65. Palmer, *Deep Blues,* p. 98.

66. Rooney, p. 124.

67. Although Little Walter left Waters's performing band in 1952 to join the Four Aces and record under his own name, he would occasionally perform with Waters in the studio throughout the 1950s. He contributed some particularly strong playing on Waters's 1954 recordings such as "Hoochie Coochie Man" and "I Just Want to Make Love to You."

68. Rooney, p. 150.

69. Berry, pp. 85–87.

70. Ibid., p. 87.

71. Ibid., p. 88.

72. Theodore Gracyk, *Rhythm and Noise: An Aesthetics of Rock* (Durham: Duke University Press, 1996), pp. 69–98.

73. George White, *Bo Diddley: Living Legend* (Surrey: Castle Communications, 1995), p. 40.

74. Mike Rowe and Bill Greensmith, "I Was Really Dedicated: An Interview with Billy Boy Arnold, part 3," *Blues Unlimited,* 128 (January/February 1978), p. 19.

75. White, p. 41.
76. Jeff Hannusch, "Bo Diddley Is a Guitarslinger," *Guitar Player,* 6 (June 1984), p. 68.
77. Tom Wheeler, *American Guitars: An Illustrated History* (New York: HarperPerennial, 1992), p. 76.
78. David Morton and Charles Wolfe, *DeFord Bailey: A Black Star in Early Country Music* (Knoxville: University of Tennessee Press, 1991), p. 112.
79. Eric Lott, *Love and Theft: Blackface Minstrelsy and the American Working Class* (New York: Oxford University Press, 1993); Robert Cantwell, *Bluegrass Breakdown: The Making of the Old Southern Sound* (New York: Da Capo Press, 1984), pp. 249–274.
80. Houston Baker, *Modernism and the Harlem Renaissance* (Chicago: University of Chicago Press, 1987), pp. 49–52.
81. Robert Christgau, "Chuck Berry," in Jim Miller (ed.), *The Rolling Stone Illustrated History of Rock 'n' Roll* (New York: Random House/Rolling Stone Press, 1980), p. 58.
82. Charles Shaar Murray, *Crosstown Traffic: Jimi Hendrix and the Rock 'n' Roll Revolution* (New York: St. Martin's Press, 1989), p. 59.
83. Diddley biographer George White has provided the most detailed, albeit still sketchy, analysis of why Berry was more appealing and acceptable to white audiences: "Diddley . . . remained firmly rooted in the ghetto: both his music and his image were too loud, too raunchy, too *black* ever to 'cross over' in the same way Berry had." White, *Bo Diddley,* p. 89.
84. Paul Gilroy, *The Black Atlantic: Modernity and Double Consciousness* (Cambridge, Mass.: Harvard University Press, 1993), p. 85.
85. Marjorie Garber, *Vested Interests: Cross-Dressing and Cultural Anxiety* (New York: HarperPerennial, 1993), p. 274.
86. One of the points that Gilroy makes in noting the intimate association of gender and race is the extent to which racial "authenticity" in musical performance or other matters is often judged as compliance with a particular notion of gendered behavior. Gilroy's comments are directed primarily at black commentators who have valued "an amplified and exaggerated masculinity" and "its relational feminine counterpart" as the "special symbols of the difference that race makes." Yet his point can also be applied to the many blues scholars, black and white, who have attributed a unique importance to the "bluesman" as the primary keeper of a distinctly African-American sensibility. Gilroy, p. 85.
87. Cub Koda, "Chuck Berry: And the Joint Was Rockin'," *Goldmine,* 25 (December 13, 1991), p. 10.
88. Berry, p. 87.
89. Ibid., pp. 90–91.

90. Tom Wheeler, "Chuck Berry: The Story," *Guitar Player,* 3 (March 1988), p. 50.

91. Berry, p. 136.

92. Shaw, p. 278.

93. Ibid., p. 143.

94. Fred Stuckey, "Chuck Berry," *Guitar Player,* 1 (February 1971), p. 23.

95. Berry's own recording of the song made it to number one on the R&B charts and number five on the pop charts; on the country charts the successful version was a cover by singer Marty Robbins, which went to number nine. Philip Ennis, *The Seventh Stream: The Emergence of Rocknroll in American Popular Music* (Hanover, N.H.: Wesleyan University Press, 1992), p. 227.

96. Greensmith and O'Neal, "Jimmy Rogers," p. 16.

97. Koda, pp. 20–22.

98. A double-stop is essentially a partial chord sounded on two consecutive strings of the guitar (ordinary chords are built on a minimum of three notes). Berry's use of double-stops was one of the principal elements of his guitar style; he used them to split the difference between single-note playing and chords, and often introduced them into his solos and fills to build rhythmic and harmonic tension through repetition.

99. Timothy Taylor, "His Name Was in Lights: Chuck Berry's 'Johnny B. Goode,'" *Popular Music,* 1 (1992), p. 27.

100. Ibid., pp. 29–30.

101. Berry, p. 157.

102. Ibid., p. 158.

103. Koda, p. 12.

104. Berry, p. 161.

5 Black Sound, Black Body

1. John Burks, "The End of a Beginning Maybe," *Rolling Stone,* 54 (March 19, 1970), p. 41.

2. Bassist Noel Redding provides some particularly sharp commentary on Hendrix's intense preoccupation with studio technologies in his autobiography, *Are You Experienced? The Inside Story of the Jimi Hendrix Experience* (New York: Da Capo, 1996). By his own admission, Redding was far less interested in the technical and technological dimensions of music, so his remembrances of time in the studio with Hendrix are marked with a certain bitterness, as in the following account of the recording of the Experience's second album, *Axis: Bold As Love:* "Jimi got totally caught up in the production side of things, but the technical end of music never

appealed to me. I'd get bored with the repetition and the whiling away of hours while they niggled over details . . . There were no pushbutton sound effects. If a phase effect was wanted the engineer . . . would send us to the pub for an hour while they set up the slightly out-of-sync interaction between two recorders which resulted in the effect" (p. 55).

3. Curtis Knight, *Jimi: An Intimate Biography of Jimi Hendrix* (New York: Praeger, 1974), p. 155.

4. David Henderson, *'Scuse Me While I Kiss the Sky: The Life of Jimi Hendrix* (New York: Bantam Books, 1981), p. 324.

5. Foremost among these were the managerial hassles that all but dominated the latter part of Hendrix's career, as his money and his freedom to maneuver were the subject of continual struggle between the guitarist and his manager, Mike Jeffery. Jeffery has become a favorite scapegoat of Hendrix aficionados in the wake of Hendrix's death, apparently with no small amount of justification. The arrangement between Hendrix and Jeffery, like the arrangement between so many black artists and their white managers, never seemed to have been properly formalized, and Jeffery consequently seems to have managed much of Hendrix's earnings into channels that were scarcely recoverable by the artist. Henderson, p. 324.

6. Paul Gilroy, *The Black Atlantic: Modernity and Double Consciousness* (Cambridge, Mass.: Harvard University Press, 1993), p. 94.

7. Robin Richman, "An Infinity of Jimis," *Life,* 14 (October 3, 1969), p. 74.

8. The main works about Hendrix are Caesar Glebbeek and Harry Shapiro, *Jimi Hendrix: Electric Gypsy* (New York: St. Martin's Press, 1990); Henderson, *'Scuse Me While I Kiss the Sky;* and Charles Shaar Murray, *Crosstown Traffic: Jimi Hendrix and the Rock 'n' Roll Revolution* (New York: St. Martin's Press, 1989). All three works try, with varying degrees of success, to deal with the issue of Hendrix's mystical outlook. Glebbeek and Shapiro's work tries hardest to explain Hendrix's ideas about spirituality, to the point of noting similarities between some of his lyrics and ideas derived from the *I Ching.* I think they go a bit too far in this direction, and try too hard to turn Hendrix himself into some sort of mystic icon. Nonetheless, the issue demands a fuller exploration than I am able to give in this chapter.

9. This performance and the entire concert of which it was a part were fortunately recorded, and released several years later (early 1990s) as part of a four-disc retrospective of Hendrix's career, *Jimi Hendrix Lifelines.* The recording includes Hendrix's stage patter, which makes numerous references to the surrounding unrest and tension between the audience and the police.

10. The Woodstock "Star-Spangled Banner" is included on the widely-distributed Woodstock album as well as in the film of the same name, both of which feature a broad range of performers from the three-day festival. Meanwhile, Hendrix's performance at Woodstock has recently been issued in its entirety on compact disc.

11. Murray, *Crosstown Traffic*, p. 24.

12. Samuel Floyd, *The Power of Black Music: Interpreting Its History from Africa to the United States* (New York: Oxford University Press, 1995), pp. 201–203. Floyd's use of the term "Signifyin(g)" is adopted from Henry Louis Gates's formulation of the term in his work, *The Signifying Monkey: A Theory of African-American Literary Criticism* (New York: Oxford University Press, 1988). I will explore Gates's concept, and Hendrix's status as a "Signifyin(g)" artist, later in this chapter.

13. My reference to the threshold is derived from Anne McClintock's *Imperial Leather: Race, Gender and Sexuality in the Colonial Contest* (New York: Routledge, 1995), p. 24.

14. Larry Neal, "The Black Arts Movement," in Addison Gayle (ed.), *The Black Aesthetic* (New York: Anchor Books, 1972), pp. 272–274.

15. Don Lee, "Toward a Definition: Black Poetry of the Sixties," *The Black Aesthetic*, p. 235.

16. Amiri Baraka, *Blues People* (New York: William Morrow and Company, 1963), p. xii.

17. Ron Wellburn, "The Black Aesthetic Imperative," *The Black Aesthetic*, p. 135.

18. Ibid., p. 133.

19. Ibid., p. 148.

20. Ibid., p. 149.

21. Paul Carter Harrison, *The Drama of Nommo: Black Theater in the African Continuum* (New York: Grove Press, 1972), p. 59.

22. Gilroy, *The Black Atlantic*, p. 80.

23. Ibid., p. 99.

24. Jay Ruby, "Jimi Hendrix," *Jazz & Pop*, 7 (July 1968), p. 17.

25. Henderson, *'Scuse Me While I Kiss the Sky*, p. 337.

26. Douglas Hall and Sue Clark, *Rock: A World as Bold as Love* (New York: Cowles Book Company, 1970), p. 160.

27. Frank Zappa, "The Oracle Has It All Psyched Out," *Life*, 26 (June 28, 1968), p. 84.

28. John Seabury, "In Search of Volume: Guitar Amplification in the '60s," in *The Electric Guitar: An Illustrated History*, edited by Paul Trynka (San Francisco: Chronicle Books, 1995), p. 84.

29. Such is the term used by Art Thompson in his recent history, *Stompbox: A History of Guitar Fuzzes, Flangers, Phasers, Echoes and Wahs* (San Francisco: Miller Freeman, 1998).

30. Jas Obrecht and Bruce Bergman, "Roger Mayer: Electronics Wizard and Designer of Effects . . . ," *Guitar Player*, 2 (February 1979), p. 48.

31. Jann Wenner and Baron Wollman, "It's Jimi Hendrix," *Rolling Stone*, 7 (March 9, 1968), p. 12.

32. Murray, pp. 148–149.

33. Ibid., p. 151.

34. Greg Tate, "The Electric Miles," *Flyboy in the Buttermilk: Essays on Contemporary America* (New York: Simon and Schuster, 1992), pp. 73–74.

35. Glebbeek and Shapiro, p. 193.

36. Robert Christgau, "Anatomy of a Love Festival," *Esquire*, 1 (January 1968), p. 154.

37. Frantz Fanon, *Black Skin, White Masks* (New York: Grove Press, 1967), p. 11.

38. Ibid., p. 112.

39. Ibid., p. 161, n25.

40. Ibid., pp. 169–170.

41. Zappa, p. 91.

42. Ibid.

43. "The Flailing, Wailing Freakout of the Hendrix Experience," *Life*, 26 (June 28, 1968), pp. 92–94.

44. My understanding of minstrelsy is based upon Eric Lott's "White Like Me: Racial Cross-Dressing and the Construction of American Whiteness," in Amy Kaplan and Donald Pease (eds.), *Cultures of United States Imperialism* (Durham: Duke University Press, 1994), pp. 474–495. The link between Hendrix's appeal and minstrelsy has been made explicit in at least one instance, that being Randy Hansen, a white guitarist from Seattle, Washington who has made a career out of imitating Hendrix's music while dressed in full regalia, including blacked-up face and arms. See Jas Obrecht, "Pro's Reply: Randy Hansen," *Guitar Player*, 7 (July 1979), pp. 6, 119ff.

45. "Bloomfield," p. 58.

46. Ibid.

47. To narrow the focus of this chapter, I have omitted any detailed account of Hendrix's life. His career involved a series of dislocations—from his hometown of Seattle, Washington, to the Southern "chitlin circuit" and then up to Harlem—before moving on to Greenwich Village where he was "discovered" by Chas Chandler, former bassist for the British blues/soul band The Animals, who moved Hendrix to London, hyped him to a consider-

able degree and produced an album, and then brought him back to the United States. Before Hendrix moved to the Village, he served as sideman for a number of African-American R&B stars like Little Richard, King Curtis, and the Isley Brothers. In these bands, he was frustrated by the lack of musical freedom as well as the fairly rigid codes imposed by many bandleaders on dress and behavior, and continually got in trouble for threatening to upstage his employers with his flashy showmanship. Only when he moved to the Village did he start his own band, though he continued to play as sideman for white bohemians like Hammond, in whose band he was playing when he was spotted by Chandler. This is the standard narrative of his early career; to fill in the details, I would refer the reader to any of the works cited in note 3.

48. Murray, p. 45.
49. "The Voice of Experience," *Newsweek*, 15 (October 9, 1967), p. 90.
50. Alfred Aronowitz, "Brash Buccaneer with a Wa-Wa," *Life*, 11 (March 15, 1968), p. 8.
51. "Wild, Wooly and Wicked," *Time*, 14 (April 5, 1968), p. 64.
52. David Henderson has offered a provocative reading of "The Show" as an element of Hendrix's artistry that was deeply rooted in African-American culture. According to Henderson, "'The Show' was the height of the performance [on tours through the South and northern venues like the Apollo] . . . This display often put both the audience and the performer in a transcendental state where improvisation came to the fore and the unexpected took everybody out." Henderson, pp. 76–77.
53. Michael Rosenbaum, "Jimi Hendrix and Live Things," *Crawdaddy*, 15 (May 1968), p. 25.
54. Ibid.
55. "Michael Bloomfield Reminisces," p. 22.
56. Matt Resnicoff, "Godhead Revisited: The Second Coming of Pete Townshend," *Guitar Player*, 9 (September 1989), pp. 83–84.
57. Murray, p. 91.
58. Glebbeek and Shapiro, p. 293.
59. Chris Welch, "Who Says Jimi Hendrix Can't Sing? (He Does!)," *Melody Maker*, (April 15, 1967), p. 3.
60. Gates, *The Signifying Monkey*, p. xxii.
61. Ibid., p. 58.
62. Ibid., p. 64.
63. Bob Dawbarn, "Second Dimension: Jimi Hendrix in Action," *Melody Maker* (March 1, 1969), p. 14.
64. Roy Hollingsworth, "Hendrix Talks," *Melody Maker* (September 5, 1970), p. 7.

6 Kick Out the Jams!

1. Chuck Eddy, *Stairway to Hell: The 500 Best Heavy Metal Albums in the Universe* (New York: Harmony Books, 1991), p. 24. The Detroit riots of July 1967 will be discussed further. As for the World Series, I am not entirely sure which World Series Eddy means—the Tigers won the 1968 Series, but that would have been far too late to have any relevance to the recording of "Looking At You," which was released in the early part of that year. My guess is that Eddy, who along with being a music critic is also a big baseball fan and a former resident of Detroit, threw in the reference to the World Series to give a nod to the Tigers without any regard to chronological sanctity. His comment still works well as a metaphor, I think, however wrong his order of events may be.

2. John Sinclair, "A Letter from Prison, Another Side of the MC5 Story, and (Incidentally) the End of an Era," *Creem,* 8 (November 28, 1969), p. 10.

3. Norman Mailer, *Miami and the Siege of Chicago: An Informal History of the Republican and Democratic Conventions of 1968* (New York: World Publishing Company, 1968), p. 142.

4. Dave Marsh, liner notes to MC5, *Back in the USA* (New York: Rhino/Atlantic, 1992 [1970]).

5. Marsh, "The MC5: Back on Shakin' Street," *Fortunate Son: The Best of Dave Marsh* (New York: Random House, 1985), p. 205.

6. Marsh, *Fortunate Son,* p. 8.

7. "MC5 on the Cusp," *Creem,* 4 (August 31, 1969), p. 14; Sinclair, "A Letter from Prison," p. 10.

8. "MC5 on the Cusp," p. 14.

9. John Sinclair, "The Penitentiary Ain't Shit to Be Afraid of," *Guitar Army: Street Writings/Prison Writings* (New York: Douglas Book Corporation, 1972), p. 194.

10. "MC5 on the Cusp," p. 15.

11. Ben Fong-Torres, "Shattered Dreams in Motor City," *Rolling Stone,* 110 (June 8, 1972), p. 32.

12. Sinclair, *Guitar Army,* p. 76.

13. Ibid.

14. Dave Marsh, Deday LaRene, and Barry Kramer, "Untitled," *Creem,* 11 (1970), p. 7. This is a collaborative essay commemorating *Creem*'s one-year anniversary, which provides an overview of the Detroit scene. By the time it was written, the Five's career had already begun its downward turn; whereas their first album, *Kick out the Jams,* had made it into the top 30 on the national charts, their second, *Back in the USA,* released very early in 1970, stalled at 137. Aside from its relative commercial failure, *Back in the*

USA also symbolized to many Five fans the decline of the band in the wake of their break with Sinclair, who had been imprisoned in July of 1969 for possession of marijuana (ostensibly; in point of fact, his conviction and ridiculous ten-year sentence probably had more to do with his political activities). Since the Detroit scene was wrapped up with the Five's career in so many ways, the Five's perceived decline was taken to be emblematic of the scene's decline as well, so that these reflections by Marsh, LaRene, and Kramer are written from the perspective of looking upon a scene that is in all likelihood past its better days. An anonymous article on Michigan bands (which appeared in the same issue of *Creem*) noted in regard to the Five, "all things being equal the MC5 are still the best rock and roll band in the country, even if they are no longer the catalyzing force they once were. We've all been hit hard by the end of innocence. Fuck." This chapter discusses the band's early years, when their political orientation and their commitment to ear-shattering noise were more explicit.

15. Sinclair, "Rock & Roll Dope," *Fifth Estate,* 19 (January 23- February 5, 1969), p. 16; William Leach, "The White Left—Serious or Not," *Fifth Estate,* 18 (January 8–22, 1969), p. 7.

16. Jerry Herron, *AfterCulture: Detroit and the Humiliation of History* (Detroit: Wayne State University Press, 1993), pp. 9–10.

17. Todd Gitlin's *The Sixties: Years of Hope, Days of Rage* (New York: Bantam Books, 1993) and William Leuchtenburg's *A Troubled Feast: American Society Since 1945* (Boston: Little, Brown and Company, 1983) are among the works that interpret the counterculture as an outgrowth of the heightened expectations that came with the longest period of continuous economic abundance in U.S. history.

18. Pam Brent, "Crow's Nest," *Creem,* 1 (1969). This issue of *Creem* is without page numbers.

19. Sinclair, "White Panther Statement," *Fifth Estate,* 14 (November 14–27, 1968), p. 8.

20. Ibid.

21. Ibid.

22. This program is reprinted in Eric Ehrmann's profile of the Five, "MC5," *Rolling Stone,* 25 (January 4, 1969), pp. 16–17. Archie Shepp is profiled in Amiri Baraka's *Black Music* (New York: William Morrow and Company, 1967).

23. Marianna Torgovnick, *Gone Primitive: Savage Intellects, Modern Lives* (Chicago: University of Chicago Press, 1990), p. 228.

24. Donald Lowe has a meticulous analysis of the mind/body split in his *History of Bourgeois Perception* (Chicago: University of Chicago Press, 1982), pp. 85–108. On the civilizing process, see Norbert Elias, *The Civi-*

lizing Process, Vol. 1: The History of Manners (New York: Urizen Books, 1978).

25. Barbara Ehrenreich, *The Hearts of Men: American Dreams and the Flight from Commitment* (New York: Anchor Press, 1983), pp. 99–116.

26. Gitlin, p. 228. Much of Gitlin's account is drawn from Abbie Hoffman's description of the same episode in *Revolution for the Hell of It* (New York: The Dial Press, 1968), p. 35. Hoffman himself was certainly in the same category of radicalism as Grogan and Sinclair; indeed, the White Panthers were a branch of the Hoffman and Jerry Rubin-led Yippies.

27. Gitlin, p. 349.

28. Sinclair, "Coat Puller," *Fifth Estate*, 7 (August 1–14, 1968), p. 5. This is a reprint of the original article to commemorate a year having passed since the riots. Sinclair's enthusiastic response to the riots was echoed, albeit with a more cynical inflection, by Peter Werbe, editor of the *Fifth Estate*. In a 1969 article by John Burks on the underground press, Werbe was quoted as saying: "'When it was burning, man you could get up on the rooftops and see the flames in all directions. It was *beautiful*. So beautiful. You've never seen anything like it.' He thought about the fires for a minute, then added—just to make sure I hadn't missed the point—'I hate this fuckin' town so much . . . I've lived in the Motor City a long time—long enough really to know what it's about, and, you know, I really hate it.'" Burks, "The Underground Press: A Special Report," *Rolling Stone*, 43 (October 4, 1969), p. 13.

29. Gitlin, pp. 234–235.

30. Ehrmann, p. 16.

31. Gitlin, p. 245. The phrase "What should whitey do?" is taken from a letter to Gitlin by Carol McEldowney.

32. Eric Lott, *Love and Theft: Blackface Minstrelsy and the American Working Class* (New York: Oxford University Press, 1993), p. 18.

33. Ibid., pp. 49–50.

34. Ibid., p. 52.

35. Rob Tyner had one of the most impressive afros to adorn any public figure in the 1960s and 1970s, especially among whites. Whether his hair was naturally that way or not, I am not sure; but the issue of the afro's association with naturalness is provocatively treated by Kobena Mercer in "Black Hair, Style Politics," in *Welcome to the Jungle: New Positions in Black Cultural Studies* (New York: Routledge, 1994).

36. Susan Hiwatt, "Cock Rock," *Twenty Minute Fandangos and Forever Changes: A Rock Bazaar*, edited by Jonathan Eisen (New York: Random House, 1971), p. 143.

37. Marjorie Garber, *Vested Interests: Cross-Dressing and Cultural Anxiety* (New York: HarperPerennial, 1993), p. 374.

38. Susan McClary, *Feminine Endings: Music, Gender, and Sexuality* (Minneapolis: University of Minnesota Press, 1991), p. 156.

39. Ibid., pp. 155–156.

40. Sinclair, "Separation Is Doom," *Guitar Army,* p. 110.

41. David Walley, "MC5 Interview," *The Age of Rock 2: Sights and Sounds of the American Cultural Revolution,* edited by Jonathan Eisen (New York: Vintage, 1970), p. 283.

42. Mailer, "The White Negro," *Advertisements for Myself* (New York: Signet, 1960), p. 310.

43. Ibid.

44. Sinclair, *Guitar Army,* p. 12.

45. Mailer, "White Negro," p. 314.

46. Walley, p. 272.

47. Sinclair, "A Letter from Prison," p. 11.

48. Difficult though it may be to measure either the breadth of the Five's audience or the depth of their enthusiasm, it is nonetheless striking, when scrolling through the pages of *Creem* and the *Fifth Estate,* how many writers were willing to testify on the band's behalf. Along with the responses already cited by Dave Marsh and Pam Brent, one could add, for instance, Dennis Frawley's description of a Five performance: "The MC5 culminated the steady rise of energy with one of their top performances kicking them out so hard that one psychedelic-induced youth leaped on stage nude for what was termed by Wayne Kramer a 'testimony by skin.'" Frawley, "Rock and Roll Revival!" *Fifth Estate,* 3 (June 12–25, 1969), p. 7. An anonymous assessment of the band in *Creem* was even more glowing: "In a sense—in a lot of senses—they are the archtypal Detroit rock and roll band . . . The way they relate to their brothers and sisters—their common culture—has inspired a lot of the people in that community to relate to each other in the same term (sic) as the 5 . . . The 5 is more a religion than just a band anyway, and the people who are behind them are behind them all the way." "MC5," *Creem,* 1 (1969), p. 5.

49. Marshall McLuhan, *The Medium Is the Massage: An Inventory of Effects* (New York: Bantam Books, 1967), pp. 8, 16.

50. Ibid., p. 111.

51. Sinclair, *Guitar Army,* p. 9.

52. Sinclair, "Motor City Music," *Jazz & Pop,* 12 (December 1970), p. 54.

53. McLuhan, *The Medium,* p. 145.

54. Torgovnick, p. 185.

55. Jacques Attali, *Noise: The Political Economy of Music,* translated by Brian Massumi (Minneapolis: University of Minnesota Press, 1985), p. 6.
56. Ibid., pp. 106, 124.
57. Ibid., p. 135.
58. Eddy, pp. 34–35.
59. Ibid., p. 35.
60. Peter McWilliams, "Contact Truss," *Creem,* 3 (1969), p. 5.
61. Richard Williams, "MC5—Still the Bad Boys of Rock," *Melody Maker* (August 8, 1970), p. 11.
62. Sinclair, *Guitar Army,* p. 104.
63. Ibid., p. 84.

7 Heavy Music

1. Chris Welch, "The Led Zeppelin Story, part two," *Melody Maker* (May 17, 1975), pp. 32–33.
2. Ibid., p. 32.
3. This despite the reputed fact that Led Zeppelin was generally met with antagonism by rock critics. The members of Zeppelin themselves often fostered the idea that they were disliked by the press, perhaps as a means of maintaining some semblance of "outsider" status with regard to the rock establishment even as they sold more albums and concert tickets than virtually any other band of the era. Ritchie Yorke, a Canadian journalist and one of the band's biographers, has also promoted this idea, though in his case the motivation seems primarily self-serving. By declaring that other critics disdained Zeppelin, he makes much of his own prescience and good judgment for having recognized the band's brilliance (and also presents their brilliance as an undisputed truth). Yet my own research into 1970s rock journalism has shown little evidence that Zeppelin was reviled by critics, and that as Robert Christgau notes, it was only at "the old hippie singer-songwriter stronghold *Rolling Stone*" that the band was condemned with any degree of regularity (and even they eventually made gestures of compromise). Ritchie Yorke, *Led Zeppelin: The Definitive Biography* (Novato, Calif.: Underwood-Miller, 1993); Robert Christgau, "Dumb Genius," *Village Voice,* 46 (November 15, 1994), p. 69.
4. For a very smart interpretation of the myths surrounding Woodstock and Altamont, see Robert Duncan's *The Noise: Notes from a Rock 'n' Roll Era* (New York: Ticknor & Fields, 1984), pp. 22–32. Especially insightful is Duncan's suggestion that both events assumed their greatest significance only after the fact, when they were packaged as records and films that purposely worked to memorialize a particular version of the 1960s. While

Woodstock was portrayed to embody a "myth of eternal youth and, indeed, of cherubic innocence triumphant," Altamont was depicted, in the form of the Maysles brothers' documentary *Gimme Shelter,* as "the maggoty underside of the acid utopia, a countermanding anti-myth to Woodstock's myth of innocence" (p. 29).

5. Matt Resnicoff, "In Through the Out Door," *Musician,* 145 (November 1990), p. 50.

6. Chris Welch, "Jimmy Page, part three," *Melody Maker* (February 28, 1970), p. 10.

7. Welch, "Jimmy Page, Paganini of the Seventies," *Melody Maker* (February 14, 1970), p. 16.

8. For a detailed discussion of the interrelationship between heavy metal and classical music, albeit one more focused on the 1980s than the 1970s, see Robert Walser's *Running with the Devil: Power, Gender, and Madness in Heavy Metal Music* (Hanover, N.H.: Wesleyan University Press, 1993), pp. 57–107. Walser posits that the main significance of guitarists' efforts to fuse rock and classical techniques is the blurring of the boundaries between "high" and "low" cultural spheres, though he also refers to the elitism and self-absorption that arise from the resulting fetishization of technique. Most relevant to my own purposes, though, is his discussion of virtuosity as a display of potency, and the ways in which that potency is often perceived to have an almost supernatural dimension (p. 76).

9. Ibid.

10. Stephen Davis, *Hammer of the Gods: The Led Zeppelin Saga* (New York: Ballantine Books, 1985), p. 8.

11. Generally, Zeppelin's concert film, *The Song Remains the Same* (1976; directed by Joe Massot and Peter Clifton), was not well regarded among the rock press. Most harsh was Dave Marsh's review in *Rolling Stone,* which condemned the film as a vanity project and condemned the band for its sadism and contempt for its audience, which Marsh took to be evident in the film. A more tongue-in-cheek response was offered by Robert Duncan in *Creem,* who concentrated the bulk of his review on the scene just described: "You know how sometimes when [Page] goes up high in a really good solo, how it can sort of take you places you've maybe never been before? (I get that effect all the time from him.) Well, that's how it is when he gets to the top [of the mountain]." Marsh, "They Probably Think This Film Is About Them," *Rolling Stone,* 227 (December 2, 1976), pp. 19, 21; Duncan, "The View from Hear," *Creem,* 8 (January 1977), pp. 50–51.

12. The mythicization of Page's interest in the occult, and especially in the notorious practitioner of "magick," Aleister Crowley, is one of the more curious elements of Led Zeppelin's history, and has gained force from

Page's continual reluctance to explain his proclivities. Stephen Davis ties Page's supposed fascination with the underworld to both Paganini and bluesman Robert Johnson, constructing a sort of transhistorical idea of the virtuoso musician as a transgressive and mysterious figure. Perhaps the strangest outgrowth of this dimension of Page's image, though, is the controversy surrounding the song "Stairway to Heaven," on which the members of the band have been charged with backward-masking Satanic messages to brainwash the minds of young listeners.

13. John Swenson with Bruce Malamut, "The Zeps Runneth Over," *Crawdaddy,* 49 (June 1975), p. 65.

14. Roy Hollingsworth, "Whole Lotta Led," *Melody Maker* (July 1, 1972), p. 25.

15. The most interesting consideration of the influence of romanticism upon rock music is Simon Frith and Howard Horne's *Art into Pop* (London: Methuen, 1987), which observes the influence of art schools upon the British rock of the 1960s and 1970s. Frith and Horne discuss the tension within the art schools between idealized notions of "art" and "commerce," and the ways in which many students of the 1960s (of whom Jimmy Page was one) adopted romanticism as a means of asserting their own marginality even as they opted to participate in the world of pop music production.

16. For a useful take on the development of musical aesthetics, and the discursive relationship between reason and unreason, see Simon Frith, "Adam Smith and Music," *New Formations,* p. 79. Robert Walser includes a suggestive analysis of the role of mysticism in heavy metal, and the furor over the possible inclusion of subliminal satanic messages in such music, in the last chapter of *Running with the Devil.* There he posits that fear of these subliminal messages is tied to the lack of an available framework among the mass of listeners for understanding music as a social discourse (p. 147), the implication being that music has been relegated by many to a realm of wordless enjoyment that should be unencumbered by disturbing effects such as those posed by musicians like Page.

17. Lawrence Kramer, *Music as Cultural Practice, 1800–1900* (Berkeley: University of California Press, 1990), p. 90.

18. Iain Chambers covers this period of time well in his book, *Urban Rhythms: Pop Music and Popular Culture* (New York: St. Martin's Press, 1985), pp. 50–83.

19. Yorke, *Led Zeppelin,* p. 44.

20. The electric guitar was still enough of a novelty in the mid-1960s to have provoked no small degree of anxiety among pop music critics. In a 1965 interview with the Yardbirds, for instance, Keith Altham posed the question, "How far do you think we can go before the machine takes over from

the musician?" and singles out the Who as a band who has "gone too far with electronic sounds." Keith Relf, singer for the band, dismissed such a notion, insisting that "The Who are creating with sounds just as surely as an artist with brush strokes. What is most important [is that] they are original." Beck then interjects that he "was experimenting with echo effects and feed-back years ago. Now it's become the thing," and expresses his admiration of the Who for their ability to draw crowds while creating their own sound. Altham, "Question-time with the Yardbirds," *New Musical Express*, 965 (July 9, 1965), p. 10.

21. Frith and Horne, *Art into Pop,* pp. 83–89.
22. Jann Wenner, "Eric Clapton," in *The Rolling Stone Interviews: Talking with the Legends of Rock and Roll, 1967–1980,* edited by Ben Fong-Torres (New York: St. Martin's, Rolling Stone Press, 1981), p. 28.
23. Chambers, *Urban Rhythms,* pp. 31–37.
24. Clapton, "Foreword" to *Damn Right I've Got the Blues: Buddy Guy and the Blues Roots of Rock-and-Roll,* by Donald Wilcock with Buddy Guy (San Francisco: Woodford Press, 1993), p. 1.
25. Steve Rosen, "Jeff Beck," *Rock Guitarists* (Saratoga: Guitar Player Books, 1978), p. 10.
26. Davis, *Hammer of the Gods,* p. 12.
27. Judith Butler, "The Lesbian Phallus and the Morphological Imaginary," *Bodies That Matter: On the Discursive Limits of Sex* (New York: Routledge, 1993), p. 58.
28. Ibid., pp. 79–80.
29. While Frith and McRobbie have put forth the most influential statement regarding cock rock, at least in quasi-academic circles, they by no means invented the term. As far as I can tell, the first recorded use of cock rock was in Susan Hiwatt's essay of the same name, cited in the previous chapter, in which Hiwatt recounts her experience as a rock fan whose encounter with feminism led her to recognize the extent to which women were marginalized as both fans and musicians within the rock community. One assumes that it already had some currency before the publication of Hiwatt's essay in 1971, and continued to do so until the publication of Frith and McRobbie's essay in 1978, although Frith and McRobbie make no reference to Hiwatt and give no background to the term. Hiwatt, "Cock Rock," *Twenty-Minute Fandangos and Forever Changes,* pp. 141–145.
30. Simon Frith and Angela McRobbie, "Rock and Sexuality," in *On Record: Rock, Pop, and the Written Word,* edited by Simon Frith and Andrew Goodwin (New York: Pantheon Books, 1990), p. 374.
31. Ibid.
32. Ibid., p. 383.

33. Frith, "Afterthoughts," *On Record,* p. 420.

34. Davis, *Hammer of the Gods,* p. 97.

35. Charles Shaar Murray, *Crosstown Traffic: Jimi Hendrix and the Rock 'n' Roll Revolution* (New York: St. Martin's Press, 1989), p. 59.

36. Ibid., p. 60.

37. Ibid.

38. This interpretation of the song's middle section has been put forth by Joy Press and Simon Reynolds in *The Sex Revolts: Gender, Rebellion, and Rock 'n' Roll* (Cambridge, Mass.: Harvard University Press, 1995), p. 115. Yet despite such flashes of insight, Press and Reynolds abandon all subtlety (as perhaps is appropriate) in their analysis of Led Zeppelin, going even farther than the critics already cited in equating the band with a destructive, violent male sexuality, while leaving any other dimensions of the band completely unexplored. Most foolishly, to my mind, they make direct comparisons between Led Zeppelin and fascism in a manner that equates the two without acknowledging any separation between performed and actual violence.

39. Ian Dove, "Herman Wooden in Mods Dress," *Billboard,* 24 (June 14, 1969), p. 22.

40. "Led Zeppelin, U.S. Tour, December 1968-January 1969," *Rolling Stone,* 501 (June 4, 1987), p. 136.

41. Another concert review, by Nick Logan, reinforces this observation: "In one way they appear to be fighting each other for dominance, in another they become as one but in the final analysis they serve to haul each other onto greater heights. Plant, with shoulder length blond curls, employs his voice as a fourth instrument. Page, a contrast with shoulder length black hair, evens the score by using his instrument as an extra voice. The result at low key is fascinating; at its high devastating." Logan, "Zeppelin and Fleetwood Take Off with a Roar," *New Musical Express,* 1173 (July 5, 1969), p. 13.

42. David Walley, "Led Zeppelin," *Jazz and Pop,* 10 (October 1969), p. 22. Plant offers a suggestive comment in this regard: "You know every vocalist is a frustrated guitarist . . . As much as I love the mike and my freedom of movement . . . I really like to play instruments." Lisa Robinson, "Led Zeppelin Dances on Air," *Creem,* 12 (May 1975), p. 70.

43. Yorke, *Led Zeppelin,* p. 55.

44. Ibid., p. 49.

45. A number of these interviews are collected in the volumes *Rock Guitarists* and *Rock Guitarists, Volume II* (Saratoga: Guitar Player Books, 1978). Frank Zappa offered a characteristically acerbic assessment of the situation in 1977, speaking of a contemporary setting "that accepts concepts like

The Super-Group, The Best Guitar Player In The World, The Fastest Guitar Player In The World, The Prettiest Guitar Player In The World, The Loudest Guitar Player In The World, The Guitar Player In The World Who Has Collected The Most Oldest Guitars In The World (some of which have been played by dead guitar players who were actually musicians), and so forth." Zappa, "Good Guitar Stuff or Stereotypifications," reprinted in *Guitar Player,* 1 (January 1987), p. 16.

46. Ritchie Yorke, "Page's Rages," *New Musical Express,* 1288 (October 2, 1971), p. 18.

47. Eve Sedgwick, *Between Men: English Literature and Homosocial Desire* (New York: Columbia University Press, 1985), p. 15.

48. Hiwatt, "Cock Rock," p. 146.

49. J. D. Considine, "Led Zeppelin," *Rolling Stone,* 587 (September 20, 1990), p. 59. Germaine Greer offers a discussion of rape that refutes any efforts at rationalization: "Many (men) believe that rape is impossible. The more simple-minded imagine that the vagina cannot be penetrated unless the woman consciously or subconsciously accepts the penetration, and so the necessary condition of rape cannot be fulfilled . . . The difficulty of getting a fully erect penis into the vagina is in direct proportion to the difficulty of overcoming the woman, either by physical force or by threat . . . or by drugging her or taking her by surprise." Greer, "Seduction Is a Four-Letter Word," in *The Madwoman's Underclothes: Essays and Occasional Writings* (New York: The Atlantic Monthly Press, 1986), p. 153.

50. Ellen Sander, *Trips: Rock Life in the Sixties* (New York: Charles Scribner's Sons, 1973), p. 122.

51. Jaan Uhelszki, "Sodom & Gomorrah in a Suitcase," *Creem* (July 1977), pp. 46–47.

52. Ibid., p. 50.

53. Pamela Des Barres, *I'm with the Band: Confessions of a Groupie* (New York: Jove Books, 1988), pp. 23–24.

54. Ibid., p. 133.

55. Ibid., p. 142.

56. Germaine Greer, "The Universal Tonguebath: A Groupie's Vision," *Oz,* 19 (1969), p. 32.

57. Greer, "What Turns Women On," in *The Madwoman's Underclothes,* p. 181.

58. Susan Whitall, "Led Zeppelin: A Psychobiograph," *Creem,* 9 (February 1979), p. 27.

59. Emily XYZ, "You Shook Me," *Village Voice,* 46 (November 15, 1994), p. 72.

60. Ibid., p. 76.

61. See especially Press and Reynolds, *The Sex Revolts.* The authors' position is somewhat complicated by the fact that they apply the term "feminine" to music by male artists such as the German group Can, yet their insistence upon maintaining a continuum of sexual/musical expression from masculine to feminine nonetheless seems to fix the terms of sexual representation too narrowly. A similar tendency can be found in Susan McClary's *Feminine Endings,* in which McClary speaks of feminine musical forms in a way that ultimately seems to uphold rather than challenge categories of gender difference.

62. John Stirn, "Which Way Pop?" *New Musical Express,* 1275 (July 3, 1971), p. 4.

63. Ibid.

64. Jim Smith, "Led Zeppelin Cause Plenty of Action," *New Musical Express,* 1284 (September 4, 1971), p. 21.

65. Ritchie Yorke, "Zeppelin: More Solid Than Ever," *New Musical Express,* 1287 (September 25, 1971), p. 6.

66. "From You to Us," *New Musical Express,* 1276 (July 10, 1971), p. 2.

67. Ibid.

68. Yorke, "Page's Rages," p. 18.

69. Take, for example, Page's remarks in a 1977 interview: "My vocation is more in composition really than anything else. Building up harmonies. Using the guitar, orchestrating the guitar like an army—a guitar army . . . I'm talking about actual orchestration in the same way you'd orchestrate a classical piece of music." Steve Rosen, "The Calculated Guitar Frenzy of Jimmy Page," reprinted in *Best of Guitar Player: Led Zeppelin* (1994), p. 14.

70. Yorke, *Led Zeppelin,* p. 128.

71. Richard Goldstein, "Also sprach Grand Funk Railroad," *Harper's,* 1457 (October 1971), p. 32.

72. Ibid.

73. Ibid., p. 36.

74. Ibid., p. 42.

75. Ibid., p. 44.

76. "The Top 100," *Rolling Stone,* 507 (August 27, 1987), p. 152. These florid words of praise stand in marked contrast to John Mendelsohn's original review of the album in *Rolling Stone,* printed in 1969, which was notable for the sarcasm that Mendelsohn brought to bear on Zeppelin's "heavy" sound. "*Led Zeppelin II* (review)," *Rolling Stone,* 48 (December 13, 1969), p. 48.

77. Davis, *Hammer of the Gods,* p. 101.

78. Ibid., p. 104.

79. My previous chapter on the MC5 was, of course, largely an effort to argue exactly this point.

80. Duncan, *The Noise,* p. 46.

81. Ibid., p. 47.

82. Jacques Attali, *Noise: The Political Economy of Music,* translated by Brian Massumi (Minneapolis: University of Minnesota Press, 1985), p. 115.

83. Ibid., p. 141.

84. Martin Millar, "Led Zeppelin and the Pixies," *Idle Worship,* edited by Chris Roberts (Boston: Faber and Faber, 1995), p. 36.

85. Ibid., p. 39.

86. Ibid., p. 40.

87. Ann Powers, "To the Misty Mountain," *Village Voice,* 46 (November 15, 1994), p. 69.

88. To be fair, Duncan himself admits this quality of the band's music, and notes that Zeppelin, having established the archetype for heavy metal with their second album, would become the genre's "most artistically adventurous group" in subsequent years (p. 43). Yet these observations are overshadowed by his broader critique of heavy metal, and are not pushed to any very interesting critical conclusions.

89. Resnicoff, "In Through the Out Door," p. 50.

90. Ibid.

91. Joe Gore, "Page's Eastern Front," *Guitar Player,* 8 (August 1993), p. 85.

92. Nick Coleman, "Stalingrad Meets Laura Ashley," *Mojo,* 12a (December 1994), p. 82.

93. Steven Feld, "Notes on 'World Beat,'" in *Music Grooves,* by Steven Feld and Charles Keil (Chicago: University of Chicago Press, 1994), p. 238.

94. Chris Welch, "The Zeppelin Remains the Same," *Melody Maker* (November 5, 1977), p. 9.

95. Although from the beginning Led Zeppelin featured acoustic songs, their third album marked a significant departure from their heavy sound, with over half the songs recorded featuring Page on acoustic guitar, including the entire second side. Just as important as the content of the album, though, was the story of its recording, which was continually recounted in interviews upon the record's release. After a strenuous bout of touring, the members of Zeppelin retreated to a remote cottage in the Welsh countryside, Bron-Yr-Aur, where they rested and composed songs. Plant described the experience: "The great thing about our stay there . . . was that there was no motion, just privacy and Nature and the beauty of the people who were there . . . The cottage has no electricity and is right away from everything. There's no road—you have to drive across the fields and mountains to get to it. We drove around the hills in a jeep in the daytime and sat

by the fire at night. We just wanted to see what we could come up with when there's nobody around." Yorke, *Led Zeppelin,* p. 110.

96. Plant voiced some of his own impressions of the setting in a 1995 interview: "Morocco is a living, pulsating entity which is changing all the time . . . But there are parts of Marrakech that carry on as they have done for thousands of years. And the music is a reflection of that, of all times and all religions, and of all the natural expectations and conditions of the people who live there. It's amazing, it's pumping, it's furious, it's anxious, it's happy, and it's far more real than anything you'll ever experience in a western city." Andy Aledort, "Led It Be," *Guitar World,* 2 (February 1995), p. 84.

97. These local musicians are the Gnaoua, who according to Nick Coleman are "a descendant tribe of migratory black Africans brought to the North of the continent as Arab slaves, whose chief function in Moroccan society is to act as therapeutic doctor-musicians." Coleman continues to describe their performance: "Somehow . . . a diplomatic bridge is rapidly built between ripe old English rocker and venerable Gnaoua doctor-musician, with the result that, cross-legged on cushions in the hive of the main square of Marrakech, Page, Plant, and Gnaoua kick up a terrific rumpus to fulfill several of the English duo's most fervid Arabesque dreams." Coleman, "Stalingrad Meets Laura Ashley," p. 82.

98. "Friends," which originally appeared on *Led Zeppelin III,* was one of two songs that Page and Plant performed and recorded with the Bombay Symphony Orchestra during a trip to India in the early 1970s in what was their earliest collaboration with local musicians. The tapes of the performances are only available on bootleg recordings.

99. Led Zeppelin, *Physical Graffiti* (Swan Song SS 2–200, 1975).

100. Mat Snow, "The Second Honeymoon," *Mojo,* 12a (December 1994), p. 95.

101. Ibid.

102. J. D. Considine, "Led Zeppelin," *Rolling Stone,* 587 (September 20, 1990), p. 60.

103. Anne McClintock, *Imperial Leather: Race, Gender and Sexuality in the Colonial Contest* (New York: Routledge, 1995), p. 22.

104. Feld, "Notes on World Beat," p. 242.

105. Edward Said, *Orientalism,* p. 55.

106. In Crowley's autobiography, the most curious instance regarding these ideas occurs in a passage in which the author suggests, "There has always been something suggesting the oriental—Chinese or ancient Egyptian" in his own appearance, and goes on to detail his longstanding involvement in the study of Eastern religions from Islam to Buddhism to Egyptian symbolism, stating that even at an early age "the East called to him," referring to

himself in the third person. Crowley, *The Confessions of Aleister Crowley,* edited by John Symonds and Kenneth Grant (New York: Arkana, 1979), p. 47.

107. William Burroughs, "Rock Magic," *Crawdaddy,* 49 (June 1975), p. 35.
108. Ibid., p. 40.
109. Chuck Eddy, *Stairway to Hell,* p. 12. As previously discussed, this was the album that Page sought to package as obscurely as possible so critics would be forced to deal with the band strictly in terms of their music. Part of that strategy was to have each band member select a symbol to represent himself rather than listing the names and instruments in more standard fashion. Page's symbol was actually a set of ancient characters, but it looked like the letters "zoso," and so the album is regularly referred to as "the zoso album," or, simply, "zoso." Donna Gaines has discussed the extent to which "zoso" became an important symbol among the suburban teens who constituted Led Zeppelin's primary audience, largely due to its indecipherable nature, and the mystery surrounding the album and Zeppelin in general. "Children of zoso are kids who just don't believe that mass culture is all that disappointing. They aren't urban trendies. They don't intellectualize their pleasures . . . They are unconcerned about things like the 'political correctness' of music, its 'socially redeeming value.' No, this stuff is spiritual, tribal." Gaines, *Teenage Wasteland: Suburbia's Dead End Kids* (New York: Pantheon, 1991), p. 181.
110. Eddy, p. 13.

Conclusion

1. "The 100 Greatest Guitarists of the 20th Century," *Musician,* 172 (February 1993), p. 43.
2. Ibid., p. 44.
3. Ibid.
4. Ibid.
5. Ibid., pp. 43–44.
6. Simon Frith, *Performing Rites: On the Value of Popular Music* (Cambridge, Mass.: Harvard University Press, 1996), pp. 16–17.
7. Simon Reynolds, *Generation Ecstasy: Into the World of Techno and Rave Culture* (Boston: Little, Brown and Company, 1998), p. 102.
8. Ibid., p. 3.
9. Ibid., p. 41.
10. James Rotondi, "Is Rock Guitar Dead . . . or Does It Just Smell Funny?" *Guitar Player,* 9 (September 1997), pp. 71–82.
11. Ibid., p. 82.

12. Paul Trynka (ed.), *The Electric Guitar: An Illustrated History* (San Francisco: Chronicle Books, 1995), pp. 142–147. Trynka writes in a brief essay on vintage guitars, "Even for modern guitar designers, '50s models have established a standard of how a guitar should look or sound—there's no doubt that original instruments will remain highly prized, and frequently copied. Forty years on from when their instruments rocked the establishment, Leo Fender's and Ted McCarty's guitars [the Stratocaster and Les Paul, respectively] have become the establishment" (p. 147).

13. Frederic Jameson, *Postmodernism, or, The Cultural Logic of Late Capitalism* (Durham: Duke University Press, 1991), p. 284.

14. George Lipsitz, *Time Passages: Collective Memory and American Popular Culture* (Minneapolis: University of Minnesota Press, 1990).

15. Jameson, p. 287.

16. This element is foreshadowed in an earlier scene in which a black busboy working at the local diner offers encouragement to George after a particularly humiliating episode, and then goes on to announce his own plans for future success. An interjection from Marty discloses the fact that this bus boy would later become mayor of the town; but when Marty suggests that the young man might someday become mayor, the white manager of the diner proclaims, "A colored mayor—that'll be the day."

17. My use of the term "noise" is rooted in the work of Jacques Attali. Bearing more explanation is my concern with silence, which in this case also derives from Attali. Specifically, I am thinking of his discussion of silence in the context of "repetition," his term for the system of mass distribution that has developed around music in the twentieth century. In one of his more dystopian moments, Attali describes the transformation of the popular dance into a concert, during which "the music is only a pretext for the noncommunication, the solitude, and the silence imposed by the sound volume and the dancing." Remove the dancing from this scene and one has, I think, a fitting description of the effect of Marty's performance upon his audience of simulated 1950s teens. As Attali says elsewhere, "controlling noise is not the same as imposing silence in the usual sense. But it is a silence in sound, the innocuous chatter of recuperable cries." Attali, *Noise: The Political Economy of Music,* translated by Brian Massumi (Minneapolis: University of Minnesota Press, 1985), pp. 118, 124.

18. Michael Chanan, *Musica Practica: The Social Practice of Western Music from the Gregorian Chant to Postmodernism* (London: Verso, 1994), p. 241.

19. Robert Walser is especially eloquent on this subject in chapter two of his study of heavy metal, *Running with the Devil: Power, Gender and Madness in Heavy Metal Music* (Hanover, N.H.: Wesleyan University Press, 1993). Asserting the need to analyze the *music* of popular music, Walser goes on

to declare that the "reception of *all* music is 'connected in a practical way with everyday life,' however hard some people may work to hide the social meanings of their music. The danger of musical analysis is always that social meanings and power struggles become the forest that is lost for the trees of notes and chords. The necessity of musical analysis is that those notes and chords represent the differences that make some songs seem highly meaningful and powerful and others boring, inept, or irrelevant" (p. 30).

20. Reynolds, pp. 9–10.
21. Christopher Small, *Music of the Common Tongue* (London: Calder, 1987), p. 50.
22. Ibid., p. 62.
23. Ibid., p. 63.
24. John Corbett, "Ephemera Underscored: Writing Around Free Improvisation," in *Jazz Among the Discourses,* edited by Krin Gabbard (Durham: Duke University Press, 1995), p. 228.
25. Ibid., p. 235.
26. As Reichel explained in a 1989 interview, "I replaced the fingerboard on my guitar with a new one with a closer succession of frets, and moved the bridge toward the fingerboard in accordance with the new, shorter scale. The result was a big portion of 'leftover' string on the other side of the bridge, and plucking there made some surprising sounds appear on the regular side." Reichel, "Crossing the Bridge," *Guitar Player,* 1 (January 1989), p. 48.
27. Reichel's musical approach can be heard to good effect on the German compact disc, *The Dawn of Dachsman . . . Plus* (Free Music Productions, 1994). The name of the album comes from another of Reichel's instrument inventions, the Dachsophone, which involves bowing pieces of carved wood and controlling the resultant sounds through the application of another, fretted piece of wood. An explanation of the dachsophone is contained in Mark Dery's article, "Forging a New Guitar Vocabulary," *Guitar Player,* 7 (July 1988), p. 61.
28. Giuseppe Colli, liner notes to Reichel, *The Dawn of Dachsman.*
29. The term "structure of desire" comes from Warren Susman, "Did Success Spoil the United States? Dual Representations in Postwar America," in *Recasting America: Culture and Politics in the Age of Cold War,* edited by Lary May (Chicago: University of Chicago Press, 1989), p. 30.
30. Paul Théberge, *Any Sound You Can Imagine: Making Music/Consuming Technology* (Hanover, N.H.: Wesleyan University Press, 1997), p. 166.

Index